GRAMMAR

OF THE

LATIN LANGUAGE

LEONHARD SCHMITZ, PH.D., F.R.S.E.

HIPPOCRENE BOOKS
NEW YORK

This title was previously published in 1851 in
Philadelphia, Pennsylvania by Lea and Blanchard
as part of their classical series.

Hippocrene Books, Inc. edition, 2004

For information, address:
Hippocrene Books, Inc.
171 Madison Avenue
New York, NY 10016

ISBN 0-7818-1040-X

Printed and bound in the United States of America.

PREFACE.

A GRAMMAR is a classified collection of the rules or laws regulating the language of which it professes to be an exposition. Every language is subject to changes, either for the better or for the worse ; and although in the case of a dead language a grammarian must consider and illustrate it mainly as it was at the time of its most perfect development, still he cannot avoid taking into consideration the earlier and later forms of words and expressions, for in many instances the language in its perfect state cannot be fully explained without recourse being had to those forms of speech out of which it has arisen. Very great advantages may also be derived, especially in the etymological part, from a comparison of the language under consideration with its sister tongues, or with its mother tongue, where the existence of this is certain. But in a grammar for young people, such comparisons must be in a great measure useless ; and all that can be done with advantage, is to apply to the language under consideration such principles as may have been established by comparative philology.

As a grammarian has only to classify and explain the phenomena or facts of the language which are generally known, he has little to add of his own ; and that which principally distinguishes him from his predecessors is the arrangement of, and the manner in which he states and explains the facts. In this alone consist his merits or demerits.

As regards arrangement, the present Grammar does not lay much claim to novelty ; the author has purposely abstained from making any material alteration in the arrangement usually adopted in grammars for schools, partly because he thinks that such alterations as have recently been introduced in school grammars are little calculated to benefit the learner, and partly because he is of opinion that sound information can be given without obliging the teacher to abandon the order to which he has been accustomed from his youth, and which he may not always be able or willing to abandon.

In the manner in which he has stated and explained the phenomena of the Latin language, the author hopes to have performed his task so as to satisfy the reasonable demands of intelligent teachers ; for he has endeavoured not only to express the facts in the most concise and perspicuous manner, but also, as far as it

(iii)

was possible, to explain and give reasons for the facts so stated. This may perhaps be objectionable to those who are in the habit of making their pupils repeat rules from grammars without concern as to whether the rules are understood or not. But for such teachers the present Grammar is not intended, for the author never contemplated that all the rules should be committed to memory *verbatim*—a process which but too often leaves the pupils, at the end of their scholastic career, as ignorant, and their minds as untrained to think, as they were at the beginning. The pupil should be led, by frequent repetition, to impress the substance of the rules upon his mind, and to understand and comprehend them by frequent application. This remark applies more especially to the rules of Syntax, for there is no way of mastering the declensions and conjugations without fully committing them to memory.

Many also may object to the fact, that the old terminology, such as *imperfect, pluperfect,* &c. has been retained, although it is faulty and incorrect. I fully admit that the ordinary grammatical terminology is anything but correct or perfect; but in what science or art is it otherwise? Do the words *epic, lyric, idyl, satire,* accurately define the kinds of poetry understood by them? Assuredly not; and yet who objects to them? The fact is, that we know what is meant by those terms, not from their strict etymological meaning, but from the notions which we have been taught to associate with them.

It is customary in some grammars to introduce elaborate discussions concerning the meaning of certain particles, and the minute differences between two or three of similar meaning; but as these are matters which, properly speaking, belong to a dictionary, all such explanations have been here avoided.

In preparing the present treatise, the writer has availed himself, as far as he thought it compatible with his own design, of the larger works of Ramshorn, Zumpt, Key, and Madvig; and to the last-mentioned author especially he is indebted for many valuable suggestions, and for many of the examples quoted in illustration of the rules. The more important rules are printed in large type, and those of less importance — exceptions to general rules, and peculiarities of poetic diction, and the like—are printed in small type, to enable the teacher and learner at a glance to see what is essential, and what not. The author's most ardent desire is, that his work may contribute something towards a more philosophical study of a language which, notwithstanding the immense progress made in philology of late years, yet continues to be taught in many places from grammars abounding in the most glaring errors and unphilosophical explanations.

CONTENTS.

(v)

INTRODUCTION.

LATIN belongs to that great family of languages which is now generally known as the Indo-Germanic or Indo-European, and which comprises the Sanscrit (the sacred language of the Hindoos), the Persian, Lithuanian, Greek, Latin, the German with all its dialects, the English, and the Celtic. All these languages stand to one another in the relation of sisters, and exhibit most striking resemblances, not only in words and inflections, but in their whole grammatical structure; none of them, however, has preserved its original character and purity in the same degree as the Sanscrit, the most ancient among them. The comparison of these languages with one another, or what is termed Comparative Philology — a field of inquiry which has been opened only in modern times—has already thrown light upon a variety of subjects which were formerly involved in utter darkness, and upon which the most erroneous notions prevailed. No department of science, however, has derived more light from this study than philology and ethnology; and it is now universally acknowledged that it is impossible to acquire profound and philosophical understanding of any one of the above languages without being able to compare it with at least one or two of its sister tongues. Many of the phenomena in the Latin and Greek languages, therefore, must remain inexplicable mysteries to those who refuse the aid of comparative philology; and all the absurd fancies and theories of the earlier etymologists and grammarians arose solely from a want of that philosophical and historical study of language, without which all speculation is, as it were, wandering on a wide sea without the guidance of the magnetic needle. Who, then, can wonder that etymology, as pursued in former times, has drawn upon itself contempt and ridicule?

In many respects every language of the Indo-Germanic stock forms by itself an organic whole, with its own historical development independent of the sister tongues. Thus the Latin language, without effacing or destroying those features by which we recognise it as a member of a great family, has passed through a peculiar course of organic development, until it became the mother tongue of the languages of south-western Europe—all of which, again, preserve the characteristic features of their common origin

In former times, it was customary to regard the Latin language as derived from the Greek, and there still are writers who, clinging to the exploded error, believe that Latin was formed mainly from the Aeolic dialect of the Greek; but comparative philology has shown most clearly that the Latin language is quite as original as the Greek and the Sanscrit. Others have endeavoured to explain the resemblance between Latin and Greek, by the supposition that both are emanations from a common stock, the language of the Pelasgians; but this is a mere hypothesis, which cannot be supported by facts. Others, again, who discovered in the Latin language words and forms of words which occur in the German and Celtic languages, have even been led to believe that a great part of the Latin language was derived from the Celts, who at an early time occupied a great portion of northern Italy. But the truth is, that the Latin language is neither a daughter of the Greek nor a mixture of any other languages, the resemblance with Greek, German, Celtic, and others, arising from the simple fact, that it is a sister of them. And if the people who spoke the Latin language were a mixed race, it can have consisted only of kindred tribes, and the mixture of these kindred tribes must have taken place at a time when they still exhibited the features of their common origin in all their freshness and purity, and before each had made any considerable progress in its own peculiar development. All the theories respecting the differences between Greek, Italian, and other elements in the Latin language, must therefore be abandoned; and even the ingenious opinion of Niebuhr, which was subsequently adopted by C. O. Müller and others, that the names of things belonging to a peaceful life are of Greek origin, and those relating to war and military life were of genuine Italian growth, is untenable; for as the one class of words is found in the Sanscrit as well as the other, and as the former does not present any essential difference from the latter, the fact that the one set of words agree in both languages, and the other not, must be regarded as purely accidental. These are the conclusions to which comparative philology has led, and which have been set forth with great clearness and precision by Dr. Georg Curtius,* an authority who is perhaps more competent than any other to pronounce an opinion on a question of comparative philology.

These results, arrived at by comparative philology, greatly affect the earliest history of Rome and of the people of Latium. The tradition that Latium was originally inhabited by different tribes, Aborigines, Siculians, and Sabines, and that the language spoken by these united tribes was as much a mixed language as

---

* In his Essay *Die Sprachvergleichung in ihrem Verhältniss zur Classischen Philologie.* Berlin: 1845. 8vo.

the nation itself was a mixed one, need not be given up, according to what was said above: all we know about those tribes tends to show that they all belonged to one great family, and that, accordingly, the language spoken in Latium was not a mixture of heterogeneous elements; but the materials were of a kindred nature, and, combined, they produced a language which has in itself as much unity as any other of the great family of languages of which it is but one. We do not mean to assert that the Latin language is not indebted to the Greek in any way, for as the Romans derived the greater part of their literature from Greece, so they also borrowed not only words, but even certain modes of expression, from the same quarter; but such things happened at a comparatively late period, and we are here speaking of the original elements of the language, such as it existed before that intimate intercourse by which, subsequently, Greece exercised her sway over the arts, literature, and civilisation of her western warlike neighbours.

The Latin language derives its name from its having been spoken by the Latins — that is, the inhabitants of Latium, on the western coast of Italy, between the rivers Tiber and Liris. This territory also contained the city of Rome, which in the course of time extended its dominion not only over Latium, but over Italy and the whole of the then known world. But although the Latins were swallowed up by the Romans, and although Rome was the ruling power, still her language being the one originally spoken in Latium, was always called the Latin, and not the Roman language; nay, even the literature of Rome was always designated by the Romans themselves as *litterae Latinae*, and not as *litterae Romanae*. The Latin language, accordingly, through the conquests made by Rome, the chief city of Latium, became in the end the language of nearly all the nations in the south-west of Europe that were subject to the Roman dominion. It was spoken all over Italy (except some parts in the south), in Spain, Portugal, France, and a great part of Switzerland and southern Germany. When, in the fifth century after the birth of Christ, the Roman Empire was broken up, and its several parts occupied by barbarians, the Latin language in Italy, France, Spain, and Portugal, which was already undergoing a process of corruption, gradually changed into the modern Italian, French, Spanish, and Portuguese. The influence of the languages spoken by the barbarians from the north and north-east also greatly contributed to this change, inasmuch as many barbarous (German) words were introduced into the countries conquered by them.

The Latin language, therefore, is the mother from whom the languages of Italy, France, Spain, and Portugal, have mainly sprung, and a knowledge of Latin is extremely useful and almost necessary to him who wishes to acquire any of the languages of south-western Europe. Through the influence of Norman-French, and other circumstances, Latin also contributed greatly to the formation of the English language, which for this reason cannot be thoroughly understood without a knowledge of Latin. During the long period of upwards of twelve hundred years, in which Latin was a living language, it had, like all other tongues, its periods of gradual and organic development and decay. The farther back we trace it, the greater shall we find the resemblances between it and its ancient sisters, the Sanscrit and Greek; and the further we follow it downwards, especially its popular dialects spoken in the countries far removed from Rome, the more shall we find it inclining towards those forms which it finally assumed in its modern derivative tongues. How long the Latin language, as such, was spoken before a literature was formed in it, we have no means of ascertaining, for the time at which the people who spoke it arrived in Italy from the east lies far beyond the reach of history; but a written literature did not spring up in Latium or at Rome till about the year B. C. 250, when Livius Andronicus and his successors began to make the Romans acquainted with the productions of the Greek Muse. We must, however, not believe that previous to that time the Romans had no literature of any kind; we have, on the contrary, the strongest possible evidence that, from a very remote period, a certain kind of native epic or ballad poetry was much cherished and cultivated by them, though none of those productions have been preserved in writing. About two centuries after Livius Andronicus, in the time of Caesar, Cicero, and Augustus, the language and literature of Rome reached the highest point of perfection; and from that time downwards literature degenerated, and the language became more and more artificial and incorrect, until at length it ceased to be a living language, and became a subject of study to the learned. In the church of Rome it remained in use as the official language, which it still is. Accordingly, during the middle ages, literature being chiefly cultivated by the priests, most works were composed in Latin; and even at the present day, a book written in this language is understood to be intelligible to educated men in all civilised countries.

WORDS AND FORMS OF WORDS.

CHAPTER I.

THE ALPHABET AND ORTHOGRAPHY.

§ 1. THE Latin language has twenty-three letters—namely, *a, b, c, d, e, f, g, h, i (j), k, l, m, n, o, p, q, r, s, t, u (v), x, y, z.* Six of them, *a, e, i, o, u,* and *y,* are vowels; the remaining seventeen are consonants. The vowels were pronounced by the Romans in their purity and fulness, as in the modern Italian and German languages.

Note 1. The two vowels *i* and *u* were not distinguished by the Romans in writing from the consonants *j* and *v, i* serving both for *i* and *j,* and *u* for *u* and *v ;* but in modern times, it has become customary to distinguish *i* and *j,* and *u* and *v,* in order to facilitate reading.

Note 2. The vowel *y* occurs only in those words which have been adopted into the Latin language from the Greek.

§ 2. Two vowels, united in such a manner as to produce only one mixed sound, form a diphthong. There are in Latin five diphthongs—namely, *ae, oe, au, ei,* and *eu.* The first three are of frequent occurrence, but *ei* is used only in a few interjections, such as *hei, eia, oiei ;* and *eu* only in the interjections *heu, heus,* and *eheu,* in *ceu, seu,* and *neu,* and in *neuter* and *neutiquam.*

Note. The diphthong *oi* is found only in *oiei ; ui* occurs only in the interjection *hui,* and in the datives *huic* and *cui.* All simple vowels are either long or short, but all diphthongs are long. If the length of a vowel is to be indicated, it is done by a horizontal line (ˉ) over it ; its shortness is marked by a curve (˘)—as *pĕcūnĭă,* money.

§ 3. The consonants were, on the whole, pronounced by the Romans just as they are written, and each consonant was probably pronounced in the same manner under all circumstances. Thus *c* was always pronounced like *k,* though we wrongly sound it as an *s* when it is followed by the vowels *e, i, y, ae,* or *oe.* In like manner, *t* was always pronounced as a pure *t,* but we now pronounce it like *sh* in words where it is followed by *i*, with another vowel after it—as *justitia*, which is pronounced *justishia*.

§ 4. Consonants are divided into two classes — namely, mutes (*mutae*), *b, c, d, f, k, p, q, t, v;* and liquids (*liquidae*), *l, m, n, r.* The sibilant *s* does not belong to either of these classes; *h* is not accounted as a distinct letter, but is a mere aspiration at the beginning of a word or syllable; *x* and *z* are double consonants, the former being composed of *c* or *g* and *s*, and the latter of *d* and *s*, though we often pronounce it merely as a soft *s*.

Note. The consonant *k* is used only in the word *kalendae* (the first day of a month), and in the names *Kaeso* and *Karthago ;* in all other words, its place is supplied by *c.* *Q* occurs only before the vowel *u*, together with which it is usually pronounced like *kw*, as *quam, quum*, though the Romans sounded the two letters only as a *k.* *Z* occurs only in words introduced into the Latin language from the Greek, such as *gaza, zona.*

§ 5. When one word ends in a vowel, and the next begins with one, there arises an inconvenience in pronunciation, which is called *hiātus*, or a yawning. To avoid this, the former of the two vowels is in poetry always thrown out (*elisio*), and in the language of common life also it seems to have been passed over. Hence we always pronounce in verse, *Saper' aude* for *Sapere aude, quoqu' et* for *quoque et, Dardanid' e muris* for *Dardanidae e muris, ultr' Asiam* for *ultro Asiam.* The same elision takes place in poetry when the second word begins with an *h*, and when the first ends in *m*—as *toller' humo* for *tollere humo, mult' ille* for *multum ille.*

§ 6. The orthography of many Latin words was not the same at all times, and there are numerous instances in which, even at the same period, words were not written in the same way by all authors. Hence we find *tamquam* and *numquam* as well as *tanquam* and *nunquam, quatuor* and *quattuor, litera* and *littera, artus* and *arctus, femina* and *foemina, fetus* and *foetus, coelum* and *caelum, obscoenus, obscaenus*, and *obscenus, plostrum* and *plaustrum.* At present, it is customary to adopt the orthography and spelling which was followed by the best of the Roman grammarians in the first centuries of the Christian era.

It must further be observed that the Romans, generally speaking, employed in their writings only capital letters, until at a very late period our small letters came into use. At present, capital letters are used only as initials—1. In proper names, and adjectives derived from them ; 2. After a full stop ; and 3. At the beginning of a verse.

If two vowels, which in ordinary circumstances form a diphthong, are to be pronounced separately, the second is marked with (¨); that is, a *diaeresis* — as *poëta*, a poet; *aër*, air; *aërius*, airy.

The Romans themselves had no other sign of punctuation than the full stop; but, in order to facilitate the reading and understanding their works, we employ in Latin the same signs (comma, colon, semicolon, and the marks of interrogation and exclamation) which are used in our own language.

CHAPTER II.

QUANTITY AND ACCENTUATION OF SYLLABLES.

§ 7. A syllable may consist of a single vowel or diphthong, or of a combination of one or more consonants with one vowel —as *i*, go; *au-ster*, south wind; *e-go*, I. A syllable is generally a part of a word, but it may also form a word by itself—as, *i*, go; *me*, me; *te*, thee; *nos*, we; *lex*, law; *rex*, king; *laus*, praise.

§ 8. Syllables are either long or short; only a few are of a doubtful nature, being sometimes used as long, and sometimes as short. The length of a syllable depends upon the vowel which it contains. In pronunciation, a long syllable is dwelt upon about twice as long as a short one; hence two short vowels, when united into a diphthong, make one long sound.

§ 9. A syllable may be long by nature (that is, by the natural length of its vowel), or by the position of its vowel (that is, when the vowel is followed by two or more consonants); in which case we are constrained to dwell upon the vowel longer than we should do if the vowel were followed only by one consonant, or by none at all. For example, *sōl* and *trādo* have their *o* and *a* long by nature; but in *făx*, *amabŭnt*, and *cŏntraho*, the *a*, *u*, and *o* are long by their position.

§ 10. All syllables containing a diphthong or a vowel which has arisen from a contraction of two others, are long — *āēdes*, a house; *lāŭs*, praise; *cōēlum*, heaven; *cōgo* (from *cŏăgo*), I compel; *mālo* (from *măgĕvŏlo*), I will rather; *tibīcen* (from *tibīĭcen*, *tibia*, while the *i* is short in *tubĭcen* (from *tuba*), a fluteplayer; *būbus* or *bōbus* (from *bŏvĭbus*), to the oxen; *jūnior* (from *jŭvĕnior*), younger.

Note. The diphthong *ae* is considered short in *prae* when compounded with words beginning with a vowel—as *praĕacutus*.

§ 11. Every vowel which is followed by another vowel
in the same word, is short, even when an *h* occurs between
them — as *dĕus*, god; *pĭus*, pious; *rŭo*, I rush; *trăho*, I draw;
vĕho, I drive.

Note. Exceptions :—
1. The *e* before *i* in the genitive and dative of the fifth declension
is long — as *diēi*, *spēi;* though it is short, according to the general
rule, in *fidĕi.*
2. *a* and *e* are long in the vocative terminations *āi* and *ēi* of words
of the second declension ending in *aius* and *eius* — as *Gāï*, *Pompēï*,
from *Gaius* and *Pompeius.*
3. *i* is long in the genitive termination *īus*—as *unīus*, *ullīus*, *nullīus*,
neutrīus; but in *alterĭus* the *i* is generally short.
4. The *a* before *i* in the obsolete genitive of the first declension is
always long—as *Musāï*, *mensāï.*
5. The first vowel in *ēheu* is always long, and in *ōhe* sometimes.
Dīus has the *i* always long, and *Dĭana* sometimes. The *i* is further
long in all the forms of the verb *fīo*, except those which contain an
r; hence *fīo*, *fīebaṃ*, *fīent*, but *fĭerem*, *fĭeri.*
6. Greek words, when adopted into the Latin language, retain their
original quantity—as *āër*, *ēos*, *herōus*, *Menelāus.* When, therefore,
the Latin *e* or *i* represent the Greek *η*, or the diphthong *ει*, the *e* and
i are always long. Hence *Brisēis*, *Medēa*, *Aenēas*, *Alexandrīa*, *Epicurēus*, *spondēus*, *Samarīa;* but when the Latin *e* or *i* answers to the
Greek *ε* or *ĭ*, they are short, as in *idĕa*, *philosophĭa.*

§ 12. It is impossible by any general rule to determine the
quantity of the radical syllables in words of more than one
syllable, and the student must here be led to learn by observation; but it must be remarked, that the vowels of radical
syllables retain the same quantity in all derivative and compound words, even when the radical vowel is changed into
another—as, *māter*, *māternus ; păter*, *păternus ; scrĭbo*, *scrĭbere*,
scrĭba, *perscrĭbere ; ămo*, *ămor*, *ămicus*, *ămicitia*, *inĭmicitia;
cădo*, *incĭdo ; caedo*, *incido ; docēbam*, *docēbamus*, *docēbamini*,
docēbantur ; amātus, *amāturus ; monĭtum*, *admonĭtio.*

Note. Exceptions :—
1. Perfects of two syllables, as well as the tenses formed from them,
have the penult long (except when the *i* of the perfect is preceded by
a vowel), though in the present tense it may be short—as *fūgi*, *lēgi*,
vīdi, *fūgeram*, *fūgissem*, *fūgisse*, from *fŭgio*, *lĕgo*, *vĭdeo;* but *rŭi*,
dirŭi, from *rŭo* and *dirŭo.* But there are seven perfects and nine
supines of two syllables, in which the penult is always short—
namely, *bĭbi*, *dĕdi*, *fĭdi*, *stĕti*, *stĭti*, *tŭli*, and *scĭdi;* and *dătum*, *rătum*,
sătum, *ĭtum*, *lĭtum*, *sĭtum*, *quĭtum*, *cĭtum*, and *rŭtum.*
2. Derivative words differ in quantity from their primitives—*a.* In
the case of perfects and supines before the terminations (*si*, *sum*, *tum*)
of which a consonant has been dropped—as in *divīsi*, *divīsum*, from
divĭdo; vīsum, from *vĭdeo; mōtum*, from *mŏveo; cāsum*, from *cădo. Pōno*,
on the other hand, makes *pŏsui*, *pŏsitum. b.* In the case of other derivative forms—as, *hūmanus*, from *hŏmo; sēcius*, from *sĕcus; rex*, *rēgis*,

rēgula, from *rĕgo ; lex, lēgis*, from *lĕgo ; suspīcio*, from *suspĭcor ; vox, vōcis*, from *vŏco ; sēdes*, from *sĕdeo ; ambĭtus*, from *ambīre, ambĭtum ; dux, dŭcis*, from *dūco ; fĭdes, perfĭdus*, from *fīdo (fĭdus, infĭdus) ; nŏta* and *nŏtare*, from *nōtus.*

3. In compound words, also, the quantity is sometimes changed— as *dejĕro* and *pejĕro*, from *jūro ; cognĭtus, agnĭtus*, from *nōtus ; pronŭbus, innŭbus*, from *nūbo.* In *connŭbium* the *u* is doubtful. All words, moreover, ending in *dĭcus* have the *i* short, though they are formed from the verb *dīco*, I say.

§ 13. Monosyllabic words ending in a vowel are long, except the enclitic particles *quĕ, vĕ, cĕ, nĕ, tĕ* (as in *tutĕ*), *psĕ* (as in *reapsĕ*), and *ptĕ* (as in *suoptĕ*).

Note. The conjunction *ne*, however, always has the *ē* long, in accordance with the rule.

§ 14. Monosyllabic substantives ending in a consonant are long—as *sōl*, the sun ; *vēr*, the spring ; *fūr*, a thief ; *jŭs*, law ; but all other monosyllabic words ending in a consonant are short—as *ŭt, ĕt, nĕc, ĭn, ăd, quĭd, sĕd, quĭs, quŏt.*

Note. Exceptions : —
1. The following substantives of one syllable have their vowel short: —*cŏr*, the heart ; *fĕl*, the bile ; *mĕl*, honey ; *vĭr*, a man ; and *ŏs*, a bone.
2. Some monosyllabic words ending in a consonant are long ; though they are not substantives—namely, *ēn, nōn, quīn, sīn, crās, plūs, cūr, pār* with its compounds ; and the adverbs ending in *ĭc* or *ūc*, as *sīc, hīc*, and *hūc.*

§ 15. The quantity of final syllables of words of more than one syllable, in declension and conjugation, as well as in derivation, can be determined by the following general rules, the details of which will be given in the chapters on the declensions, the conjugations, and derivation : —

§ 16. The termination *a* in nouns is short—as *mensă, lignă, animaliă, Palladă ;* but it is long in the ablative singular of the first declension (*mensā*) ; in the vocative of those Greek words of the first declension which end in the nominative in *as*—as *Aeneā ;* in the imperative of verbs of the first conjugation—as *amā, laudā ;* and in the indeclinable words *intrā, extrā, ergā, anteā, praetereā, proptereā, trigintā, quadragintā,* and others. It is short in the words *ĭtă, quĭă, eĭă,* and *pută* in the sense of 'for example.'

§ 17. The termination *e* is generally short—as *patrĕ, matrĕ, currĕ, scribĕ, nempĕ, propĕ, facilĕ, difficilĕ, legerĕ ;* but it is long in the ablative of the fifth declension—as *diē, faciē ;* in the imperative of the second conjugation—as *valē, vidē, monē, docē ;* in all adverbs formed from adjectives ending in *us*—as *doctē, rectē, doctissimē, optimē,* also in *ferē, fermē, ohē ;* and lastly, in words borrowed from the Greek language when they end in *η*—as *crambē, Tempē, Circē.* The adverbs *benĕ, malĕ*, however, always have their final *e* short, and *infernĕ* and *supernĕ* sometimes.

§ 18. The termination *i* is commonly long—as in *puerī, patrī, fructuī, vidī;* it is short only in the vocative of Greek words which end in the nominative in *is*—as *Parĭ* (from *Paris*), *Alexĭ* (from *Alexis*); and in the words *nisĭ, quasĭ*, and *cuĭ* (when used as a word of two syllables). In the following words it may be used either long or short:—*mihĭ, tibĭ, sibĭ, ibĭ, ubĭ.* *Ubĭ*, in composition, also has the *i* sometimes long and sometimes short—as *ubĭque*, but *ubĭcunque*, and *necubĭ, sicubĭ, ubĭvis, ubĭnam.*

§ 19. The termination *o*, in the first person of verbs, and in the nominative of substantives of the third declension, may be used long or short, though it is more commonly long—as *amŏ, amaverŏ, sermŏ, virgŏ.* It is always long in the dative and ablative singular of the second declension; further, in *ambō*, and in adverbs—as *porrō, quō, falsō, quandō, idcircō, vulgō, omnīnō, ergō*—except *modŏ* (and its compounds, as *tantummodŏ, quomodŏ, dummodŏ*), *citŏ, immŏ.* It is also short in *duŏ*, two; *octŏ*, eight; *egŏ*, I; *cedŏ*, say; *endŏ* (obsolete for *in*).

Note. Greek words ending in ω naturally have the *o* long when introduced into Latin—as *Iō, echō, Sapphō.*

§ 20. The termination *u* is always long—as in *cornū, diū, fructū, vultū.*

§ 21. The termination *y* occurs only in a very few Greek words, and is always short—as in *molÿ.*

§ 22. All final syllables ending in a single consonant, except *s*, are short—as *donĕc, illŭd, consŭl, amĕm, amĕr, amatŭr, amabăm, carmĕn, forsăn, agĕr, patĕr, satŭr, capŭt.* Exceptions are *alēc, lĭēn, pār* and its compounds, as *dispār,* and adverbs formed from *ille* and *iste, illīc, illāc, illōc, istīc.*

Note. Greek words introduced into Latin retain their original quantity—as *aēr, cratēr, aethēr, Sirēn, georgicōn;* but the termination ωρ is shortened in Latin into *ŏr;* as *Hectŏr, rhetŏr.*

§ 23. Final syllables ending in *s* require special rules. The termination *as* is generally long—as in *mensās, aetās, amās;* but it is short in *anăs*, in Greek words ending in *as* which form their genitive in *ădis*—as *Iliăs, Pallăs;* and in the Greek accusative plural of the third declension, as *heroăs.*

§ 24. The termination *es* is generally long—as in *cladēs, aedēs, monēs, docēs, regēs, seriēs, amēs, dicēs, quotiēs.* It is, however, short—1. In the nominative singular of those words of the third declension which form their genitive in *ĕtis, ĭtis*, or *ĭdis*—as *segĕs, milĕs, obsĕs;* 2. In *ĕs* (thou art, from *sum*) and its compounds—as *abĕs, adĕs, potĕs;* 3. In *penĕs* (in the power of or with), and in all Greek nominatives plural of the third declension—as *craterĕs, Arcadĕs;* and 4. In Greek neuters ending in *es*—as *Cynosargĕs, Hippomanĕs.*

Note. The words *abiēs, ariēs,* and *pariēs,* have their final syllable long, although they make their genitive in *ĕtis.*

§ 25. The termination *is* is generally short — as *ignĭs, regĭs, facilĭs, dicĭs, tegĭs;* but it is long —1. In the dative and ablative plural — as in *mensīs, puerīs, populīs, vobīs, nobīs;* and in the accusative plural of the third declension, where it is sometimes used instead of *ēs*—as *omnīs* for *omnēs;* 2. In the second person singular of the present of the fourth conjugation — as *audīs, punīs;* and in the verbs *vīs, sīs* (and its compounds, *adsīs, absīs, praesīs*), *fīs, velīs, nolīs, malīs;* 3. In the nominative of proper names of the third declension which increase in the genitive and retain a long *ī*—as *Quirīs (Quirītes), Samnīs (Samnītes), Salamīs (Salamīnis), Eleusīs (Eleusīnis), Simoīs (Simoëntis).*

Note. The second person of the perfect subjunctive and future perfect may be used either long or short — as *amaverĭs, legerĭs, monuerĭs, audiverĭs.*

§ 26. The termination *os* is long, except in the words *compŏs, impŏs,* and in those Greek words in which the termination ος is retained in Latin—as *Delŏs, Seriphŏs, Erinnyŏs* (genitive of *Erinnys*).

§ 27. The termination *us* is generally short—as *annŭs, populŭs, corpŭs, vetŭs, fontibŭs, legibŭs, senatŭs, tenŭs, funditŭs;* but it is long —1. In the genitive singular and in the nominative and accusative plural of the fourth declension—as *senatūs* (gen.), *quercūs* (nom. or accus. plur.) : 2. In the nominative of words of the third declension which retain *u* long in the genitive — as *virtūs, virtūtis; palūs, palūdis; tellūs, tellūris:* 3. In those cases of Greek words where the Latin *us* answers to the Greek diphthong ους—as *Sapphūs* (gen. of *Sappho*), *Melampūs;* but *Oedipŭs* has the *u* short notwithstanding.

§ 28. The termination *ys* occurs only in Greek words, and is short, except in a very few instances in which *ys* is a contraction for *yis.*

§ 29. A syllable, though naturally short, may become long by its vowel being followed by two or more consonants (see § 9). It makes no difference whether the two consonants following a vowel belong to the same word or to different words —as *amabŭnt, făx, dāntis, inferrētque, passŭs sum.*

§ 30. When in the same word a vowel is followed by two consonants, the first of which is a mute, and the second a liquid, the position is termed weak (*positio debilis*); that is, the vowel may be pronounced either long or short—as *pătris*, *tenĕbrae*, *mediŏcris*, *vĕpres*, *pŏples*, *Ătlas*, *assēcla*.

Note 1. It need hardly be observed, that if a vowel before a mute and a liquid be naturally long, it always remains so—as in *salūbris*, *delūbrum*, *ambulācrum*, *lavācrum*.

2. The consonant *j* alone has the power of making the preceding vowel long, because it was probably pronounced, like *x* and *z*, as a double consonant—hence *mājor*, *ējus;* but in the compounds of *jugum* it nevertheless leaves the preceding vowel short—as *bĭjugus*, *quadrĭjugus*.

3. *Qu* is never treated as two consonants, though we commonly pronounce it like *kw*. See § 4, note.

§ 31. In consequence of the prevailing practice in modern languages, we are inclined, in pronouncing Latin, to place the accent always upon a long syllable, as in most modern languages the accented syllables are usually long. But in the ancient languages, quantity and accent have no connection with one another, and a short syllable may have the emphatic accent, while a long syllable in the same word is not accented at all. Generally speaking, there is in every word one syllable which has the accent; that is, which is pronounced more emphatically than the rest. This accent may be either the acute (') or circumflex (ˆ). These signs, however, are not used either in printing, or in writing Latin.

Note 1. In some editions of the Latin classics, vowels are marked with ^, to indicate that they are long; but this is an injurious practice, because it might mislead the beginner, making him believe that such a vowel is accented, when it is not. Mere length should always be indicated by ¯.

2. Some words have no accent at all—namely, 1. Those particles called enclitics which always attach themselves to other words, and never appear by themselves—as *que, ve, ne, ce;* 2. All prepositions, when they are placed before the case which they govern — as *per úrbem, propter moénia*, but *moénia propter*.

§ 32. Words of one syllable have the circumflex, if their vowel is naturally long; in all other cases they have the acute.

§ 33. In words of two syllables, the accent is always on the penultima; and in those of three or more syllables, it is on the penultima, if this be long; but if the penultima be short, it goes back to the last but two (antepenultima): the last syllable of a word never has the accent. The penultima has the circumflex when its vowel is naturally long, and that of the last syllable short; but if the last is long, the penultima can have only the acute. The antepenultima can never have any other accent than the acute. Examples: *Rômă, Rómă, hó mŏ, léctŭs, Rōmânŭs, Rōmánōs, Metéllŭs, mŏribŭs, carminiuŭs, hŏminēs.*

Note. A syllable having the circumflex is dwelt upon by the voice longer than one which has only the acute, though the vowels should be pronounced with equal emphasis in each case—as in *légo,* I read, and *lēgo,* I despatch; *pálus,* a marsh, and *pâlus,* a post. The length of a syllable by position does not come into consideration in the rules about accent. The right accentuation of syllables is a great help to the beginner in determining the quantity. Those syllables of a word which have no accent at all are said to have the grave accent (`).

CHAPTER III.

THE DIFFERENT CLASSES OF WORDS OR PARTS OF SPEECH.

§ 34. The words of the Latin language are divided into nine classes—namely, 1. Substantives; 2. Adjectives; 3. Pronouns; 4. Numerals; 5. Verbs; 6. Adverbs; 7. Prepositions; 8. Conjunctions; and 9. Interjections.

§ 35. The first four of these classes may be comprised under the common name of Nouns, and, with some exceptions among the numerals, they are capable of inflection, called *declension.* Verbs also are capable of an inflection, which is called *conjugation.* The remaining four classes, and some of the numerals, are not capable of inflection, but retain the same form under all circumstances.

§ 36. Declension and conjugation consist mainly in the change of termination. The various relations expressed by these terminations are marked by separate words in those languages which have no inflections, or too few to express all those relations—as *patris domus,* the house *of* the father; *coluisti Deum,* thou *hast* reverenced God.

§ 37. The Latin language has no article; hence we can only gather from the context as to whether, for example, *homo* must be translated *the* man or *a* man.

CHAPTER IV.

SUBSTANTIVES AND THEIR GENDERS.

§ 38. A substantive is the name of a person or thing which we can perceive by our senses, or which we conceive in our mind as a distinct and independent existence—as *mensa*, a table ; *liber*, a book ; *domus*, a house ; *Julius*, Julius ; *populus*, a people ; *virtus*, valour ; *justitia*, justice ; *amicitia*, friendship.

§ 39. Substantives are either generic terms—that is, names applied to whole classes of persons or things which have certain qualities or peculiarities in common ; or proper names— that is, names given to individual persons or things without any regard to their qualities. *Equus*, horse, is a term applied to every animal possessing certain qualities ; but *Julius* and *Roma* are the names of a particular person and of a particular place ; and if several persons bear the name of Julius, it is not because they have certain qualities in common, as in the case of the name *horse*, but is merely accidental.

§ 40. All objects designated by substantives are either living beings or things ; and as all living beings are either male or female, their names in language are either masculine or feminine. The names of things having no sex, should accordingly be of neither gender—that is, they should be neuter —but by a kind of personification, the Latin language, in common with many others, assigns the masculine or feminine gender even to names of things.

Note. The names of inanimate things are generally neuter in the English language, but in a few instances we also adopt the personifying system of the Latins—thus, a ship, a country, a town, the moon, are treated as feminine words ; while the sun, time, and death are regarded as masculines.

§ 41. The gender of Latin substantives may be ascertained partly from their meaning and partly from their terminations. We shall here confine ourselves to the rules by which the gender can be ascertained from the meaning of substantives, reserving those concerning the terminations for the chapters on the declensions. It is necessary to know the genders of Latin substantives, because adjectives, pronouns, and numerals, when joined to a substantive, must accommodate themselves to it, by assuming a termination corresponding with the gender of the substantive—as *pater bon*us, a good father ; *filia bon*a, a good daughter ; *corpus san*um, a healthy body.

§ 42. Names of men, male beings, rivers, winds, and months, are masculine, whatever their termination may be—as *vir*, a man; *scriba*, a scribe; *poëta*, a poet; *consul*, a consul; *Deus*, God; *aries*, a ram; *verres*, a boar; *taurus*, a bull; *Tiberis*, the Tiber; *Albis*, the Elbe; *Sequăna*, the Seine; *Etesiae*, the passage winds; *Auster*, south-wind; *Januarius*, January; *September*, September.

Note. Exceptions:—
1. Among the names of rivers, a few are feminines—as *Allia*, *Matrona* (Marne), *Albula*, *Lethe*, *Styx*.
2. Some substantives, which do not originally signify living beings, but were in the course of time applied to them by custom, retain their original gender, as determined by their termination—as, *mancipium* (neut.), a slave; *scortum* (neut.), a prostitute.; *operae* (fem.), labourers; *vigiliae* and *excubiae* (fem.), sentinels; *copiae* (fem.), troops; *auxilia* (neut. pleur.), auxiliary troops.
3. A few names of rivers ending in *r*, being neither Latin nor Greek, are neuter—as *Elaver*.
4. The names of months are, properly speaking, adjectives, to which the masculine substantive *mensis* must be understood.

§ 43. Names of women, female beings, whatever their terminations may be, are feminine—as *femina*, a woman; *uxor*, a wife; *soror*, a sister; *socrus*, mother-in-law; *dea*, a goddess; *nympha*, a nymph; *Glycerium*, *Leontium*, two names of females. Most of the names of trees, towns, countries, islands, and precious stones, are likewise feminine—as *cedrus*, a cedar; *pinus*, a fir-tree; *fagus*, a beech-tree; *ficus*, a fig-tree; *Corinthus*, Corinth; *Tyrus*, Tyre; *Lacedaemon*, Lacedaemon; *Aegyptus*, Egypt; *Salamis*, Salamis; *Delos*, Delos; *smaragdus*, emerald.

Note. Exceptions:—
1. Names of trees and plants in *er*, belonging to the third declension, are neuter—as, *siler*, the spindle-tree; *cicer*, small pulse; *papaver*, poppy; but *oleaster*, a wild olive-tree, and *pinaster*, a wild pine-tree, which belong to the second declension; *styrax*, the storax-tree, and many other names of trees and shrubs in *us* of the second declension—are masculine—as *amarantus*, amaranth; *asparagus*, asparagus; *calamus*, reed; *dumus*, a brier; *helleborus*, the hellebore; *intubus*, succory; *rhamnus*, buckthorn; *spinus*, the sloe. *Robur*, an oak-tree, is neuter.
2. The following names of towns are masculine:—a. All plural names ending in *i*—as *Argi* (Argos), *Delphi*, *Veii*, *Parisii;* b. Five names ending in *o*—namely, *Hippo* (Regius), *Narbo*, *Frusino*, *Sulmo*, and *Croto;* c. All names of towns ending in *um* and *on* are neuter—as *Tarentum*, *Beneventum*, *Tusculum*, *Ilion;* d. All names of towns ending in *a*, and forming their genitive in *orum*, are neuter—as *Leuctra*, *Susa*, *Ecbatana;* e. All names of towns ending in *e* and *ur*, together with *Tuder*, are likewise neuter—as *Caere*, *Reate*, *Praeneste*, *Anxur*, *Tibur*.
3. All names of countries ending in *um*, and the plurals in *a*, are neuter—as *Latium*, *Samnium*, *Bactra;* the name *Delta* is likewise neuter. The names *Bosporus*, *Pontus*, and *Hellespontus*, are masculine.

§ 44. Indeclinable substantives, the names of the letters of the alphabet, and all words which, without being substantives, are used as such (provided they do not refer to persons, as in the case of *boni*, good men), are neuter—as *fas*, divine right; *nefas*, an act contrary to the laws of religion; *gummi*, gum; *pascha*, easter; *sinapi*, mustard; *pondo*, a pound; *o longum*, a long o; *Graecum digamma*, the Greek digamma; *hoc ipsum diu*, this very word *diu*, or long; *illud paene*, that word *paene*, or almost.

Note. The names of the letters of the alphabet are sometimes used as feminine, the feminine substantive *litera* being understood. It must be observed, that the neuter gender of words mainly depends upon their terminations, whence we must refer the student to the rules of gender in the chapters on the declensions.

§ 45. Some substantives denoting persons, without any distinction of sex being thought of, are masculine—as *hostis*, an enemy, whether it be a man or a woman; *testis*, a witness; *civis*, a citizen; *sacerdos*, a priest or priestess; *comes*, a companion; *conjux*, a wife or a husband; *heres*, an heir or heiress; *parens*, a parent (either father or mother). But if the person designated by any of these words is to be described as a female, they are used as feminine.

§ 46. Some substantives (called *substantiva mobilia*) receive different terminations according as they designate male or female beings. Thus many masculine substantives ending in *tor* have a feminine in *trix*, and some ending in *us* or any other termination have a feminine in *a*—as *victor*, a conqueror, and *victrix*, a female conqueror; *ultor*, an avenger, and *ultrix*, a female avenger; *coquus*, a male cook, and *coqua*, a female cook; *magister*, a teacher, and *magistra*, a female teacher; *rex*, a king, and *regina*, a queen; *avus*, a grandfather, and *avia*, a grandmother. The same is the case with many names of animals—as *agnus*, a male lamb, and *agna*, a female lamb; *cervus*, a stag, and *cerva*, a hind or doe; *equus*, a horse, and *equa*, a mare; *lupus*, a he-wolf, and *lupa*, a she-wolf; *leo*, a lion, and *lea* or *leaena*, a lioness. It should, however, be observed, that when the sex is not to be particularly pointed out, the masculine form is commonly used.

Note 1. Most names of animals have only one form, which is used both for the male and female; and if the particular sex is to be specified, it is done by an adjective—as *anas mas*, a male duck; *anas femina*, a female duck; *vulpes mas* or *mascula*, a male fox; *canis rabida*, a rabid bitch.

2. Some names of animals are altogether different words when they denote female animals—as *taurus*, a bull, *vacca*, a cow; *aries*, a ram, *ovis*, a ewe; *hoedus*, a he-goat, *capra* or *capella*, a she-goat; *catus*, a tom-cat, *felis*, a female cat.

3. Some names of animals have a masculine and a feminine form, without either having reference to any particular sex—as *coluber* and *colubra*, a serpent; *luscinia* and *luscinius*, a nightingale; *simius* and *simia*, a monkey. Others, again, have only one form, but may be used at discretion, either as masculines or as feminines, and that without any regard to difference of sex—as *anguis* and *serpens*, a serpent; *dama*, a fallow-deer; *talpa*, a mole; *sus*, a pig; *tigris*, a tiger; though *sus* is more commonly feminine, and *tigris* masculine.

CHAPTER V.

GENERAL OBSERVATIONS ON THE DECLENSION OF SUBSTANTIVES.

§ 47. By declension a language expresses the different relations in which a noun is placed to other words. These relations are indicated in Latin by terminations, while the English language is in most cases obliged to express them by separate words called prepositions — as *patr*ı, *to* the father; *patr*ıs, *of* the father; *patr*ᴇ, *by* or *from* the father.

§ 48. There are six great or general relations which the Latin language can indicate by such terminations, and it accordingly has six cases — namely, the Nominative, Genitive, Dative, Accusative, Vocative, and Ablative — which are distinguished from one another by their terminations.

§ 49. The Nominative denotes the person or the thing spoken of; that is, the subject of a sentence—as *Deus creavit mundum*, God has created the world, where *Deus* (God) is the nominative, or the subject.

The Genitive denotes possession, or any of the relations which are expressed in English by *of* — as *patris domus*, the father's house, where *patris* is the genitive; *amor Dei*, the love of God, where *Dei* is the genitive.

The Dative denotes the person or thing for which or to which anything is or is done; as *pater dat filio librum*, the father gives to the son a book, where *filio* is the dative (to the son).

The Accusative denotes the person or thing in which an action terminates, or which is the object of an action—as in the above example, *pater dat filio librum*, where *librum* (a book) is the accusative, and the object of the action of giving.

The Vocative is used in addressing an object — as *Deus*, O God! *mater*, O mother! or simply, mother!

The Ablative, which is peculiar to the Latin language, expresses a variety of relations, such as separation, instrumentality, time, place, &c., which we express by the prepositions *from, by, with, in, at,* &c.

Note. The nominative and vocative are termed in Latin *casus recti,* the upright or independent cases ; and the four others *casus obliqui,* oblique or dependent cases, because they are always dependent upon or governed by other words.

§ 50. A substantive may either denote a single person or thing, or it may denote many—as *house, houses.* In the former case, it is said to be in the Singular, and in the latter, in the Plural. The Latin language, accordingly, has two numbers, the singular and the plural; and in each number a noun has six cases; that is, six cases in the singular, and six in the plural.

Note. If the Latin language were perfect, it would have twelve different terminations for each substantive—six for the singular, and six for the plural—but we shall see hereafter that this is not the case.

§ 51. There are five modes in which nouns are declined, and the language, accordingly, has five declensions. In order to determine to which of these five declensions a noun belongs, it is necessary to know its termination in the genitive singular. Words belonging to the first declension, end, in the genitive singular, in *ae ;* those belonging to the second, in *ī ;* those of the third, in *ĭs ;* those of the fourth, in *ūs ;* and those of the fifth, in *eï.*

Note 1. There are other marks, also, which may show to what declension a word belongs, such as the termination of the nominative singular and the gender ; but no sign is so safe and universal a guide as the genitive singular, for which reason it is marked in all dictionaries.

2. The only exceptions to the above rule about the termination of the genitive singular occur in the case of pronouns and numerals, which for this reason require to be considered separately.

§ 52. Certain points are common to all declensions—namely,

1*st.* All neuter nouns have the nominative, accusative, and vocative, alike, and in the plural these cases end in *ă.* Neuters, however, occur only in the second, third, and fourth declensions.

2*d.* The accusative singular of all declensions ends in *m,* and the accusative plural in *s,* except in the case of neuters, which have the accusative like the nominative.

3*d.* The vocative, both in the singular and the plural, is like the nominative, except in words ending in *us,* belonging to the second declension.

4*th.* The genitive plural of all declensions ends in *um.*

5*th.* The dative plural in all declensions is like the ablative plural.

§ 53. The following table shows the terminations of all the cases in all declensions:—

SINGULAR.

	1st.	2d.	3d.	4th.	5th.
Nom.	ă (ē,ās,ēs)	us,er(nt.um)	a,e,o,c,l,n,r,	ŭs (nt. ŭ)	ēs
Gen.	ae (ēs)	ī	ĭs [s,t,x	ūs	eï
Dat.	ae	ō	ī	uī	eï
Acc.	am (ēn)	um (nt. um)	em (im)	um (nt. ŭ)	em
Voc.	like Nom.	ĕ, er (nt. um)	like Nom.	like Nom.	like Nom.
Abl.	ā (ē)	ō	ĕ or ī	ŭ	ē

PLURAL.

Nom.	ae	ī (nt. ă)	ēs (nt. ă or iă)	ūs (nt. uă)	ēs
Gen.	ārum	ōrum	um or ium	uum	ērum
Dat.	īs	īs	ĭbus	ĭbus or ŭbus	ēbus
Acc.	ās	ōs (nt. ă)	like Nom.	like Nom.	like Nom.
Voc.	like Nom.	like Nom.	like Nom.	like Nom.	like Nom.
Abl.	like Dat.	like Dat.	like Dat.	like Dat.	like Dat.

In order to decline any noun, it is only necessary to know the genitive, which consists of the stem of the word and the termination: the stem remains the same in all the cases, and the termination is the only part of the word which is changed.

CHAPTER VI.

FIRST DECLENSION.

§ 54. All Latin nouns (adjective and substantive) belonging to the first declension, terminate in the nominative singular in ă, and form their genitive in ae.

Note. There are a few Greek words ending in ās, ē, ēs, which were introduced by the Romans into their language; and the declension of these is somewhat different from that of genuine Latin words.

The following examples may serve as specimens:—

SINGULAR.	PLURAL.
Nom. *mens-ă*, the (or a) table.	Nom. *mens-ae*, the tables.
Gen. *mens-ae*, of the (or a) table.	Gen. *mens-ārum*, of the tables.
Dat. *mens-ae*, to the (or a) table.	Dat. *mens-īs*, to the tables.
Acc. *mens-am*, the (or a) table.	Acc. *mens-ās*, the tables.
Voc. *mens-ă*, table!	Voc. *mens-ae*, tables!
Abl. *mens-ā*, from, with, or by the (or a) table.	Abl. *mens-īs*, from, with, or by the tables.

SINGULAR.	PLURAL.
Nom. *vi-ă*, the (or a) road.	Nom. *vi-ae*, the roads.
Gen. *vi-ae*, of the (or a) road.	Gen. *vi-ārum*, of the roads.
Dat. *vi-ae*, to the (or a) road.	Dat. *vi-īs*, to the roads.
Acc. *vi-am*, the (or a) road.	Acc. *vi-ās*, the roads.
Voc. *vi-ă*, road!	Voc. *vi-ae*, roads!
Abl. *vi-ā*, from, with, or by the	Abl. *vi-īs*, from, with, or by the
(or a) road.	roads.

Words to be used as Exercises.

Penna, a wing or feather; *epistola*, a letter; *hora*, an hour; *porta*, a gate; *victoria*, victory; *silva*, a forest; *fuga*, flight; *uva*, a grape; *tabula longa*, a long tablet; *epistola scripta*, a written letter. All the feminine forms of adjectives and participles ending in *a* follow the first declension.

Note 1. The first declension is sometimes called the *a* declension, because the termination *a*, which appears in the nominative, is retained in all the other cases, though in some it disappears, being contracted with another vowel contained in the termination, as we shall see presently.

2. The genitive singular terminated in early Latin, as in Greek, in *ās* (a contraction for *aes*)—as in *aurās*, and in the expressions *pater familiās* (father of a family), *mater familiās* (mother of a family), and *filius familiās* (a son belonging to a family), which continued to be used by the best writers of the Golden Age.

3. All the cases now ending in *ae* (genitive and dative singular, and nominative and vocative plural) at one time ended in *aï*, which was subsequently contracted into *ai* or *ae*. The genitive singular in *ai*, which the poets used as two syllables with a long penult (*āï*), occurs even in Virgil and some of the later poets. See § 11, note 4.

4. The termination of the ablative *ā*, is a contraction for *aë*, whence the *a* is long.

5. Some words, more especially the Greek patronymics and the Latin compounds with *gena* and *cola*, form their genitive plural in *um* instead of *arum*, e.g. *terrigenum* for *terrigenarum; coelicolum* for *coelicolarum; Aeneadum* for *Aeneadarum.*

6. The dative and ablative plural of feminine nouns in *a* originally ended in *ābus*, which was subsequently contracted into *is;* but the ancient form was preserved in a few words, to distinguish them from the masculines which follow the second declension, and must make their dative and ablative plural in *is*, as *dea* (a goddess), *filia* (a daughter), *anima* (soul), *liberta* (freedwoman), *equa* (a mare), *mula* (a mule), which make their dative and ablative *deābus, filiābus, animābus, libertābus, equābus, mulābus*, if the gender is not sufficiently clear from the context. The feminines of *duo* (two), and *ambo* (both), likewise make their dative and ablative plural *duābus* and *ambābus.*

§ 55. The Greek words in *ās, ēs*, and *ē*, are declined like the following specimens. Many of them are proper names, and have no plural; but those which have a plural, form it like the genuine Latin substantives:—

Nom.	*Aene-ās.*		Nom.	*Anchīs-ēs.*
Gen.	*Aene-ae.*		Gen.	*Anchis-ae.*
Dat.	*Aene-ae.*		Dat.	*Anchis-ae.*
Acc.	*Aene-am* or *Aene-an.*		Acc.	*Anchis-ēn* or *Anchis-am.*
Voc.	*Aene-ā.*		Voc.	*Anchis-ē* or *Anchis-ă.*
Abl.	*Aene-ā.*		Abl.	*Anchis-ē* or *Anchis-ā.*

SINGULAR.			PLURAL.	
Nom.	*epitom-ē,* an abridgment.		Nom.	*epitom-ae,* abridgments.
Gen.	*epitom-ēs.*		Gen.	*epitom-ārum.*
Dat.	*epitom-ae.*		Dat.	*epitom-īs.*
Acc.	*epitom-ēn.*		Acc.	*epitom-ās.*
Voc.	*epitom-ē.*		Voc.	*epitom-ae.*
Abl.	*epitom-ē.*		Abl.	*epitom-īs.*

Note 1. The following Greek words of this declension are those most common in Latin:—*Boreas* (north wind), *Gorgias, Midas, Pythagoras; planetes* (a planet), *cometes* (a comet), *dynastes* (a ruler), *satrapes* (a satrap), *sophistes* (a sophist), *anagnostes* (a reader), *Thersites,* and all patronymics—that is, words derived from the name of a person, and denoting origin or descent from him—they end in *des,* as *Aeneades,* a son or descendant of·Aeneas ; *Pelīdes,* a son or descendant of Peleus ; *Priamīdes,* a son or descendant of Priam ; *Tydīdes,* a son or descendant of Tydeus. Lastly, such words as *aloë,* the aloe ; *crambe,* cabbage ; *Circe, Danaë, Phoenīce, Penelope, Daphne.*

2. Words in *as* make the accusative in *am,* more especially in prose ; whereas in poetry they prefer *an.* Words in *ās* and *ēs* generally form the vocative by simply omitting the *s;* but proper names and patronymics in *es* sometimes terminate in *a,* which is properly long, but also occurs as short, according to the analogy of genuine Latin words.

3. The ablative of words in *es* is either *ē* or *ā,* but the former occurs more frequently in poetry, and the latter in prose.

4. Many words which are originally Greek, and should end in *e* and *es,* have in the course of time become completely Latinised, and are therefore declined as genuine Latin words—as *epistola,* a letter ; *poëta,* a poet. Others, however, are sometimes used with their Greek, and sometimes with a Latin termination—as *Creta* and *Crete, Penelopa* and *Penelope, musica* and *musice, grammatica* and *grammatice, rhetorica* and *rhetorice,* though the termination *a* seems to be preferable.

5. The beginner must be cautioned against the belief that all Greek names in *es* follow the first declension. Besides the patronymics, there are few Greek names that follow the first declension, and even many of those which in Greek belong to the first are declined in Latin after the third declension, such as *Alcibiades, Euripides, Aeschines, Apelles, Xerxes, Astyages.* Some, again, as *Orestes,* may follow either the first or third declension ; *acinaces* (a Persian sword) follows the third, and *satrapes* the first declension, though its genitive is sometimes *satrapis.*

§ 56. Words of this declension ending in *ă* or *ē* are feminine, and those ending in *ās* or *ēs* are masculine.

Note. Some words in *a* denoting male beings are masculine—as *aurīga* (the driver of a coach), *collēga* (a colleague), *nauta* (a sailor), *poëta* (a poet), *scriba* (a scribe), *agricola* (a husbandman), *parricīda* (a murderer), *incola* (an inhabitant), *advĕna* (a comer, or one who arrives). Names of rivers in *a* are masculine, according to the general rule (§ 42); but *Allia, Albula*, and *Matrŏna* (the Marne), are nevertheless feminine. *Hadria* (the Adriatic Sea) is likewise masculine.

CHAPTER VII.

SECOND DECLENSION.

§ 57. Latin nouns (both substantives and adjectives) which form their genitive by the termination *i*, belong to the second declension. In the nominative, the masculines end in *us*, or *er*, and the neuters in *um*. *Vir* (a man), with its compounds —as *Trevir, triumvir*, and the adjective *saţur* (sated or full, fem. *satŭra*, neut. *satŭrum*), are the only words in *ir* and *ur* belonging to this declension.

The following examples may serve as specimens:—

SINGULAR.	PLURAL.
Nom. *hort-us*, the garden.	Nom. *hort-ī*, the gardens.
Gen. *hort-ī*, of the garden.	Gen. *hort-ōrum*, of the gardens.
Dat. *hort-ō*, to the garden.	Dat. *hort-īs*, to the gardens.
Acc. *hort-um*, the garden.	Acc. *hort-ōs*, the gardens.
Voc. *hort-ĕ*, o garden!	Voc. *hort-ī*, o gardens!
Abl. *hort-ō*, from, with, or by the garden.	Abl. *hort-īs*, from, with, or by the gardens.

SINGULAR.	PLURAL.
Nom. *ager*, a field.	Nom. *agr-ī*, fields.
Gen. *agr-ī*, of a field.	Gen. *agr-ōrum*, of fields.
Dat. *agr-ō*, to a field.	Dat. *agr-īs*, to fields.
Acc. *agr-um*, a field.	Acc. *agr-ōs*, fields.
Voc. *ăger*, o field!	Voc. *agr-ī*, o fields!
Abl. *agr-ō*, from, with, or by a field.	Abl. *agr-īs*, from, with, or by fields.

SINGULAR.	PLURAL.
Nom. *puer*, the boy.	Nom. *puer-ī*, the boys.
Gen. *puer-ī*, of the boy.	Gen. *puer-ōrum*, of the boys.
Dat. *puer-ō*, to the boy.	Dat. *puer-īs*, to the boys.
Acc. *puer-um*, the boy.	Acc. *puer-ōs*, the boys.
Voc. *puer*, o boy!	Voc. *puer-ī*, o boys!
Abl. *puer-ō*, from, with, or by the boy.	Abl. *puer-īs*, from, with, or by the boys.

SINGULAR.	PLURAL.
Nom. *vĭr*, the man.	Nom. *vir-ī*, the men.
Gen. *vir-ī*, of the man.	Gen. *vir-ōrum*, of the men.
Dat. *vir-ō*, to the man.	Dat. *vir-īs*, to the men.
Acc. *vir-um*, the man.	Acc. *vir-ōs*, the men.
Voc. *vir*, o man!	Voc. *vir-ī*, o men!
Abl. *vir-ō*, from, with, or by the man.	Abl. *vir-īs*, from, with, or by the men.

SINGULAR.	PLURAL.
Nom. *templ-um*, the temple.	Nom. *templ-ă*, the temples.
Gen. *templ-ī*, of the temple.	Gen. *templ-ōrum*, of the temples.
Dat. *templ-ō*, to the temple.	Dat. *templ-īs*, to the temples.
Acc. *templ-um*, the temple.	Acc. *templ-ă*, the temples.
Voc. *templ-um*, o temple!	Voc. *templ-ă*, o temples!
Abl. *templ-ō*, from, with, or by the temple.	Abl. *templ-īs*, from, with, or by the temples.

Words to be used as Exercises.

Agnus, a lamb; *annus*, a year; *coquus*, a cook; *corvus*, a raven; *digitus*, a finger; *dolus*, a trick; *dominus*, the master or owner; *equus*, a horse; *famulus*, a man-servant; *fluvius*, a river; *gladius*, a sword; *herus*, a master; *legatus*, an ambassador; *modus*, measure or manner; *murus*, a wall; *nervus*, sinew or string; *ramus*, a branch; *servus*, a slave; *ventus*, the wind; *antrum*, a cave; *astrum*, a star; *bellum*, a war; *donum*, a gift; *initium*, the beginning; *judicium*, the judgment; *membrum*, a limb; *monstrum*, a monster or prodigy; *ovum*, an egg; *tergum*, the back. Respecting the peculiarity in the declension of neuters, see above, § 52.

Note. The adjective *satur* is declined like *vir*, the case endings being merely added to the nominative.

§ 58. Most of the words of this declension ending in *er*, have the *e* only in the nominative and vocative, like *ager*, where it is inserted for the purpose of facilitating the pronunciation; but in the other cases they throw it out. The following are those which retain the *e* in all cases :—*adulter*, an adulterer; *socer*, father-in-law; *gener*, son-in-law; *Liber*, the god Liber or Bacchus; *liberi* (plur.), children (but *libri*, books, from *liber*); *vesper*, evening; the adjectives *asper*, rough; *liber*, free; *lacer*, torn; *miser*, miserable; *prosper*, prosperous; *tener*, tender; and all nouns compounded with *fer* and *ger* (from *fero* and *gero*)—as *mortifer*, deadly; *armiger*, bearing arms; and lastly, the names of nations—*Iber*, an Iberian, and *Celtiber*, a Celtiberian, and the Greek word *presbyter*, an elder. *Dexter*, right, and *Mulciber* (a surname of Vulcan), sometimes retain the *e* in the oblique cases, and sometimes drop it.

Note 1. The second declension is sometimes called the *o* declension; for in the first place, several cases end in *o;* in the second, those which now end in *um* and *us*, anciently ended in *om* and *os;* and lastly, even the cases which now end in *i* or *is*, seem at one time to have ended in *oe* and *oes*, as may be inferred from a comparison of the second Latin with the second Greek declension. The *o* therefore originally appeared in all the case endings of the second declension.

2. Substantives ending in the nominative singular in *ius* and *ium*, should make their genitive in *ii;* but in early Latin they had only a single *i* — as *Appius*, gen. *Appi; consilium* (counsel), gen. *consili; ingenium* (talent), gen. *ingeni*. This form is constantly employed even in the poems of Virgil and Horace; but at a later time, the genitive was generally formed in *ii*.

3. The following adjectives and pronouns, the masculine and neuter of which follow the second, and the feminine the first declension, make their genitive in all the three genders in *īus*, and the dative in *ī:* — *unus*, one ; *solus*, alone ; *totus*, all ; *ullus*, any ; *nullus*, none ; *alius*, another ; *alter*, one of two ; *uter*, either ; *neuter*, neither ; together with the compounds of *uter* and *alter*—such as *uterque*, each of two ; *utervis utercunque, uterlibet*, whichever of two ; e.g. *unus*, gen. *unīus*, dat. *unī; solus*, gen. *solīus*, dat. *solī*. In all their other cases they follow the declensions named above. The *i* before *us* in the genitive is sometimes shortened; and this is most frequently the case with *alter*, gen. *alterĭus*. Some writers, as Caesar, now and then decline *alius, nullus*, &c., regularly after the second declension.

4. Proper names in *ius* form their vocative in *ī*—as *Mercurius*, voc. *Mercurī; Julius*, voc. *Julī; Caius*, voc. *Caï; Pompeius*,voc. *Pompēï*. Among common nouns this vocative occurs only in *filius* (a son), voc. *filī; genius*, voc. *genī*, and *Feretrius*, voc. *Feretrī*. Greek names in *ius* (Greek ειος)—as *Arīus, Heraclīus*, and Greek adjectives in *ius*, make their vocative regularly in *ie*. *Meus* (my) forms the vocative *mī;* and *deus* (God), is always in the vocative like the nominative. The poets sometimes also make the vocative of other words in *us* like the nominative.

5. The genitive plural of some substantives sometimes ends in *ūm* (the Greek ων), instead of *orum*. This is the case especially with such as denote money, weight, or measure—such as *nummus*, a piece of money ; *sestertius*, a sesterce ; *denarius*, a denarius ; *talentum*, a talent; *medimnus*, a medimnus or bushel; all of which make their genit. plur., especially when accompanied by numerals, in *um*—as *nummum, sestertium, denarium, talentum*, &c. In like manner we often find *liberum* (of children), *deum* (of gods), *fabrum* (of workmen), *virum* (of men), instead of *liberorum, deorum, fabrorum, virorum*. The distributive numerals, as *bini* (two each time), *terni* (three each time), *quaterni* (four each time), generally make their genitive in *um* instead of *orum*. Poets often form the gen. plur. of nations in the same manner—as *Argivum, Danaum*, and *Pelasgum* for *Argivorum, Pelasgorum, Danaorum*. Compare §54, note 5. It should be observed that in early Latinity the genitive plural regularly ended in *um* (Greek ων), and not in *orum*.

6. The word *deus* (God) may form the nom., dat., and ablat. plural *dei, deis;* but it more commonly has *dii* and *diis*, or the contracted forms *dī* and *dīs*.

7. Greek names of towns and islands, and also a few common nouns of the second declension, sometimes retain in Latin their original ter-

mination *ŏs* and *ŏn* in the nom. and accus. singular, instead of assuming the Latin endings *us* and *um*, e.g. *Delos*, acc. *Delon; scorpios*, acc. *scorpion; Paros*, acc. *Paron*, &c., though the Latin endings *us* and *um* are also used. The same is the case with neuter names, as *Ilion* and *Ilium*. A few Greek words in *os* make their plural in *oe* (Greek οι), as *Locroe canephoroe*, for *Locri canephori*. Some Greek neuter nouns, which are used as titles of books, as *Georgica, Bucolica*, make their genit. plural in the Greek fashion, in *ōn*, as *Georgicōn, Bucolicōn;* the same occurs, though very rarely, in the case of names of nations, as *Theraeōn* for *Theraeorum*.

8. Greek proper names, which are declined in Greek according to what is called the second Attic declension (in ως), either take the Latin termination *us*, and are declined regularly like *hortus*, or they end in the nom. in *ōs*, and in the accus. in *ōn*—as *Tyndareus* or *Tyndareōs; Androgeus* or *Androgeōs; Athōs* accordingly has its accus. *Athōn;* but both *Androgeōs* and *Athōs* are also declined according to the third declension, making the genitive *Androgeōnis* and *Athōnis*.

9. Greek proper names in *eus* (Greek ευς), as *Orpheus, Prometheus*, are either declined like *hortus*, except that they form the vocative in *eu;* or they follow the third Greek declension, as *Orpheus*, gen. *Orphĕōs*, dat. *Orphĕī* or *Orphei* (as a bissyllabic word), acc. *Orphĕă*, voc. *Orpheu;* but the Greek forms occur almost exclusively in poetry. The name *Perseus* is declined in the following manner:—gen. *Persei*, dat, *Perseo* and *Persi* (from the nom. *Perses*, of the third declension), acc. *Persea* or *Perseum*, abl. *Perseo* (or *Perse* and *Persa*).

§ 59. The nouns of the second declension in *us, er, ir,* and *ur,* are masculine, and those in *um* and the Greek ones in *ŏn* are neuter.

Note. The following words in *us* form an exception to this rule.

1. The names of towns and islands in *us* are feminine—as *Corinthus, Ephesus*, Rhodus (See § 43). To these must be added the names of some countries in *us*—as *Aegyptus, Chersonesus, Epirus, Peloponnesus*, though *Canōpus* is masculine.

2. The names of trees, and of certain shrubs and precious stones, are feminine, e.g. *fagus*, beech; *ficus*, a fig-tree; *malus*, an apple-tree; *pirus*, a pear-tree; *pomus*, an apple-tree; *populus*, a poplar, *ulmus*, elm-tree; *papyrus*, the papyrus plant; *juniperus*, juniper; *amethystus*, amethyst. See § 43.

3. The following feminines must be remembered separately:—*alvus*, belly; *carbăsus*, linen; *colus*, distaff (is sometimes masc.); *humus*, earth; *vannus*, a corn van.

4. Some Greek words which have been adopted into the Latin language retain the fem. gender which they have in Greek—as *methŏdus*, method; *periŏdus*, period; *atŏmus*, an atom; *antidŏtus*, antidote; *dialectus*, dialect; *diamĕtrus*, diameter; *dipthongus*, diphthong; *paragrăphus*, paragraph.

5. The following words in *us* are neuter:—*virus*, juice or poison; *vulgus*, the common people (is, however, sometimes used as a masc.), *pelagus*, the sea.

CHAPTER VIII.

THIRD DECLENSION.

§ 60. The third declension presents greater difficulties than either the first or second; for in these the stem and the termination are distinguishable even in the nominative, and their declension consists only in changing the termination of the nominative in the oblique cases. But in the third declension this is not the case; for the nominative either presents the pure stem without any termination at all, or an *s* (either with or without a euphonic *i* or *e*) is added to the stem; or lastly, the stem is altogether disguised in the nominative, so that one of the oblique cases must be known, in order to distinguish the stem from the termination. All words of the third declension, however, end in the genitive in *is*.

Note. The addition of *s* to the stem for the purpose of forming the nominative, produces considerable changes; for when the stem ends in *c* or *g*, they are united with the *s* into *x*, as *grex* from the stem *greg*, *rex* from *reg*, and *judex* from *judic*. In the last instance the *i* also is changed into *e;* and in the case of *nox* from *noct*, the *t* is thrown out for the sake of euphony. When the stem ends in *t* or *d*, these letters are thrown out before the *s*, as in *aetas* from *aetat*, *miles* from *milit*, *amans* from *amant, dens* from *dent, praeses* from *praesid*. In many cases a euphonic *i* or *e* is inserted between the final consonant of the stem and the *s*, as in *avis*, *navis*, and *ovis*, for *avs*, *navs*, and *ovs; caedes* and *clades*, for *caeds* and *clads*. In some words, the *s* in the nominative is only the representative of *r* (*r* and *s* being convertible in the early language), and belongs to the stem, as in *corpus*, that is, *corpor; decus*, that is, *decor; flos* for *flor, honos* for *honor, labos* for *labor*, &c.

§ 61. We may accordingly divide the nouns of the third declension into the following five classes:—

1. Nouns in which the nominative itself is the stem, so that the terminations of the oblique cases are merely added to it. Examples:—

	SINGULAR.		PLURAL.
Nom.	*consul,* the consul.	Nom.	*consul-ēs,* the consuls.
Gen.	*consŭl-is.*	Gen.	*consul-um.*
Dat.	*consul-ī.*	Dat.	*consul-ĭbus.*
Acc.	*consul-em.*	Acc.	*consul-ēs.*
Voc.	*consul.*	Voc.	*consul-ēs.*
Abl.	*consul-ĕ.*	Abl.	*consul-ĭbus.*

SINGULAR.	PLURAL.
Nom. *honor*, the honour.	Nom. *honor-ēs*, the honours.
Gen. *honor-ĭs*.	Gen. *honor-um*.
Dat. *honor-ĭ*.	Dat. *honor-ĭbus*.
Acc. *honor-em*.	Acc. *honor-ēs*.
Voc. *honor*.	Voc. *honor-ēs*.
Abl. *honor-ĕ*.	Abl. *honor-ibus*.

SINGULAR.	PLURAL.
Nom. *animal* (neut.), an animal.	Nom. *animal-ia*, animals.
Gen. *animal-ĭs*.	Gen. *animal-ĭum*.
Dat. *animal-ĭ*.	Dat. *animal-ĭbus*.
Acc. *animal*.	Acc. *animal-ia*.
Voc. *animal*.	Voc. *animal-ia*.
Abl. *animal-ī*.	Abl. *animal-ĭbus*.

Note. Stems ending in *l* and *r* never take any additional nominative termination. Respecting the neuter termination of the plural *ia*, and the ablat. sing. *i*, see below, §§ 65 and 66.

2. Nouns in which *s* is added to the stem, without any further change to form the nominative. Examples:—

SINGULAR.	PLURAL.
Nom. *urb-s*, a city.	Nom. *urb-ēs*, cities.
Gen. *urb-ĭs*.	Gen. *urb-ium*.
Dat. *urb-ĭ*.	Dat. *urb-ĭbus*.
Acc. *urb-em*.	Acc. *urb-ēs*.
Voc. *urb-s*.	Voc. *urb-ēs*.
Abl. *urb-ĕ*.	Abl. *urb-ĭbus*.

SINGULAR.	PLURAL.
Nom. *grex* (i. e. *greg-s*), a flock.	Nom. *greg-ēs*, flocks.
Gen. *greg-ĭs*.	Gen. *greg-um*.
Dat. *greg-ĭ*.	Dat. *greg-ĭbus*.
Acc. *greg-em*.	Acc. *greg-ēs*.
Voc. *grex*.	Voc. *greg-ēs*.
Abl. *greg-ĕ*.	Abl. *greg-ĭbus*.

SINGULAR.	PLURAL.
Nom. *radix* (i. e. *radic-s*), a root.	Nom. *radic-ēs*, roots.
Gen. *radĭc-ĭs*.	Gen. *radic-um*.
Dat. *radic-ĭ*.	Dat. *radic-ĭbus*.
Acc. *radic-em*.	Acc. *radic-ēs*.
Voc. *radix*.	Voc. *radic-ēs*.
Abl. *radic-ĕ*.	Abl. *radic-ĭbus*.

SINGULAR.	PLURAL.
Nom. *dux* (i. e. *duc-s*), a leader.	Nom. *duc-ēs*, leaders.
Gen. *duc-ĭs*.	Gen. *duc-um*.
Dat. *duc-ĭ*.	Dat. *duc-ĭbus*.
Acc. *duc-em*.	Acc. *duc-ēs*.
Voc. *dux*.	Voc. *duc-ēs*.
Abl. *duc-ĕ*.	Abl. *duc-ĭbus*,

3

3. Nouns in which an *e* or *i* is inserted between the stem and the *s* of the nominative.   Words of this description, which are very numerous, consist in the nominative of the stem and the termination *is* or *es*, and thus resemble in their declension the nouns of the first and second declensions, having in the oblique cases of the singular the same number of syllables as in the nominative.   Examples:—

SINGULAR.	PLURAL.
Nom. *nav-ĭs*, a ship.	Nom. *nav-ēs*, ships.
Gen. *nav-ĭs*.	Gen. *nav-ĭum*.
Dat. *nav-ī*.	Dat. *nav-ĭbus*.
Acc. *nav-em*.	Acc. *nav-ēs*.
Voc. *nav-ĭs*.	Voc. *nav-ēs*.
Abl. *nav-ĕ*, or *nav-ī*.	Abl. *nav-ĭbus*.

SINGULAR.	PLURAL.
Nom. *clad-ēs*, a defeat.	Nom. *clad-ēs*, defeats.
Gen. *clad-ĭs*.	Gen. *clad-ĭum*.
Dat. *clad-ī*.	Dat. *clad-ĭbus*.
Acc. *clad-em*.	Acc. *clad-ēs*.
Voc. *clad-ēs*.	Voc. *clad-ēs*.
Abl. *clad-ĕ*.	Abl. *clad-ĭbus*.

4. Nouns in which the *s* of the nominative causes the final consonants of the stem (*d, t*) to be thrown out.   Sometimes, also, the *i* in the final syllable of the stem is changed into *e*.   Examples:—

SINGULAR.	PLURAL.
Nom. *aeta-s* (for *aetat-s*), age.	Nom. *aetat-ēs*, ages.
Gen. *aetat-ĭs*.	Gen. *aetat-um*.
Dat. *aetat-ī*.	Dat. *aetat-ĭbus*.
Acc. *aetat-em*.	Acc. *aetat-ēs*.
Voc. *aeta-s*.	Voc. *aetat-ēs*.
Abl. *aetat-ĕ*.	Abl. *aetat-ĭbus*.

SINGULAR.	PLURAL.
Nom. *mile-s*,(for *milit-s*),a soldier.	Nom. *milit-ēs*, soldiers.
Gen. *milit-ĭs*.	Gen. *milit-um*.
Dat. *milit-ī*.	Dat. *milit-ĭbus*.
Acc. *milit-em*.	Acc. *milit-ēs*.
Voc. *mile-s*.	Voc. *milit-ēs*.
Abl. *milit-ĕ*.	Abl. *milit-ĭbus*.

SINGULAR.	PLURAL.
Nom. *lau-s* (for *laud-s*), praise.	Nom. *laud-ēs*, praises.
Gen. *laud-ĭs*.	Gen. *laud-um*.
Dat. *laud-ī*.	Dat. *laud-ĭbus*.
Acc. *laud-em*.	Acc. *laud-ēs*.
Voc. *lau-s*.	Voc. *laud-ēs*.
Abl. *laud-ĕ*.	Abl. *laud-ĭbus*.

SINGULAR.	PLURAL.
Nom. *glan-s* (for *gland-s*), acorn.	Nom. *gland-ēs*, acorns.
Gen. *gland-ĭs.*	Gen. *gland-ĭum.*
Dat. *gland-ĭ.*	Dat. *gland-ĭbus.*
Acc. *gland-em.*	Acc. *gland-ēs.*
Voc. *glan-s.*	Voc. *gland-ēs.*
Abl. *gland-ĕ.*	Abl. *gland-ĭbus.*

SINGULAR.	PLURAL.
Nom. *fron-s*(for *front-s*),forehead.	Nom. *front-ēs*, foreheads.
Gen. *front-ĭs.*	Gen. *front-ĭum.*
Dat. *front-ī.*	Dat. *front-ĭbus.*
Acc. *front-em.*	Acc. *front-ēs.*
Voc. *fron-s.*	Voc. *front-ēs.*
Abl. *front-ĕ.*	Abl. *front-ĭbus.*

SINGULAR.	PLURAL.
Nom. *nepo-s* (for *nepot-s*), grand-	Nom. *nepot-ēs*, grandsons.
Gen. *nepot-ĭs.* [son.	Gen. *nepot-um.*
Dat. *nepot-ī.*	Dat. *nepot-ĭbus.*
Acc. *nepot-em.*	Acc. *nepot-ēs.*
Voc. *nepo-s.*	Voc. *nepot-ēs.*
Abl. *nepot-ĕ.*	Abl. *nepot-ĭbus.*

5. Nouns in which the stem, for the sake of euphony, is disguised in the nominative either by the omission of its final consonant, or by the addition of a euphonic vowel, or by the change of one vowel into another. Examples:—

SINGULAR.	PLURAL.
Nom. *sermo* (for *sermon*), conver-	Nom. *sermon-ēs*, conversations.
Gen. *sermon-ĭs.* [sation.	Gen. *sermon-um.*
Dat. *sermon-ī.*	Dat. *sermon-ĭbus.*
Acc. *sermon-em.*	Acc. *sermon-ēs.*
Voc. *sermo.*	Voc. *sermon-ēs.*
Abl. *sermon-ĕ.*	Abl. *sermon-ĭbus.*

SINGULAR.	PLURAL.
Nom. *homo* (for *homin*), man.	Nom. *homin-ēs*, men.
Gen. *homin-ĭs.*	Gen. *homin-um.*
Dat. *homin-ī.*	Dat. *homin-ĭbus.*
Acc. *homin-em.*	Acc. *homin-ēs.*
Voc. *homo.*	Voc. *homin-ēs.*
Abl. *homin-ĕ.*	Abl. *homin-ĭbus.*

SINGULAR	PLURAL.
Nom. *pat-e-r* (for *patr*), father.	Nom. *patr-ēs*, fathers.
Gen. *patr-ĭs.*	Gen. *patr-um.*
Dat. *patr-ī.*	Dat. *patr-ĭbus.*
Acc. *patr-em.*	Acc. *patr-ēs.*
Voc. *pat-e-r.*	Voc. *patr-ēs.*
Abl. *patr-ĕ.*	Abl. *patr-ĭbus.*

3

	SINGULAR.			PLURAL.	
Nom.	*nomen* (for *nomin*, neut.),		Nom.	*nomin-ă*, names.
Gen.	*nomin-ĭs.*	[name.		Gen.	*nomin-um.*
Dat.	*nomin-ī.*			Dat.	*nomin-ĭbus.*
Acc.	*nomen.*			Acc.	*nomin-ă.*
Voc.	*nomen.*			Voc.	*nomin-ă.*
Abl.	*nomin-ĕ.*			Abl.	*nomin-ĭbus.*

	SINGULAR.			PLURAL.	
Nom.	*caput* (for *capit*, neut.) head.		Nom.	*capit-ă*, heads.
Gen.	*capit-ĭs.*			Gen.	*capit-um.*
Dat.	*capit-ī.*			Dat.	*capit-ĭbus.*
Acc.	*caput.*			Acc.	*capit-ă.*
Voc.	*caput.*			Voc.	*capit-ă.*
Abl.	*capit-ĕ.*			Abl.	*capit-ĭbus.*

	SINGULAR.	
Nom.	*lac* (for *lact*, neut.), milk.	
Gen.	*lact-ĭs.*	
Dat.	*lact-ī.*	Has no plural.
Acc.	*lac.*	
Voc.	*lac.*	
Abl.	*lact-ĕ.*	

Note 1. The nouns of this class comprise all neuter nouns in *e*—as *mare*, the sea ; *sedile*, a seat ; *monile*, a necklace ; as well as the neuters of adjectives in *is* and *er;* for in all these cases the *e* is a simple addition to the root.

2. As the letters *r* and *s* were convertible in the early language, it is clear that such words as *mos* (gen. *moris*), *flos* (gen. *floris*), *corpus* (gen. *corporis*), *decus* (gen. *decoris*), *litus* (gen. *litoris*), and *nemus* (gen. *nemoris*), *tellus* (gen. *telluris*), present the pure stem in the nominative, *mos* being identical with *mor*, and *corpus* with *corpor*.

3. No neuter noun of the third declension assumes *s* as the termination of the nominative ; they either present the pure stem—as *animal*, *calcar*, *corpus* (*corpor*)*;* or they disguise it in some other manner—as *nomen* (for *nomin*), *mare* for *mar*, *lac* for *lact*, *caput* for *capit*, *vulnus* for *vulner*, *sidus* for *sider.*

§ 62. We shall now subjoin a list of the terminations as they appear in the nominative, adding to each its genitive and the gender, so far as it can be determined by the ending.

1. Nouns ending in *a* are neuter; they are of Greek origin, and their stem ends in *at*, so that their genitive is *atis*—as *poëma, poëmatis.*

2. Nouns ending in *al* are neuter, and form their genitive by adding *is* to the nominative, which is the pure stem — as *animal, animālis.* *Sal,* however, is commonly masculine (rarely neuter), like the proper name *Hannibal,* and makes its genitive *sălis,* like *Hannibălis.*

3. Nouns ending in *ar* are neuter, and form their genitive

by adding *is* to the nominative, which is the pure stem—as
calcar (spur), genit. *calcăris*. In some, the syllable *ar* preceding the termination is short—as *jubar, ăris*, ray or beam ;
nectar, ăris, nectar. The following words in *ar* are masculine :—*Caesar, ăris ; Arar, ăris ;* and *lar, lăris*, a household
god ; *par, păris*, a companion or equal ; and its compounds
—as *dispar, dispăris*.
4. Nouns ending in *as* are feminine, and their stem ends in
at ; they make their genitive in *ātis*—as *aetas, aetātis*. In
like manner are declined the adjectives in *as* derived from
names of towns—as *Arpinas, ătis*, an inhabitant of Arpinum. *Anas*, a duck, however, makes its genitive *anătis ;*
as (a copper coin), makes *assis ; mas* (a male being), *maris ;*
vas (a surety), *vădis ;* and *vas* (a vessel) is neuter, and makes
its genitive *vāsis*.

Note. Greek feminines in *as* make their genitive in *ădis*—as *lampas,*
ădis (a lamp). So also the names of peoples—as *Arcas, ădis*, and
Nomas, ădis. Greek masculines in *as* generally make their genitive
in *antis*, their stem ending in *ant*—as *gigas* (a giant), *gigantis; ada-*
mas (diamond), *adamantis*. A few neuters in *as* end in the genitive
in *ătis*, the stem ending in *at*—as *erysipelas, erysipelătis*.

5. Nouns ending in *ax* are from a *stem* in *ac*, and form their
genitive by changing the *s* contained in the *x* into *is*, and
are feminine—as *pax* (peace), *pācis ; fornax* (oven), *fornā-*
cis ; fax (a torch), *făcis*. All adjectives in *ax* make their
genitive in the same way. Greek words in *ax* are generally masculine, but *limax* (a snail) is feminine.
6. Nouns ending in *c* are neuter ; but there are only two, *lac*
(milk), gen. *lactis ;* and *alec* (pickle, brine), gen. *alēcis*.
7. Nouns in *e* are neuter, and make their genitive by changing *e* into *is*—as *mare* (the sea), gen. *maris ; facile* (easy),
gen. *facilis*. (Compare § 61, note 1.)
8. The few nouns ending in *el* represent the pure root, forming their genitive by adding *is*, but the *l* is at the same
time doubled. They are neuter—as *mel* (honey), gen. *mel-*
lis ; fel (bile), gen. *fellis*.
9. Nouns in *en*, forming their genitive in *ĭnis*, are generally
neuter ; but the following are masculine :—*pecten*, a comb ;
flamen, a kind of priest ; *cornĭcen*, a player on the horn ;
fidĭcen, a player on the lyre or harp ; *tibĭcen*, a flute-player ;
tubĭcen, a trumpeter ; and the adjective *oscen*, singing.
Those which make their genitive in *ēnis* are masculine—as
ren (kidney), gen. *rēnis ;* but *Siren* (a fabulous female being)
and *Troezen* (a Greek town) are of course feminine.

10. Nouns in *er* either represent the pure stem, and only add *is* in the genitive; or the *e* before the *r* is only euphonic, and is thrown out in the genitive. Those of the first class, making their genitive in *ĕris*, are generally masculine—as *carcer*, *carcĕris;* but the following are neuter :—*cadāver*, a dead body ; *tuber*, a swelling ; *uber*, udder ; *verbera* (a plur., the singular *verber* does not occur), blows ; and all botanical names—as *acer*, maple-tree ; *papaver*, poppy ; *piper*, pepper. But *mulier*, *muliēris*, a woman, is of course feminine. The adjectives *degener* (degenerate), *pauper* (poor), and *uber* (fertile), likewise make their genitive in *ĕris*. Those of the second class, which throw out the *e* in the genitive, are generally masculine — as *venter* (belly), gen. *ventris*. But *linter*, a boat, is sometimes feminine. In the same manner are declined all substantives in *ter* (except *later*, gen. *lateris*); and all adjectives in *er*, which make their feminine in *is*, and the neuter in *e*—as *acer*, *alacer*, October, November. The two neuters *ver* (spring), and *iter* (journey), make their genitive *vēris* and *itinĕris*.

Note. Greek words in *ter* represent the pure stem, and form their genitive by simply adding *is* to the genitive—as *cratēr*, gen. *cratēris*.

11. Nouns ending in *es* must be divided into two classes, for the *es* is either only the nominative termination (the *e* being merely euphonic), which in the genitive is changed into *is;* or the consonant *t* or *d* has been thrown out before the *s* in the nominative, and reappears in the genitive. Those of the former class are commonly feminine — as *caedes* (murder), gen. *caedis ; clades* (defeat), gen. *cladis ;* but *palumbes* (wood-pigeon) is both masculine and feminine ; and *vepres* (a thorn-bush, commonly plur.), *verres* (a boar), and the names of rivers, as *Euphrates*, *Araxes*, are masculine. (Compare § 42.)
In those nouns in which a *t* or *d* has been dropped before the *s* of the nominative, the *e* either belongs to them, or has arisen from a euphonic change of *i* into *e*—as *paries*, gen. *parietis*, and *miles*, gen. *militis*. Those which make their genitive in *ĭtis* are masculine—as *miles* (a soldier), *eques* (a horseman), gen. *equĭtis; hospes* (a guest), gen. *hospĭtis ;* but *merges, ĭtis* (a sheaf of corn) is feminine. In like manner are declined nearly all adjectives in *es*—as *dives* (rich), *sospes* (safe), *superstes* (surviving), &c. Those which make their genitive in *ĕtis* are partly masculine and partly feminine—as *paries*, *pariĕtis*, masc. (a wall); *seges*, *segĕtis*, fem. (a field); *aries*, masc. (a ram); *interpres*, masc. (an

interpreter). In like manner are declined the following adjectives : — *hebes*, dull ; *indiges*, native ; *praepes*, swift ; *teres*, round or smooth.

In those nouns in which the *d* of the stem has been dropped before *s*, the *e* likewise either belongs to the stem, or is a euphonic change for *i*—as *pes* (foot), gen. *pĕdis ;* and *obses* (hostage), gen. *obsĭdis.* Words of this kind are commonly masculine ; but *merces*, *mercēdis* (reward), *quies*, *quiētis* (quiet), and its compound *requies* (tranquillity), are feminine. The adjectives *deses* and *reses* are declined like *obses*, and *locuples* like *quies*.

Note. Ceres, gen. *Cerĕris*, *pubes* and *impubes*, gen. *pubĕris*, and *impubĕris*, do not belong to this class ; for the *s* being the same as *r*, they present the pure stem in the nominative.

Some Greek masculine words in *ēs* make their genitive in *ētis*—as *lebes*, gen. *lebētis* (a kettle) ; *tapes*, a carpet : *magnes*, magnet ; *Tunes*, a town in Africa. A few in *ēs* are neuter —as *cacoëthes*, a malign ulcer.

12. Nouns ending in *ex* are formed from the stem *ec* or *eg*, and accordingly change the *x* in the genitive either into *cis* or *gis*. In some of them, the *e* belongs to the stem, while in others it is a euphonic change of *i* into *e*—as *rex*, *rēgis ; prex*, *prĕcis ; apex*, *apĭcis.* Most of those which make their genitive in *ĭcis* are masculine — as *apex*, the extreme point ; but the following are feminine : — *ilex*, a species of oak ; *carex*, sheer-grass ; *forfex*, a pair of scissors ; *vitex*, the chaste-tree ; and *pellex*, a mistress. Some are used both as masculine and feminine — as *imbrex*, shingle ; *obex*, a bolt ; *cortex*, rind ; *silex*, flint-stone ; but *atriplex*, the herb orage, is neuter.

Those in which the stem ends in *g* are not very numerous, and are chiefly masculine — as *rex*, *rēgis*, a king ; *remex*, *remĭgis*, a rower ; *grex*, *grĕgis* (a flock) ; *Lelex*, *Lelēgis ;* but *lex*, *lēgis* (law), is feminine. *Supellex*, gen. *supellectĭlis*, is irregular and feminine.

13. Nouns ending in *i* are neuter, and of Greek origin. They change the *i* in the genitive into *is* — as *sinapi* (mustard), gen. *sinapis ;* or into *ĭtis*—as *oxymeli* (a mixture of vinegar and honey), gen. *oxymelitis.*

14. Nouns ending in *il* represent the pure root, are masculine, and form their genitive by simply adding *is* to the nominative—as *pugil* (a pugilist), gen. *pugĭlis ; vigil* (watchful), gen. *vigĭlis.*

15. Nouns ending in *is* must be divided into two classes. In

the first, the termination *is* is simply added to the stem, the
s being the nominative ending, and the *i* a euphonic addition—as in *navis,* from *nav-i-s.* In the second class of words,
the *s* of the nominative has caused more or less important
changes in the stem — as in *cuspis* for *cuspid-s,* *sanguis* for
sanguin-s, and *cinis* for *ciner* (where the *e* is changed into *i,*
and *r* converted into its equivalent *s*).
Nouns of the first class have their genitive like the nominative, and are chiefly feminine—as *navis* (ship), gen. *navis;*
avis (bird), gen. *avis;* *vallis* (valley), gen. *vallis.* But many
of them are masculine — as *amnis,* river; *axis,* axis; *callis,*
path (sometimes used as a fem.); *canalis,* canal; *cassis,*
hunter's net; *caulis,* stalk; *collis,* hill; *crinis,* hair; *ensis,*
sword; *fascis,* bundle; *finis,* end (sometimes fem. in the sing.,
but never in the plur.); *follis,* a pair of bellows; *funis,* rope;
fustis, club; *ignis,* fire; *mensis,* month; *orbis,* circle; *panis,*
bread; *pis is,* fish; *postis,* a post; *scrobis,* pit; *sentis,* thorn-
bush; *torquis* (also *torques* as fem.), chain; *torris,* a fire-
brand; *unguis,* nail; *vectis,* lever; *vermis,* worm. Further,
a number of adjectives which are used as substantives, a
masculine substantive being understood—as *annalis (liber),*
chronicle; *natalis (dies),* birthday; *molaris (lapis* or *dens),* a
millstone or grinder; *pugillares (libri),* tablet for writing;
Aprilis (mensis), April. The compounds of *as,* as *decussis,*
ten asses, and some others which are masculine on account
of their meaning—as *hostis,* enemy; *testis,* witness; *Tiberis,*
the river Tiber. *Canis* (dog), and *anguis* (snake), are used
oftener as masculine than as feminine; and *corbis* (basket),
and *clunis* (buttock or haunch), are both masculine and
feminine. All adjectives in *is* are declined in the same
manner, the genitive being like the nominative—as *facilis,*
gen. *facilis;* *acris,* gen. *acris.* Greek feminine substantives
in *is* derived from verbs are generally declined in the same
manner — as *poësis,* gen. *poësis;* also the names of towns
composed with *polis,* as *Neapolis,* and other names of females
ending in *is.*
Those nouns in *is* in which the *d* or *t* of the stem was
thrown out before the *s* in the nominative, form their genitive in *idis* and *itis,* and are mostly feminine — as *cuspis*
(point), gen. *cuspidis;* *cassis* (helmet), gen. *cassidis;* *pyra-
mis* (pyramid), gen. *pyramidis; lis* (dispute), gen. *litis;*
Samnis, gen. *Samnitis; Dis,* gen. *Ditis; Quiris,* gen. *Qui-
ritis. Lapis* (a stone), gen. *lapidis,* and *Phasis,* the name
of a river, are masculine.
A few masculines in *is* make their genitive in *inis,* an *n*
having dropped out before the *s* of the nominative --as

sanguis (blood), gen. *sanguĭnis ; pollis* (fine flour, not used in the nom.), gen. *pollĭnis.*

Some, again, which end in *is,* have changed the ending *er* of the stem into *is,* and accordingly make their genitive in *ĕris* —as *cinis* (ashes), gen. *cinĕris ;* so also *cucumis,* cucumber ; *pulvis,* dust ; *vomis* (also *vomer*), ploughshare.

Note 1. *Semis,* half an as, has the genitive *semissis,* the stem being *semiss;* but no Latin word is allowed to end in a double consonant. The word *glis* makes its genitive *glīris,* and *vis* its plural *vīres,* the *s* in the nominative being equivalent to *r.* *Vis,* however, is irregular besides.

2. Some Greek names in *is* make their genitive in *īnis*—as *Sala-mis,* gen. *Salamīnis;* and others in *entis*—as *Simoïs,* gen. *Simoëntis.*

16. Nouns ending in *ix* are feminine. As they are formed from a stem ending in *c* or *g,* the *x* is changed in the genitive either into *cis* or *gis*—as *salix* (willow), gen. *salĭcis ; radix* (root), gen. *radīcis ; strix* (a fabulous bird), gen. *strīgis.* The following are masculine : —*calix, ĭcis,* cup ; *fornix, ĭcis,* vault ; while *varix* (a swollen vein) is both masculine and feminine. *Phoenix,* the name of a bird, as well as of a people, is masculine. *Nix* (snow), gen. *nĭvis,* is irregular.

17. Nouns ending in *o* represent the stem but imperfectly, for sometimes an *n* has been thrown out after *o*—as in *sermo* (conversation), gen. *sermōn-is ;* and sometimes the *o* represents a stem ending in *in*—as *virgo* (maiden), gen. *virgĭn-is.* We must accordingly distinguish between two classes :-

The words of the first class make their genitive in *ōnis,* and are generally masculine—as *sermo.* But those which end in *io,* and are derived from verbs, are feminine—as *lectio,* the reading ; *oratio,* the speaking or speech ; *legio* (from *lĕgo,* I select), a legion ; *regio* (from *rego,* I direct), a district ; *natio* (from *nascor*), a nation ; so also *communio* (from the adjective *communis*), community ; and *consortio* (from *con-sors*) : but all other substantives in *io* are masculine—as *ves-pertilio,* bat ; *scipio,* staff ; *pugio,* dagger ; *septemtrio,* north. Some words of this class are masculine, notwithstanding their being names of towns—as *Sulmo, Narbo,* and *Vesontio.* (§ 43, note 2.) A few words have the *o* short in the genitive —as *Macedo,* gen. *Macedŏnis ;* and *Seno,* gen. *Senŏnis.*

Words of the second class change the *o* of the nominative into *ĭnis* in the genitive ; this is the case chiefly in those which end in the nominative in *do* and *go,* and most of them are feminine—as *hirundo* (swallow), gen. *hirundĭnis ; imago* (image), gen. *imagĭnis ; Carthago* (Carthage), gen.

Carthagĭnis. The following, however, are masculine :—
ordo, order; *cardo,* bolt; *margo,* margin. *Cupido,* as the
name of a god, is masculine ; in the sense of 'love' or 'desire' it is feminine, though poets sometimes use it as a masculine. The following masculines also make their genitive
in *ĭnis,* like those in *do* and *go*—namely, *homo,* man ; *nemo*
(i.e. *ne homo,* no man) ; *turbo,* whirlwind ; and *Apollo.* The
following words in *do* and *go,* on the other hand, are masculine, and make their genitive in *ōnis :*—*praedo,* robber ;
spado, eunuch ; *ligo,* spade ; *mango,* slave-dealer ; *harpăgo,*
a hook. The feminine *caro* (flesh) alone is irregular, making
its genitive *carnis.*

18. The only noun ending in *ol* is the masculine *sōl* (the sun),
gen. *sōlis.*

19. All nouns in *on* are Greek masculines, making their genitive, according to the Greek, either in *ōnis, ŏnis,* or *ontis*—
as *Babylōn,* gen. *Babylōnis ; Ctesiphon,* gen. *Ctesiphontis ;
Chalcedon,* gen. *Chalcedŏnis.*

20. Nouns ending in *or* represent the pure stem in the nominative, and form their genitive by adding simply *is* to it.
Those in which the *o* is long are generally masculine—as
dolor (pain), gen. *dolōris ;* but the following are feminine
by their meaning :—*soror,* sister ; *uxor,* wife. All the comparatives of adjectives are declined in the same manner as
facilior and *facilius* (more easy), gen. *faciliōris.* Nouns in
which the *o* is short are generally neuter—as *aequor* (surface
of the sea), gen. *aequŏris ; marmor* (marble), gen. *marmŏris ;
ador* (spelt), gen. *adŏris ;* but *arbor, ŏris,* tree, is feminine ;
and *rhetor, ŏris,* teacher of oratory, masculine.

Note. It must be observed that in many words ending in *or,* the
more ancient termination was *os*—hence *arbor* and *arbos, honor* and
honos, lepor and *lepos, labor* and *labos.* In *cor* (heart), the stem is *cord*
—hence the genitive *cordis,* as in its compounds *concors* and *discors.*

21. Nouns ending in *os* either represent the pure stem (the *s*
being equivalent to *r*), or a *t* or *d* has been thrown out before
the *s.* The former accordingly make their genitive in
ōris, and are masculine—as *mos* (manner), gen. *mōris ; flos*
(flower), gen. *flōris ;* but *os* (mouth), gen. *ōris,* is neuter.
Those in which a *t* or *d* has been thrown out in the nominative, are sometimes feminine—as *cos* (whetstone), gen.
cōtis ; dos (dowry), gen. *dōtis ;* and sometimes masculine—
as *sacerdos* (priest), gen. *sacerdōtis ; custos* (guardian), gen.
custōdis. The adjectives *compos* and *impos* have *compŏtis* and
impŏtis. Bōs (ox) has *bŏvis,* and *ŏs* (bone), *ossis.* Compare
above, *Note* to No. 20.

Note. A few Greek words in *ŏs* are neuter, and occur only in the nominative and accusative—as *epŏs*, an epic poem. Others in *ōs* are masculine—as *herōs* (a hero), gen. *herōis*.

22. Nouns ending in *ox* have a stem ending in *c* or *g*, and accordingly make their genitive either in *cis* or *gis*. They are mostly feminine — as *vox* (voice), gen. *vōcis; celox* (a swift-sailing ship), gen. *celōcis*. In like manner are declined the adjectives in *ox*—as *atrox*, fierce ; *velox*, swift ; *praecox* (precocious), however, has *praecŏcis*. Names of nations are of course masculine—as *Cappadox*, *Cappadŏcis ; Allobrox, Allobrŏgis.* The feminine *nox* (night) alone has *noctis.*

23. Nouns ending in *ul* represent the pure stem, and are masculine — as *consul* (consul), gen. *consŭlis; exsul* (exile), gen. *exŭlis ; praesul* (one who goes before), gen. *praesŭlis.*

24. Nouns ending in *ur* represent the pure stem, and make their genitive by simply adding *is*. The following are masculine :—*fur* (thief), gen. *fŭris; furfur* (bran), gen. *furfŭris; turtur* (turtle-dove), gen. *turtŭris ; vultur* (vulture), gen. *vultŭris ; augur* (augur), gen. *augŭris ;* and the adjective *cicur, ŭris,* tame. The following are neuter :—*fulgur* (lightning), gen. *fulgŭris ; Tibur, ŭris ; robur* (strength), gen. *robŏris ; ebur* (ivory), gen. *ebŏris ; femur* (loin), gen. *femŏris ; jecur* (liver), gen. *jecŏris.*

Note. Here again it must be observed that *u* and *o* are only euphonic varieties of the same sound, *jecur* being the same as *jecor* or *jecus.*

25. Nouns ending in *us* must be divided into two classes. In some the stem ending in *d* or *t* has lost these letters before the *s* of the nominative, and accordingly recovers them in the genitive. All of these are feminine—as *virtus* (virtue), gen. *virtūtis; salus* (safety), gen. *salūtis; palus* (marsh), gen. *palūdis; incus* (anvil), gen. *incūdis. Pecus* (cattle), gen. *pecŭdis ;* the adjective *intercus* makes the genitive *intercŭtis.* In others the *us* of the nominative represents the stem *ur, or,* or *er,* and most of these are neuters—as *jus* (law), gen. *jūris; crus* (leg), gen. *crūris* (and so also *pus,* viscous matter ; *rus,* country ; *tus,* incense) ; *corpus* (body), gen. *corpŏris ; decus* (ornament), gen. *decŏris ; genus* (kind or species), gen. *genĕris ; vulnus* (wound), gen. *vulnĕris.* The following form exceptions in regard to gender :—*Ligus, ŭris,* a Ligurian, and the plural *Lemŭres,* spectres ; and *lepus, ŏris,* a hare, are masculine ; *tellus, ŭris* (earth), and *Venus, ĕris,* are feminine.

The following words are of a different kind, the *s* in the nominative being simply added to the stem : — *sus* (pig), gen. .*suis; grus* (crane), *gruis*. We may here also notice the only two Latin words ending in *aus* — namely, *laus*, praise, and *fraus*, fraud, in which a *d* is dropped before *s*, so that their genitive is *laudis, fraudis*. Both are feminine. Some Greek names of places in *us* make their genitive in *untis* — as *Pessinus,* gen. *Pessinuntis;* and others, especially compounds of πούς, make their genitive in *ŏdis* — as *tripus* (tripod), gen. *tripŏdis*. But *Oedipus* is commonly declined after the second declension, and *polypus* (a polype) always.

26. Nouns ending in *y* are neuter, and of Greek origin, and form their genitive by simply adding *is* to the nominative — as *misy* (vitriol), gen. *misyis*. Those in *ys* are likewise Greek, and mostly feminine ; their genitive is either *yis* or *ȳdis* — as *chelys* (lyre), gen. *chelyis; chlamys* (cloak), *chlamȳdis*. *Othrys,* gen. *Othryis,* being the name of a mountain, is masculine.

27. Nouns in *yx* are all Greek, and make their genitive in *ȳcis, ȳcis, ȳgis, ȳgis,* or *ȳchis,* according as their stem in Greek ends in *c, g,* or *ch*. They are generally masculine — as *calyx* (cup of a flower), gen. *calȳcis;* but *sandyx, ȳcis* (a red colour), is often used in Latin as feminine. The following also are sometimes used as feminines : — *bombyx, ȳcis,* silkworm ; *sardonyx, ȳchis,* a precious stone.

28. Nouns ending in *ns* have a stem ending either in *t* or *d,* which letters have been dropped before the *s*. Those whose stem ends in *t,* accordingly form their genitive in *ntis,* and are generally masculine — as *mons* (mountain), gen. *montis*. The following, however, are feminine, which in some arises from the fact of their being adjectives or participles, to which a feminine substantive is understood : — *gens,* family or nation ; *lens,* a kind of pulse ; *mens,* mind ; *frons,* forehead ; *bidens,* a sheep of two years old ; *serpens* (namely, *bestia*), a snake ; *continens* (namely, *terra*), the continent. To this class of words belong all participles and adjectives in *ns*.

Those of which the stem ends in *d,* and which make their genitive in *ndis,* are feminine—as *glans* (acorn), gen. *glandis; frons* (foliage), gen. *frondis; juglans* (walnut), gen. *juglandis*.

29. Nouns ending in *bs* have their stem ending in *b,* the *s* being only the sign of the nominative, so that their genitive ends in *bis;* their gender is feminine—as *urbs* (town), gen. *urbis*. So also the adjective *caelebs,* gen. *caelĭbis*.

30. Nouns ending in *ps* are formed from a stem ending in *p*, the *s* being only the sign of the nominative. The *ps* is usually preceded by *e*, which is a euphonic change for *i*; e.g. *daps* (fem. food), gen. *dapis*. The following are used both as masculine and feminine:—*adeps* (fat), gen. *adĭpis*; *forceps* (a pair of tongs), gen. *forcĭpis*. In like manner are declined all adjectives in *ceps*, which are derived from *capio* —as *princeps* (though *auceps* makes *aucŭpis*); while those derived from *caput*—as *anceps*, *praeceps*, *biceps*, and *triceps*, make their genitive in *cĭpĭtis*—as *ancĭpĭtis*, *praecĭpĭtis*, &c. Some, as *stirps*, make their genitive *stirpis*.

Note. Greek nouns in *ps* are generally masculine, and their declension in Latin is on the same principle as in the Greek language —as *hydrops* (dropsy), gen. *hydrōpis*; *Pelops*, gen. *Pelŏpis*; *gryps*, gen. *grȳphis*.

31. The only word in *ms* is the feminine *hiems* (winter), which makes its genitive *hiemis*. There is likewise only one in *ls* —*puls* (pap), gen. *pultis*.
32. Nouns ending in *rs* have their stem ending in *t*, which has been dropped before *s*. They are feminine—as *ars* (art), gen. *artis*; but Mars (a contraction for *Mavors*) is of course masculine. In like manner are declined the adjectives in *ers*—as *iners*, gen. *inertis*.
33. The only nouns in *t* are *caput* (head), and its compounds *occiput* and *sinciput*, which are all neuters. The *u* being only a euphonic change for *i*, their genitive is *capitis*, *occipitis*, *sincipitis*. Compare above, No. 30.
34. Nouns in *x*, preceded by a consonant, are feminine, and their stem ends in *c*—as *arx* (citadel), gen. *arcis*; *falx* (sickle), gen. *falcis*. Those ending in *unx* (derived from *uncia*) are masculine—as *deunx*, eleven-twelfths of an as; so also *quincunx*, *septunx*. *Calx*, limestone, and *lynx*, lynx, are sometimes masculine, and sometimes feminine.

Note. Some Greek words of this kind make their genitive in *gis*, their stem ending in *g*—as *sphinx* (a sphinx), gen. *sphingis*; *phalanx* (phalanx), gen. *phalangis*; *syrinx* (a reed or tube), gen. *syringis*.

CHAPTER IX.

PECULIAR FORMATION OF CERTAIN CASES IN THE THIRD DECLENSION, AND OF GREEK WORDS FOLLOWING THIS DECLENSION.

§ 63. The genitive of the third declension ends in *ĭs;* but there are some Greek proper names in *es* not increasing in the genitive, which in the best Latin writers make the genitive in *i* instead of *is*—as *Aristoteles, Isocrates, Neocles, Achilles, Ulixes, Praxiteles;* gen. *Aristoteli, Isocrati, Neocli, Achilli, Ulixi, Praxiteli.* Some writers even make the genitive of such names end in *eï* or *ei*, as if their nominative ended in *eus*—as *Achillēi, Alyattei, Ulixei.* Those names in *es*, however, which increase in the genitive, invariably make their genitive in *is*—as *Laches*, gen. *Lachētis.*

§ 64. Some words in *is*, which make their genitive in *is* without any increase, have in the accusative *im* instead of *em*. This is the case commonly with *amussis*, a ruler; *buris*, a crooked piece of wood forming the trunk of a plough; *cucumis*, cucumber; *ravis*, hoarseness; *sitis*, thirst; *tussis*, cough; *vis*, force; and in the names of towns and rivers in *is*—as *Hispalis, Tiberis, Albis, Baetis.* The following have more frequently *im* than *em:*—*febris*, fever; *pelvis*, basin; *puppis*, stern of a ship; *restis*, rope; *turris*, tower; *securis*, axe; while *clavis*, key, *messis*, harvest, and *navis*, ship, have more frequently *em* than *im.*

Note. Many Greek words and proper names in *is* likewise make their accusative in *im* (or *in*). See § 70, note 2.

§ 65. Many Latin words make the ablative singular in *ī* instead of *ĕ*, and some may have either termination.
(*a*). The following have the ablative in *i* exclusively:—
1. All those words which make their accusative singular in *im* instead of *em*—as *amussis, buris, sitis*, &c. See § 64.
2. All neuter nouns ending in the nominative singular in *e, ı, al*, and *ar*—as *mare* (sea), abl. *mari; sinapi* (mustard), abl. *sinapi; calcar* (spur), abl. *calcari; animal*, abl. *animali; dulce* (sweet), abl. *dulci.*

Note. Masculines having any of these terminations, however, make their ablative as usual in *e*—as *sal* (salt), abl. *sale; nectar*, abl. *nectare;* and the neuter *far* (grain) also has *farre.* The neuter names of towns ending in *e* make their abl. invariably in *e*—as *Praeneste, Reate, Caere.*

Poets even make the ablative of *mare* sometimes end in *e*, like the nominative. It may be observed, in general, that the terminations *i* and *e* were originally the same, and that the one is only a softened form of the other; whence we find both *Carthagini* and *Carthagine* in the sense of ' at Carthage.'

3. All adjectives of two and three terminations (those ending in *is, e,* and *er, is, e*) — as *facilis* and *facile,* both make the ablative *facili; gracilis* and *gracile,* abl. *gracili; acer, acris,* and *acre,* all make their ablative *acri.* The same is the case with all substantives in *is,* which are originally adjectives — as *familiaris,* a friend; and *natalis,* birthday.

Note. Some of these substantives, however, which are originally adjectives, as *aedilis,* sometimes make their ablative in *e ;* and when they occur as proper names — as *Juvenalis, Martialis, Celer* — they invariably have their ablative in *e.* Poets, however, sometimes take licenses in regard to the adjectives mentioned in the rule, using *e* where we should expect *i,* and *i* where we should expect *e.*

(*b*). The following words make their ablative both in *e* and *i :* —

1. Those substantives which may form their accusative singular, both in *em* and *im*—as *febris, pelvis, puppis, clavis, messis,* &c. See § 64. But *restis* has always *reste,* and *securis* always *securi.*

2. All adjectives and participles which have only one termination for all three genders — as *prudens,* abl. *prudente* and *prudenti; amans,* abl. *amante* and *amanti; iners,* abl. *inerte* and *inerti; felix,* abl. *felice* and *felici; Arpinas,* abl. *Arpinate* and *Arpinati.* The *i,* however, is generally preferred, except in the abl. absolute, where we always find *e* — as *Romulo regnante* (in the reign of Romulus), and never *regnanti.* The ending *e* is also preferred when these adjectives or participles are used as substantives.

Note. The following adjectives of this class, however, invariably make their ablative in *e :* — *compos, impos, caelebs, deses, pauper, princeps, pubes* (gen. *ĕris*), and *superstes. Ales* and *dives* generally have *e,* and *vetus* and *uber* frequently, while the adjectives *par* and *memor* always have *i.*

3. All comparatives of adjectives — as *major* and *majus,* abl. *majore* and *majori,* though the termination *e* is usually preferred.

Note. There are also some other words not mentioned in the rules here given, which now and then make their ablative in *i* — as *ignis,* fire; *vis,* bird; *imber,* rain; *supellex,* furniture; *rus,* country. It must be remembered that *i* is usually the more ancient form, and that in early times the ablative perhaps generally terminated in *i.* Compare § 65 (*a*), 2., note 1.

§ 66. All neuter substantives ending in *e, al,* and *ar,* make the nominative, accusative, and vocative plural in *ia* instead of *a*—as *mare* (sea), plur. *maria; animal,* plur. *animalia; calcar,* plur. *calcaria.* The same is the case with the neuter of adjectives and participles in the positive — as *elegans,* neut. plur. *elegantia; iners,* neut. plur. *inertia; animans,* neut. plur. *animantia. Vetus* alone has *vetera,* and *complures* (several) both *complura* and *compluria.*

§ 67. The genitive plural of some words ends in *ium* instead of *um.* This is the case—

1. In substantives ending in *es* and *is,* which do not increase in the genitive, but merely change the termination of the nominative into *is*—as *aedes,* house ; *crinis,* hair; gen. plur. *aedium, crinium.*

Note. The following words, however, form exceptions, making their genitive in *um,* and not in *ium :*—*ambāges,* a round-about way ; *strues,* heap ; *vates,* a prophet or poet ; *canis,* dog ; *juvenis,* a youth. *Volucris* (bird) has most commonly *um ;* and the following have frequently *um* instead of *ium :*—*apis,* bee ; *sedes,* seat ; *mensis,* month.

2. In the following nouns, which must be remembered separately :—*imber,* rain ; *linter,* boat ; *venter,* belly ; *uter,* bag ; and *caro,* flesh ; genitive plural *imbrium, lintrium, ventrium, carnium.*

3. In all monosyllabic nouns ending in *s* or *x* preceded by a consonant — as *mons,* mountain ; *arx,* citadel ; *urbs,* town ; which make *montium, arcium, urbium.* The same is the case with the following monosyllabic words :—*glis, lis, mas, mus, os* (gen. *ossis*), *vis, faux* (not used in the nom. sing.), *nix, nox,* and sometimes also *fraus.*

Note. Opum, from the obsolete *ops,* forms an exception. The Greek words *gryps, lynx,* and *sphinx,* likewise make their genitive plural only in *um. Lares* (from *Lar*) has both *Larum* and *Larium.*

4. In nouns ending in *ns* and *rs,* whether they consist of one or more syllables—as *cliens,* client ; *cohors,* cohort ; *amans,* loving ; *solers,* industrious ; gen. plur. *clientium, cohortium, amantium, solertium.* Those in *ns,* however, admit both *um* and *ium.* Those which are properly participles, when used as substantives, prefer *ium* to *um* — as *adolescens, sapiens ;* gen. *adolescentium, sapientium. Parens,* however, has more frequently *parentum* than *parentium.*

5. In all neuter substantives ending in *e, al,* and *ar,* and in all those adjectives and participles which make their neuter plural in *ia* — as *animal,* gen. plur. *animalium ; mare, marium ; calcar, calcarium ; acer, acris* and *acre, acrium ;*

facilis and *facile, facilium; felix, felicium; elegans, elegantium; iners, inertium.*

Note. The adjectives *quadrupes, versicolor, anceps, praeceps, princeps, opifex,* and all those derived from *facio* and *capio,* make their genitive plural in *um.* Adjectives ending in *ns* also sometimes make their genitive in *um;* and poets use the same termination even in the case of adjectives in *is* — as *coelestum* for *coelestium,* from *coelestis.* *Celer* (quick) likewise makes its genitive only in *um.*

6. In names of peoples ending in *is* and *as*—as *Quiris, Arpinas, Fidenas;* gen. plur. *Quiritium, Arpinatium, Fidenatium.* The same is the case with the plurals *penates* (household gods), and *optimates* (nobles), which generally make their genitive in *ium,* and rarely in *um.* Other substantives in *as* also, as *civitas,* sometimes make their genitive in *ium,* though *um* is preferable.

7. The names of Roman festivals, which are neuter plurals ending in *alia,* make their genitive either in *ium,* according to the third declension, or in *orum,* according to the second — as *Floralia,* gen. *Floralium* or *Floraliorum; Bacchanalia,* gen. *Bacchanalium* or *Bacchanaliorum.* So also *ancile* (a shield fallen from heaven), and *vectigal* (revenue), make either *ancilium* and *vectigalium,* or *anciliorum* and *vectigaliorum.*

§ 68. Greek neuter substantives in *ma* commonly make the dative and ablative plural in *is* instead of *ibus* — as *poëma* (a poem), dat. and abl. plur. *poëmatis* instead of *poëmatibus.*

Note. Bos (ox), which has in the genitive plural *boum,* makes the dative and ablative plural *būbus* or *bōbus,* which are contractions for *bovibus;* and *sus* (a pig), makes *subus,* a contraction for *suibus.*

§ 69. The accusative plural of masculine and feminine nouns which make their genitive plural in *ium,* frequently ended, in the early times of the Latin language, in *ĭs* or *eis* instead of *es,* though *es* also was in use. Hence we find *omnis* and *omneis, classis* and *classeis,* along with *omnes* and *classes.*

§ 70. Among the Greek nouns which follow the third declension, there are many, especially proper names, which retain certain terminations peculiar to them in the Greek language, where they likewise follow the third declension. The following are the principal peculiarities of this kind :—

1. The genitive singular of Greek words is made by poets sometimes in *os* instead of *is.* This is more especially the case with words ending in *is* or *as,* making their genitive in Greek in *idos* and *ados*— as *Thetis,* gen. *Thetidos; Pallas, Pallados;* and also with those in *ys,* gen. *yos*—as *Thetys,* gen. *Thetyos.*

Proper names of females ending in *o*—as *Io, Sappho,* generally have

4   c

the Greek genitive in *ūs* (*ους*)—as *Iūs, Sapphūs;* in the dative and accusative these names generally end in *ō*, and rarely in *onem* and *oni*.

2. The accusative singular sometimes ends, as in Greek, in *a* instead of *em*. In prose this is chiefly the case with some proper names, and only a few common nouns—as *Agamemnŏna, Babylōna, Periclea, Troezēna*, from *Agamemnon, Babylon, Pericles, Troezen*. The words *aër* and *aether* generally make their accusative in *a* even in prose ; but poets adopt the same practice also in a great many other words— as *herōa, thorāca*, from *herōs* and *thorax*.

Greek nouns in *is*, which make their genitive in *is* without any increase, make their accusative singular either in *im* (which is the Latin form), or in *in* (the Greek form)— as *poësis*, acc. *poësim* or *poësin; Charybdis*, acc. *Charybdim* or *Charybdin*. Those nouns in *is*, which make their genitive in *idis*, make their accusative according to the Greek either in *im* (*in*) or *ida* (rarely *idem*) — as *Paris*, gen. *Paridis*, acc. *Parin* or *Parida* or *Paridem*. Those, on the other hand, which in Greek have only *ida* in the accusative, are formed in Latin either in *ida* or *idem*, but never in *im* or *in*—as *tyrannis*, acc. *tyrannidem* or *tyrannida; Aeneïs*, acc. *Aeneïda* or *Aeneïdem*. Greek names in *tis*, however, have either *im* (*in*) or *idem* (*ida*)—as *Phthiotis*, acc. *Phthiotim* (*Phthiotin*) or *Phthiotidem* (*Phthiotida*).

Words in *ys*, gen. *yis*, have the accusative singular even in prose either in *ym* or *yn*— as *Othrys*, acc. *Othrym* or *Othryn; Halys*, acc. *Halym* or *Halyn*.

Greek nouns in *es*, which make their genitive in *is*, and which in Greek follow the first declension, make their accusative sometimes in *em* and sometimes in *en*—as *Aeschines*, acc. *Aeschinem* or *Aeschinen; Mithridates*, acc. *Mithridatem* or *Mithridaten*. The same is the case with those names in *es*, which in Greek follow the third declension, but make their accusative either in *en* or *ea* — as *Xenocrates*, acc. *Xenocratem* or *Xenocraten; Hippocrates*, acc. *Hippocratem* or *Hippocraten; Sophocles*, acc. *Sophoclem* or *Sophoclen*. The termination *en*, however, is much less frequent than *em*.

Greek names in *es*, gen. *ētis*, make their accusative regularly in *etem*, which, however, they may contract into *em* — as *Thales*, acc. *Thaletem* or *Thalem* (whence also in the ablat. *Thale* instead of *Thalete*).

3. The vocative in Greek words is generally like the nominative, as in all Latin words of the third declension; but those ending in *is*, *ys*, and *eus*, generally throw off the *s* in the vocative—as *Phyllis*, voc. *Phylli; Alexis*, voc. *Alexi; Cotys*, voc. *Coty; Orpheus*, voc. *Orpheu*. Names of men ending in *as*, gen. *antis*, usually make their vocative in *ā* — as *Calchas*, voc. *Calchā*. Those in *es* may have the vocative like the nominative, or throw off the *s*—as *Carneades*, voc. *Carneades* or *Carneade; Chremes* (gen. *Chremētis*), voc. *Chremes* or *Chreme*. But poets often deviate from these rules, making the vocative, according to the general rule, like the nominative.

4. The termination *es* of the nominative plural is sometimes used short, like the Greek *ες*, whereas the Latin termination *es* is always long.

5. The genitive plural sometimes ends in *ōn* instead of *um;* but this is chiefly the case in titles of books — as *Metamorphoseōn* from *Metamorphosis; epigrammatōn* from *epigramma; Bucolicōn, Georgicōn*, from *Bucolica, Georgica*.

6. The dative plural of Greek names occasionally takes the ending *si* or *sin*—as *Troasin, Charisin,* for *Troadibus, Charitibus.*

7. The accusative plural in poetry frequently, and sometimes also in prose, takes the Greek termination *as* instead of *es*—as *pyramidas, Aethiopas, Arcadas,* for *pyramides, Aethiopes, Arcades.* The same is often done with names which are not Greek—as *Allobrŏgas* and *Sintonas,* from *Allobrox* and *Sinton.*

8. A few Greek neuters in *as* and *es* make the nominative and accusative plural in *ē* (*η*)—as *melos,* plural *melē.* Of the same kind is the plural name *Tempē.*

CHAPTER X.

FOURTH DECLENSION.

§ 71. The fourth declension is only a modification of the third. The stem of the words belonging to it ends in *u,* which is retained in all cases; but the vowel of the terminations generally coalesces with the *u* of the stem into *ū,* or one of the vowels is thrown out. The nominative of masculines and feminines always ends in *us,* and of neuters in *u.*

The following may serve as specimens of the fourth declension :—

	SINGULAR.		PLURAL.
Nom.	*fructŭ-s,* fruit.	Nom.	*fructū-s,* fruits.
Gen.	*fructū-s.*	Gen.	*fructŭ-um.*
Dat.	*fructū-i.*	Dat.	*fructĭ-bus.*
Acc.	*fructu-m.*	Acc.	*fructū-s.*
Voc.	*fructŭ-s.*	Voc.	*fructū-s.*
Abl.	*fructū.*	Abl.	*fructĭ-bus.*

	SINGULAR.		PLURAL.
Nom.	*cornū,* horn.	Nom.	*cornŭ-ă,* horns.
Gen.	*cornū-s.*	Gen.	*cornŭ-um.*
Dat.	*cornū (cornū-i).*	Dat.	*cornĭ-bus.*
Acc.	*cornū.*	Acc.	*cornŭ-ă.*
Voc.	*cornū.*	Voc.	*cornŭ-ă.*
Abl.	*cornū.*	Abl.	*cornĭ-bus.*

Words to be used as Exercises.

Actus, action ; *coetus,* assembly ; *cursus,* course ; *gradus,* step ; *lusus,* play ; *magistratus,* magistracy ; *motus,* movement ; *sensus,* sense ; *sumptus,* expenditure ; *vultus,* countenance. The following are the only neuters:—*genu,* knee ; *gelu,* cold ; *veru,* a spit, broach ; and *pecu* (the same as *pecus, ŏris,* or *ŭdis*), cattle.

Note 1. The ending *ūs* in the genitive singular is a contraction for *uis*, which is still found in the earliest writers—as *sumptuis, senatuis, nuruis.* In some cases the genitive of this declension is made to end in *i*, as if the word belonged to the second declension—as *fructi, quaesti, senati, tumulti, adventi.* It may be observed in general, that many words belonging to the fourth declension are sometimes either wholly or partially declined according to the second.

It was formerly believed that the genitive singular of neuters was like the nominative; but examples in which the genitive ends in *us* are numerous.

2. The dative termination *ui* is by some writers contracted into *ū*— as *equitatu* for *equitatui.* In neuter nouns, the contracted form is used almost exclusively. The ablative in *ū* is likewise a contraction for *ue.*

3. The genitive plural is occasionally made in *um*, instead of *uum* —as *passum, currum,* for *passuum, curruum.*

4. The dative and ablative plural of the following words end in *ŭbus* instead of *ĭbus:*—*acus,* needle; *arcus,* arch; *lacus,* lake; *quercus,* oak; *specus,* cave; *pecu,* cattle; *artus,* limb; *partus,* birth; *tribus,* tribe; and *veru,* spit. *Portus* (harbour) has both *portibus* and *portubus.*

5. Some names of trees in *us*—as *cupressus,* cypress; *ficus,* fig-tree; *laurus,* laurel; *pinus,* a pine-tree, are either entirely declined according to the second declension, or take from the fourth declension only those cases which end in *u* and *us;* that is, the genitive and ablative singular, and the nominative and accusative plural. (Compare § 81. 4.) The word *domus* (a house) is declined in the following manner:—

	SINGULAR.		PLURAL.
Nom.	*domŭs.*	Nom.	*domūs.*
Gen.	*domūs.*	Gen.	*domŭum* or *domōrum.*
Dat.	*domŭi* (rarely *domo*).	Dat.	*domĭbus.*
Acc.	*domum.*	Acc.	*domōs* (rarely *domūs*).
Voc.	*domŭs.*	Voc.	*domūs.*
Abl.	*domō* (rarely *domu*).	Abl.	*domĭbus.*

The form *domi* is only used in the sense of ' at home.'

§ 72. Words of the fourth declension ending in *us* are masculine; those which end in *u* are neuters without exception. The following in *us*, however, are feminine:—*acus,* needle; *anus,* old woman; *colus,* distaff; *domus,* house; *manus,* hand; *nurus,* daughter-in-law; *penus,* provision; *porticus,* portico; *quercus,* oak; *tribus,* tribe; *socrus,* mother-in-law, and sometimes also *specus,* a cave. The two plural nouns, *idus* (gen. *iduum*), the 13th or 15th day of a month; and *quinquatrus* (gen. *quinquatruum*), a certain Roman festival, are likewise feminine.

Note. Colus also occurs as a masculine, and *specus* as a neuter, though only in the nominative and accusative. Instead of *penus,* there are two other forms—*penum,* gen. *peni;* and *penus,* gen. *penŏris.*

CHAPTER XI.

FIFTH DECLENSION.

§ 73. The fifth declension is, like the fourth, only a modification of the third. The stem of the words belonging to it ends in *e*, to which an *s* is added, to form the nominative. The number of words of this declension is very limited ; their genitive is formed by changing the *es* of the nominative into *ei*. The following may serve as specimens :—

SINGULAR.		PLURAL.	
Nom. *rē-s*, a thing.		Nom. *rē-s*, things.	
Gen. *rĕ-ī*.		Gen. *rē-rum*.	
Dat. *rĕ-ī*.		Dat. *rē-bus*.	
Acc. *re-m*.		Acc. *rē-s*.	
Voc. *rē-s*.		Voc. *rē-s*.	
Abl. *rē*.		Abl. *rē-bus*.	

SINGULAR.		PLURAL.	
Nom. *diē-s*, day.		Nom. *diē-s*, days.	
Gen. *diē-ī*.		Gen. *diē-rum*.	
Dat. *diē-ī*.		Dat. *diē-bus*.	
Acc. *die-m*.		Acc. *diē-s*.	
Voc. *diē-s*.		Voc. *diē-s*.	
Abl. *diē*.		Abl. *diē-bus*.	

Words to be used as Exercises.

Species, appearance ; *spes*, hope ; *acies*, battle array ; *effigies*, image ; *facies*, face ; *series*, a series.

Note 1. The words *dies* and *res* are the only nouns of this declension which have the plural complete. The words *acies, facies, effigies, species, spes*, and *glacies*, are used throughout the singular ; but in the plural they occur only in the nominative and accusative ; and all other words of this declension have no plural at all — as *caries*, rottenness ; *fides*, faith ; *macies*, leanness ; *rabies*, madness ; *scabies*, itch ; *pernicies*, destruction ; *superficies*, surface.

2. The ancient termination of the genitive singular was *is* — as *dieis*, which was contracted into *dies* (whence *Diespiter*, i. e., *Diei pater*), or changed into the usual form *diei* by dropping the *s*. The form *diei* was further contracted even by the best writers into *die* or *dii*, and that both in the genitive and dative. Hence the expression *tribuni plebi* (from *plebes*), the tribunes of the plebs. The e in the genitive and dative is long when it is preceded by a vowel, as in *diēi;* but short when preceded by a consonant, as in *rĕī*.

3. Some words have two forms, one of which follows the first, and

the other the fifth declension—as *materia* and *materies*, *barbaria* and *barbaries*, *mollitia* and *mollities*, *luxuria* and *luxuries*. Such words are termed *abundantia*.

§ 74. All words of the fifth declension are feminine, except *dies*, which in the singular is both masculine and feminine, but in the plural masculine only. The compound *meridies* (mid-day) is masculine only : it does not occur in the plural.

CHAPTER XII.

PECULIARITIES IN DECLENSION—DEFECTIVE AND IRREGULAR DE-CLENSION.

§ 75. There are a few compound words, consisting of two distinct nouns put together, without any change. In such compound words, which are termed spurious compounds (because the two words may be separated by the interposition of a third), each of the two elements is declined according to the declension to which it belongs — as *respublica* (republic), gen. *reipublicae* (the first word belonging to the fifth, and the second to the first declension) ; *jusjurandum* (oath), gen. *jurisjurandi* (the first word belonging to the third, and the second to the second declension). Of the same kind are the pronouns *quisquis* and *unusquisque*, &c. See § 117.

§ 76. Proper names, and such common nouns as express a thing or an idea in its totality, without regard to the various objects in which the idea is manifested, are generally used only in the singular, in Latin as well as in English — as *justitia*, justice ; *humanitas*, humanity ; *senectus*, old age ; *fames*, hunger ; *quies*, rest ; *plebs* and *vulgus*, common people ; *supellex*, furniture ; *aurum*, gold ; *ferrum*, iron ; *triticum*, wheat ; *oleum*, oil ; *sanguis*, blood.

Note 1. When, however, words of this kind change their original meaning, and denote different kinds of the thing designated by the word itself, they may have a plural — as *aera* (from *aes*, bronze), statues of bronze ; *cerae* (from *cera*, wax), wax tablets ; *mortes*, deaths, or cases of death ; *vina*, different kinds of wine. Poets, however, go much further in their use of the plural, and sometimes it does not differ at all with them from the singular — as *silentia* (silence), for *silentium* ; *murmura* (murmur), for *murmur* ; *flamina* (blast), for *flamen* ; *corda* (heart), for *cor* ; *ora* (face), for *os* ; *pectora* (breast), for *pectus* ; and others.

2. Nouns expressing abstract ideas are further used in the plural, when an idea is conceived as appearing in more than one person or thing, or when it is to be suggested that the same idea manifests itself

in different ways—as *adventūs imperatorum*, the arrival of the commanders ; *exitūs bellorum*, the different issues of wars ; *odia hominum*, the various manifestations of hatred in men ; *invidiae multitudinis*, the various ways in which envy displays itself in the multitude. On the same principle we find such plurals as *nives* (from *nix*, snow) ; *grandines* (from *grando*, hail) ; *imbres* (from *imber*, rain or shower) ; *frigora* (from *frigus*, cold).

3. Proper names also are used in the plural when several persons bearing the same name are spoken of, or when several men are figuratively called by the name of one whom they resemble—as *Licinii*, the men bearing the name *Licinius; Scipiones*, the persons bearing the name of *Scipio; multi Cicerones*—that is, many men as distinguished by their oratory, as Cicero; *pauci Catilinae*, few men as bad as *Catiline*.

§ 77. Some words are used only in the plural, either because they designate a number of individual things or persons — as *majores*, ancestors; or because they originally conveyed the idea of repetition, or of a thing consisting of several parts—as *arma* (gen. *armorum*), armour ; *fides* (gen. *fidium*), lyre. The following notes contain classified lists of the principal words of this kind :—

Note 1. The following, which denote living beings, are used only in the plural :—*liberi*, children ; *gemini*, twins ; *majores*, ancestors ; *posteri*, descendants ; *primores* and *proceres*, the principal persons or chieftains ; *inferi*, inhabitants of the lower regions ; *superi*, inhabitants of Olympus ; *coelites*, inhabitants of heaven ; *penates*, household gods ; *manes*, spirits of the dead ; *excubiae*, outposts or sentinels. If it is to be specified that only an individual is meant, it must be expressed by 'one of the children,' 'one of the ancestors,' &c.—as *unus liberorum, unus e majoribus*, &c.

2. The following denote parts of the human body :—*artūs*, limbs : *cani* (properly an adjective, to which *capilli* is understood), gray hair ; *exta, intestina*, and *viscera*, the intestines ; *praecordia*, midriff ; *ilia*, the loins.

3. The following denote things which were conceived by the Romans as consisting of several parts : —*arma*, armour ; *armamenta*, tackling ; *balneae*, a bathing-house ; *cancelli*, balusters or rails ; *casses*, a hunter's net ; *clathri*, railing ; *cunae, cunabula*, and *incunabula*, cradle ; *exuviae*, spoil ; *fides*, lyre ; *fori*, a row of seats ; *loculi*, repository ; *manubiae*, booty ; *moenia*, wall of a town ; *phalĕrae*, ornaments of a horse ; *salinae*, salt-works ; *scopae*, broom ; *sentes*, briar ; *spolia*, spoils or booty ; *virgulta*, bush.

4. Names of days and festivals :—*calendae*, the first day of a month ; *nonae*, the fifth, and sometimes the seventh day of a month ; *idūs*, the thirteenth or fifteenth of a month ; *feriae*, a holiday ; *nundinae*, a market-day ; *Bacchanalia, Saturnalia, Floralia, Ambarvalia*, all of which are names of Roman festivals.

5. The following must be noticed separately :—*ambāges*, a roundabout way ; *argutiae*, witticism ; *crepundia*, toy ; *deliciae*, delight ; *dirae*, curse ; *divitiae*, wealth ; *exsequiae*, funeral ; *epulae*, meal ; *fasti*, calendar ; *grates*, thanks ; *induciae*, truce ; *inferiae*, sacrifice offered to the dead ; *insidiae*, ambuscade; *inimicitiae*, enmity; *nuptiae*, wedding ; *tenebrae*, darkness ; *blanditiae*, flattery ; *illecebrae*, a bait.

6. The names of many towns occur only in the plural, probably because such towns were conceived to have arisen out of a union of two or more townships, or because the name of the people was used as the name of the town inhabited by them—as *Veii, Athenae, Leuctra, Gades, Delphi, Leontini, Parisii.*

7. Some names of mountains also are used only in the plural—as *Alpes, Acroceraunia;* and according to the same analogy, poets sometimes use names of Greek mountains as neuter plurals, which should be masculine and singular—as *Taygĕta* for *Taygĕtus.*

§ 78. Some words denote in the singular, as usual, a single object; but in the plural express both a plurality of such objects and an aggregate of the same or similar objects, which in many cases we express in English by a substantive in the singular—as *litera*, a letter of the alphabet; *literae*, both letters of the alphabet, and a letter or epistle; *auxilium*, help, aid; *auxilia*, auxiliary troops.

The following list contains the principal words of this kind:—

SINGULAR.	PLURAL.
aedes, a temple.	*aedes*, temples and a house.
aqua, water.	*aquae*, waters and medicinal springs.
carcer, prison.	*carceres*, prisons, and the barriers of a race-course.
castrum (more commonly *castellum*), a fort.	*castra*, a camp.
comitium, a part of the forum.	*comitia*, the assembly of the people.
copia, abundance.	*copiae*, provisions or troops.
facultas, power to do a thing.	*facultates*, property.
finis, end.	*fines*, boundary or territory.
fortuna, fortune.	*fortunae*, gifts of fortune.
gratia, favour.	*gratiae*, thanks.
hortus, garden.	*horti*, gardens and pleasure-grounds, or country seat.
impedimentum, an obstacle.	*impedimenta*, obstacles, and baggage of an army.
ludus, a game or pastime.	*ludi*, games, or a public exhibition on the stage or in the circus.
naris, nostril.	*nares*, the nose.
natalis (scil. *dies*), birthday.	*natales*, a man's descent or origin.
opera, work.	*operae*, labourers.
opis (gen. from the obsolete *ops*), help.	*opes*, wealth, power.
pars, part.	*partes*, parts, and a party.
rostrum, a beak or pointed front of a ship.	*rostra*, a place in the Roman forum, which was adorned with the beaks of ships, and from which the orators addressed the people.
sal, salt.	*sales*, wit.
tabula, a board or table.	*tabulae*, boards, and a register or document.

§ 79. A few nouns do not admit of any inflection; hence they are termed *indeclinable*. Words of this kind are the names of thè letters of the alphabet, both in Latin and Greek —as, *alpha, beta, gamma*. To these must be added the following:—*fas*, divine right; *nefas*, wrong; *instar*, weight, importance, validity; *mane*, the morning; *caepe*, onion; *gummi*, gum; *pondo*, weight or pound. The same is the case with the neuter nouns in *os* and *es*, and the plurals in *e*, which are taken from the Greek—as *chaos*, chaos; *cacoëthes*, and *Tempe*. As to the gender of indeclinable words, see § 44.

Note 1. All these indeclinable words may be used in the oblique cases, but the case is then usually indicated by some accompanying adjective or•pronoun. Instead of the indeclinable *gummi*, we also find the feminine *gummis* (gen. *gummis*), and the neuter *gumen ;* instead of *caepe*, we also have the feminine *caepa* (gen. *caepae*). Instead of the neuter indeclinable form *Argos* (a town in Argolis), Latin writers also use *Argi*, as a plural of the second declension.
2. Foreign words, such as Hebrew names, which occur chiefly in Christian writers, often take a Latin termination, for the purpose of rendering declension possible. Sometimes this is done in the nominative as well as in the oblique cases—as *Abrahamus*, gen. *Abrahami;* but sometimes the foreign form is retained in the nominative ; but the oblique cases take a Latin termination—as *David*, gen. *Davidis*. *Jesus* makes the accusative *Jesum;* in all the other cases it is *Jesu*. If such Hebrew words have no termination analogous to those occurring in the Latin and Greek languages, they may be used as indeclinables ; but where there are such terminations, as in *Joannes, Maria, Moses, Judas*, they are declined after the first or third declension.
3. *Pondo*, which was mentioned above among the indeclinable nouns, is properly the ablative of *pondus* or *pondum*, and accordingly signifies 'in weight.' But in the sense of 'pound,' it is used also as a plural—as *quinque pondo*, five pounds.

§ 80. Some nouns are indeed capable of inflection, but do not possess all the cases, and are therefore termed defectives in case. This arises either from the fact, that certain cases of a word, in consequence of its signification, cannot occur in the language, and partly from other less obvious causes. The following is a classified list of the principal words of this kind : —

1. The nominative is wanting to the following words, of which we shall give only the genitive, though the other cases also occur:—*dapis*, food (from *daps*); *dicionis*, dominion (from *dicio*); *frugis*, fruit (from *frux*); *internecionis*, destruction (from *internecio*); *opis*, help (from *ops*); *pollinis*, fine flour (from *pollen*); *stipis*, little money (from *stipes*).
2. The following words occur only in certain cases of the singular:—*Fors* (chance), in the nominative and ablative

forte, by chance, or accidentally. *Impĕtis* and *impĕte,* the genitive and ablative of an obsolete nominative *impes* (vehemence), for which *impetus* is commonly used. *Lues* (an epidemic), occurs only in the nominative, accusative (*luem*), and ablative (*lue*).

3. The following occur only in certain cases of the singular and plural:— From the obsolete *sordes* (filth), we have only the accusative and ablative singular, *sordem* and *sorde ;* but the plural is complete. From the obsolete *vepres* (a thorn-bush), we have only the accusative and ablative singular, *veprem* and *vepre ;* but the plural is complete. Of the obsolete *vicis* or *vix* (change), there exist the genitive, accusative, and ablative singular, *vicis, vicem,. vice ;* the plural is complete, except that the genitive is wanting. *Vis* (force) exists in the nominative, accusative, and ablative singular, *vis, vim, vi ;* but the plural, *vires, virium, viribus,* &c. is complete.

4. The following words occur in the singular in the ablative only, and, generally speaking, only in poetry : *ambāge, compĕde, fauce, obice, prece, verbere.* The last two occur also in prose. Terence also uses the dative *preci,* and Ovid the genitive *verberis.* But generally speaking, these words occur in all the cases of the plural.

5. The following words also are used only in the ablative singular :—*sponte* (impulse), always with a possessive pronoun, as *mea sponte,* of my own accord ; *sua sponte,* of his own accord. A number of verbal substantives of the fourth declension, occurring always joined either to a genitive or to a possessive pronoun—as *jussu populi,* by command of the people ; *mandatu Caesaris,* by the order of Caesar ; *rogatu meo,* at my request. So also *natu,* joined with *magnus, major, maximus,* and the expressions *in promptu, in procinctu, concessu, permissu, efflagitatu,* and others.

Note 1. Some nouns occur only in one particular case, and that only in peculiar expressions—as *dicis,* in *dicis causa,* for the sake of appearance ; *nauci* (gen.), in *non nauci facio,* I do not consider it worth a farthing ; and *non nauci est,* it is not worth a farthing. To these must be added some datives of verbal substantives of the fourth declension, which occur only in connection with *esse* and *duci*—as *derisui esse,* to be a subject of derision ; *contemptui esse,* to be a subject of contempt ; so also *ostentui, despicatui duci,* or *esse.* Of the same kind are *infitias ire,* to deny ; *suppetias ferre,* to bring succour ; *venum dare,* to sell ; and *venum ire,* to be sold—the accusatives *infitias, suppetias,* and *venum,* being the only forms of these words that exist.

2. *Secus* (sex), joined with the adjectives *virile* and *muliebre,* is used as an indeclinable expression, and may accordingly be put in apposition to any case. *Repetundarum* and *repetundis* (the genitive and

ablative of the participle *repetundae*—namely, *pecuniae*) are the only forms used in the sense of 'moneys extorted in an illegal manner.' The plural *grates* (thanks), and the plural of some monosyllabic neuters, as *aera, jura, rura, farra*, occur only in the nominative and accusative, and that chiefly in poetry. A few monosyllabic words of the third declension, as *cor, cos, rus, sal, sol, vas* (gen. *vadis*), have no genitive plural.

§ 81. Some words have in the nominative two or three different terminations, in consequence of which they belong to different declensions, and sometimes also are of different genders—as *eventus* and *eventum*, an event; *jugulus* and *jugulum*, the throat; *luxuria* and *luxuries*, luxury.

Note. Several words of this kind have already been noticed—such as *laurus*, gen. *lauri* and *laurūs* (See § 71, note 5), and those Greek words which may have either a Greek or a Latin termination—as *grammatice* and *grammatica*. (See § 55, note 4.)

1. In the second declension, some masculines in *us* have at the same time a neuter form in *um*—as *callus* and *callum*, a wart; *commentarius* and *commentarium*, a memoir; *jugulus* and *jugulum*, throat; *lupinus* and *lupinum*, lupine; *porrus* and *porrum*, leek; *cubitus* and *cubitum*, the elbow, or a cubit; *balteus*, and more rarely *balteum*, a belt; *baculum*, rarely *baculus*, a stick; *clipeus*, rarely *clipeum*, a shield; *angiportus* and *angiportum*, a narrow lane; *tonitrus* and *tonitruum*, *vallus* and *vallum*, *rictus* and *rictum*.

2. The following words belong either to the first or to the second declension, according to their terminations: *menda* and *mendum*, a fault; *vespera* and *vesper*, evening (the ablative, however, is commonly *vespere* or *vesperi*, according to the third declension; while *vesper*, the evening star, entirely belongs to the second); *aranea* and *araneus*, a spider; *essedum* and *esseda*, a travelling carriage.

3. The following words belong either to the first or to the fifth declension, according as they end in *ia* or *ies*:—*barbaria* and *barbaries*, a barbarous country; *mollitia* and *mollities*, effeminacy; *luxuria* and *luxuries*, luxury; *materia* and *materies*, matter, though the latter usually signifies timber. The genitive and dative singular of these words is rarely found inflected according to the fifth declension. (Compare § 73, note 3.)

4. Some verbal substantives of the fourth declension in *us* have another form in *um*, following the second declension —as *eventus* and *eventum*, an occurrence; *suggestus* and *suggestum*, the hustings. (Compare § 71, note 5.)

5. The following must be noticed separately:—

Plebs and *plebes*, gen. *plebis* and *plebei*, or contracted, *plebi;* the former following the third, and the latter the fifth declension.

Jugerum (an acre), of the second declension, has certain forms belonging to the third—namely, ablative *jugere*, genitive plural *jugerum*, and dative and ablative *jugeribus*.

Fames (hunger) belongs to the third declension, but has in the ablative always *famē*, according to the fifth, instead of *famĕ*.

Requies (rest), gen. *requietis*, but makes the accusative and ablative both *requietem*, *requiete* and *requiem*, *requiē*.

Gausăpe, *gausăpis*, and *gausăpum* (a piece of woollen cloth), are neuter; the first two forms belong to the third, and the third to the second declension; but there also exists the feminine *gausapa* of the first, and the masculine *gausapes*, gen. *is*, of the third declension.

Praesēpe, gen. *praesēpis* (a manger), is neuter; but *praesēpes*, gen. *praesēpis*, is feminine, and *praesēpium* is neuter.

Tapes, gen. *tapētis* (a carpet), is masculine; but *tapēte*, gen. *tapētis* and *tapētum*, are neuter.

Ilia (a neut. plur.), the loins, makes its genitive plural *ilium* and *iliorum*, and the dative and ablative *ilibus* only.

6. Some words have not only different terminations in the different cases, but the stem itself is different; so that they may be regarded as different words; e.g.—

Femur (thigh), gen. *femŏris* and *femĭnis* (from the obsolete *femen*).

Jecur (liver), gen. *jecoris;* but also *jecinŏris*, *jocinŏris*, and *jocinĕris*.

Juventus and *juventa* (youth), gen. *juventutis* and *juventae*, while *Juventas* (the goddess of youth) makes *Juventatis*.

Senectus and *senecta* (old age), gen. *senectutis* and *senectae;* but the latter, like *juventae*, is used only in poetry.

Pecus (cattle), when feminine, makes the genitive *pecŭdis;* when neuter, *pecŏris*. There is also a plural *pecua*, dat. and abl. *pecubus*.

Penus (provisions), gen. *penŏris*, plur. *penŏra;* but it is also a feminine of the fourth declension, gen. *penŭs*, and a neuter, *penum*, of the second. The two last forms do not occur in the plural.

Colluvio and *colluvies* (a mass of filth flowing together), are both feminine; the former of the third, and the latter of the fifth declension.

Scorpio and *scorpius* (a scorpion), are both masculine; the former of the third, and the latter of the second declension.

Note. Some Greek words, on being adopted into the Latin language, retained their original termination, and at the same time received a Latin one — as *crater* (a vessel for mixing wine and water), gen. *cratēris*, and the Latin form *cratēra, ae; elephas* (elephant), gen. *elephantis*, and the Latin form *elephantus, i;* the masculine *tiāras* (the tiara), and the Latin feminine *tiāra; delphin* (a dolphin), and *delphinus*.

§ 82. Some substantives, though they have only one form in the singular, have in the plural either two forms of different genders, or one form only, which, however, differs in gender from the singular:—

Jocus (a joke), plur. *joci* and *joca*.
Locus (a place), plur. *loca*, places, but *loci*, passages in books; this distinction, however, is not always observed.
Carbasus (fem. linen), plur. *carbasa*, sail.
Coelum (heaven), plur. *coeli*.
Frenum (bit), plur. *freni* and *frena*.
Rastrum (a hatchet), plur. *rastri* and *rastra*.
Ostrea (oyster), plur. *ostreae* and *ostrea*.
Sibilus (a hissing), plur. *sibili*, and in poetry *sibila*.
Tartarus (the lower world), plur. in poetry *Tartara*.
Balneum (bath), plur. *balneae*, a public bath-house.
Epulum (a solemn feast), plur. *epulae*, a meal.
Vas (a vessel), belongs to the third declension, but follows in the plural the second, *vasa, vasorum, vasis*.

Note. The only substantives of a really irregular declension are *Jupiter* (or *Juppiter*), which makes its genitive *Jŏvis*, the remaining cases being regularly formed from *Jovis; senex* (an old man) makes its genitive *sĕnis; nix* (snow), *nĭvis; supellex* (furniture), gen. *supellectilis;* and *vis* (violence), though it makes the accusative and ablative *vim* and *vi*, yet has the plural *vires, virium, viribus*, &c.

CHAPTER XIII.

TERMINATIONS AND DECLENSION OF ADJECTIVES.

§ 83. Adjectives are words which denote qualities, peculiarities, and properties of persons or things, provided these qualities, peculiarities, &c. are not regarded as independent existences. In *fortis miles* (a brave soldier), the word *fortis* is an adjective, denoting the quality as connected with, or attached to, the soldier ; but *fortitudo* (bravery), which likewise denotes a quality, is yet not an adjective, but a substantive, because the quality expressed by *fortitudo* is regarded as an independent existence.

§ 84. An adjective, therefore, is commonly joined to a substantive, with which it agrees in gender, number, and case. In order to make it agree in gender, an adjective should have three different terminations to mark the genders. This, however, is not always the case, for some adjectives have only two terminations to mark the gender, the first for the masculine and feminine, and the second for the neuter; while a large number have only one termination for all the genders.

Note. What is here said of adjectives, holds good also of participles, which, as far as their form is concerned, must be regarded, and are treated, as adjectives.

§ 85. There are only two classes of adjectives which have three distinct terminations for the three genders — namely, those in *us* and *er*, both forming the feminine in *a* and the neuter in *um*—as *bonus* (good), fem. *bona*, neut. *bonum; amatus* (beloved), fem. *amata*, neut. *amatum; liber* (free), fem. *libera*, neut. *liberum; niger* (black), fem. *nigra*, neut. *nigrum.* To these must be added the single adjective *satur*, fem. *satura*, neut. *saturum.* (§ 57, note 1.)

Those adjectives which retain the *e* before the *r* in the genitive singular (see § 58), also retain that vowel in the feminine and neuter — as in *liber, libera, liberum;* while those which throw it out in the genitive, also drop it in the feminine and neuter—as *niger, nigra, nigrum.*

Respecting the declension of these adjectives, it must be observed that the masculine and neuter forms follow the second declension, but the feminine in *a* the first.

Note. It has already been observed that there are a number of adjectives and pronouns in *us, a, um*, which make their genitive in all genders in *ius*, and their dative in *i*, though they are regular in all other respects. (See § 58, note 3.)

§ 86. There are, however, thirteen adjectives in *er* which make their feminine in *is*, and the neuter in *e*, all of which forms follow the third declension. (Compare § 65 (*a*) 2 and 3; § 67. 5.) The three genders can be distinguished only in the nominative singular, since the declension of the masculine is quite the same as that of the feminine. These adjectives are :—

Masc.	Fem.	Neut.
acer,	acris,	acre (gen. acris), sharp.
alacer,	alacris,	alacre (gen. alacris), cheerful.
campester,	campestris,	campestre (gen. campestris), belonging to a plain
celeber,	celebris,	celebre (gen. celebris), famous. [or field.

Masc.	Fem.	Neut.
celer,	celeris,	celere (gen. celeris), swift.
equester,	equestris,	equestre (gen. equestris), equestrian.
paluster,	palustris,	palustre (gen. palustris), marshy.
pedester,	pedestris,	pedestre (gen. pedestris), on foot.
puter,	putris,	putre (gen. putris), rotten.
saluber,	salubris,	salubre (gen. salubris), wholesome.
silvester,	silvestris,	silvestre (gen. silvestris), woody.
terrester,	terrestris,	terrestre (gen. terrestris), earthy.
volucer,	volucris,	volucre (gen. volucris), swift, winged.

Note 1. These adjectives seem originally to have had only two terminations, *is* for both the masculine and feminine, and *e* for the neuter ; and there are instances even in the very best writers, though chiefly in prose, in which the masculine ends, like the feminine, in *is*, as Cic. *De Divin.* ii. 4: *locus celebris*, a famous place ; Caes. *De Bell. Gall.* ii. 18, and vi. 34.

2. The names of months ending in *er* are likewise adjectives of this kind—as *September, October, November, December*, the masculine substantive *mensis* (month) being understood to each of them. The feminine of these names of months occurs rarely in any other connection except with the plurals *calendae* and *idus*—as *calendae Septembres, idus Novembres;* but Horace also uses *libertas Decembris*, the freedom enjoyed in December. The neuter is never used.

§ 87. Adjectives in *is*, and the comparatives in *ior*, have only two terminations—one for the masculine and feminine, and the second for the neuter. Those in *is* make their neuter in *e*, and the comparatives in *ior* make their neuter in *ius*—as *levis* (masc. and fem.) *leve* (neut.), light ; *pulchrior* (masc. and fem.), *pulchrius* (neut.), handsomer. All the forms of these adjectives belong to the third declension ; both *levis* and *leve* making their genitive *levis*, and *pulchrior* as well as *pulchrius* make *pulchrioris*. (Compare § 65 (a) 3, (b) 3.)

Note. There are twelve adjectives which have double forms ; one in *us, a, um*, and the other in *is, e*—namely :—

Bijugus, a, um, and *bijugis, e*, with two yokes.
Exanimus, a, um, and *exanimis, e*, dead.
Hilarus, a, um, and *hilaris, e*, cheerful.
Imbecillus, a, um, and *imbecillis, e*, weak, imbecile.
Imberbus, a, um, and *imberbis, e*, without a beard.
Inermus, a, um, and *inermis, e*, unarmed.
Infrenus, a, um, and *infrenis, e*, without a bridle.
Multijugus, a, um, and *multijugis, e*, with many yokes.
Quadrijugus, a, um, and *quadrijugis, e*, with four yokes.
Semiermus, a, um, and *semiermis, e*, half-armed.
Semianimus, a, um, and *semianimis, e*, half-dead.
Unanimus, a, um, and *unanimis, e*, unanimous.

The adjectives *acclivis, declivis*, and *proclivis*, are sometimes likewise used as adjectives of three terminations, in *us, a, um;* but only very rarely.

§ 88. All other adjectives have only one termination for all genders, and all belong to the third declension. (Compare § 65 (*b*) 2.) For example, *sapiens*, wise ; *felix*, happy ; *legens*, reading; *concors*, unanimous; *atrox*, atrocious; *locuples*, rich ; *memor*, remembering. But although in these adjectives the neuter is like the two other genders, still it differs from them by having, according to the general rule, the nominative, accusative, and vocative singular alike, and by the same cases of the plural ending in *ia;* hence the neuter nominative, accusative, and vocative of *prudens* is *prudens*, and the same cases in the plural are all *prudentia*. (Compare §§ 66 and 67.) *Vetus* (old), gen. *veteris*, alone makes the plural *vetera*.

Note 1. The neuter plural of adjectives of one termination occurs only in those ending in *ns, as, rs, ax, ix*, and *ox;* and in numerals ending in *plex*—as *elegantia* (from *elegans*), *sapientia* (from *sapiens*), *Larinatia* (from *Larinas*), *solertia* (from *solers*), *concordia* (from *concors*), *tenacia* (from *tenax*), *felicia* (from *felix*), *atrocia* (from *atrox*), *simplicia* (from *simplex*). To these must be added the following :—*anceps*, of two sides or doubtful ; *praeceps*, precipitous ; *locuples*, rich ; *par*, equal ; *hebes*, blunt ; *teres*, round ; *versicolor*, of different colours. Some adjectives of one termination, which generally have no neuter plural, are nevertheless used with neuter substantives in the dative and ablative plural—as *supplicibus verbis*, with suppliant words ; *puberibus* (from *pubes*), *foliis*, with full-grown leaves.

2. Some adjectives have different forms, one being of three terminations, and the other of one—as *opulentus, a, um* (wealthy), and *opulens; violentus, a, um* (violent), and *violens*. *Dives* (rich) is properly an adjective of one termination ; but there is also a contracted form *dis* (gen. *ditis*), which makes its neuter *dite*, though it is of very rare occurrence.

3. A number of nouns which are in reality substantives, especially those ending in *tor* (fem. *trix*), and those compounded with *fex* (from *facio*), and *cola* (from *colo*), are sometimes joined to other substantives, as if they were adjectives—as *victor exercitus*, a victorious army ; *ultrices deae*, the avenging goddesses ; *artifex motus*, an artistic movement ; *turba incola*, the inhabiting crowd, or crowd of inhabitants. These expressions, however, occur more frequently in poetry than in prose. Some substantives of this kind, when used as adjectives, even form a neuter plural—as *victricia arma* (victorious arms), just as if *victrix* were a real adjective of one termination. Poets often take greater license, employing not only such words as *senex* (an old man), and *juvenis* (a young man), in the sense of ' old' and ' young :' even the Greek patronymics in *as* and *is* are used by them as mere adjectives—as *Pelias hasta*, a Pelian spear ; that is, a spear made of wood grown on Mount Pelion ; *Ausonis ora*, the Ausonian coast ; *Hesperides aquae*, Hesperian (western) waters.

4. The following adjectives are indeclinable :—
Frugi (discreet), properly a dative of the obsolete *frux;* hence *homo frugi, hominis frugi, homines frugi*, &c.
Nequam (good for nothing) occurs only as a neuter in connection with the verbs *esse* and *habere*.

Opus and *necesse* (necessary) are likewise indeclinable, and occur only in connection with *esse*.

Praesto (ready or at hand) occurs only with *esse*.

Semis (and a half) occurs only in connection with numerals; and the conjunction *et* (and) being omitted, must be rendered by 'and a half'—as *recipe uncias quatuor semis*, take four ounces and a half.

Potis, neut. *pote* (able), occurs only in the nominative in connection with the verb *esse*, with which it is contracted into *posse* (to be able.)

Damnas (condemned) is used only as a law term in connection with the imperatives *esto* and *sunto*.

5. The following adjectives are deficient, having either not all cases or not both numbers:—

Of the feminine *cetera*, neut. *ceterum* (the other), the masculine nominative *ceterus* is not used; but all the other cases both of the singular and plural are very common.

The genitive *primoris* (of the first) has no nominative; but in the plural it is very common in the sense of 'chiefs' or 'leaders.'

Of *sontis*, *puberis*, and *seminěcis* (guilty, full-grown, and half-dead), the nominative *sons*, *pubes*, and *seminex*, do not occur.

The words *exlex*, lawless; *exspes*, hopeless, occur only in the nominative.

Pauci (a few) and *plerique* (many, or the greater number) are used only in the plural; but the singular now and then occurs in connection with collective substantives—as *pleraque nobilitas*, the greater part of the nobility; *pleraque juventus*, the greater part of the youths; *plerusque exercitus*, the greater part of the army. *Plerique* has no genitive, but that of *plurimi* supplies its place.

The vocatives *macte* and *macti* are the only forms that occur of this adjective. It is said to be a compound of *magis* and *auctus*, so that its meaning is 'more increased,' or simply 'increased.'

CHAPTER XIV.

COMPARISON OF ADJECTIVES.

§ 89. As adjectives denote qualities, and as the same quality existing in two different persons or things may be in a higher degree in the one than in the other; and again, as among many persons or things possessing the same quality, one may possess it in the highest degree, every language has some means or other to express these different degrees. Their number is three — the *Positive*, *Comparative*, and *Superlative*. The positive is the adjective in its fundamental form — as *bonus*, good; *felix*, happy; *fortis*, brave. When a comparison is instituted between two persons or things in regard to a quality they have in common, or when the same quality exist-

5   c 2

ing in the same object is compared with itself at different times, and when the result of the comparison is that the quality exists in one object in a higher degree than in the other, or at one time in a higher degree than at another, the comparison is expressed by the comparative ; *e.g.*, he is *wiser* than his brother ; he is *wiser* now than he ever has been. When a comparison is instituted between more than two objects in regard to a quality which they have in common, and when the result of the comparison is that one possesses the quality in a higher degree than the others, or we may say in the highest degree, this degree is the superlative ; *e.g.*, he is the *most* diligent of all my pupils ; Socrates was the *wisest* of all the Greeks. In all these points the Latin language follows the same principle as the English.　　　　　-

Note. In one point, however, the Latin language differs—namely, when we compare two different qualities existing in the same object, we in English put only one of the adjectives in the comparative, while the Latin language has them both in the comparative ; *e.g.*, my friend is *more learned* than *just*, where the Latin is *juster — amicus meus doctior est quam justior.* The Latin language, moreover, frequently employs the comparative in an elliptical manner, where we should say either ' too' or ' rather'—as *doctior,* ' more learned,' namely, than should be ; that is, ' rather learned,' or ' too learned.' In like manner the Latin language is very partial to the use of the superlative (as all southern nations are apt to speak in strong terms) where we simply say ' very'—as *doctissimus* may either mean ' the most learned man' or ' a very learned man.' It should be observed that when the result of a comparison between two objects in regard to a common quality is that both possess the same in an equal degree, the comparison is indicated, in Latin as in English, not by the comparative, but by certain particles joined to the positive ; *e.g.*, he is *as* learned as his brother, *aeque* doctus est *ac* frater ; he is *as* learned *as* he is troublesome, *aeque* doctus est *ac* molestus.

§ 90. The comparative degree is formed in Latin by the termination *ior* (for the masculine and feminine) and *ius* (for the neuter) being added to the stem of the adjective, as it appears in any of the oblique cases — as *opulentus,* comp. *opulent-ior, ius ; sapiens,* comp. *sapient-ior, ius ; sagax,* comp. *sagac-ior, ius ; liber,* comp. *liber-ior, ius ; pulcher,* comp. *pulchr-ior, ius ; levis,* comp. *lev-ior, ius.* Those adjectives in *er* which lose the *e* in the oblique cases, of course lose it also in the comparative—as in *liber, liberior,* and *pulcher, pulchrior.* Sinister (left) alone has *sinisterior,* although its genitive is *sinistri.* All comparatives follow the third declension, making their genitive in *oris.* (Compare § 65 (*b*) 3.)

Note. From the comparative of some adjectives there is formed a sort of diminutive by attaching to the neuter the termination *culus—*

as *durus* (hard), comp. *durius*, dim. *duriusculus* (a little harder); *grandis* (grand), comp. *grandius*, dim. *grandiusculus* (a little grander).

§ 91. The superlative is formed by adding the termination *issĭmus, a, um,* to the stem of the adjective, as it appears in any of the oblique cases—as *opulentus,* sup. *opulent-issimus, a, um; sapiens,* sup. *sapient-issimus, a, um; sagax,* sup. *sagac-issimus, a, um; levis,* sup. *lev-issimus, a, um.*

Note. In early Latinity, the termination of the superlative was *issŭmus,* which form still occurs in poetry, and in Sallust, who is generally partial to ancient forms of words.

§ 92. All adjectives ending in *er* make the superlative by adding *rĭmus, a, um,* to the masculine nominative of the positive—as *pulcher,* sup. *pulcherrimus; liber,* sup. *liberrimus; acer,* sup. *acerrimus; celeber,* sup. *celeberrimus.* *Vetus* (old, gen. *veter-is*) likewise makes its superlative *veterrimus,* and *nuperus* (late, from *nuper*), *nuperrimus.* *Maturus* (early) has two forms in the superlative, *maturissimus* and *maturrimus,* but the latter especially in the adverb *maturrime.*

§ 93. The following adjectives in *lis—facilis* (easy), *difficilis* (difficult), *gracilis* (slender, thin), *humilis* (humble, low), *similis* (similar), and *dissimilis* (dissimilar)—form their superlative by adding *limus* to the stem—as *facil-limus, difficil-limus, simil-limus,* &c. All other adjectives in *lis* form their superlative in the regular manner—as *utilis,* sup. *util-issimus.*

§ 94. Adjectives ending in *dĭcus, fĭcus,* and *vŏlus* (from the verbs *dico, facio,* and *volo*), make the comparative by changing *us* into *entiŏr,* and the superlative by changing *us* into *entissimus,* just as if the positive ended in *ens—* as *maledicus* (slanderous), comp. *maledicentior,* sup. *maledicentissimus; munificus* (munificent), comp. *munificentior,* sup. *munificentissimus; malevolus* (ill-disposed), comp. *malevolentior,* sup. *malevolentissimus.* The two adjectives *egēnus* (poor or needy) and *provĭdus* (provident), likewise form their comparative and superlative from *egens* and *providens,* so that they have *egentior, egentissimus,* and *providentior, providentissimus.*

The masculine and neuter of all superlatives follow the second declension, and the feminine the first.

Note. The participles of the present ending in *ns,* and those of the perfect passive in *us,* are likewise capable of forming degrees of comparison, if they have the meaning of an adjective—as *amans* (loving), comp. *amantior,* sup. *amantissimus; doctus* (taught or learned), comp. *doctior,* super. *doctissimus.* But the future participle in *rus* and the gerundive in *dus* have no degrees of comparison.

§ 95. Some adjectives form their degrees of comparison in

ᴀn irregular manner, or rather from obsolete words and different stems—as,

Positive.	Comparative.	Superlative.
Bónus, good,	*melior, ius*,	*optimus, a, um.*
Malus, bad,	*pejor, pejus*,	*pessimus, a, um.*
Magnus, great,	*major, majus*,	*maximus, a, um.*
Multus, much,	*plus* (gen. *pluris*),	*plurimus, a, um.*
	plural, *plures, plura.*	
Parvus, small,	*minor, minus*,	*minimus, a, um.*
Nequam, good for nothing,	*nequior, ius*,	*nequissimus, a, um.*
Frugi, cheerful,	*frugalior, ius*,	*frugalissimus, a, um.*

Senex (an old man) and *juvenis* (a young man), although substantives, yet have a comparative *senior* and *junior*, but no superlative, the place of which is supplied by *natu maximus* and *natu minimus*.

Note. Multus properly signifies 'much,' but in poetry it is also used in the sense of 'many'—as *multa tabula*, many a table ; *multa victima*, many a victim. The same is the case with *plurimus*, which in the singular signifies 'a great many'—as *plurima avis;* that is, *plurimae aves*, a great many birds. Both words, however, commonly occur only in the plural. The comparative *plus* exists in the singular only in the neuter gender (nom. and acc. *plus*, gen. *pluris*, and abl. *plure*), and is used as a substantive ; but the plural *plures* (masc. and fem.), *plura* (neut.), is complete, gen. *plurium*, dat. *pluribus*, &c.

§ 96. Some adjectives have two irregular forms of the superlative, and sometimes with a slight difference in meaning—as,

Positive.	Comparative.	Superlative.
exterus, being without,	*exterior*, outer,	*extrēmus* (rarely *extĭmus*), the last.
inferus, being below,	*inferior*,	*infĭmus*, or contracted, *ĭmus*.
superus, being above,	*superior*,	*supremus*, the last in point of time, and *summus*, the highest.
posterus, one who follows,	*posterior*,	*postremus*, the last, and *postumus*, one born after his father's death.

Note. Some of the four positives here given, such as *inferus, superus*, and *posterus*, do not occur in the nominative masculine, but the other genders and the oblique cases do occur. The plural *exteri* is used in the sense of 'foreign ;' *superi* in the sense of 'the gods of heaven ;' *inferi* in the sense of 'the gods of the lower world ;' ănd *posteri* in the sense of 'descendants.'

§ 97. There are a few comparatives and superlatives to which there is no adjective in the positive, and which are generally derived from adverbs, though some of them cannot be derived either from adjectives or from adverbs—namely,

Comparative.	Superlative.
citerior, situated on this side,	*citimus*, from the adverb *citra*.
ulterior, placed beyond,	*ultimus*, from the adverb *ultra*.
interior, interior,	*intimus*, from the adverb *intra*.
propior, nearer,	*proximus*, from the adverb *prope.*
deterior, inferior,	*deterrimus*, the lowest.
ocior, quicker,*	*ocissimus*, from the Greek ὠκύς.
potior, preferable,	*potissimus*, from the obsolete *potis*, § 87, note 4.
prior, first of two,	*primus*, from the adverb *prae*.
sequior, *sequius*, or *secius*, less good,	——, from the adverb *secus*.
anterior, being before another,	——, from the adverb *ante*.

Note 1. The following adjectives have a superlative, but no com-parative :—*diversus* (different), *diversissimus; falsus* (false), *falsissi-mus; inclĭtus* (famous), *inclitissimus; novus* (new), *novissimus; sacer* (sacred), *sacerrimus*. *Vetus* has *veterrimus*, but *vetustus*, which has the same meaning, furnishes the comparative *vetustior*, and has also a superlative *vetustissimus*.

2. Many adjectives, especially such as are derived from verbs, and end in *ĭlis* and *bĭlis*, together with those in *ĭlis*, derived from sub-stantives, have a comparative, but not a superlative. But this rule is not without exceptions, among which may be mentioned *amabilis* (amiable), *nobilis* (noble), *ignobilis* (ignoble), *mobilis* (moveable), *fer-tilis* (fertile), *utilis* (useful).

§ 98. There are many adjectives which cannot have any degrees of comparison at all, because they denote qualities which cannot be conceived to exist in a higher or lower degree than that in which they commonly appear. This is chiefly the case with those which denote the material of which something is made, origin, and a definite time — as *aureus*, golden ; *argenteus*, made of silver ; *ligneus*, wooden ; *Romanus*, Roman ; *paternus*, paternal ; *hibernus*, winterly ; *hodiernus*, belonging to this day ; *vivus*, alive ; *exanimis*, dead ; *caecus*, blind ; *sinister*, left-handed ; *ater*, black ; *surdus*, deaf ; *jejunus*, not having breakfasted ; and many others. But it must be observed that when such words assume a figurative meaning, a comparative may still be used : *e. g.*, *caecus*, in the sense of 'a person who cannot see,' has no comparative ; but when it denotes moral blindness, we may say, *e. g.*, 'this man is more blind to the truth than another.' So, also, *sinister* cannot have a comparative in its primary meaning, but in the sense of 'awkward' it may have one.

§ 99. Many adjectives do not form their degrees of com-parison in the ordinary way, by means of terminations, partly because the affixing of the terminations to the stem would produce a disagreeable sound, and partly for other less obvious reasons. Adjectives of this class express the comparative degree by adding the adverb *magis* (more), and the superlative by adding *maxime* (most), to the positive—as pos. *idoneus* (fit), comp. *magis idoneus,* sup. *maxime idoneus.* This is the case—

1. With all adjectives ending in *us,* in which the *us* is preceded by a vowel—as *idoneus; dubius,* doubtful; *necessarius,* necessary.

Note. As *qu* counts only for *c* or *k* (see § 4, note), adjectives in which *us* is preceded by *qu* have their regular comparative and superlative—as *antiquus* (ancient), *antiquior, antiquissimus.* Some adjectives ending in *uus* also sometimes form their degrees of comparison in the ordinary way—as *strenuus* (strenuous), *strenuior, strenuissimus; assiduus* (assiduous), *assiduior, assiduissimus;* so also *vacuus* (empty), *exiguus* (small). Adjectives in *ius* rarely form their degrees, but if they do, they cast out the *i* of the stem — as *noxius* (hurtful), comp. *noxior* for *noxiior; industrius* (industrious), comp. *industrior* for *industriior; egregius* (distinguished), comp. *egregior* for *egregiior.* Of those in *ius,* the only ones which have a superlative, are *egregius, egregiisimus,* and *pius* (pious), *piisimus.*

2. Many adjectives which are compounds of verbs or substantives, such as those ending in *ger,* and *fer* (from *gero,* and *fero*), and many others — as *ignivomus,* fire-spitting; *degener,* degenerate; *discolor,* of different colours; *inops,* poor; *magnanimus,* generous. Those ending in *dicus, ficus,* and *volus* (from *dico, facio, volo;* see § 94), however, as well as those compounded with *ars, mens,* and *cor,* may have their regular degrees — as *iners, sollers, demens, amens, concors, discors, vecors.*

3. Most derivative adjectives ending in *ālis, āris, bundus, ĭcus, ĭlis, ĭdus, īnus, īvus, ōrus, tĭmus, ŭlus* — as *naturalis,* natural; *furibundus,* full of fury; *modicus,* moderate; *senilis,* peculiar to an old man; *rabidus,* rabid; *peregrinus,* foreign; *furtivus,* thievish; *canorus,* sonorous; *querulus,* quarrelsome; *legitimus,* legitimate. To these must be added the adjectives, ending in *ātus,* derived from substantives — as *barbatus,* bearded; *cordatus,* prudent or wise.

Note. There are several exceptions to this rule. Some of these adjectives have both the comparative and the superlative—as *liberalis* (liberal), *hospitalis* (hospitable), *divinus* (divine). Others have only the comparative—as *rusticus* (rustic), *aequalis* (equal), *capitalis* (mortal), *popularis* (popular), *regalis* (kingly), *salutaris* (wholesome), *civilis* (belonging to a citizen), *tempestivus* (in proper time).

4. The following adjectives have no regular degrees, though there are no apparent reasons for the deficiency, and they

must, accordingly, be remembered separately : — *almus*, nourishing; *caducus*, falling or fragile; *calvus*, bald ; *curvus*, crooked ; *ferus*, wild ; *gnarus*, knowing ; *lacer* and *mutilus*, mutilated ; *lassus*, tired ; *mediocris*, middling ; *memor*, mindful : *mirus*, wonderful ; *navus*, industrious ; *rudis*, rude ; *trux*, fierce.

Note. Sometimes an adjective, instead of being put in the superlative, has *per* (the Greek περὶ, beyond or above measure) prefixed to it —as *permagnus*, *percommodus*. Others take *prae* in a similar sense— as *praegelidus* (very cold). Adjectives thus compounded with *per* or *prae* have no degrees of comparison, except *praeclarus* (illustrious), which is treated as a simple adjective, and accordingly has its degrees *praeclarior* and *praeclarissimus*. It should further be observed that poets sometimes form the comparative and superlative of such adjectives as usually form their degrees in the regular manner by the adverbs *magis* and *maxime*.

CHAPTER XV.

NUMERALS.

§ 100. Most numerals are in reality adjectives denoting number — as one man (*unus homo*), the first man (*primus homo*), *terni milites*, three and three soldiers together ; *duplex numerus*, the double number. Only one class of numerals belongs to the adverbs — as *semel*, once ; *bis*, twice ; *ter*, thrice. All numerals are divided into six classes : — 1. *Cardinal numerals*, or those which simply denote the number of objects, and answer to the question ' how many ?'—as one, two, three ; 2. *Ordinal numerals*, or those indicating the order or succession of objects—as the first, second, third ; 3. *Distributive numerals*, or those which denote how many each time — as *terni*, three each time ; 4. *Multiplicative numerals*, denoting how many fold a thing is—as *triplex*, threefold ; 5. *Proportional numerals*, denoting how many times more one thing is than another — as *triplum*, three times as much ; and lastly, 6. *Adverbial numerals*, denoting how many times a thing happens or is done — as *quater*, four times.

§ 101. The first three cardinal numerals—*unus, a, um* (one) ; *duo, duae, duo* (two); and *tres, tria*— are declinable ; the rest, up to two hundred, are indeclinable ; but from two hundred up to a thousand they are declinable, and have three terminations for the three genders. *Mille*, one thousand, is an indeclinable adjective, but it has a plural, *millia,* which is declinable, and used as a substantive. The Latin language has no words to express any higher units than 1000 ; such as a million, billion, &c. must be expressed by a paraphrase in the form of a multiplication. Hence a million is said to be 'ten times a hundred thousand,' *decies centena millia ;* two millions, accordingly, is *vicies centena millia*—that is, twenty times a hundred thousand ; *centies centena millia,* a hundred times a hundred thousand—that is, ten millions, &c.

The following table contains the principal cardinal numerals, according to which all others may be formed :—

1.	I.	*unus, una, unum.*
2.	II.	*duo, duae, duo.*
3.	III.	*tres, tria.*
4.	IIII. or IV.	*quatuor.*
5.	V.	*quinque.*
6.	VI.	*sex.*
7.	VII.	*septem.*
8.	VIII.	*octo.*
9.	IX. or VIIII.	*novem.*
10.	X.	*decem.*
11.	XI.	*undecim.*
12.	XII.	*duodecim.*
13.	XIII.	*tredecim,* or *decem et tres (tria),* or *tres (tria) et de-*
14.	XIV.	*quatuordecim.* [*cem.*
15.	XV.	*quindecim.*
16.	XVI.	*sedecim, sexdecim,* or *decem et sex.*
17.	XVII.	*decem et septem,* or *septemdecim.*
18.	XVIII.	*decem et octo,* or *duodeviginti.*
19.	XIX.	*decem et novem,* or *undeviginti.*
20.	XX.	*viginti.*
21.	XXI.	*unus (a, um) et viginti,* or *viginti unus (a, um).*
22.	XXII.	*duo (duae) et viginti,* or *viginti duo (duae).*
23.	XXIII.	*tres (tria) et viginti,* or *viginti tres (tria).*
24.	XXIV.	*quatuor et viginti,* or *viginti quatuor.* [*ginti octo.*
28.	XXVIII.	*duodetriginta,* more rarely *octo et viginti,* or *vi-*
29.	XXIX.	*undetriginta,* more rarely *novem et viginti,* or *vi-*
30.	XXX.	*triginta.* [*ginti novem.*
31.	XXXI.	*unus (a, um) et triginta,* or *triginta unus (a, um).*
40.	XL.	*quadraginta.*
50.	L.	*quinquaginta.*
60.	LX.	*sexaginta.*
70.	LXX.	*septuaginta.*
80.	LXXX.	*octoginta.*
90.	XC.	*nonaginta.*
99.	IC. or XCIX.	*nonaginta novem,* or *novem et nonaginta,* or *unde-*
100.	C.	*centum.* [*centum.*
101.	CI.	*centum et unus (a, um),* or *centum unus.*
102.	CII.	*centum et duo (duae),* or *centum duo.*
200.	CC.	*ducenti, ae, a.*

300.	CCC.	*trecenti, ae, a.*
400.	CCCC.	*quadringenti, ae, a.*
500.	D. or IƆ.	*quingenti, ae, a.*
600.	DC.	*sexcenti, ae, a.*
700.	DCC.	*septingenti, ae, a.*
800.	DCCC.	*octingenti, ae, a.*
900.	DCCCC.	*nongenti, ae, a.*
1000.	M. or CIƆ.	*mille.*
?000.	CIƆCIƆ. or MM.	*duo millia,* or *bis mille.*
3u00.	CIƆCIƆCIƆ. or MMM.	*tria millia,* or *ter mille.*
5000.	IƆƆ.	*quinque millia,* or *quinquies mille.*
10,000.	CCIƆƆ.	*decem millia,* or *decies mille.*
100,000.	CCCIƆƆƆ.	*centum millia,* or *centies mille.*

Note 1. It is unnecessary here to inquire into the origin of the Latin symbols for numbers; suffice it to say, that M alone seems to be a real letter, and the initial of *mille.* The other leading symbols are I = 1, V = 5, X = 10, L = 50, C = 100, IƆ or D = 500, M or CIƆ = 1000. In reading the Latin symbols, the following points must be observed:—1. Two symbols of equal value are added together—as II = 2, CC = 200. 2. A symbol of less value before one of greater is subtracted—as IX = 9, XC = 90. 3. A symbol of less value after one of greater is added—as XI = 11, CX = 110. 4. Each inverted C (Ɔ) after the symbol IƆ (500), indicates that the latter must be multiplied by ten, so that IƆƆ is 5000, and IƆƆƆ, 50,000. 5. When we place as many C before I as there are inverted Ɔ after it, we double the number—as IƆƆ = 5000, but CCIƆƆ = 10,000; again, IƆƆƆ = 50,000, but CCCIƆƆƆ = 100,000; and a million would accordingly be expressed by CCCCIƆƆƆƆ.

2. From the above table it will be seen that in all the numbers between 20 and 100 we may put the smaller number either with *et* before the greater, or without the *et* after the greater—as *viginti unus,* or *unus et viginti,* twenty-one, or one-and-twenty. For the numbers 18, 19, 28, 29, 38, 39, 48, 49, 58, 59, 68, 69, 78, 79, 88, 89, 98, 99, the expressions in the form of a subtraction by means of *de* are more frc quent than the others. Hence it is more advisable to say, *duodeviginti, undeviginti, duodetriginta, undetriginta, undecentum,* &c. than *decem et octo, decem et novem, octo et viginti, novem et viginti,* &c. Above 100, the greater number always precedes the smaller either with or without *et*—as *mille unus,* or *mille et unus; centum sexaginta,* or *centum et sexaginta; mille trecenti nonaginta novem,* or *mille et trecenti nonaginta novem.*

§ 102. In regard to the declension of *unus, a, um,* it has already been remarked (§ 58, note 3) that it is one of those adjectives which form the genitive in all genders in *ius,* and the dative in *i;* and that in the other cases the masculine and neuter follow the second declension, and the feminine the first.

Note. It should be observed, however, that now and then we meet with the genitive masculine *uni,* and with the dative *uno,* or in the feminine *unae;* but these are irregularities. Notwithstanding its meaning, the numeral *unus* occurs also in the plural (*uni, unae, una*), but only when joined to such substantives as have no plural—as *unae*

D

nuptiae, one marriage ; *unae literae*, one letter ; *una castra*, one camp. The singular as well as the plural of *unus* is also used in the sense of alone,' or ' the same'—as *uni Romani*, the Romans alone ; *unis moribus*, with the same manners ; *unus Gracchus*, Gracchus alone.

§ 103. *Duo* and *tres* of course occur only in the plural, and are declined as follows :—

	Masc.	Fem.	Neut.		M. & F.	Neut.
Nom.	*duo,*	*duae,*	*duo.*	Nom.	*tres,*	*tria.*
Gen.	*duōrum,*	*duārum,*	*duōrum.*	Gen.	*trium,*	*trium.*
Dat.	*duōbus,*	*duābus,*	*duōbus.*	Dat.	*trĭbus,*	*trĭbus.*
Acc.	*duōs* (or *duo*),	*duās,*	*duo.*	Acc.	*tres,*	*tria.*
Abl.	*duōbus,*	*duābus,*	*duōbus.*	Abl.	*trĭbus,*	*trĭbus.*

Note. The word *ambo, ambae, ambo* (both) is declined like *duo.* The genitive plural of *duo* is sometimes *duum*, instead of *duorum*— as *duum millium*, of two thousand.

§ 104. *Centum* itself is indeclinable, but *ducenti, ae, a ; trecenti, ae, a ; quadringenti*, &c. down to *nongenti*, are all plural adjectives, the masculine and neuter of which follow the second declension, and the feminine the first. *Mille* is commonly treated as an indeclinable adjective, and is accordingly joined to any case of a substantive ; but it has a complete plural, *millia*, gen. *millium*, dat. *millibus*, &c. which is regarded as a substantive of the neuter gender—as *duo millia, tria millia, quatuor millia, multa millia*, &c. and is accordingly followed by the genitive of the objects counted—as *tria millia militum,* 3000 soldiers.

Note. Mille also is sometimes used as a substantive, followed by a genitive—as *mille militum*, 1000 soldiers ; but this generally happens only in sentences where *mille* is either nominative or accusative. In the other cases, it does not occur except in connection with *millia;* e.g., *cum octo millibus peditum, mille equitum*, ' with 8000 foot and 1000 horse ;' where *mille*, like *millibus*, is in the ablative. When smaller (adjective) numerals follow after *millia*, and the name of the objects counted follows after the smaller numerals, it is in the same case as *millia*, and not in the genitive—as *caesi sunt tria millia sexcenti viginti milites* (for *militum*)—' there were slain 3620 soldiers ;' but if the name of the objects counted precedes the word *millia*, it is commonly in the genitive—as *Caesar Gallorum duo millia quingentos sex cepit*—'Caesar took 2506 Gauls prisoners.'

The expressions *bis mille, ter mille, quater mille*, &c. occur more commonly in poetry than in prose.

§ 105. Ordinal numerals are adjectives of three terminations —masculine *us*, feminine *a*, neuter *um*. With the exception of *primus* and *secundus*, they are all formed from the cardinal numerals. The following table contains the principal ordinal numerals, according to which all the others may be formed :—

1. *primus*, the first.
2. *secundus* or *alter*, the second.
3. *tertius*, the third.
4. *quartus*, the fourth.
5. *quintus*, the fifth.
6. *sextus*, the sixth.
7. *septimus*, the seventh.
8. *octavus*, the eighth
9. *nonus*, the ninth.
10. *decimus*, the tenth.
11. *undecimus*, the eleventh.
12. *duodecimus*, the twelfth, &c.
13. *tertius decimus*, rarely *decimus et tertius.*
14. *quartus decimus*, rarely *decimus et quartus*, &c.
15. *quintus decimus.*
16. *sextus decimus.*
17. *septimus decimus.*
18. *duodevicesimus*, rarely *octavus decimus.*
19. *undevicesimus*, rarely *nonus decimus.*
20. *vicesimus* (or *vigesimus*).
21. *unus et vicesimus* (*una et vicesima*, *unum et vicesimum*), more rarely *primus et vicesimus*, or *vicesimus primus.*
22. *alter* (rarely *secundus*) *et vicesimus*, *vicesimus alter*, or *duo et*
23. *tertius et vicesimus*, or *vicesimus tertius.* [*vicesimus.*
24. *quartus et vicesimus*, or *vicesimus quartus*, &c.
28. *duodetricesimus*, more rarely *octavus et vicesimus*, and *vicesimus octavus.*
29. *undetricesimus*, more rarely *nonus et vicesimus*, and *vicesimus*
30. *tricesimus*, or *trigesimus.* [*nonus.*
31. *primus et tricesimus*, *tricesimus primus*, or *unus et tricesimus.*
   (See above, 20.) [*tricesimus octavus.*
38. *duodequadragesimus*, more rarely *octavus et tricesimus*, or
39. *undequadragesimus*, more rarely *nonus et tricesimus*, or *tri-*
40. *quadragesimus.* [*cesimus nonus.*
50. *quinquagesimus.*
60. *sexagesimus.*
70. *septuagesimus.*
80. *octogesimus.*
90. *nonagesimus.*
100. *centesimus.*
101. *centesimus primus.*
110. *centesimus decimus.*
124. *centesimus vicesimus quartus.*
200. *ducentesimus.*
300. *trecentesimus.*
400. *quadringentesimus.*
500. *quingentesimus.*
600. *sexcentesimus.*
700. *septingentesimus.*
800. *octingentesimus.*
900. *nongentesimus.*
1000. *millesimus.*
2000. *bis millesimus.*
3000. *ter millesimus*, &c

10,000. *decies millesimus.*
100,000. *centies millesimus.*
1,000,000. *decies centies millesimus.*

Note 1. *Primus* is properly a superlative, and denotes 'the first among many.' There is another form, *prior*, properly a comparative, which accordingly is used only when two objects are spoken of. When only two objects are spoken of, 'the second' is always expressed by *alter:* otherwise *alter—alter* means 'the one—the other.' In the word *unusetvicesimus,* the *unus* is declinable like *vicesimus;* but sometimes we find *unetvicesimus, unetvicesima,* in which the *un* remains unchanged throughout all cases. In such forms as *undetricesimus,* and *duodetricesimus,* the *un* and *duo* are indeclinable.

2. The years before and after the birth of Christ, after the foundation of Rome, or of any other era, are expressed in Latin by ordinal numerals—as 1847 is *anno millesimo octingentesimo quadragesimo septimo;* all words being here in the ablative.

3. From ordinal numerals are derived a class of numerals in *ānus,* to which the English language has nothing corresponding — as *primanus, secundanus, tertianus, vicesimanus,* &c. ; they denote the division or class to which any one belongs, but are chiefly used to denote the particular legion to which a Roman soldier belonged—as *vicesimanus,* one who belongs to the 20th legion. In consequence of the word *legio* being understood, the first numeral in a compound is generally feminine — as *tertiadecimanus,* one of the 13th legion ; *quarta decimanus,* one of the 14th legion ; *tertia et vicesimanus,* one of the 23d legion ; but we also find such forms as *unetvicesimanus, duoetvicesimanus.*

§ 106. Distributive numerals answer to the question *quoteni?* 'how many each time?' They are used only in the plural, and are adjectives of three terminations, *i, ae, a.* The English language has no corresponding numerals, but has recourse to circumlocution—as *terni milites,* three soldiers each time.

The following table contains the leading distributive numerals :—

1. *singuli, ae, a,* one each time, or one by one.	19. *noveni,* or *undeviceni.*
2. *bini,* two each time.	20. *vicēni.*
3. *terni (trini),* three each time.	21. *viceni, singuli.*
4. *quaterni.*	22. *viceni bini,* &c.
5. *quini.*	30. *tricēni.*
6. *seni.*	40. *quadragēni.*
7. *septēni.*	50. *quinquageni.*
8. *octōni.*	60. *sexageni.*
9. *novēni.*	70. *septuageni.*
10. *dēni.*	80. *octogeni.*
11. *undēni.*	90. *nonageni.*
12. *duodēni.*	100. *centēni.*
13. *terni deni.*	200. *duceni.*
14. *quaterni deni,* &c.	300. *treceni.*
18. *octoni deni,* or *duodeviceni.*	400. *quadringeni.*
	500. *quingeni.*

600. *sexceni.*	1000. *singula millia,* or simply
700. *septingeni.*	2000. *bina millia.* [*millia.*
800. *octingeni.*	3000. *terna millia.*
900. *nongeni.*	10,000. *dena millia.*

Note 1. The genitive of all these numerals in the masculine and neuter is more commonly *um* than *orum.* Instead of the compound numerals *viceni bini,* &c. we may also say, *bini et viceni,* or *bini viceni,* &c. 'A thousand each time,' 'two thousand each time,' &c. should, according to analogy, be expressed by *milleni, bis milleni,* &c.; but this form does not occur, and instead of it, we find the forms given in the table, *singula millia, bina millia, terna millia,* &c. Instead of *singula millia,* we also find simply *millia,* provided the distributive meaning is clear from the context—as *singulis millia talenta dedit,* 'he gave to each a thousand talents.' For the same reason we may use the cardinal numerals instead of the distributives in any case where the distributive nature is indicated by any other word (especially *singuli*) in the clause—as *singulis denarii trecenti* (for *treceni*) *imperabantur.*

2. Distributives are used instead of cardinals when joined to substantives which have no singular, or of which the plural has a different meaning from that of the singular—as *bina castra,* two camps ; *binae litterae,* two letters ; *binae aedes,* two houses. In this case, however, it is customary to use *uni, ae, a,* and *trini, ae, a,* instead of *singuli* and *terni.* Words which have a different meaning in the singular and plural deserve particular attention, e.g. *binae litterae* signifies two letters or epistles, but *duae litterae,* two letters of the alphabet ; *duae aedes,* two temples, but *binae aedes,* two houses.

3. Distributives, from the nature of their meaning, are employed in multiplication in connection with the adverbial numerals—as *bis bina,* twice two ; *quater septeni dies,* four times seven days ; *bis seni pueri,* twice six boys. In poetry, however, cardinal numerals are often used in multiplication instead of distributives—as *bis quinque* for *bis quini,* twice five.

4. Distributive numerals are sometimes used in speaking of things which exist in pairs—as *bini oculi,* the two eyes. Poets even go so far as to use them entirely in the sense of cardinal numerals—as *bina hastilia,* two lances ; and sometimes also use them in the singular —as *binum corpus,* a double body ; *septeno gurgite,* with a sevenfold whirlpool.

5. There is a class of numeral adjectives ending in *ārius* which are derived from distributive numerals ; they denote of how many equal parts or units a thing consists—as *numerus binarius,* a number consisting of two units ; *versus senarius,* a verse consisting of six equal parts or feet ; *nummus denarius* (or *denarius* alone), a coin containing ten equal parts ; *vir octogenarius,* a man who has lived eighty years. On the same analogy we should have *singularius* and *millenarius;* but the forms *singularis* and *milliarius* are more commonly used.

§ 107. Multiplicative numerals answering to the question 'how many fold?' (*quotuplex?*) all end in *plex,* and are adjectives of the third declension (gen. *plicis*), and of one termination only for all genders. Few of them seem to have been in use ; the following are those which occur in Latin writers:—

simplex, simple.	*quincuplex*, fivefold.
duplex, twofold.	*septemplex*, sevenfold.
triplex, threefold.	*decemplex*, tenfold.
quadruplex, fourfold.	*centumplex*, a hundredfold.

§ 108. Proportional numerals answer to the question *quotŭplus?* 'how many times more?' They are adjectives ending in *plus, a, um;* but we scarcely ever find them in any other than the neuter gender. The only numerals of this class which occur in Latin writers are :—

1. *simplus, a, um*, simple.	7. *septuplus*, seven times as much.
2. *duplus, a, um*, twice as much.	8. *octuplus*, eight times as much.
3. *triplus*, thrice as much.	10. *decuplus*, ten times as much.
4. *quadruplus*, four times as much.	100. *centuplus*, a hundred times as
5. *quinquiplus*, five times as much.	much.

§ 109. Adverbial numerals denoting repetition answer to the question 'how often?' *quoties* or *quotiens?* As adverbs, they are not susceptible of any inflection.

1. *semel*, once.	23. *ter et vicies* or *vicies ter*,
2. *bis*, twice.	30. *tricies*. [&c.
3. *ter*, thrice.	40. *quadragies*.
4. *quater*, four times.	50. *quinquagies*.
5. *quinquies*, five times, &c.	60. *sexagies*.
6. *sexies*, (or *sexiens*).	70. *septuagies*.
7. *septies* (or *septiens*, &c).	80. *octogies*.
8. *octies*.	90. *nonagies*.
9. *novies*.	100. *centies*.
10. *decies*.	130. *centies tricies* or *centies et*
11. *undecies*.	200. *ducenties*. [*tricies.*
12. *duodecies*.	300. *trecenties*.
13. *terdecies* or *tredecies*.	400. *quadringenties*.
14. *quaterdecies* or *quatuordecies*.	500. *quingenties*.
15. *quinquiesdecies* or *quindecies*.	600. *sexcenties*.
16. *sexiesdecies* or *sedecies*.	700. *septingenties*.
17. *septies decies*.	800. *octingenties*.
18. *duodevicies* or *octiesdecies*.	900. *nongenties*.
19. *undevicies* or *noviesdecies*.	1000. *millies*.
20. *vicies*.	2000. *bis millies*, &c.
21. *semel et vicies* or *vicies semel*.	10,000. *decies millies*.
22. *bis et vicies* or *vicies bis*.	100,000. *centies millies*.

Note 1. Besides the above adverbial numerals, which are formed from cardinal numerals, there are some others from ordinal numerals, which end in *o* (abl.) and *um* (accus. neut.)—as *primum* and *primo, secundum* and *secundo,* tertium and *tertio, quartum* and *quarto,* &c. *Primum* generally signifies 'for the first time,' and *primo* 'at first,' or 'at the beginning.' Instead of *secundum,* 'for the second time,' *iterum* is used; *secundo* signifies 'secondly,' but it is more common to use *deinde* or *tum* instead of it. In the remaining numbers, the forms ending in *o* are scarcely ever used. ' For the last time' is *ultimum, postremum,* or *extremum.*

2. There are regular series of compound substantives, formed of numerals and the substantives *annus* (year), *dies* (day), and *vir* (man) — as *biennium, triennium, quadriennium, sexennium, septuennium,* a period of two, three, four, six, and seven years; *biduum, triduum, quatriduum,* a space of two, three, and four days. There were at Rome several commissions composed of two, three, or more persons, and the different commissioners, accordingly, were called *duumviri, tresviri* or *triumviri, quatuorviri, quinqueviri, decemviri, quindecimviri, centumviri,* &c. A member of such a commission was called *duumvir, triumvir, decemvir,* &c. To these compounds we may add the derivative adjectives *bimus, trimus,* and *quadrimus,* a child of two, three, and four years.

§ 110. Fractional numbers are always expressed in Latin by *pars* (part) — as *dimidia pars,* $\frac{1}{2}$; *tertia pars,* $\frac{1}{3}$; *quarta pars,* $\frac{1}{4}$; *quinta pars,* $\frac{1}{5}$; *sexta pars,* $\frac{1}{6}$, &c. When the number of parts in a fractional number is less by one than the number of parts into which the whole is divided — as $\frac{2}{3}, \frac{3}{4}, \frac{4}{5}$, &c. the fractions are expressed simply by *duae, tres, quatuor,* &c. to which must be understood *partes,* and it must be conceived thus: two parts out of three, three parts out of four, four parts out of five, &c. All other fractions are expressed just as in English — as $\frac{2}{5}$, *duae quintae;* $\frac{3}{5}$, *tres quintae;* $\frac{4}{7}$, *quatuor septimae;* $\frac{5}{7}$, *quinque septimae,* &c. *partes* being understood. Sometimes, however, fractions are expressed by circumlocution — as $\frac{1}{8}$, *dimidia quarta,* one-half of a fourth; $\frac{5}{6}$, *dimidia pars et tertia*—that is, one-half and one-third.

CHAPTER XVI.

PRONOUNS.

§ 111. Pronouns are words which supply the place of a substantive, or refer to a substantive mentioned either before or after—as *Ego,* I; *tu,* thou; *nos,* we; *vos,* they; *homo* QUI *laudat,* the man *who* praises; *ille vir,* that man. The pronouns *ego, tu, nos,* and *vos,* supplying the place of names, may be regarded as substantives, and convey a full meaning by themselves; whence they are called *substantive pronouns,* or, less correctly, *personal pronouns.* All other pronouns may be regarded as adjectives, their meaning not being complete without a substantive either expressly added or understood. Hence their different forms for the different genders, to accommodate themselves to the substantives to which they belong.

§ 112. All pronouns are divided into seven classes.

1. Substantive pronouns—as *ego, tu, nos, vos.*

2. Adjunctive pronouns—as *ipse, ipsa, ipsum,* self.

3. Demonstrative pronouns—as *hic, haec, hoc,* this; *iste, ista, istud,* that; *ille, illa, illud,* that; *is, ea, id,* and its derivative, *idem, eadem, idem.*

4. Possessive pronouns—*meus, a, um; tuus, a, um; suus, a, um; noster, nostra, nostrum; vester, vestra, vestrum.*

5. Relative pronouns—*qui, quae, quod,* and its compounds, *quicumque* and *quisquis.*

6. Interrogative pronouns — *quis, quae, quid,* and *qui, quae, quod.*

7. Indefinite pronouns—as *aliquis, aliqua, aliquid* and *aliquod; quidam, quaedam, quiddam* and *quoddam; quispiam, quaepiam, quidpiam* and *quodpiam,* and the compound *aliquispiam; quisquam* (masc. and fem.), *quidquam; quivis, quaevis, quidvis* and *quodvis; quilibet, quaelibet, quodlibet* and *quidlibet; quisque, quaeque, quodque,* and all other compounds of *qui* and *quis.*

§ 113. Substantive pronouns always stand by themselves, and are not joined to substantives. *Ego* denotes the person speaking — that is, the first person; and *tu* the person spoken to, or the second person. In English, we have also a pronoun of the third, or the person spoken of—namely, *he, she,* and *it;* but the Latin language has no substantive pronoun for the third person in the nominative; and if it is to be expressed at all, its place must be supplied by the demonstrative pronouns *is* or *ille.* In the oblique cases, however, there are forms for the third person. The declension of the substantive pronouns is very peculiar:—

SINGULAR.

First Person.	Second Person.	Third Person.
Nom. *ĕgo,* I.	*tū,* thou.	is wanting.
Gen. *meī,* of me.	*tuī,* of thee.	*suī,* of himself, herself, itself.
Dat. *mĭhi,* to me.	*tĭbi,* to thee.	*sĭbi,* to himself, herself, itself.
Acc. *mē,* me.	*tē,* thee.	*sē,* himself, herself, itself.
Voc. is wanting.	*tū,* thou.	is wanting.
Abl. *mē,* with, by, from, or in me.	*tē,* with, by, from, or in thee.	*sē,* with, by, from, or in himself, &c.

PLURAL.

First Person.	Second Person.	Third Person.
Nom. *nōs*, we.	*vōs*, you.	is wanting.
Gen. *nostrī*, or *nostrum*, of us.	*vestrī*, or *vestrum*, of you.	*suī*, of themselves.
Dat. *nōbīs*, to us.	*vōbīs*, to you.	*sĭbi*, to themselves.
Acc. *nōs*, us.	*vōs*, you.	*sē*, themselves.
Voc. is wanting.	*vōs*, you.	is wanting.
Abl. *nōbīs*, with, by, from, or in us.	*vōbīs*, with, by, from, or in you.	*sē*, with, by, from, or in themselves.

Note 1. What we have given here as the pronoun of the third person is properly a reflective pronoun; that is, one which refers either to the subject of the clause in which it occurs, or if it appears in an inserted clause, to the subject of the leading clause—as *Cato se interfecit,* 'Cato killed himself,' the *se* referring to Cato, the subject; *amicus meus contemnebat divitias, quod se felicem reddere non possent* —'my friend despised wealth, because it could not make him happy,' the *se* referring to my friend, the subject of the leading clause. Wherever there is no such reference to the subject, but where the pronoun refers to a different person or thing from the subject, the oblique cases must be taken from *is, ea, id,* or from *ille, illa, illud*—as *ubi ad hostem accessit, interfecit eum*—'when he came near the enemy, he slew him,' the *eum* not referring to the subject, but to *hostem.*

2. All forms of the substantive pronoun, except the genitives plural, and the nominative and vocative singular *tu,* may take the suffix *met,* which answers in meaning to the English 'self,' and makes the pronouns emphatic—as *egomet,* I myself; *mihimet,* to myself; *sibimet,* to himself; *nobismet,* to ourselves. The emphasis is sometimes strengthened by the addition of *ipse*—as *sibimet ipsi, nobismet ipsis,* &c. *Tu* is made emphatic by the suffix *te*—as *tute,* thou thyself; but *met* is sometimes added to *te*—as *tutemet,* thou thyself. The forms *me, te,* and *se,* are frequently doubled — as *meme, tete, sese,* without these pronouns thereby becoming particularly emphatic.

3. The genitives *mei, tui, sui, nostri, vestri,* are properly genitives of the neuter of the possessive pronouns *meum, tuum, suum, nostrum, vestrum,* so that *mei* properly means 'of my being;' that is, 'of me.' The genitives plural *nostrum* and *vestrum* are used only in a partitive sense—as 'every one of us,' *unusquisque nostrum;* but 'he remembers us,' *nostri reminiscitur.*

4. In the dative singular of the first person poets often employ a contracted form, *mi* instead of *mihi;* but it is rarely used in prose.

§ 114. The adjunctive pronoun *ipse, ipsa, ipsum,* is commonly joined to substantives, and other pronouns, and is declined as follows, the plural being quite like that of adjectives in *us, a, um:*—

	SINGULAR.				PLURAL.		
	Masc.	Fem.	Neut.		Masc.	Fem.	Neut.
Nom.	*ipse,*	*ipsă,*	*ipsum.*	Nom.	*ipsi,*	*ipsae,*	*ipsa.*
Gen.	*ipsius,*	*ipsius,*	*ipsius.*	Gen.	*ipsorum,*	*ipsarum,*	*ipsorum.*
Dat.	*ipsī,*	*ipsī,*	*ipsī.*	Dat.	*ipsis,*	*ipsis,*	*ipsis.*
Acc.	*ipsum,*	*ipsam,*	*ipsum.*	Acc.	*ipsos,*	*ipsas,*	*ipsa.*
Abl.	*ipsō,*	*ipsā,*	*ipsō.*	Abl.	*ipsis,*	*ipsis,*	*ipsis.*

6

Note. In the early language, and in the comic poets, the masculine nominative singular is sometimes *ipsus* instead of *ipse*. *Ipse* is in reality a compound of *is, ea, id,* and the suffix *pse;* hence we find in early writers such forms as *eapse* (nom. and abl. fem.), *eopse* (abl. masc.), *eumpse,* and *eampse,* for *ipsa, ipso, ipsum,* and *ipsam.* This, also, accounts for the expression *reapse;* that is, *re eapse* or *re ipsa.*

§ 115. Demonstrative pronouns point to an object. *Hic, haec, hoc,* points to an object near to the speaker, and accordingly answers to the English ‘this;’ whereas, *ille, illa, illud,* points to a more distant object, and answers to the English ‘that,’ or ‘you.’ *Iste, ista, istud,* generally refers to the person spoken to, or to things connected with him, and is accordingly termed the demonstrative of the second person. As by using *hic,* a speaker may also point to himself, *hic, haec, hoc,* is sometimes called the demonstrative of the first person, while *ille, illa, illud,* pointing to a distant object, or the one spoken of, is termed the demonstrative of the third person. *Is, ea, id,* generally refers to something mentioned before, being almost equivalent to ‘the person or thing mentioned before,’ or it is followed by an explanatory relative clause, as in English ‘he who,’ *is qui.* This pronoun can hardly be called a demonstrative. *Idem, eadem, idem,* ‘the same,’ expresses unity or identity; this word, too, is, properly speaking, not a demonstrative pronoun.

The declension of these pronouns has many peculiarities.

| | SINGULAR. | | | PLURAL. | | |
	Masc.	Fem.	Neut.	Masc.	Fem.	Neut.
Nom.	*hic,*	*haec,*	*hŏc.*	*hī,*	*hae,*	*haec.*
Gen.	*hūjus,*	*hūjus,*	*hūjus.*	*hōrum,*	*hārum,*	*hōrum.*
Dat.	*hūīc,*	*hūīc,*	*hūīc.*	*hīs,*	*hīs,*	*hīs.*
Acc.	*hunc,*	*hanc,*	*hŏc.*	*hōs,*	*hās,*	*haec.*
Abl.	*hōc,*	*hāc,*	*hŏc.*	*hīs,*	*hīs,*	*hīs.*

| | SINGULAR. | | | PLURAL. | | |
	Masc.	Fem.	Neut.	Masc.	Fem.	Neut.
Nom.	*ĭs,*	*eă,*	*ĭd.*	*iī (eī),*	*eae,*	*eă.*
Gen.	*ējus,*	*ējus,*	*ējus.*	*eōrum,*	*eārum,*	*eōrum.*
Dat.	*eī,*	*eī,*	*eī.*	*iīs (eīs),*	*iīs (eīs),*	*iīs (eīs).*
Acc.	*eum,*	*eam,*	*ĭd.*	*eōs,*	*eās,*	*eă.*
Abl.	*eō,*	*eā,*	*eō.*	*iīs (eīs),*	*iīs (eīs),*	*iīs (eīs).*

Ille, illa, illud, and *iste, ista, istud,* are both declined like *ipse* (§ 114) — as gen. *illius,* dat. *illī,* &c.; *istius, isti,* &c. *Idem, eădem, ĭdem,* being composed of *is, ea, id,* with the suffix *dem,* is declined like *is, ea, id,* with *dem* attached to it — as gen. *ejusdem,* dat. *eidem,* acc. *eundem, eandem, idem,* &c. The *n* in *eundem* and *eandem* is merely a euphonic change for *eumdem eamdem,* and so also in the genitive plural *eorundem* and *earundem.*

Note 1. The *c* in the various forms of *hic, haec, hoc, hunc,* &c. is a remnant of an ancient suffix or enclitic, for the original form was *hicĕ, haecĕ, hocĕ;* hence in early Latinity we still find such forms as *hancĕ, hacĕ.* But in the best authors, the *ce* is found attached to those cases only which end in *s*—as *hujusce, hisce, hosce, hasce,* and renders the meaning of these forms more emphatic. When the interrogative particle *ne* is attached in addition to the *ce,* the *e* of the latter is changed into *i*—as *hicĭne, hocĭne.* The dative singular *huic* is usually pronounced as one syllable, but later poets sometimes count it as two short syllables, *hŭĭc.*

2. The nominative plural masculine *ei,* instead of *ii* (from *is*), occurs very rarely, and in the compound *idem* never. In the dative plural, also, *eis* is much more rare than *iis.* The two *i* in *ii, iidem,* and *iisdem,* were pronounced as one long *i.*

3. Instead of *ille,* there existed in early Latin the form *ollus,* of which *olli* (dat. sing., and nom. plur.) still occurs in Virgil, and *ollos* and *olla* in an imitation of the ancient language in Cicero. Instead of the genitive *illius, istius,* and the dative *illi, isti,* we sometimes find in the early writers, genitive *illi, isti,* dative *illae, istae,* and in the fem. plur. *illaec* and *istaec* (originally *illaece* and *istaece*), for *illae* and *istae.* For in the ancient language, both *ille* and *iste,* like *hic,* took the demonstrative suffix *ce*—as *illic, illaec, illoc,* or *illuc; istic, istaec, istoc;* and we still find such forms as *istace, istisce, illace, illisce, illosce, illasce;* but even the best writers use *istunc, istanc, illunc, illanc;* the ablative *istoc, istac, illoc, illac,* and the neuter plural *istaec* and *illaec.* When the interrogative particle *ne* is added, the *e* of the *ce* is changed into *i*—as *istucine, instocine, istoscine, illicine, illancine.*

4. The demonstrative particle, when a word by itself, is *ecce* or *en,* 'lo' or 'behold;' and these compounded with forms of *is, ea, id, ille,* and *iste,* make *eccum, eccam, eccos, eccas,* (for *ecce eum, eam, eos, eas*); *ellum, ellam, ellas, ellos* (for *en illum, illam, illas, illos*); and *eccillum, eccistam* (for *ecce illum, istam*), which were very common in the language of ordinary life, and often occur in Plautus and Terence.

§ 116. The possessive pronouns are real adjectives of three terminations—masculine *us* or *er,* feminine *a,* neuter *um;* and the masculine and neuter follow the second, and the feminine the first declension. They are—*meus, mea, meum,* my; *tuus, tua, tuum,* thy; *suus, sua, suum,* his; *noster, nostra, nostrum,* our; *vester, vestra, vestrum,* your. *Meus,* however, makes the vocative singular masculine *mi,* instead of *mee.* (Compare § 58, note 4.)

Note 1. Some forms of these pronouns take the suffix *pte* (the Greek ποτε) to strengthen their meaning—as *suopte, suapte, meopte, tuopte, nostrapte. Suus,* in all its cases, takes the suffix *met,* with quite the same meaning—as *suŏmet, suamet,* &c. Sallust, however, also uses *meămet.*

2. There is a class of possessive pronouns ending in *as* (for all genders), genitive *ātis*—as *nostras, vestras,* and *cujas;* they signify 'belonging to our, your, whose country, family, or party;' so that *nostrates* means our countrymen, or the men of our party or family

3. The possessive interrogative *cujus, cuja, cujum* (whose?) occurs only in the nominative and accusative singular (*cujum, cujam, cujum*), the ablative singular feminine *cuja*, and in the nominative and accusative plural fem. *cujae, cujas;* but it is found only in early Latinity and in legal phraseology.

§ 117. The relative pronoun *qui, quae, quod*, 'who' or 'which,' generally refers to a noun in another clause, and introduces an explanatory clause—as Socrates, *who* was the wisest of the Athenians, was sentenced to death. Its declension is as follows :—

	SINGULAR.				PLURAL.		
	Masc.	Fem.	Neut.		Masc.	Fem.	Neut.
Nom.	quī,	quae,	quod.	Nom.	quī,	quae,	quae.
Gen.	cūjus,	cūjus,	cūjus.	Gen.	quōrum,	quārum,	quōrum.
Dat.	cūī,	cūī,	cūī.	Dat.	quĭbus,	quĭbus,	quĭbus.
Acc.	quem,	quam,	quod.	Acc.	quōs,	quās,	quae.
Abl.	quō,	quā,	quō.	Abl.	quĭbus,	quĭbus,	quĭbus.

The compound *quicunque, quaecunque, quodcunque* (from *cum* or *quum* and *que*, 'whenever'), signifies 'whoever' or 'whichever;' and *quisquis* (masc. and fem.) *quidquid* (neut.) denotes 'every one who.' *Quicunque*, in all its genders, is joined to substantives, and is accordingly treated as an adjective ; *quisquis* is likewise sometimes joined to substantives, but *quidquid* never, and is accordingly regarded as a substantive. *Quicunque* is declined like *qui, cunque* being merely affixed to the cases—as *cujuscunque, cuicunque, quemcunque, &c.* ; but sometimes one or two other words are inserted between the relative and the suffix *cunque*—as *quo ea me cunque ducet*, 'whithersoever she may lead me.' *Quisquis* commonly occurs only in the nominative masculine, the nominative and accusative neuter (*quidquid*), and in the ablative masculine and neuter (*quoquo*). *Quemquem, quibusquibus*, and *quaqua*, are found only very rarely. From the genitive, which must have been *cujus-cujus*, there has been formed, by a sort of contraction, *cuicui*, which occurs in the expression *cuicuimodi*, 'in any way,' for *cujuscujusmodi*.

Note. A more ancient form for the genitive and dative *cujus* and *cui* was *quojus* and *quoi;* the dative *cūī*, as a word of two syllables, occurs only in very late writers. The ancient ablative singular for all genders was *quī*, which is used by the best writers when the preposition *cum* (with) is appended to the ablative—as *quicum*, for *quocum* or *quacum;* and in certain phrases, when the relative is used in the neuter gender without a substantive to which it refers—as *vix reliquit qui efferretur*—'he scarcely left (means) wherewith he could be buried ;' *habeo, qui utar*—'I have (means) which I may use.' Instead of the ablative plural *quibus*, there is a more ancient form, *quīs* or *queis*, which often occurs in poetry and late prose writers.

§ 118. There are two interrogative pronouns, *quis, quae, quid,* and *qui, quae, quod,* the latter of which in form is entirely the same as the relative pronoun. The former has the nature of a substantive, and is therefore not joined to a substantive, but used by itself, while the latter, having the nature of an adjective, is joined to substantives — as *quid facis?* 'what art thou doing?' — *quod facinus commisit?* 'what crime has he committed?' This distinction is strictly observed in regard to the neuter *quid* and *quod;* but less strictly in regard to *quis* and *qui,* especially in clauses containing an indirect question, for there *qui* is often used for *quis,* and *quis* for *qui.* The declension of the interrogative pronouns is the same as that of the relative. When a question is to be expressed with a certain degree of impatience, the particle *nam* is attached to *quis*—as *quisnam, quaenam, quidnam,* or *quodnam,* 'who then?' or 'what then?' The difference between *quidnam* and *quodnam* is the same as between *quid* and *quŏd.*

Note. The ablative singular for all genders, *quī,* as in the case of the relative pronoun (§ 117, note), occurs only in the sense of 'in what manner?' or 'how?'—as *qui fit?* 'how does it happen?'—*qui convenit?* 'how is it consistent?'

§ 119. The indefinite pronouns express an indefinite generality. They have been enumerated in § 112. Their declension is, on the whole, the same as that of the relative pronoun.

The most common indefinite pronoun is *aliquis, aliqua, aliquid,* and *aliquod* (some one). For the masculine there is also a form, *aliqui,* which, however, is not often used. The neuter, *aliquid,* has the nature of a substantive, and *aliquod* that of an adjective; whence it is joined to substantives. The masculine *aliquis* is used both as a substantive and as an adjective. The feminine singular and the neuter plural differ in termination from the relative pronoun, being *aliqua,* and not *aliquae,* which is the feminine plural. There is also a simple form without the prefix *ali* (from *alius,* or the obsolete form, *alis,* neut. *alid.*); namely, *quis, quae, quid,* and *qui, qua, quod,* which is declined like the relative, except that the feminine is both *quae* and *qua,* and the neuter plural likewise both *quae* and *qua.* *Quid* is used only as a substantive, and *quod* as an adjective. *Quis* may be used in both senses — as *dicat quis,* 'some one may say;' *si quis dux,* 'if any general.' It may be said, in general, that this simple indefinite occurs only after the particles *si, nisi, ne, num,* and after the relatives *quo, quanto,* and *quum,* though even the best writers sometimes use *aliquis* after them.

Another indefinite pronoun is *ecquis, ecqua, ecquid,* and *ecqui,*

ecquae, ecquod (from *en* and *quis*), signifying ' whether any one.'
A strengthened form is *ecquisnam* or *numquisnam*.

Quidam, quaedam, quiddam, and *quoddam,* ' a certain one.'
The form *quiddam* is a substantive, and *quoddam* an adjective. It is declined like the relative, gen. *cujusdam,* dat.
cuidam, &c.

Aliquispiam, or *quispiam, quaepiam, quidpiam,* and *quodpiam.*
Quispiam is chiefly used as a substantive, but *aliquispiam* occurs also as an adjective, and *quidpiam* is used only as a substantive.

Quisquam (masc. and fem.), *quidquam* (neut.), ' any one,' occurs only in negative clauses, or at least has always a negative meaning. *Quisquam* is used both as a substantive and as an adjective with names of persons — as *scriptor quisquam,* ' any writer ;' *quisquam Gallus,* '.any Gaul ;' but it has no plural.
Ullus, which has the same meaning as *quisquam,* occurs only as an adjective, excepting a few passages.

Quivis, quilibet (any one who pleases, from *vis,* ' thou wilt,'
and *libet,* ' it pleases'), and *quisque* (every one), are declined like the relative ; when used as substantives, they make the neuter *quid,* and when used as adjectives, *quod.*

Unusquisque, unaquaeque, unumquidque, and *unumquodque,*
' every one,' is declined in both the words of which it is composed—as gen. *uniuscujusque,* dat. *unicuique,* acc. *unumquemque,*
unamquamque, &c.

Quicunque, quaecunque, quodcunque, ' whosoever' or ' whichsoever,' has no neuter *quidcunque.*

Quisquis, quidquid (also written *quicquid*), generally occurs only in these two forms, and only as a substantive. Its place is supplied by *quicunque,* which has the same meaning. (See
§ 117.)

§ 120. Besides the pronouns above enumerated, there are a number of others, commonly termed pronominal adjectives, which may conveniently be discussed here. They are—

Uter, utra, utrum, ' which of two,' and its compounds *uter-vis, uterlibet, utercunque* (whichever of the two you please),
uterque (each of two or both), and *alteruter* (either the one or the other). They are all declined like *uter,* gen. *utrius,* dat.
utri (See § 58, note 3). In *alteruter,* sometimes both words are declined, and sometimes the latter only—as gen. *alterius utrius,*
acc. *alterum utrum,* or *alterutrum.*

Neuter, neutra, neutrum (that is, *ne* or *non uter*), ' neither of two,' is declined like *uter.*

Alter, altĕra, altĕrum, ' one of two,' or ' the other' (§ 105, note
1), gen. *alterius,* dat. *alteri,* &c.

Alius, alia, aliud, 'another,' gen. *alīus,* dat. *alii.* It is never used in speaking of two; hence it is 'another,' and not 'the other.'

Ullus, ulla, ullum, 'any,' gen. *ullīus,* dat. *ulli,* &c.

Nullus, a, um (that is, *ne* or *non ullus*), 'none' or 'no one.'

Note 1. Many of these adjectives which form their genitive in *ius,* and the dative in *i* (§ 58, note 3), are found in the best writers making their genitive, according to the first and second declensions, in *i* and *ae,* and the dative in *o* and *ae*—as in Caesar: *alterae legioni,* for *alteri legioni;* and *nullo consilio,* for *nulli consilio.*

2. *Nullus* is used both as an adjective and a substantive; but *nemo* (gen. *neminis,* from *ne* and *homo,* 'no man') is generally a substantive; and where it is joined to other substantives, the latter may be regarded as in apposition to it—as *nemo scriptor,* 'no one who is a writer;' *nemo Gallus,* 'no one who is a Gaul.' *Nemo* is always joined in this manner with names of nations—as *nemo Romanus.* The neuter *nihil* (nothing, contracted *nil*) makes its genitive *nihili,* dat. *nihilo,* and belongs to the second declension.

3. *Uterque* signifies 'both,' when each side or party consists only of one—as *uterque miles,* 'both soldiers,' or 'each of the two soldiers;' but when each of the two sides or parties consists of several persons or things, the plural must be used—as *utrique,* 'both parties,' implying that each consisted of several individuals. The plural is often used even when there is only one person or thing on each side.

§ 121. There is another class of pronominal adjectives, denoting the nature, size, or number of things. Some of them can express the same idea in a demonstrative, relative, interrogative, indefinite form; and those in which this is the case are termed correlatives, as—

Demonstrative.	Relative and Interrog.	Indefinite.
talis, e, such a one.	*qualis, e,* as, or of what kind.	*qualiscunque* and *qualislibet,* of whatever kind.
tantus, a, um, so great.	*quantus, a, um,* as great, or how great?	*quantuscunque* and *quantuslibet,* however great.
tot (indeclinable), so many.	*quot,* as many, or how many?	*quotcunque* and *quotquot,* however many.
totidem, just as many.	*quotus, a, um,* which in the series?	

There are a few with the prefix *ali*—as *aliquantus,* of a certain or tolerable greatness; *aliquot,* some or a few; which may likewise be classed among the indefinite pronominal adjectives.

Note. From *tantus* and *quantus* are formed the diminutives *tantulus, a, um, quantulus, a, um, quantuluscunque* and *aliquantulum.*

§ 122. From pronouns are formed a number of pronominal

adverbs, denoting place where? place whither? and the place whence?—the way and manner in which anything is done, or time.

1. Pronominal adverbs denoting the place *where* anything is done:—*ibi*, here or there; *hic*, here; *istic*, there, near you; *illic*, in that place; *ibīdem*, in the same place; *alibi*, elsewhere; *ubi*, where; *ubicunque* and *ubiubi*, wherever; *alicubi*, somewhere; *uspiam* and *usquam*, anywhere; *nusquam*, nowhere; *utrobīque*, in both places; *ubīvis* and *ubilibet*, anywhere; *ubīque*, everywhere. All these adverbs ending in *i* (those in *c* have the demonstrative enclitic *ce* attached) are properly ancient datives or locatives, denoting place where?

2. Pronominal adverbs denoting the place *whither* anything proceeds:—*eo*, thither; *huc*, hither; *istuc* and *isto*, to the place where you are; *illuc* and *illo*, thither, or to the place where he (or it) is; *eodem*, to the same place or part; *alio*, to another place; *quo*, to which place; *utro*, to which of two places; *quocunque, quoquo*, to which place soever; *quovis, quolibet*, to whichever place you please; *aliquo*, to some place; *utroque*, to both places; *usquam*, to any place; *nusquam*, to no place.

3. Pronominal adverbs denoting the place *whence* anything proceeds:—*inde*, thence; *hinc*, from this place; *istinc*, from that place where you are; *illinc*, from that place where he or it is; *indidem*, from the same place; *aliunde*, from another place; *unde*, whence; *undecunque, undeunde*, whencesoever; *alicunde*, from some place; *utrinque*, from both sides or places; *undique*, from any or all sides; *undelibet*, whencesoever you please.

4. Pronominal adverbs denoting the way or manner in which anything is done:—*eā*, in that way; *hac, istac, illac,* or *illā, eādem, ita, sic, ut, aliā, quā, qui, quācunque, quāquā, aliquā, quāvis,* and *quālibet*.

Note. All these forms are properly ablatives of the feminine, to which the substantive *viā* or *ratione* may be understood. They also appear in the compounds *eatenus* and *quatenus*.

5. Pronominal adverbs denoting time:—the demonstrative *tum* or *tunc*, then; the interrogative *quando*, when? *ecquando*, whether ever; the relative *quum*, when; the indefinite *aliquando*, at some time; *quandocunque* and *quandōque*, whenever; *unquam*, ever; *nunquam*, never.

Note. When the indefinites composed with *ali* are preceded by *si, nisi, ne,* or *num,* the prefix *ali* is generally dropped—as *necubi*, 'that not somewhere;' *ne quo*, for *ne aliquo; ne cunde,* for *ne alicunde; ne qua,* for *ne aliqua; ne quando,* for *ne aliquando.* (Compare § 119.)

6. Pronominal adverbs of degree:—as *tam*, so, so much; *quam*, as, as much, or how much? *quantumvis* or *quamvis*, however much; and the compound *adeo*, to that degree.
7. Pronominal adverbs of number:—*toties*, so often; *quoties*, as often, or how often? *quotiescunque*, however often; *aliquoties*, sometimes.
8. Pronominal adverbs of cause:—*eo*, *hoc*, for this reason; *quod* or *quia*, because; *cur*, why?

CHAPTER XVII.

THE VERB.

§ 123. A verb is a word which denotes that a person or thing (the subject of a sentence) is in a certain state or condition, performs an action, or is acted upon. A verb accordingly always implies existence and time; because whatever exists, exists in time. For example: I *sleep*—that is, I *am* asleep at the present *time;* I *sat* all day long—that is, I *was* sitting all day long in past time; I have *worked* vigorously—that is, I *have been* (in past time) vigorously at work; I *purchase* a book —that is, I perform the act of purchasing now (present time), he *is esteemed* by his friends (here 'he,' the subject, is acted upon by his friends, at the present time).

§ 124. Verbs which denote a state or condition are termed *neuter*, or, better, *intransitive* verbs. Some verbs denoting action also are intransitive, if the action terminates in the subject, and does not require an object to complete its meaning. For example—'I run,' 'I walk,' are actions, but complete in themselves, and without requiring an object. Verbs, on the other hand, which denote actions, and require an object upon which the action is performed, are called *transitive verbs*—as 'I purchase,' 'I strike;' these are actions requiring an object, and cannot be fully understood unless that object is mentioned or understood from the context—as 'I purchase a house,' 'I strike the offender.'

§ 125. The object of a transitive verb is generally in the accusative. The object in which the action terminates may also be considered as the subject in a state of suffering the action. Hence every transitive verb has an *active* and a *passive* form. 'I *strike* you,' therefore, is the active form, but ' you *are struck* by me' is the passive form; so also 'I read the book,' and 'the book is read.' Intransitive verbs, on the other hand, generally have no passive form; and when it does occur, it is only as an impersonal verb, no subject being mentioned on whom the action is performed—as *curritur*, 'running is taking place;' or, as we should say, 'they' or 'people run.'

Note 1. Sometimes a verb which is naturally intransitive may acquire a figurative meaning which is transitive, and in this case it naturally may have an object and a regular passive—as *excedo* properly signifies 'I go out,' and is intransitive; but in the sense 'I exceed,' it is transitive, and requires an object—as *excedo modum*, 'I exceed the measure;' *modus exceditur*, 'the measure is exceeded.' Sometimes verbs have different forms for the transitive and intransitive meaning—as *albēre*, to be white, and *albare*, to make white; *fugĕre*, to flee, and *fugāre*, to put to flight; *placēre*, to be pleasing, and *placare*, to make a person be pleased; *jacēre*, to lie down, and *jacĕre*, to throw down, &c.

2. In the case of a transitive verb, the person performing the action (the subject) may at the same time be the person acted upon (object) —as *amo me*, I love myself; *amat se*, he loves himself. In this case a verb is said to be used in a reflective sense. Many verbs assume (like the Greek middle voice) a passive form to express their reflective meaning—as *delector*, I delight myself, or am delighted; *fallor*, I am deceived, or deceive myself; *moveor*, I am moved, or move myself; *mutor*, I alter myself, or am altered; *vertor*, I turn myself, or am turned.

§ 126. There is a peculiar and rather numerous class of verbs in Latin which have a passive form, but an active (either transitive or intransitive) meaning. They are called *Deponents*—as *imitor*, I imitate; *hortor*, I admonish; *morior*, I die; *reminiscor*, I remember; *fateor*, I confess; and many others. A great many of them are in reality passives, or verbs used in a reflective sense—such as *vehor*, I ride in a carriage, properly signifies 'I am carried;' *versor*, I stay in a place, properly signifies 'I turn myself.' (Compare § 125, note 2.)

§ 127. A few verbs, on the other hand, have an active form, but are passives in meaning—as *fio*, I become, or am made; *vapulo*, I am beaten; *veneo*, I am sold—and such are called *neuter passives*. Some again have a passive form in the past participle, and the tenses formed from it, though in meaning, as well as in all their other forms, they are active—as *audeo*, I dare; *fido*, I trust; *gaudeo*, I rejoice; *soleo*, I am wont; their perfects, therefore, being *ausus sum, fisus sum, gavisus sum, solitus sum*. These are termed *Semideponents*.

§ 128. The Latin language has four modes or *moods* of representing a state or action, and each of them is indicated by special forms of the verb.

1. The *Indicative* represents a state or action simply as a fact —as *laudo*, I praise; *laudavi*, I have praised; *laudabo*, I shall praise; *laudor*, I am praised.

2. The *Subjunctive* represents a state or action as a mere possibility, as a conception of the mind, or as a wish—LAUDET
aliquis, some one may praise ; *opto ut* VENIAT, I wish that he
may come ; *veniat,* let him come !

3. The *Imperative* represents a state or action in the form of a
command—as *lauda,* praise ; *scribite,* write ye.

4. The *Infinitive* represents a state or action in its most general and indefinite form, without ascribing it to any subject
—as *laudare,* to praise ; *laudavisse,* to have praised ; *scribĕre,*
to write ; *scripsisse,* to have written.

§ 129. Besides these moods, a verb has certain forms which
must be classed among nouns, at least as far as their form is
concerned, and are accordingly declinable. These are—

1. The *Supine,* which has an accusative in *um,* and an ablative
in *u,* but no other cases — as *amatum* and *amatu ; lectum* and
lectu ; auditum and *auditu.* The supine, to which there is
nothing analogous in the English verb, represents, like the
infinitive, the state or action only in a general way ; its use,
which is very limited, will be explained under Syntax.

2. The *Gerund* likewise expresses a state or action in a general
way. It is, like the supine, a verbal noun ending in *dum,*
but it is used only in its oblique cases—as gen. *amandi,* dat.
amando, acc. *amandum,* abl. *amando.*

3. The *Participles* are in form adjectives derived from verbs,
but at the same time retain the notion of time which is in-
herent in every verb. A verb may have two participles in
the active, and two in the passive. Those in the active are
the participle of the present ending in *ns* for all genders,
and the participle of the future ending in *urus, a, um ;* the
former represents the action as going on or in progress, and
the latter as going to take place in future—as *amans,* loving ;
scribens, writing ; *amaturus,* one who is going to love, or is
about to love ; *scripturus,* one who is going to write, or is
about to write. The two participles of the passive are the
past participle ending in *us, a, um,* and what is now called
the gerundive (formerly the participle of the future) ending
in *dus, da, dum ;* the former represents an action in a state
of completion, the latter that it is going on, or must take
place—as *amatus,* loved ; *scriptus,* written ; *auditus,* heard ;
amandus, one who is to be loved ; *scribendus,* one who is to
be written ; *audiendus,* one who is to be heard ; *in scribenda
epistola,* in writing a letter.

Intransitive verbs, having no regular passive voice, cannot
have either of the passive participles ; but their neuter is
nevertheless used in connection with the verb ' to be,' *esse*—

as *cursum est,* running has taken place, or people have been running; *currendum est,* there is a necessity for running. These expressions are of the same kind as the impersonal form of the passive of intransitive verbs. (See § 125.) De-ponent verbs have all the four participles — as *imitans,* imi-tating; *imitatus,* having imitated; *imitaturus,* one who is about to imitate; and *imitandus,* one who is to be imitated.

Note. Respecting the declension of participles, see the chapters on declension; and respecting their degrees of comparison, § 94, note.

§ 130. Every state or action takes place at a certain time; that is, is represented either as past, or as present, or as future. But in each of these times a state or action may be described as completed, or as in progress; hence arise six forms or *Tenses* to describe the different times and relations of a state or action; and a verb is said to have six tenses, which might occur in all the moods. The Latin language has its six tenses, both in the active and passive, only in the Indicative; the Subjunctive has only five; the Infinitive three; and the Im-perative only two. Three of these tenses represent a state or action as not completed or in a state of progress, and the three remaining as completed. The former three are—

(a). The PRESENT, *laudo,* I praise, or am praised; and *laudor,* I am praised; the action not being terminated at the pre-sent time.

(b.) The IMPERFECT, *laudabam,* I praised, or was praising; and *laudabar,* I was being praised; the action is past, but is re-presented as not completed in past time.

(c). The FUTURE, *laudabo,* I shall praise, or shall be praising; *laudabor,* I shall be praised; the action is future, but not described as completed in future time.

The following three tenses express a completed action:—

(a). The PERFECT, *laudavi,* I have praised; *laudatus sum,* I have been praised, denote a past action completed at the present time.

(b). The PLUPERFECT, *laudaveram,* I had praised; and *laudatus eram,* I had been praised, denote a past action completed in past time.

(c). The FUTURE PERFECT, *laudavero,* I shall have praised; and *laudatus ero,* I shall have been praised, denote a com-pleted action in future time.

These tenses, on the whole, have the same meaning in the different moods in which they occur.

§ 131. When a state or action is ascribed to one person or thing, the verb is in the singular; when to two or more, in the plural—as I praise, *laudo;* we praise, *laudamus.* A state or action further may be assigned to the person or persons speaking (*I* or *we*), to the person or persons spoken to (*thou* or *you*), and to the person or persons spoken of (*he, she, it,* or *they*). There are accordingly three persons in the singular, and three in the plural, which are commonly distinguished by the terms, the first, second, and third person plural or singular. The two numbers occur in all moods except the infinitive, and the three different persons only in the indicative and subjunctive; the imperative has only the second and third persons, and the infinitive does not assign an action to any person at all. The pronouns I, thou, he (she, it), we, you, they, are usually not expressed in Latin, as they are sufficiently marked by the terminations of the verb itself; they are expressed only when they have a particular emphasis.

§ 132. To put a verb through the active and passive voice, through its moods, tenses, numbers, and persons, is called to *conjugate* or to decline it. Conjugation consists mainly in the change of terminations. These terminations may be classified, according to the persons, in the active as well as in the passive voice. In the active, the first person singular, in all the tenses and moods, except the imperative, terminates in *o, i,* or *m;* in the passive in *r :* the second person singular in the active in *s* or *sti ;* in the passive in *ris :* the third person singular active in *t ;* in the passive in *tur :* the first person plural active ends in *mus ;* in the passive in *mur :* the second person plural active ends in *tis ;* and in the passive in *mini ;* the third person plural active ends in *nt ;* and in the passive in *ntur.*

Note. What has been said here applies, in the case of those tenses which are formed by means of an auxiliary verb and a participle, only to the auxiliary verb.

§ 133. The different manners in which the terminations marking the moods, tenses, numbers, and persons are united with the stem of verbs, and the difference among the stems themselves, render it necessary to divide verbs into four classes; hence there arise four conjugations :—

(*a*). The first conjugation, which may be termed the *a* conjugation, comprises all verbs the stem of which ends in *a,* which in the first person of the present indicative is contracted with the *o* of the termination into *o,* and in the present subjunctive is changed into *ē*—as *amo, amem,* from the stem *ama ;* but in all other forms of the verb it reappears— as in *ama-s,* thou lovest · *ama-t,* he loves · *ama-re.* to love.

The infinitive of verbs of this conjugation accordingly al
ways ends in *āre*.

Note. The *a* of the stem may be preceded by a consonant, as in
ama, or by a vowel, as *creāre*, to create ; *cruciāre*, to torment ; *sinu-
are*, to fold.

(*b*). The second, also called the *e* conjugation, comprises all
verbs the stem of which ends in *e*—as *mone-o*, I admonish ;
monē-re, to admonish ; *doce-bam*, I taught ; *docē-re*, to teach.
The infinitive of this conjugation always ends in *ēre*.

(*c*). The third or consonant conjugation comprises all verbs
the stem of which terminates in a consonant or the vowel *u*
—as *scrib-o*, I write ; *scrib-ĕre*, to write ; *minu-o*, I lessen ;
minu-ĕre, to lessen. A few insert an *i* in the present indicative and the tenses formed from it—as *cap-i-o*, I take ;
present subjunctive, *cap-i-am;* imperfect indicative, *cap-i-
ebam;* future indicative, *cap-i-am;·* participle present, *cap-i-
ens;* but in all other tenses the *i* is thrown out. The infinitive of verbs of the third conjugation invariably ends in *ĕre*
—as *facio, facĕre.*

(*d*). The fourth conjugation, also called the *i* conjugation, comprises those verbs the stem of which ends in *i*, which is retained in all moods and tenses—as *audi-o*, I hear ; *audi-ebam*,
I heard ; *audi-vi*, I have heard ; *audi-re*, to hear. The infinitive invariably ends in *īre*.

Note 1. As it is impossible to discover the conjugation to which a
verb belongs from the present indicative—since *creo* and *moneo*, *capio*
and *audio*, *lĕgo* and *lēgo*, appear to belong to the same conjugation,
though they belong to different ones—it is customary always to mention the infinitive : *āre*, indicating the first ; *ēre*, the second ; *ĕre*, the
third ; and *īre*, the fourth conjugation.

2. As the stem of verbs of the first and second conjugations ends
in a vowel, the terminations are simply added to the stem—as *amo*,
ama-s, *ama-t*, *ama-mus*, *ama-tis*, *ama-nt; mone-o*, *mone-s*, *mone-t*,
mone-mus, *mone-tis*, *mone-nt*, and so also in the passive ; but in the
third conjugation a connecting vowel is required to step in between
the stem and the termination—as *leg-o*, *leg-i-s*, *leg-i-t*, *leg-i-mus*,
leg-i-tis, *leg-u-nt*. The fourth conjugation likewise sometimes requires a connecting vowel—as in *audi-e-bam*, *audi-u-nt*. Verbs of
the second conjugation generally throw out the *e* of the stem in the
perfect—as *mon-ui*, I have admonished ; and in the supine they
change it into *ĭ*—as *monĭ-tum.*

§ 134. The present indicative in all the four conjugations
ends in *o*, the infinitives in *āre*, *ēre*, *ĕre*, *īre*. But in order to be
able to form the complete conjugation of a verb, it is necessary, in addition to the present and infinitive, to know the
perfect indicative and the supine, since several other tenses
are formed from them.

The perfect is formed in the first and fourth conjugations by simply adding *vi* to the stem, *amā-vi, audī-vi.* In the second conjugation the *e* of the stem is thrown out, and the termination *ui* is added—as *mone-o, mon-ui.* In the third conjugation the perfect ends sometimes in *i*, sometimes in *si*, and sometimes in *ui.* The verbs of which the stem ends in *u* simply add *i* to it—as *minu-o, minu-i.* Those of which the stem ends in a consonant take *si.* When the stem ends in *c, g, h,* or *qu,* these consonants coalesce with *s* into *x*—as *dic-o, dixi; reg-o, rexi; veho, vexi; coquo, coxi; b* before *s* is changed into *p*—as *scrib-o, scripsi;* and *d* is thrown out—as *laed-o, lae-si;* but sometimes also the *s* must give way —as in *defend-o, defend-i,* instead of *defend-si.* The perfect in *ui* occurs chiefly in verbs ending in *lo* and *mo*—as *alo, alui; molo, molui; gemo, gemui.*

Note 1. Some verbs, the stem of which ends in a consonant, make their perfect by simply adding *i*—as *lĕgo, lēgi; ĕmo, ēmi;* and it should be observed that all verbs of this kind lengthen the vowel of the penult when it is short, as in the two examples just mentioned: the only verbs in which the vowel of the penult remains short are—*bĭb-i, fĭd-i, scĭd-i,* and *tŭl-i,* from *bibo, findo, scindo,* and *fero.* (Comp. § 12, note 1.)

2. Some verbs which make their perfect in *i* have a reduplication; that is, the first consonant of the verb with the vowel following it (in case of its being *o* or *u*), or with *ĕ*, is prefixed to the word—as *curro, cucurr-i; posco, poposc-i; cano, cĕcin-i; parco, pĕperc-i; fallo, fĕfell-i.* Compounds of such verbs generally have no reduplication; the only exceptions are the compounds of *do, sto, disco, posco,* and some compounds of *curro.* Lastly, in some verbs the reduplication is somewhat irregular—as in *stĕt-i,* from *sto,* I stand; *stĭt-i,* from *sisto,* I cause to stand; *spopond-i,* from *spondeo* (of the second conjugation), I promise.

§ 135. The supine is formed in the first, third, and fourth conjugations, by adding *tum* (abl. *tu*) to the stem of the verb —as *am-o, ama-tum, em-o, em-tum, audi-tum.* It must, however, be observed that *b* before *t* is hardened into *p;* and *g, h,* and *qu,* into *c*—as *scrib-o, scrip-tum; leg-o, lec-tum; trah-o, trac-tum; coqu-o, coc-tum.* Verbs of the third conjugation, of which the stem ends in *d,* make their supine in *sum* (abl. *su*), before which the *d* is thrown out—as *laed-o, lae-sum; claud-o, clau-sum.* Verbs of the second conjugation change the *e* of the stem into *ĭ* before *tum*—as *mone-o, moni-tum.*

Note 1. *Figo* has irregularly *fixum; pingo, pictum; relinquo, relictum;* and *stringo, strictum;* though in the last three the *n* seems to be thrown out, because it does not belong to the root of the word, as is the case also in *vinco,* and *fundo,* which make their perfects *vici, fudi.*

2. Whenever the perfect of a verb ends in *ui,* to whatever conjugation it may belong, the supine has an *ĭ* before *tum*—as *mon-eo,* perf. *mon-ui,* sup. *moni-tum; dom-o,* perf. *dom-ui,* sup. *dom-i-tum; gem-o,*

perf. *gem-ui*, sup. *gem-i-tum*. But when the *u* in *ui* belongs to the stem, the *u* remains—as in *minu-o*, perf. *minu-i*, sup. *minū-tum*.

§ 136. It now remains to show how from the four principal forms of a verb—namely, the present, perfect, infinitive, and supine—all the remaining forms are derived.

(*a*). From the present are formed—

1. The present subjunctive active, by changing in the first conjugation the *o* into *em*—as *am-o, am-em ;* and in the three other conjugations into *am* — as *mone-o, mone-am; leg-o, leg-am; audi-o, audi-am.*

2. The present indicative passive, by the addition of *r*—as *am-o, am-or ; mone-o, mone-or ; leg-o, leg-or ; audi-o, audi-or.*

3. The present subjunctive passive, by changing the *m* of the present subjunctive active into *r*—as *am-em, am-er ; mone-am, mone-ar ; leg-am, leg-ar ; audi-am, audi-ar.*

4. The imperfect indicative active, in the first and second conjugations, by adding *bam* to the stem ; and in the third and fourth, by prefixing the connecting vowel *ē* before *bam* —as *am-o, ama-bam; mone-o, mone-bam; leg-o, leg-e-bam; audi-o, audi-e-bam.*

5. The imperfect indicative passive, by changing the *m* of the imperfect indicative active into *r*—as *ama-bar, mone-bar, leg-e-bar, audi-e-bar.*

6. The future indicative active, in the first and second conjugations, by adding *bo* to the stem—as *ama-bo, mone-bo;* in the third and fourth, by changing the *o* of the present into *am*—as *leg-o, leg-am ; fac-i-o, fac-i-am ; audi-o, audi-am.*

7. The future indicative passive, in the first and second conjugations, by adding *r* to the *bo* in the future indicative active—as *ama-bor, mone-bor ;* in the third and fourth conjugations, by changing the *m* of the future indicative active into *r*—as *leg-ar, audi-ar.*

8. The participle present, by adding *ns* to the stem ; in addition to which, however, in the third and fourth conjugations, the connecting vowel *e* steps in between the stem and the termination *ns*—as *ama-ns, mone-ns, leg-e-ns, audi-e-ns.* From this participle, again, is formed the gerund and gerundive, by changing *s* into *dum* and *dus*—as *ama-ndus* and *ama-ndum*, &c.

(*b*). From the perfect are formed—

1. The perfect subjunctive active, by changing the *i* of the perfect into *ĕrim*—as *ama-vi, ama-verim; mon-ui, mon-uerim ; leg-i, leg-erim ; audi-vi, audi-verim.*

2. The pluperfect indicative active, by changing the *i* of the

perfect into *ĕram* — as *ama-vi, ama-veram; mon-ui, mon-ueram; leg-i, leg-eram; audi-vi, audi-veram.*

3. The pluperfect subjunctive active, by changing the *i* of the perfect into *issem* — as *ama-vi, ama-vissem; mon-ui, mon-uissem; leg-i, leg-issem; audi-vi, audi-vissem.*

4. The future perfect active, by changing *i* into *ĕro* — as *ama-vi, ama-vero; mon-ui, monu-ero; leg-i, leg-ero; audi-vi, audi-vero.*

5. The perfect infinitive active, by changing *i* into *isse* — as *ama-vi, ama-visse; mon-ui, monu-isse; leg-i, leg-isse; audi-vi, audi-visse.*

(*c*). From the present infinitive active are formed—

1. The imperfect subjunctive active, by adding *m* to the termination *re* — as *ama-re, ama-rem; mone-re, mone-rem; leg-e-re, leg-e-rem; audi-re, audi-rem.*

2. The imperfect subjunctive passive, by adding *r* to the termination of the infinite *re* — as *ama-re, ama-rer; mone-re, mone-rer; leg-e-re, leg-e-rer; audi-re, audi-rer.*

3. The imperative active, by dropping the termination *re* — as *ama-re, amā; mone-re, monē; leg-e-re, legĕ; audi-re, audī.*

4. The imperative passive, which in all conjugations is quite like the infinitive active.

5. The infinitive present passive, by changing *re* into *ri* — as *ama-re, ama-ri; mone-re, mone-ri; audi-re, audi-ri;* but in the third conjugation the two syllables *ĕre* are changed into *i*— as *leg-e-re, leg-i.*

(*d*). From the supine are formed—

1. The participle perfect passive, by changing *um* into *us, a, um* — as *ama-tum, ama-tus, a, um; moni-tum, moni-tus, a, um; lec-tum, lec-tus, a, um; audi-tum, audi-tus, a, um.*

2. The participle future active, by changing *um* into *ūrus, a, um* — as *ama-tum, ama-turus, a, um; moni-tum, moni-turus, a, um; lec-tum, lec-turus, a,um; audi-tum, audi-turus, a, um.*

Note 1. The supine actually occurs in very few verbs, but its existence is always presupposed when either of the participles derived from it is found.

2. Some tenses cannot be formed without the auxiliary verb *Esse*, ' to be.' These tenses are in the active, the future subjunctive, and the future infinitive, which consist of the participle future active with *esse;* and in the passive, the perfect indicative and subjunctive, the pluperfect indicative and subjunctive, the future perfect, and the perfect infinitive, which consist of the participle perfect passive with *esse.*

CHAPTER XVIII.

THE VERB ESSE, TO BE.

§ 137. *Esse* is the only Latin auxiliary verb. It is also used as a verb by itself, denoting existence. Its conjugation is irregular; for the perfect, and the tenses derived from it, are formed from the obsolete verb *fuo* (Greek φύω), and the remaining tenses from the stem *ĕs* (which also appears in the Greek verb εἰμὶ, I am); so that the present *sum, sim, sumus, sunt, sis, sit,* &c. are shortened forms for *es-um, es-im, es-umus, es-unt, es-is, es-it,* &c. It must further be observed, that the *s* of the stem is in some forms changed into *r,* as is most common in the Latin language — as *eram, ero,* for *esam, eso. Esse* has neither gerund nor supine.

PRINCIPAL FORMS.

PRESENT INDICATIVE.	PERFECT.	PRESENT INFINITIVE.
sum.	*fuī.*	*esse.*

INDICATIVE MOOD.	SUBJUNCTIVE MOOD.

PRESENT.

Sing. *sum,* I am	Sing. *sim,* I am, or may be
ĕs, thou art	*sīs,* thou art, or mayst be
est, he (she or it) is.	*sĭt,* he is, or may be.
Plur. *sŭmus,* we are	Plur. *sīmus,* we are, or may be
estis, you are	*sītis,* you are, or may be
sunt, they are.	*sint,* they are, or may be.

IMPERFECT.

Sing. *ĕr-am,* I was	Sing. *ess-em,* I was, might, or should be
ĕr-ās, thou wert	*ess-ēs,* thou wert, mightst, or shouldst be
ĕr-at, he (she or it) was.	*ess-ĕt,* he was, &c.
Plur. *ĕr-āmus,* we were	Plur. *ess-ēmus,* we were, &c.
ĕr-ātis, you were	*ess-ētĭs,* you were, &c.
ĕr-ant, they were.	*ess-ent,* they were, &c.

FUTURE.

Sing. *ĕr-o,* I shall be	Sing. *fŭtūrus (a, um) sim,* I shall be, or may be about to be
ĕr-is, thou wilt be	*futurus sis,* thou wilt be, or mayst be about to be
ĕr-it, he will be.	*futurus sit,* he will be, &c.

INDICATIVE.	SUBJUNCTIVE.

FUTURE.

Plur. *ĕr-ĭmus*, we shall be

  ĕr-ĭtis, you will be

  ĕr-unt, they will be.

Plur. *futuri (ae, a) simus*, we shall be, &c.

  futuri sītis, you will be, &c.

  futuri sint, they will be, &c.

PERFECT.

Sing. *fu-ī*, I was, or have been

  fu-istī, thou wert, or hast been

  fu-it, he was, or has been.

Plur. *fu-ĭmus*, we were, or have been

  fu-istis, you were, or have been

  fu-ērunt, or *fu-ēre*, they were, or have been.

Sing. *fu-ĕrim*, I have been, or may have been

  fu-ĕris, thou hast been, or mayst have been

  fu-ĕrit, he has been, &c.

Plur. *fu-ĕrĭmus*, we have been, &c.

  fu-ĕrĭtis, you have been, &c.

  fu-ĕrint, they have been, &c.

PLUPERFECT.

Sing. *fu-ĕram*, I had been

  fu-ĕrās, thou hadst been

  fu-ĕrăt, he had been.

Plur. *fu-ĕrāmus*, we had been

  fu-ĕrātĭs, you had been

  fu-ĕrant, they had been.

Sing. *fu-issem*, I had been, or I might or should have been

  fu-issēs, thou hadst been, or thou mightst or wouldst have been

  fu-issĕt, he had been, &c.

Plur. *fu-issēmus*, we had been, &c.

  fu-issētis, you had been, &c.

  fu-issent, they had been, &c.

FUTURE PERFECT.

Sing. *fu-ĕro*, I shall have been

  fu-ĕris, thou wilt have been

  fu-ĕrit, he will have been.

Plur. *fu-ĕrĭmus*, we shall have been

  fu-ĕrĭtis, you will have been

  fu-ĕrint, they will have been.

The Subjunctive does not exist.

IMPERATIVE MOOD.

PRESENT.	FUTURE.

Sing. *ĕs*, be thou.

Plur. *es-tĕ*, be ye.

Sing. *es-to*, thou shalt be

  es-to, he shall be.

Plur. *es-tōtĕ*, you shall be

  sunto, they shall be.

INFINITIVE MOOD.

Present infinitive, *esse*, to be.

Perfect infinitive, *fu-isse*, to have been.

Future infinitive, *fūtūrum, am, um,* * *esse*, or *fore*, to be about to be.

* In mentioning the infinitive of a compound tense, it is customary to give the participle in the acc., because this case usually accompanies the infinitive.

PARTICIPLES.

Present, does not exist.

Future, *fŭ-tūrus, a, um,* one who is to be, or is about to be.

REMARKS.

Note 1. The participle present, if it did exist, should be *es-ens* or *sens,* as it actually does occur in the compounds *ab-sens,* absent (from *absum*), and *prae-sens,* present (from *praesum*). But there is a philosophical term *ens,* gen. *entis* (a being), which is regarded as originally the present participle of *esse.*

2. The compounds *absum,* I am away from ; *adsum,* I am present ; *desum,* I am wanting or missing ; *insum,* I am in ; *intersum,* I am between or among ; *obsum,* I am against or in the way ; *praesum,* I am before or at the head ; *prosum,* I am useful ; *subsum,* I am under ; *supersum,* I am over, I am left ; are all conjugated like the simple *sum.* *Prosum,* however, inserts a euphonic *d* wherever the *pro* is followed by the radical vowel *e*—as *pro-d-est, pro-d-eram, pro-d-essem, pro-d-ero, pro-d-esse;* but *prosum, prosim, profui,* &c. are regular. *Possum* (I am able, or I can) is composed of *potis sum* or *pot sum;* but its conjugation is irregular.

3. Instead of the forms of the present subjunctive given above, we find in the earliest Latin writers the forms *siem, sies, siet,* and *sient;* and somewhat more frequently the forms *fuam, fuas, fuat* or *fuvat,* and *fuant,* which are formed from the obsolete *fuo.* The forms *escit* and *escunt* (that is, *esit* and *esunt*), for the future *erit* and *erunt,* are quite obsolete.

4. Instead of the infinitive *futurum (am, um) esse,* there is another form, *fŏre* (connected with *fuo*) ; and instead of the imperf. subjunctive *essem,* we have (likewise from *fuo*) *fŏrem, fŏres, fŏret,* and *fŏrent,* which are frequently used by the best writers, especially in conditional clauses. Instead of the usual perfect, we find in the earliest writers the forms *fuvimus, fuverint, fuvissent,* &c.

CHAPTER XIX.

THE FOUR CONJUGATIONS.

§ 138. The following specimens of the four conjugations may serve as examples according to which all other regular verbs are inflected. *Lego,* although it has a slight irregularity (see § 135, note 1), has been chosen as an example for the third conjugation, because its very irregularity renders unnecessary all change of the stem, which might tend to confound the learner rather than assist him :—

THE VERB. **99**

FIRST CONJUGATION.
ACTIVE VOICE.

PRESENT.	PERFECT.	SUPINE.	INFINITIVE.
ămŏ.	ămā-vī.	ămā-tum.	ămā-rĕ.

INDICATIVE.	SUBJUNCTIVE.

PRESENT.

Sing. ămŏ, I love
 amā-s, thou lovest
 amă-t, he loves.
Plur. amā-mus, we love
 amā-tis, you love
 ama-nt, they love.

Sing. am-em, I love, or may love
 am-ēs, thou lovest, or mayst love
 am-ĕt, he loves, or may love.
Plur. am-ēmus, we love, or may love
 am-ētis, you love, or may love
 am-ent, they love, or may love.

IMPERFECT.

Sing. amā-bam, I was loving or loved
 amā-bās, thou wert loving or lovedst
 amā-băt, he was loving or loved.
Plur. amā-bāmŭs, we were loving or loved
 amā-bātĭs, you were loving or loved
 amā-bant, they were loving or loved.

Sing. amā-rem, I loved, might, or should love
 amā-rēs, thou lovedst, mightst, or shouldst love
 amā-rĕt, he loved, might, or should love.
Plur. amā-rēmŭs, we loved, might, or should love
 amā-rētĭs, you loved, might, or should love
 amā-rent, they loved, might, or should love.

FUTURE.

Sing. amā-bo, I shall love

 amā-bĭs, thou wilt love

 amā-bĭt, he will love.

Plur. amā-bĭmus, we shall love

 amā-bĭtis, you will love

 amā-bunt, they will love.

Sing. amā-tūrus (a, um) sim, I shall love, or may be about to love
 amā-tūrus (a, um) sis, thou wilt love, or mayst be about to love
 amā-tūrus (a, um) sit, he will love, &c.
Plur. amā-tūri (ae, a) simus, we shall love, &c.
 amā-tūri (ae, a) sitis, you will love, &c.
 amā-tūri (ae, a) sint, they will love, &c.

PERFECT.

Sing. amā-vī, I loved, or have loved
 amā-vistī, thou lovedst, or hast loved
 amā-vit, he loved, or has loved.

Sing. amā-vĕrim, I have loved, or may have loved
 amā-vĕris, thou hast loved, or mayst have loved
 amā-vĕrĭt, he has loved, &c.

INDICATIVE.   SUBJUNCTIVE.

PERFECT.

Plur. *amā-vīmus*, we loved or have | Plur. *amā-vĕrĭmus*, we have loved,
loved | &c.
amā-vistis, you loved, or | *amā-vĕrĭtĭs*, you have loved,
have loved | &c.
amā-vērunt, or *amā-vēre*, | *amā-vĕrint*, they have loved,
they loved, or have loved. | &c.

PLUPERFECT.

Sing. *amā-vĕram*, I had loved | Sing. *amā-vissem*, I had, might,
  | or should have loved
amā-vĕras, thou hadst loved | *amā-vissēs*, thou hadst,
  | mightst, or shouldst have
  | loved
amā-vĕrăt, he had loved. | *amā-vissĕt*, he had, &c.
Plur. *amā-vĕrāmus*, we had loved | Plur. *amā-vissēmus*, we had, &c.
amā-vĕrātĭs, you had loved | *amā-vissētis*, you had, &c.
amā-vĕrant, they had loved. | *amā-vissent*, they had, &c.

FUTURE PERFECT.

Sing. *amā-vĕro*, I shall have loved
amā-vĕrĭs, thou wilt have
loved
amā-vĕrĭt, he will have
loved.
Plur. *amā-vĕrĭmus* we shall have | The Subjunctive does not exist.
loved
amā-vĕrĭtĭs, you will have
loved
amā-vĕrint, they will have
loved.

IMPERATIVE.

PRESENT.   FUTURE.

Sing. *amā*, love thou. | Sing. *amā-to*, thou shalt love
  | *amā-to*, he shall love.
Plur. *amā-tĕ*, love ye. | Plur. *amā-tōte*, ye shall love
  | *ama-nto*, they shall love.

INFINITIVE.

Present, *amā-rĕ*, to love.
Perfect, *amā-visse*, to have loved.
Future, *amā-tūrum* (*am, um*) *esse*, to be about to love.

GERUND.

Gen. *ama-ndī*, of loving.
Dat. *ama-ndō*, to loving.
Acc. *ama-ndum*, loving.
Abl. *ama-ndō*, with or by loving.

SUPINE.

amā-tum (in order), to love ; and *amā-tu*, to be loved.

PARTICIPLES.

Present, *ama-ns*, loving.
Future, *amā-tūrus*, being about to love.

PASSIVE VOICE.

INDICATIVE.	SUBJUNCTIVE.

PRESENT.

Sing. *amŏr*, I am loved

    amā-rĭs, or *re*, thou art loved

    amā-tŭr, he is loved.

Plur. *amā-mŭr*, we are loved

    amā-mĭnī, you are loved

    amā-ntŭr, they are loved.

Sing. *am-ēr*, I am loved, or may be loved

    am-ērĭs, or *am-ērĕ*, thou art loved, or mayst be loved

    am-ētŭr, he is loved, &c.

Plur. *am-ēmŭr*, we are loved, &c.

    am-ēmĭnī, you are loved, &c.

    am-entŭr, they are loved, &c.

INPERFECT.

Sing. *amā-bǎr*, I was loved, or was being loved

    amā-bārĭs, or *bāre*, thou wert loved, &c.

    amā-bātŭr, he was loved, &c.

Plur. *amā-bāmŭr*, we were loved, &c.

    amā-bāmĭnī, you were loved, &c.

    amā-bạntŭr, they were loved, &c.

Sing. *amā-rĕr*, I was, might be, or should be loved

    amā-rērĭs, or *rērĕ*, thou wert, mightst be, or shouldst be loved

    amā-rētŭr, he was, &c.

Plur. *amā-rēmŭr*, we were, &c.

    amā-rēmĭnī, you were, &c.

    amā-rentŭr, they were, &c.

FUTURE.

Sing. *amā-bŏr*, I shall be loved

    amā-bĕrĭs, or *bĕrĕ*, thou wilt be loved

    amā-bĭtŭr, he will be loved.

Plur. *amā-bĭmŭr*, we shall be loved

    amā-bĭmĭnī, you will be loved

    amā-buntŭr, they will be loved.

The subjunctive is wanting.

PERFECT.

Sing. *amā-tŭs* (*ǎ, um*) *sum*, I was, or have been loved

    amā-tŭs (*ǎ, um*) *es*, thou wert, or hast been loved

    amā-tŭs (*ǎ, um*) *est*, he was, or has been loved.

Plur. *amā-tī* (*ae, ǎ*) *sumus*, we were, &c.

    amā-tī (*ae, ǎ*) *estis*, you were, &c.

    amā-tī (*ae, ǎ*) *sunt*, they were, &c.

Sing. *amā-tŭs* (*ǎ, um*) *sim*, I have been, or may have been loved

    amā-tŭs (*ǎ, um*) *sis*, thou hast been, &c.

    amā-tŭs (*ǎ, um*) *sit*, he has been, &c.

Plur. *amā-tī* (*ae, ǎ*) *simus*, we have been, &c.

    amā-tī (*ae, ǎ*) *sitis*, you have been, &c.

    amā-tī (*ae, ǎ*) *sint*, they have been, &c.

INDICATIVE.	SUBJUNCTIVE.

PLUPERFECT.

Sing. *ama-tus (a, um) eram,* I had been loved

ama-tus (a, um) eras, thou hadst been loved

ama-tus (a, um) erat, he had been loved.

Plur. *ama-ti (ae, a) eramus,* we had been loved

ama-ti (ae, a) eratis, you had been loved

ama-ti (ae, a) erant, they had been loved.

Sing. *ama-tus (a, um) essem,* I had been, might, or should have been loved

ama-tus (a, um) esses, thou hadst been, &c.

ama-tus (a, um) esset, he had been, &c.

Plur. *ama-ti (ae, a) essemus,* we had been, &c.

ama-ti (ae, a) essetis, you had been, &c.

ama-ti (ae, a) essent, they had been, &c.

FUTURE PERFECT.

Sing. *ama-tus (a, um) ero,* I shall have been loved

ama-tus (a, um) eris, thou wilt have been loved

ama-tus (a, um) erit, he will have been loved.

Plur. *ama-ti (ae, a) erimus,* we shall have been loved

ama-ti (ae, a) eritis, you will have been loved

ama-ti (ae, a) erunt, they will have been loved.

The subjunctive is wanting.

IMPERATIVE.

PRESENT.	FUTURE.

Sing. *amā-rĕ,* be thou loved.

Plur. *amā-mĭnĭ,* be ye loved.

Sing. *amā-tŏr,* thou shalt be loved
amā-tŏr, he shall be loved.

Plur. *amā-bĭmĭnĭ,* ye shall be loved.

amā-ntŏr, they shall be loved.

INFINITIVE.

Present, *amā-rī,* to be loved.
Perfect, *ama-tum (am, um) esse,* to have been loved.
Future, *ama-tum iri,* to be about to be loved.

PARTICIPLES.

Perfect,   *ama-tus, a, um,* loved.
Gerundive,   *ama-ndus,* deserving or requiring to be loved.

SECOND CONJUGATION.
ACTIVE VOICE.

PRESENT.	PERFECT.	SUPINE.	INFINITIVE.
mŏnē-ŏ.	*mŏn-ŭī.*	*mŏnĭ-tum.*	*mŏnē-rĕ.*

INDICATIVE.	SUBJUNCTIVE.

PRESENT.

Sing. *mŏne-o,* I advise

  mŏnē-s, thou advisest

  mŏnē-t, he advises.
Plur. *mŏnē-mus,* we advise
  mŏnē-tis, you advise
  mŏnē-nt, they advise.

Sing. *monĕ-am,* I advise, or may
  advise
  monĕ-ās, thou advisest, or
  mayst advise
  monĕ-ăt, he advises, &c.
Plur. *monĕ-āmus,* we advise, &c.
  monĕ-ātis, you advise, &c.
  monĕ-ant, they advise, &c.

IMPERFECT.

Sing. *monē-bam,* I was advising,
  or I advised
  monē-bās, thou wert advising, or advisedst
  monē-băt, he was advising,
  &c.
Plur. *monē-bāmŭs,* we were advising, &c.
  monē-bātĭs, you were advising, &c.
  monē-bant, they were advising, &c.

Sing. *monē-rem,* I advised, might,
  or should advise
  monē-rēs, thou advisedst,
  mightst, or wouldst advise
  monē-rĕt, he advised, &c.
Plur. *monē-rēmus,* we advised,
  &c.
  monē-rētis, you advised, &c.

  monē-rent, they advised,
  &c.

FUTURE.

Sing. *monē-bo,* I shall advise

  monē-bĭs, thou wilt advise

  monē-bĭt, he will advise
Plur. *monē-bĭmŭs,* we shall advise

  monē-bĭtis, you will advise.

  monē-bunt, they will advise.

Sing. *monĭ-tūrus (a, um) sim,* I
  shall, or may be about to
  advise
  monĭ-tūrus (a, um) sis, thou
  wilt, or mayst be about to
  advise
  monĭ-tūrus (a, um) sit, he
  will, &c.
Plur. *monĭ-tūri (ae, a) simus,* we
  shall, &c.
  monĭ-tūri (ae, a) sitis, you
  will, &c.
  monĭ-tūri (ae, a) sint, they
  will, &c.

PERFECT.

Sing. *monŭī,* I advised, or have
  advised
  mon-ŭistī, thou advisedst,
  or hast advised
  mon-ŭit, he advised, &c.

Sing. *mon uĕrim,* I have, or may
  have advised
  mon-uĕrĭs, thou hast, or
  mayst have advised
  mon-uĕrĭt, he has advised,
  &c.

INDICATIVE. SUBJUNCTIVE.

PERFECT.

Plur. *mon-ŭĭmŭs*, we advised, &c. | Plur. *mon-ŭĕrĭmŭs*, we have ad
vised, &c.

mon-ŭĭstĭs, you advised, &c. | *mon-ŭĕrĭtĭs*, you have ad
vised, &c.

mon-ŭērunt, or *ēre*, they ad- | *mon-ŭĕrint*, they have ad
vised, &c. | vised, &c.

PLUPERFECT.

Sing. *mon-ŭĕrăm*, I had advised | Sing. *mon-uissem*, I had, might,
or should have advised

mon-ŭĕrās, thou hadst ad- | *mon-uissēs*, thou hadst,
vised | mightst, or shouldst have
advised

mon-ŭĕrăt, he had advised. | *mon-uissĕt*, he had advised,
&c.

Plur. *mon-ŭĕrāmŭs*, we had ad- | Plur. *mon-uissēmŭs*, we had ad-
vised | vised, &c.

mon-ŭĕrātĭs, you had advised | *mon-uissētĭs*, you had ad-
vised, &c.

mon-ŭĕrant, they had ad- | *mon-uissent*, they had ad-
vised. | vised, &c.

FUTURE PERFECT.

Sing. *mon-ŭĕro*, I shall have advised
mon-ŭĕrĭs, thou wilt have
advised
mon-ŭĕrĭt, he will have advised.

Plur. *mon-ŭĕrĭmŭs*, we shall have | The Subjunctive is wanting.
advised
mon-ŭĕrĭtĭs, you will have
advised
mon-ŭĕrint, they will have
advised.

IMPERATIVE.

PRESENT. FUTURE.

Sing. *monē*, advise thou. | Sing. *monē-to*, thou shalt advise
monē-to, he shall advise.

Plur. *monē-te*, advise ye. | Plur. *monē-tōte*, ye shall advise
mone-nto, they shall advise.

INFINITIVE.

Present, *mŏnē-rĕ*, to advise.
Perfect, *mŏn-ŭissĕ*, to have advised.
Future, *mŏnĭ-tūrum* (*am, um*) *esse*, to be about to advise.

GERUND.

Gen. *mone-ndī*, of advising.
Dat. *mone-ndō*, to advising.
Acc. *mone-ndum*, advising.
Abl. *mone-ndō*, with, in, or by advising.

monĭ-tum (in order), to advise; and *monĭ-tū*, to be advised.

PARTICIPLES.

Present, *mone-ns*, advising.
Future, *monĭ-tūrus, a, um*, being about to advise.

PASSIVE VOICE.

INDICATIVE.	SUBJUNCTIVE.

PRESENT.

Sing. *monĕ-or*, I am, or am being advised
monē-rĭs, or *re*, thou art advised
monē-tŭr, he is advised.
Plur. *monē-mŭr*, we are advised
monĕ-mĭnī, you are advised
mone-ntŭr, they are advised.

Sing. *monĕ-ar*, I am advised, or may be advised
mone-ārĭs, or *ārĕ*, thou art advised, or mayst be advised
mone-ātŭr, he is advised,&c.
Plur. *mone-āmŭr*, we are advised, &c.
mone-āmĭnī, you are advised, &c.
mone-antŭr, they are advised, &c.

IMPERFECT.

Sing. *monē-băr*, I was advised, or was being advised
monē-bārĭs, or *bāre*, thou wert advised, &c.
monē-bātŭr, he was advised.
Plur. *monē-bāmŭr*, we were advised
monē-bāmĭnī, you were advised
monē-bantŭr, they were advised.

Sing. *monē-rĕr*, I was advised, might, or should be advised
monē-rērĭs, or *rere*, thou wert advised, mightst, or shouldst be advised
monē-rētŭr, he was advised, &c.
Plur. *monē-rēmŭr*, we were advised, &c.
monē-rēmĭnī, you were advised, &c.
monē-rentŭr, they were ad vised, &c.

FUTURE.

Sing. *monē-bŏr*, I shall be advised
monē-bĕrĭs, or *bĕrĕ*, thou wilt be advised
monē-bĭtŭr, he will be advised.
Plur. *monē-bĭmŭr*, we shall be advised
monē-bĭmĭnī, you will be advised
monē-buntŭr, they will be advised.

The subjunctive is wanting.

INDICATIVE.   SUBJUNCTIVE.

PERFECT.

Sing. *mŏnĭ-tŭs (a, um) sum,* I was, | Sing. *monĭ-tŭs (a, um) sim,* I have
or have been advised | been, or may have been
                                | advised
monĭ-tus (a, um) es, thou | *monĭ-tus (a, um) sis,* thou
wert, or hast been ad- | hast been, or mayst have
vised | been advised
monĭ-tus (a, um) est, he was, | *monĭ-tus (a, um) sit,* he has
&c. | been, &c.
Plur. *monĭ-ti (ae, a) sumus,* we | Plur. *monĭ-ti (ae, a) simus,* we
were, &c. | have been, &c.
monĭ-ti (ae, a) estis, you | *monĭ-ti (ae, a) sitis,* you
were, &c. | have been, &c.
monĭ-ti (ae, a) sunt, they | *monĭ-ti (ae, a) sint,* they
were, &c. | have been, &c.

PLUPERFECT.

Sing. *monĭ-tŭs (a, um) eram,* I had | Sing. *monĭ-tŭs (a, um) essem,* I had
been advised | been, might, or should
                                | have been advised.
monĭ-tus (a, ŭm) eras, thou | *monĭ-tus (a, um) esses,* thou
hadst been advised | hadst been, &c.
monĭ-tŭs (a, ŭm) erat, he | *monĭ-tus (a, um) esset,* he
had been advised. | had been, &c.
Plur. *monĭ-ti (ae, a) eramus,* we | Plur. *monĭ-ti (ae, a) essemus,* we
had been advised | had been, &c.
monĭ-ti (ae, a) eratis, you | *monĭ-ti (ae, a) essetis,* you
had been advised | had been, &c.
monĭ-ti (ae, a) erant, they | *monĭ-ti (ae, a) essent,* they
had been advised. | had been, &c.

FUTURE PERFECT.

Sing. *monĭ-tŭs (a, um) ero,* I shall
have been advised
monĭ-tus (a, um) eris, thou
wilt have been advised
monĭ-tus (a, um) erit, he will
have been, &c.   The subjunctive is wanting.
Plur. *monĭ-ti (ae, a) erimus,* we
shall have been, &c.
monĭ-ti (ae, a) eritis, you
will have been, &c.
monĭ-ti (ae, a) erunt, they
will have been, &c.

IMPERATIVE.

PRESENT.   FUTURE.

Sing. *monē-rĕ,* be thou advised. | Sing. *monē-tor,* thou shalt be ad-
                                | vised
                                | *monē-tor,* he shall be advised.
Plur. *monē-mĭnĭ,* be ye advised. | Plur. *monē-bĭmĭnĭ,* ye shall be ad-
                                | vised
                                | *mone-ntor,* they shall be ad-
                                | vised.

INFINITIVE.

Present, *monē-rī*, to be advised.
Perfect, *monĭ-tum (am, um) esse*, to have been advised.
Future, *monĭ-tum, irī*, to be about to be advised.

PARTICIPLES.

Perfect, *mŏnĭ-tŭs, a, um*, advised.
Gerundive, *mŏne-ndŭs, a, um*, deserving, or requiring to be advised.

THIRD CONJUGATION.

ACTIVE VOICE.

PRESENT.	PERFECT.	SUPINE.	INFINITIVE.
lĕg-ŏ.	*lĕg-ĭ.*	*lec-tum.*	*lĕg-ĕrĕ.*

INDICATIVE.	SUBJUNCTIVE.

PRESENT.

Sing. *leg-ŏ*, I read
    leg-ĭ-s, thou readest

    leg-ĭ-t, he reads.
Plur. *leg-ĭ-mŭs*, we read
    leg-ĭ-tĭs, you read
    leg-u-nt, they read.

Sing. *leg-am*, I read, or may read
    leg-ās, thou readest, or mayst read
    leg-ăt, he reads, &c.
Plur. *leg-āmŭs*, we read, &c.
    leg-ātĭs, you read, &c.
    leg-ant, they read, &c.

IMPERFECT.

Sing. *leg-ē-bam*, I read, or was reading
    leg-ē-bās, thou readest, or wert reading
    leg-ē-băt, he read, &c.
Plur. *leg-ē-bāmŭs*, we read, &c.
    leg-ē-bātĭs, you read, &c.
    leg-ē-bant, they read, &c.

Sing. *leg-ĕ-rem*, I read, might, or should read
    leg-ĕ-rēs, thou readest, mightst, or wouldst read
    leg-ĕ-rĕt, he read, &c.
Plur. *leg-ĕ-rēmŭs*, we read, &c.
    leg-ĕ-rētĭs, you read, &c.
    leg-ĕ-rent, they read, &c.

FUTURE.

Sing. *leg-am*, I shall read

    leg-ēs, thou wilt read

    leg-ĕt, he will read.
Plur. *leg-ēmŭs*, we shall read

    leg-ētĭs, you will read

    leg-ent, they will read.

Sing. *lec-tūrŭs (a, um) sim*, I shall, or may be about to read
    lec-tūrus (a, um) sis, thou wilt, or mayst be about to read
    lec-tūrus (a, um) sit, he will, &c.
Plur. *lec-tūri (ae, a) simus*, we shall, &c.
    lec-tūri (ae, a) sitis, you will, &c.
    lec-tūri (ae, a) *sint*, they will, &c.

INDICATIVE.   SUBJUNCTIVE.

PERFECT.

Sing. *leg-ĭ*, I read, or have read Sing. *leg-ĕrim*, I have read, or may have read

 leg-istĭ, thou readst, or hast read *leg-ĕrĭs*, thou hast read, or mayst have read

 lēg-ĭt, he read, or has read.   *leg-ĕrĭt*, he has read, &c.

Plur. *leg-ĭmŭs*, we read, or have read Plur. *leg-ĕrĭmus*, we have read, &c.

 leg-istĭs, you read, or have read   *leg-ĕrītĭs*, you have read &c.

 leg-ērunt, or *ēre*, they ıead, or have read.   *leg-ĕrint*, they have read, &c.

PLUPERFECT.

Sing. *leg-ĕram*, I had read Sing. *leg-issem*, I had, might have, or should have read

 leg-ĕrās, thou hadst read   *leg-issēs*, thou hadst, mightst, or wouldst have read

 leg-ĕrăt, he had read.   *leg-issĕt*, he had read, &c.

Plur. *leg-ĕrāmŭs*, we had read Plur. *leg-issēmŭs*, we had read, &c.

 leg-ĕrātĭs, you had read   *leg-issētĭs*, you had read, &c.

 leg-ĕrant, they had read.   *leg-issent*, they had read, &c.

FUTURE PERFECT.

Sing. *leg-ĕro*, I shall have read
 leg-ĕrĭs, thou wilt have read
 leg-ĕrĭt, he will have read.
Plur. *leg-ĕrĭmŭs*, we shall have read The subjunctive is wanting.
 leg-ĕrītĭs, you will have read
 leg-ĕrint, they will have read.

IMPERATIVE.

PRESENT.   FUTURE.

Sing. *leg-ĕ*, read thou. Sing. *leg-ĭ-to*, thou shalt read
        leg-ĭ-to, he shall read.

Plur. *leg-ĭ-te*, read ye. Plur. *leg-ĭ-tōte*, you shall read
        leg-u-nto, they shall reaɑ.

INFINITIVE.

Present, *leg-ĕrĕ*, to read.
Perfect, *leg-isse*, to have read.
Future, *lec-tūrum* (*am*, *um*) *esse*, to be about to read.

GERUND.

Gen. *leg-e-ndĭ*, of reading.
Dat. *leg-e-ndō*, to reading.
Acc. *leg-e-ndum*, reading.
Abl. *leg-e-ndō*, with, by, or in reading.

SUPINE.

lec-tum (in order) to read; *lec-tū*, to be read.

PARTICIPLES.

Present, *leg-e-ns*, reading.
Future, *lec-tūrus*, about to read.

PASSIVE VOICE.

INDICATIVE.
SUBJUNCTIVE.

PRESENT.

Sing. *leg-or*, I am read

leg-ĕ-rĭs, or *rĕ*, thou art read

leg-ĭtŭr, he is read.

Plur. *leg-ĭ-mŭr*, we are read

leg-ĭ-mĭnī, you are read

leg-u-ntŭr, they are read.

Sing. *leg-ăr*, I am read, or I may
be read
leg-ārĭs, thou art read, or
mayst be read
leg-ātŭr, he is read, or may
be read.

Plur. *leg-āmŭr*, we are read, or
may be read
leg-āmĭnī, you are read, or
may be read
leg-antŭr, they are read, or
may be read.

IMPERFECT.

Sing. *leg-ē-băr*, I was read, or was
being read
leg-ē-bārĭs, or *bārĕ*
leg-ē-bātŭr.

Plur. *leg-e-bāmŭr*
leg-ē-bāmĭnī
leg-ē-bāntŭr.

Sing. *leg-ĕ-rĕr*, I was read, might
be read, or should be read
leg-ĕ-rērĭs, or *rērĕ*
leg-ĕ-rētŭr.

Plur. *leg-ĕ-rēmŭr*
leg-ĕ-rēmĭnī
leg-ĕ-rentŭr.

FUTURE.

Sing. *leg-ăr*, I shall be read
leg-ērĭs, or *ērĕ*
leg-ētŭr.

Plur. *leg-ēmŭr*
leg-ēmĭnī
leg-entŭr.

The subjunctive is wanting.

PERFECT.

Sing. *lec-tŭs (a, um) sum*, I was
read, or have been read
lec-tus (a, um) es
lec-tus (a, um) est.

Plur. *lec-tī (ae, a) sumus*
lec-ti (ae, a) estis
lec-ti (ae, a) sunt.

Sing. *lec-tus (a, um) sim*, I have,
or may have been read
lec-tus (a, um) sis
lec-tus (a, um) sit.

Plur. *lec-ti (ae, a) simus*
lec-ti (ae, a) sitis
lec-ti (ae, a) sint.

INDICATIVE.	SUBJUNCTIVE.

PLUPERFECT.

Sing. *lec-tus (a, um) eram*, I had been read
  lec-tus (a, um) eras
  lec-tus (a, um) erat.
Plur. *lec-ti (ae, a) eramus*
  lec-ti (ae, a) eratis
  lec-ti (ae, a) erant.

Sing. *lec-tus (a, um) essem*, I had been, might, or should have been read
  lec-tus (a, um) esses
  lec-tus (a, um) esset.
Plur. *lec-ti (ae, a) essemus*
  lec-ti (ae, a) essetis
  lec-ti (ae, a) essent.

FUTURE PERFECT.

Sing. *lec-tus (a, um) ero*, I shall have been read
  lec-tus (a, um) eris
  lec-tus (a, um) erit.
Plur. *lec-ti (ae, a) erimus*
  lec-ti (ae, a) eritis
  lec-ti (ae, a) erunt.

The subjunctive is wanting.

IMPERATIVE.

PRESENT.

Sing. *leg-ĕrĕ*, be thou read.

Plur. *leg-ĭ-mĭnī*, be ye read.

FUTURE.

Sing. *leg-ĭ-tŏr*, thou shalt be read
  leg-ĭ-tŏr, he shall be read.
Plur. *leg-ē-mĭnī*, ye shall be read
  leg-u-ntor, they shall be read.

INFINITIVE.

Present, *leg-ī*, to be read.
Perfect, *lec-tum (am, um) esse*, to have been read.
Future, *lec-tum iri*, to be about to be read.

PARTICIPLES.

Perfect, *lec-tŭs, a, um*, read.
Gerundive, *leg-e-ndus, a, um*, requiring, or deserving to be read.

FOURTH CONJUGATION.

ACTIVE VOICE.

PRESENT.	PERFECT.	SUPINE.	INFINITIVE.
audĭ-ŏ̆.	*audī-vī.*	*audī-tum.*	*audī-rĕ.*

INDICATIVE.	SUBJUNCTIVE.

PRESENT.

Sing. *audi-o*, I hear
  audĭ-s
  audĭt.
Plur. *audī-mŭs*
  audī-tĭs
  audi-u-nt.

Sing. *audi-ăm*, I hear, or may hear
  audi-ās
  audi-ăt.
Plur. *audi-āmŭs*
  audi-ātĭs
  audi-ant.

INDICATIVE.   SUBJUNCTIVE.

IMPERFECT.

Sıng. *audĭ-ē-bam,* I heard, or was   Sing. *audī-rem,* I heard, might, or
hearing   should hear
    audi-ē-bās   *audī-rēs*
    audi-ē-băt.   *audī-rĕt.*
Plur. *audi-ē-bāmŭs*   Plur. *audī-rēmŭs*
    audi-ē-bātĭs   *audī-rētĭs*
    audi-ē-bant.   *audī-rent.*

FUTURE.

Sing. *audi-am,* I shall hear   Sing. *audī-tūrus (a, um) sım,* I
                                 shall, or may be about to
                                 hear
    audĭ-ēs   *audī-tūrus (a, um) sis*
    audĭ-ĕt.   *audī-turus (a, um) sit.*
Plur. *audĭ-ēmŭs*   Plur. *audī-turi (ae, a) simus*
    audĭ-ētĭs   *audī-turi (ae, a) sitis*
    audĭ-ent.   *audī-turi (ae, a) sint.*

PERFECT.

Sing. *audī-vī,* I heard, or have   Sing. *audī-vĕrim,* I have heard, or
heard   may have heard
    audī-vistī   *audī-vĕris*
    audī-vĭt.   *audī-vĕrit.*
Plur. *audī-vĭmŭs*   Plur. *audī-vĕrĭmŭs*
    audī-vistĭs   *audī-vĕrĭtĭs*
    audī-vērunt, or *vērĕ.*   *audī-vĕrint.*

PLUPERFECT.

Sing. *audī-vĕram,* I had heard   Sing. *audī-vissem,* I had heard, or
                                 I might or should have
                                 heard
    audī-vĕrās   *audī-vissēs*
    aᵘdī-vĕrăt.   *audī-vissĕt.*
Plur. *aᵤdī-vĕrāmŭs*   Plur. *audī-vissēmŭs*
    audī-vĕrātĭs   *audī-vissētĭs*
    audī-vĕrant.   *audī-vissent*

FUTURE PERFECT.

Sing. *audī-vĕro,* I shall have heard
    audī-vĕrĭs
    audī-vĕrit.   The subjunctive is wanting.
Plur. *audī-vĕrĭmŭs*
    audī-vĕrĭtĭs
    audī-vĕrint

IMPERATIVE.

PRESENT.   FUTURE.

Sıng. *audī,* hear thou.   Sing. *audī-to,* thou shalt hear
                                  audī-to, he shall hear
Plur. *audī-tĕ,* hear ye.   Plur. *audī-tōtĕ,* you shall hear
                                  audi-u-nto, they shall hear.

8   E 2

INFINITIVE.

Present, *audĭ-rĕ*, to hear.
Perfect, *audĭ-vissĕ*, to have heard.
Future, *audĭ-tūrum (am, um) esse,* to be about to hear.

GERUND.

Gen. *audi-e-ndī,* of hearing.
Dat. *audi-e-ndō,* to hearing.
Acc. *audi-e-ndum,* hearing.
Abl. *audi-e-ndō,* with, by, or in hearing.

SUPINE.

audĭ-tum, (in order) to hear ; *audĭ-tū,* to hear.

PARTICIPLES.

Present, *audi-e-ns,* hearing.
Future, *audĭ-tūrus,* about to hear.

PASSIVE VOICE.

INDICATIVE.	SUBJUNCTIVE.

PRESENT.

Sing. *audi-ọr,* I am heard

   audĭ-rĭs, or *rĕ*
   audĭ-tŭr.
Plur. *audĭ-mŭr*
   audĭ-mĭnī
   audi-u-ntur.

Sing. *audi-ăr,* I am heard, or **may be heard**
   audi-ārĭs
   audi-ātŭr.
Plur. *audi-āmŭr*
   audi-āmĭnī
   audi-antŭr.

IMPERFECT.

Sing. *audi-ē-bar,* I was heard, or being heard
   audi-ē-bārĭs, or *bārĕ*
   audi-ē-bātŭr.
Plur. *audi-ē-bāmŭr*
   audi-ē-bāmĭnī
   audi-ē-bantŭr.

Sing. *audĭ-rĕr,* I was heard, might, or should be heard
   audĭ-rērĭs, or *rērĕ*
   audĭ-rētŭr.
Plur. *audĭ-rēmŭr*
   audĭ-rēmĭnī
   audĭ-rentŭr.

FUTURE.

Sing. *audi-ăr,* I shall be heard
   audi-ērĭs
   audi-ētŭr.
Plur. *audi-ēmŭr*
   audi-ēmĭnī
   audi-entŭr.

The subjunctive is wanting.

INDICATIVE.   SUBJUNCTIVE.

PERFECT.

Sing. *audī-tŭs (a, um) sum,* I was
 heard, or have been heard
 audi-tus (a, um) es
 audi-tus (a, um) est.
Plur. *audi-tī (ae, a) sumus*
 audi-ti (ae, a) estis
 audi-ti (ae, a) sunt.

Sing. *audī-tŭs (a, um) sim,* I have
 been heard, or may have
 been heard
 audi-tus (a, um) sis
 audi-tus (a, um) sit.
Plur. *audi-tī (ae, a) simus*
 audi-ti (ae, a) sitis
 audi-ti (ae, a) sint.

PLUPERFECT.

Sing. *audī-tūs (a, um) eram,* I had
 been heard
 audi-tus (a, um) eras
 audi-tus (a, um) erat.
Plur. *audi-tī (ae, a) eramus*
 audi-ti (ae, a) eratis
 audi-ti (ae, a) erant.

Sing. *audī-tŭs (a, um) essem,* I had
 been heard, might, or
 should have been heard
 audi-tus (a, um) esses
 audi-tus (a, um) esset.
Plur. *audi-tī (ae, a) essemus*
 audi-ti (ae, a) essetis
 audi-ti (ae, a) essent.

FUTURE PERFECT.

Sing. *audī-tŭs (a, um) ero,* I shall
 have been heard
 audi-tus (a, um) eris
 audi-tus (a, um) erit.
Plur. *audi-tī (ae, a) erimus*
 audi-ti (ae, a) eritis
 auditi (ae, a) erunt.

The subjunctive is wanting.

IMPERATIVE.

PRESENT.

Sing. *audī-rĕ,* be thou heard.-

Plur. *audī-mĭnī,* be ye heard.

FUTURE.

Sing. *audī-tŏr,* thou shalt be heard
 audī-tŏr, he shall be heard.
Plur. *audĭ-ēmĭnī,* ye shall be heard
 audĭ-untŏr, they shall be
 heard.

INFINITIVE.

Present, *audī-rī,* to be heard.
Perfect, *audī-tum (am, um) esse,* to have been heard.
Future, *audī-tum, iri,* to be about to be heard.

PARTICIPLES.

Perfect, *audī-tŭs, a, um,* heard.
Gerundive, *audĭ-e-ndŭs,* deserving, or requiring to be heard.

CHAPTER XX.

DEPONENT VERBS.

§ 139. Deponent verbs (compare § 126) being in form passives, are conjugated like the passives of other verbs, and follow one of the four conjugations, according as their stem ends.
Those of which the stem ends in *ā*, *ē*, and *ī*, follow the first,
second, and fourth conjugations, and all the rest belong to the
third. But the conjugation of a deponent verb has more
forms than the ordinary passive; for it has not only the supine
and the gerund, but four participles: the participle present—
as *hortans* (admonishing), denoting the action in progress;
hortatus (one who has admonished), denoting the action as
completed; *hortaturus* (one who is about to admonish), describing an action as future; and the gerundive *hortandus* (one
who is to be admonished), which has a passive meaning, and
accordingly is formed only of those deponents which have a
transitive signification. In the neuter gender, however, it
occurs also from intransitive verbs.

Note 1. Many deponents have also an active form with an active
meaning—as *pasco*, I give food, and *pascor*, I take food, or feed myself; *veho*, I carry, and *vehor*, I am carried, or I ride; *verto*, I turn,
and *vertor*, I turn myself, or I am turned. The participle present of
all such verbs has a twofold meaning; so that *vehens* may mean
either 'carrying' or 'riding,' and *vertens* either 'turning' or 'turning
myself.' Some deponents of this kind are occasionally used as real
passives—as *comitor*, I am accompanied; *fabricantur*, they are made
or manufactured; *populari*, to be plundered.
   2. Real deponents, on the other hand—that is, those which are not
derivable from an active form—are rarely used in a passive sense,
though *adūlor*, *aspernor*, *arbitror*, *criminor*, and *ulciscor*, occur as
passives in Cicero and Sallust; and the following perfect participles
are used in a passive sense by the best authors: *abominatus*, *adeptus*,
auspicatus, *amplexus*, *complexus*, *commentus*, *commentatus*, *confessus*,
despicatus, *detestatus*, *eblanditus*, *ementitus*, *expertus*, *exsecratus*, *in-
terpretatus*, *ludificatus*, *meditatus*, *metatus*, *mensus* (*dimensus*), *mode-
ratus*, *opinatus* (*necopinatus*), *pactus*, *partitus*, *perfunctus*, *periclitatus*,
stipulatus, *testatus*, *ultus* (*inultus*), and some others which are found
only in poetry and writers of inferior authority.

§140. DEPONENTS OF THE FOUR CONJUGATIONS.

	FIRST CONJUGATION.	SECOND CONJUGATION.	THIRD CONJUGATION.	FOURTH CONJUGATION.

INDICATIVE.

	FIRST CONJUGATION.	SECOND CONJUGATION.	THIRD CONJUGATION.	FOURTH CONJUGATION.
Present,	*hort-or*, I admonish.	*vere-or*, I fear.	*ut-or*, I use.	*parti-or*, I distribute.
	hort-āris (e), &c.	*verē-ris (e)*, &c.	*ut-ĕ-ris*, &c.	*parti-ris*, &c.
	like *am-or*.	like *mone-or*.	like *leg-or*.	like *audi-or*.
Imperfect,	*hortā-bar*.	*verē-bar*.	*ut-ē-bar*.	*parti-ē-bar*.
Future,	*hortā-bor*.	*verē-bor*.	*ut-ar*.	*parti-ar*.
Perfect,	*hortā-tus (a, um) sum*.	*verī-tus (a, um) sum*.	*u-sus (a, um) sum*.	*parti-tus (a, um) sum*.
Pluperfect,	*horta-tus, (a, um) eram*.	*verī-tus (a, um) eram*.	*u-sus (a, um) eram*.	*parti-tus (a, um) eram*.
Fut. Perfect,	*horta-tus (a, um) ero*.	*verī-tus (a, um) ero*.	*u-sus (a, um) ero*.	*parti-tus (a, um) ero*.

SUBJUNCTIVE.

	FIRST CONJUGATION.	SECOND CONJUGATION.	THIRD CONJUGATION.	FOURTH CONJUGATION.
Present,	*hort-er*.	*vere-ar*.	*ut-ar*.	*parti-ar*.
Imperfect,	*hortā-rer*.	*verē-rer*.	*ut-ē-rer*.	*parti-rer*.
Future,	*hortā-tūrus (a, um) sim*.	*verī-turus (a, um) sim*.	*u-sūrus (a, um) sim*.	*parti-tūrus (a, um) sim*.
Perfect,	*horta-tus (a, um) sim*.	*verī-tus (a, um) sim*.	*u-sus (a, um) sim*.	*parti-tus (a, um) sim*.
Pluperfect,	*horta-tus (a, um) essem*.	*verī-tus (a, um) essem*.	*u-sus (a, um) essem*.	*parti-tus (a, um) essem*.
Fut. Perfect,	*horta-tus (a, um) ero*.	*verī-tus (a, um) ero*.	*u-sus (a, um) ero*.	*parti-tus (a, um) ero*.

	FIRST CONJUGATION.	SECOND CONJUGATION.	THIRD CONJUGATION.	FOURTH CONJUGATION.
IMPERATIVE.				
Present,	*hortā-re.*	*verē-re.*	*ut-ĕre.*	*partī-re.*
Future,	*hortā-tor.*	*verē-tor.*	*ut-ĕ-tor.*	*partī-tor.*
INFINITIVE.				
Present,	*hortā-rī.*	*verē-rī.*	*ut-ī.*	*partī-rī.*
Perfect,	*horta-tum (am, um) esse.*	*verĭ-tum (am, um) esse.*	*u-sum (am, um) esse.*	*parti-tum (am, um) esse.*
Future,	*horta-turum (am, um) esse.*	*verĭ-turum (am, um) esse.*	*u-surum (am, um) esse.*	*parti-turum (am, um) esse.*
SUPINE.				
	horta-tum, horta-tu.	*verĭ-tum, verĭ-tu.*	*u-sum, us-u.*	*partĭ-tum, partĭ-tu.*
GERUND.				
	horta-ndum, &c.	*vere-ndum, &c.*	*ut-e-ndum, &c.*	*parti-e-ndum, &c.*
PARTICIPLES.				
Present,	*horta-ns.*	*vere-ns.*	*ut-e-ns.*	*parti-e-ns.*
Perfect,	*hortā-tus, a, um.*	*verĭ-tus, a, um.*	*u-sus, a, um.*	*partĭ-tus, a, um.*
Future,	*horta-turus, a, um.*	*verĭ-turus, a, um.*	*u-surus, a, um.*	*parti-turus, a, um.*
Gerundive,	*horta-ndus, a, um.*	*vere-ndus, a, um.*	*ut-e-ndus, a, um.*	*parti-e-ndus, a, um.*

CHAPTER XXI.

PECULIAR, CONTRACTED, AND ANTIQUATED FORMS OF CONJUGATION.

§ 141. The perfects ending in *vi*, as well as the tenses formed from them (namely, the pluperfect, future perfect, and the infinitive perfect), sometimes appear in a syncopated form—that is, the *v* is thrown out, and the two vowels thus following one another are contracted into one. This is the case—

1. When in the first conjugation *vi* or *ve* is followed by *r* or *s*, the *v* is omitted, and the *a* of the stem is contracted with *i* or *e* into *ā*—as *amasti, amasse, amārim, amārunt, amāram, amāro*, for the ordinary forms *amavisti, amavisse, amaverim, amaverunt, amaveram*, and *amavero*. The same is the case with verbs of the second and third conjugations forming their perfects in (*ē*)*vi*—as *flestis, flērunt, flēram*, &c. ; *nesti, nestis, nerunt; deleram, decresse*, for *flevistis, fleverunt, fleveram*, &c. ; *nevisti, nevistis, neverunt; deleveram, decrevisse*. So also *sīris, sīrit*, for *siveris, siverit*, from *sino*, ‑I allow. Perfects ending in (*o*)*vi* are generally not contracted, and the only verbs in which a contraction does occur are *nōvi* (from *nosco*) and the compounds of *moveo*—as *nosti, norunt, noram, norim*, for *novisti, noverunt, noveram, noverim* (but we never find *noro* for *novero*); *commosse* for *commovisse*, from‑*commoveo*.

2. In verbs making their perfect in (*ī*)*vi*, the *v* is simply thrown out when *s* follows—thus, *audivisse, audivissem*, become *audiisse, audiissem;* but here, too, the best writers contract the two *i* into one—as *audisse, audissem;* so also *petisse* or *petiisse*, from *peto*, perf. *petīvi*. In those forms where the *v* is followed by *e*, the *v* is thrown out without any contraction taking place—as *audierunt, audieram, desierunt, definieram, quaesieram*, for *audiverunt, audiveram, desiverunt, definiveram, quaesiveram.* · Before the termination *it* the *v* is rarely omitted, and, generally speaking, only in poetry—as *audiit* for *audivit, muniit* for *munivit.*

Note 1. A few of the perfects ending in *iit* (for *ivit*) are contracted by poets into *it*, whereby they acquire the appearance of the third person singular of the present—as *desit, abit, obit, perit, edormit*, for *desiit,‑abiit, obiit, periit, edormiit.* Similar contractions occur in the first and second conjugations—as *donāt* for *donavit, enarramus* for *enarravimus, flemus* for *flevimus.*

2. Perfects of the third conjugation ending in *si* (*xi*), and the tenses formed from them, sometimes throw out *si* when it is followed by *s*—as *evasti* for *evasisti*, *dixti* for *dixisti*, *divisse* for *divisisse*. In cases where, by this process, three *s* or two *s* and one other consonant would meet together, one *s* is omitted—as *abscessem* for *abscessissem*, *dixe* for *dixisse*, *accestis* for *accessistis*, *consumpset* for *consumpsisset*. Similar forms are—*percusti* for *percussisti*, *abstraxe* for *abstraxisse*, *surrexe* for *surrexisse*, *erepsemus* for *erepsissemus*. But all such forms occur only in early Latinity and in poetry.

3. In the third person plural of the perfect indicative active we very often find the termination *ēre* for *ērunt*—as *amavēre, monuēre, legēre, audivēre*, for *amavērunt, monuērunt, legērunt, audivērunt*. In these forms the *v* is never thrown out. It should be observed that poets sometimes use the termination *erunt* with the *e* short—as *stetĕrunt* for *stetērunt*.

§ 142. The second person singular in passive and deponent verbs generally ends in *ris*; but another termination equally common is *re*—as *amabaris* and *amabare; amareris, amarere; amaberis, amabere*; but in the second person of the present indicative the termination *re* occurs very rarely—as *arbitrare* for *arbitraris*. In the fourth conjugation *re* is never used for *ris* in the present indicative.

§ 143. Verbs of the third conjugation, of which the stem ends in a consonant, usually take *e* in the present imperative ; but the verbs *dico*, I say ; *duco*, I lead ; *facio*, I do ; and *fero*, I bear, form their imperatives without *e*—as *dic, duc, fac, fer*. The same is the case in their compounds—as *educ*, from *educo; affer* and *refer*, from *affero* and *refero*. Of *facio*, only those compounds follow this rule in which the *a* is retained—as *calefac* from *calefacio;* but all the other compounds in which the *a* is changed into *i* are regularly formed—as *confice, perfice, effice*, from *conficio, perficio, efficio*.

Note. *Face* sometimes occurs in poetry; *dice* and *duce* more rarely. *Scio* (I know) commonly has only the future imperative, *scito* and *scitote;* the present, *sci* and *scite*, are not in use.

§ 144. Many verbs of the third and fourth conjugations take *u* as the connecting vowel instead of *e* in forming the gerundive. This is done especially when *i* precedes—as *fac-i-undus* for *faci-e-ndus ; poti-u-ndus* for *poti-e-ndus ;* but we also find *divid-u-ndus, reg-u-ndus*, for *divid-e-ndus, reg-e-ndus ;* and *dic-u-ndus* for *dic-e-ndus*.

§ 145. Some verbs, chiefly intransitive (both active and deponent), form a sort of participle in *bundus, a, um*. In the first conjugation, where this form occurs most frequently, *bundus* is added to the stem—as *cuncta-bundus, delibera-bundus, mira-bundus*, &c. In the third conjugation either *i* or *e* is prefixed to *bundus*—as *fur-i-bundus, mor-i-bundus, frem-e-bundus, trem-e-bundus.* In the second and fourth conjugations such participles scarcely ever occur. Their meaning is like that of the present participle, but somewhat stronger; so that *furibundus* is 'full of fury,' whereas *furens* is only 'furious.' When they are derived from transitive verbs, they may, like other participles, govern the case of their verb.

§ 146. It now only remains to notice a few antiquated forms of conjugation which are met with in the early Latin writers, and in certain solemn forms of expression:—

1. The present infinitive passive is sometimes lengthened by the addition of the syllable *er* — as *amarier, mercarier, labier, scribier.*

2. The imperfect indicative, both in the active and passive of the fourth conjugation, was in ancient times formed without the connecting vowel *e*—as *scibam* and *largibar* for *sciebam* and *largiebar; nutribam* and *lenibam* for *nutriebam* and *leniebam.*

3. The future indicative, both in the active and passive of the fourth conjugation, was sometimes formed, as in the first and second conjugations, by simply adding *bo* to the stem—as *servibo, opperibor,* for *serviam, opperiar.*

4. In the present subjunctive active we sometimes find the ancient termination *im, is, it,* especially in the case of the verb *edo* (I eat), which now and then has *edim* for *edam;* and the verb *do* (I give) and its compounds, which make the subjunctive *duim.* But this occurs almost exclusively in ancient forms of prayers and curses—as *di duint* (may the gods grant); *di te perduint* (may the gods destroy thee). This termination *im, is, it,* has been preserved in the ordinary language in the case of the verb *esse* (*sim, sis, sit*), in all the perfects subjunctive of the active, and in the subjunctives *velim, nolim, malim,* and *ausim.*

5. The imperative future of passive, but more especially of deponent verbs, sometimes had an active termination—as *arbitrato, utito, nitito,* for *arbitrator, utitor, nititor;* so also *censento* for *censentor; utunto, tuento,* for *utuntor, tuentor.* In the second and third persons singular we sometimes find such forms as *hortamino, veremino,* for *hortator* and *veretor; progredimino* and *praefamino* for *progreditor* and *praefator.*

6. In the first three conjugations we sometimes find peculiar forms of the perfect subjunctive and the future perfect. In the first conjugation we find (*a*)*ssim* and (*a*)*sso* for (*a*)*verim* and (*a*)*vero;* in the second, (*e*)*ssim* and (*e*)*sso* for *uerim* and *uero;* and in the third, *sim* and *so* for *erim* and *ero;* e.g. *creassim* and *creasso* (for *creaverim, creavero*), *licessit* (*licuerit*), *prohibessit* (*prohibuerit*), *capso* (*cepero*), *axim* and *axo* (*egerim, egero*), *faxim* and *faxo* (*fecerim, fecero*). The origin of the forms in *so* is not quite certain; some believe that they are futures made in the same way as in Greek, by adding the termination *so* to the stem; but though this is the case in some, it is evident that others also change the stem in the same manner as is done in the perfect; and it is moreover certain that the meaning of the forms in *so* is that of a future perfect (Cic. *De Senect.,* 1). For these reasons we prefer considering them as future perfects, and those in *sim* as perfects subjunctive. They seem to have arisen from the change of *r* into *s,* and a syncope—as *levavero, levaveso, levasso.* A few remnants of such

F

formations remained in use, especially in poetry, even in the best period of the language—as *faxo* (from *facio*), expressing a threat or promise ; *faxim, faxis, faxit, faximus, faxitis, faxint*, expressing a wish. So also *ausim* (from *audeo*), expressing a doubtful statement —as *ausit*, ' he might be inclined to venture.'

CHAPTER XXII.

CONJUGATION BY PERIPHRASIS OR CIRCUMLOCUTION.

§ 147. A conjugation by circumlocution might be formed by means of the verb *esse* in conjunction with any participle ; but it must be observed, at the outset, that the Latin language does not possess that conjugation which is formed in English by means of the participle present and the verb *esse ;* so that I am loving, I was loving, &c. cannot be expressed in Latin otherwise than by the simple forms *amo, amabam*, &c.—*amans sum, amans eram*, &c. not being used.

§ 148. *Esse*, in combination with the participle perfect passive, is used to form some of the ordinary tenses of the passive voice, as has been seen above—as perf. *amatus sum* and *amatus sim ;* pluperf. *amatus eram* and *amatus essem ;* fut. perf. *amatus ero ;* infin. perf. *amatum esse.* But instead of *sum, eram, ero*, and *esse*, we also find the forms *fui, fueram, fuero*, and *fuisse*, in quite the same sense as the forms of the tenses denoting an incomplete action ; so that *amatus sum* is equivalent to *amatus fui, amatus eram* to *amatus fueram, amatus ero* to *amatus fuero*, and *amatum esse* to *amatum fuisse.* Hence, as far as form is concerned, we here have a complete periphrastic conjugation ; but those tenses which are formed by means of the perfect tenses of *esse* do not differ in meaning from those formed by means of those tenses of *esse* which denote an action in progress.

Note. There is, however, one case in which the distinction must be observed. The participle of the perfect passive, both in Latin and English, sometimes entirely loses its character of a participle, and becomes a real adjective ; and then the tenses of *esse*, when joined to it, naturally retain their original meaning as much as when they are joined to any other adjective. Thus if we take *positus* in the sense of the adjective, 'situate,' *positus est* and *positus fuit, positus erat* and *positus fuerat, positus erit* and *positus fuerit*, &c. are very different in meaning, the original meaning of each tense of *esse* being strictly preserved.

§ 149. A real and complete periphrastic conjugation is formed by means of the verb *esse* and the participle future active. Throughout this conjugation the action is represented as one that will take place, or is to take place ; *e.g.*—

INDICATIVE.	SUBJUNCTIVE.
Present, *dicturus sum*, I am about to say.	Present, *dicturus sim*, I am about to say, or may be about to say.
Imperfect, *dicturus eram*, I was about to say.	Imperfect, *dicturus essem*, I was, might be, or should be, about to say.
Future, *dicturus ero*, I shall be about to say.	No future.
Perfect, *dicturus fui*, I was, or have been, about to say.	Perfect, *dicturus fuerim*, I have been, or may have been, about, &c.
Pluperfect, *dicturus fueram*, I had been about to say.	Pluperfect, *dicturus fuissem*, I had been, might, or should have been, about to say.
Fut. Perf. *dicturus fuero*, I shall have been, &c.	No future perfect.

Note. The future perfect (*dicturus fuero*) is scarcely ever used ; and the future, or in some instances the present subjunctive, supplies its place. It has been already seen in the tables of the conjugations that *scripturus sim* and *scripturum esse* are used to supply the place of the future subjunctive and the future infinitive. No passive can be formed of this periphrastic conjugation ; but its place can be supplied by longer circumlocutions—as *futurum est ut dicatur*, or *in eo est ut dicatur; futurum erat*, or *in eo erat ut diceretur*, &c.

§ 150. A second real and complete periphrastic conjugation is formed by means of the verb *esse* combined with the neuter of the gerundive ; and in this conjugation the action is invariably represented as necessary, and the person by whom it is to be performed is, expressed by the dative case. For example :—

INDICATIVE.

Present, *mihi scribendum est*, I must write.
Imperfect, *mihi scribendum erat*, I was obliged to write.
Future, *mihi scribendum erit*, I shall be obliged to write.
Perfect, *mihi scribendum fuit*, I was, or have been, obliged to write.
Pluperfect, *mihi scribendum fuerat*, I had been obliged to write.
Fut. Perf. *mihi scribendum fuerit*, I shall have been obliged to write.

In like manner are formed the subjunctive—as *scribendum sit, scribendum esset, scribendum fuerit, scribendum fuisset*, and the infinitive, *scribendum fuisse*.

CHAPTER XXIII.

VERBS OF THE FIRST CONJUGATION FORMING THEIR PERFECT AND SUPINE DIFFERENTLY FROM THE GENERAL RULE.

§ 151. Many verbs do not form the perfect and supine according to the rules laid down in §§ 134 and 135. Sometimes there is a difference in the termination which is appended to the stem, sometimes the stem itself undergoes a change, and sometimes both kinds of irregularities appear together in the same verb. Thus *juvo*, instead of *juva-vi*, makes its perfect *juvi*, and instead of its supine *juvatum*, makes *jutum*. Again, *frango* makes its perfect *fregi*, and its supine *fractum*. These and similar peculiarities render it necessary for the beginner to make himself acquainted with the following lists of verbs. It must, however, be observed, that whatever the apparent irregularity in the perfect and supine may be, the tenses formed from these two are derived from them according to the general rules. (§ 136, *b* and *d*.) We shall in the subjoined lists give only the simple verbs, because, generally speaking, derivative and compound verbs are conjugated like the simple ones. Where, however, the compounds present any difference, these shall be added. There will be found some verbs which have either no perfect or no supine, or neither of them, and in such cases the tenses derived from those two generally do not exist.

Note. The irregularities (if they may be so called) which we are here speaking of, have for the most part arisen from the fact, that the perfect and supine are formed from a more ancient and simpler stem than that which appears in the present; the stem of the present being extended and increased. This extension or increase of the stem consists most frequently—1. In the addition of a vowel (*a*, *e*, or *i*) to it— as *son* (*sono*, sound), increased *sona*, but the perfect *sonui*, and the supine *sonitum*; *rid* (*rideo*, laugh), increased *ride*, but the perfect *risi*, and the supine *risum*; *ven* (*venio*, come), increased *vĕni*, but the perfect *vēni*, supine *ventum*: 2. In the addition of *n* to the stem—as *si*, strengthened *sin* (*sino*, allow), perfect *sīvi*, supine *sĭtum*; or in the insertion of *n* before the final consonant of the stem, the *n* being sometimes, for reasons of euphony, changed into *m*—as *frang* (original stem *frag*), *frango* (I break), but perfect *frēgi*, supine *fractum*; *rump* (original stem *rup*), *rumpo* (break), but perfect *rūpi*, supine *ruptum*. A few verbs also have a reduplication in the present, which disappears in the perfect and supine—as *gi-gno*, perfect *genui*, supine *genitum* (from the stem *gen*); *si-sto*, perfect *stĭti*, supine *statum* (from the stem *sta*). A similar reduplication occurs very frequently in Greek.

The verbs *uro* (*ussi, ustum*) and *gero* (*gessi, gestum*) have not an extended stem but the *s* of the stem is only changed into its equivalent *r* in the present. Some other merely apparent irregularities in the perfect and supine arise simply from the concurrence of the final letter of the stem with the *s* and *t* with which the terminations of the perfect and supine begin. (See §§ 134 and 135.) The supine, lastly, sometimes adds the termination *tum* to the stem without the connecting vowel, where, according to analogy, we should expect *ĭtum*.

The supine itself is rarely used in Latin, and of many verbs, accordingly, no supine occurs in the Latin writers whose works have come down to us; but its existence is nevertheless presupposed wherever we find any of the forms derived from it, such as the participle perfect passive, or the participle future active.

§ 152. The following verbs of the first conjugation and their compounds form their perfect and supine in *ui* and *ĭtum*, as if they belonged to the second conjugation :—

crĕpo,	*crĕpui,*	*crepĭtum,*	make a harsh noise.
discrepo,	*discrepui,* oftener *discrepavi,*	*discrepĭtum,*	differ.
increpo,	*increpavi,* or *increpui,*	*increpatum,* or *increpĭtum,*	scold.
cŭbo,	*cŭbui,*	*cŭbĭtum,*	lie down.

Sometimes we also find *cubavi* and *incubavi*. When compounds of *cubo* take an *m* before *b*, as in *incumbo*, they follow the third conjugation. (§ 156.)

dŏmo,	*dŏmui,*	*dŏmĭtum,*	tame, or subdue.
sŏno,	*sŏnui,*	*sŏnĭtum,*	sound (part. fut. *sŏnātūrus*).
tŏno,	*tŏnui,*	*tŏnĭtum,*	thunder. *Intono* has a partic. *intonatus*.
vĕto,	*vĕtui,*	*vĕtĭtum,*	forbid.

The following have the supine either regular, or throw out the vowel *a :—*

mĭco,	*mĭcui,*	————	dart, glitter.
ēmico,	*ēmĭcui,*	*ēmĭcatum,*	dart forth.
dīmĭco,	*dīmĭcavi,*	*dīmĭcatum,*	fight.
frĭco,	*frĭcui,*	*fricatum,* or *frictum,*	rub.
sĕco,	*sĕcui,*	*sectum,*	cut (partic. fut. *secaturus*).
nĕco,	*nĕcavi,*	*nĕcatum,*	kill; but *eneco* has *enecui* and *enecavi*, as well as *enecui, enectum.*

The following must be remembered separately :—

jŭvo,	*jūvi,*	*jūtum,*	support, assist (partic. fut. *jŭvaturus*).
lăvo,	*lāvi,*	*lavatum, lautum, lōtum,*	wash. There is also an infinitive *lavĕre* for *lavare.*

pŏto,	pŏtāvi,	{ pōtum, or } { pōtātum, }	drink. *Potus* means both one who has been drunk and one who has drunk.

do,   dĕdi,   dătum, inf. dăre, give. Many of the compounds of *do* belong to the third conjugation—as *reddo, addo.* (Compare § 146, 4, and § 158.)

sto,	stĕti,	stātum,	stand.
obsto,	obstĭti,	obstĭtum,	stand in the way of.
praesto,	praestĭti,	praestĭtum,	perform, excel (part. fut. *prae-*
antesto,	antestĕti,	———	stand before. [*staturus*).
disto,		———	be at a distance.
plico,	———	———	fold.
duplĭco,	duplĭcavi,	duplĭcatum,	double.
applĭco,	{ applicavi, or } { applicui, }	{ applicatum, or } { applicĭtum, }	apply.

The verbs *jūro* (swear) and *coeno* (sup) have a perfect participle which, like *potus*, has an active meaning—*juratus*, ' one who has sworn,' and *coenatus*, 'one who has supped.'

CHAPTER XXIV.

VERBS OF THE SECOND CONJUGATION FORMING THEIR PERFECT AND SUPINE DIFFERENTLY FROM THE GENERAL RULE.

§ 153. Many verbs of the second conjugation are defective, having no supine, and many have neither perfect nor supine, nor of course any of the forms derived from them. The irregularity consists in either the perfect or supine, or in both of them, being formed as in verbs of the third conjugation. The learner must be reminded that the regular termination of the perfect is *ui*, and of the supine *ĭtum;* the short *i* before *tum* is sometimes thrown out. Verbs having a *v* before the *e* of the stem are contracted in the perfect and supine—as *moveo, mōvi, mōtum,* for *mŏvui, mŏvĭtum.*

The following form the perfect by adding *vi*, and the supine by adding *tum* to the stem, like the regular verbs of the first and fourth conjugations, except that *ē* before *tum* is sometimes changed into *ĭ :*—

dēleo,	dēlēvi,	dēlētum,	destroy.
fleo,	flēvi,	flētum,	weep.
neo,	nēvi,	nētum,	spin.
compleo (from the } obsolete *pleo*), }	complēvi,	complētum,	fill up.
vieo,	viēvi,	viētum,	hoop a vessel.

áboleo,	*abolēvi,*	*abolĭtum,*	âbolish.
exoleo,	*exolēvi,*	*exolētum,*	fade.
inoleo,	*inolēvi,*	{ *inolētum,* or *inolĭtum,*	come into use.
obsoleo,	*obsolēvi,*	*obsolētum,*	grow out of use.

Verbs in which the *e* of the stem is preceded by *v* form the perfect and supine by a sort of contraction, the perfect ending in *vi,* and the supine in *tum,* which terminations are added to the stem after the removal of the *e* :—

căveo,	*cāvi,*	*cautum,*	take care.
făveo,	*favi,*	*fautum,*	favour.
fŏveo,	*fōvi,*	*fōtum,*	cherish.
moveo,	*mōvi,*	*mōtum,*	move.
vŏveo,	*vōvi,*	*vōtum,*	vow.
păveo,	*pāvi,*	———	dread.
ferveo,	{ *fervi,* or *ferbui,*	———	glow, boil.
conniveo,	{ *connīvi,* or *connixi,*	———	wink, connive.

The following have the perfect regular, but throw out the vowel *i* before the *tum* of the supine :—

dŏceo,	*dŏcui,*	*doctum,*	teach.
tĕneo,	*tĕnui,*	*tentum,*	hold.
misceo,	*miscui,*	{ *mistum,* or *mixtum,*	mix.
torreo,	*torrui,*	*tostum,*	toast.
sorbeo,	*sorbui,*	*sorptum,*	sip. [pass. also *censītŭs.*
censeo,	*censui,*	*censum,*	value, believe. The part. perf.

The following make the perfect in *i,* and the supine in *sum* :—

prandeo,	*prandi,*	*pransum,*	breakfast (partic. *pransus,* one
sĕdeo,	*sēdi,*	*sessum,*	sit. [who has breakfasted).
video,	*vīdi,*	*vīsum,*	see.
strīdeo,	*strīdi,*	———	whistle, hiss (also *strido, stridĕre*).

The following form the perfect and supine in the same manner, but take a reduplication in the perfect, which, however, does not occur in their compounds :—

mordeo,	*mŏmordi,*	*morsum,*	bite.
pendeo,	*pĕpendi,*	*pensum,*	hang.
spondeo,	*spŏpondi,*	*sponsum,*	engage to give.
tondeo,	*tŏtondi,*	*tonsum,*	shear.

The following make the perfect in *si,* and the supine in *tum* :—

augeo,	*auxi,*	*auctum,*	increase.
indulgeo,	*indulsi,*	*indultŭm,*	indulge.
torqueo,	*torsi,*	*tortum,*	twist.

Verbs which have the perfect in *si*, and the supine in
sum :—

ardeo,	arsi,	arsum,	burn.
haereo,	haesi,	haesum,	cling.
jŭbeo,	jussi,	jussum,	command.
măneo,	mansi,	mansum,	remain.
mulceo,	mulsi,	mulsum,	stroke, caress.
mulgeo,	mulsi,	mulsum,	milk.
rīdeo,	rīsi,	rīsum,	laugh.
suādeo,	suāsi,	suāsum,	advise.
tergeo,	tersi,	tersum,	wipe.

The following make the perfect in *si*, but have no supine :—

algeo,	alsi,	——	shiver with cold.
frīgeo,	frixi,	——	freeze with cold.
fulgeo,	fulsi,	——	shine brightly.
turgeo,	tursi,	——	swell.
urgeo,	ursi,	——	press, urge.
luceo,	luxi,	——	shine.
lugeo,	luxi,	——	mourn.

The following must be noticed separately :—

cieo, *cīvi*, *cĭtum*, stir up ; also *cio*, *cīvi*, *cītum*. In the compounds we also have, e.g., *concieo* and *concio;* but the forms of the second conjugation are hardly ever used, except in the present indicative. *Excire* has both *excītum* and *excĭtum*.

audeo,	ausus sum,	venture (a semideponent).
gaudeo,	gavisus sum,	rejoice (a semideponent).
soleo,	solitus sum,	am in the habit (a semideponent).

Verbs (mostly intransitive) which have neither perfect nor supine :—

adoleo, kindle.
aveo, desire.
calveo, am bald.
cāneo, am gray.
cēveo, wag the tail.
denseo, grow thick.
flāveo, am yellow.
foeteo, stink.
hĕbeo, am dull.
hūmeo, am damp.
lacteo, suck.

līveo, am pale.
(*mĭneo*), *immĭneo*, am imminent.
maereo, mourn.
polleo, am strong.
promĭneo, am prominent.
rĕnīdeo, shine.
scăteo, gush forth.
squāleo, am dirty.
uveo, am juicy.
vĕgeo, am gay.

The following deponents of the second conjugation also
form their supine in an unusual manner :—

făteor,	fassum,	confess.
profĭteor,	professum,	profess.
mĭsĕreor,	mĭsĕritum and mĭsertum,	pity.
reor,	rătum,	think.

CHAPTER XXV.

VERBS OF THE THIRD CONJUGATION FORMING THEIR PERFECT AND
SUPINE DIFFERENTLY FROM THE GENERAL RULE.

§ 154. In treating of verbs of the third conjugation, it is particularly necessary to remember the general rules respecting the formation of the perfect and supine (§ 134, &c.) It was observed that verbs, the stem of which ends in *u* (or *v*), form their perfect by simply adding *i* to the stem, and their supine by adding *tum*—as *minuo*, perf. *minui*, sup. *minūtum;* *solvo, solvi, solūtum.*

The following verbs of this kind are regular, but want the supine : —

arguo, I accuse (*argutus*, clear, is an adjective).
luo, pay, atone for (has, however, a part. fut. *luiturus.* Some compounds form the supine regularly — as *ablūtum, dilūtum, elūtum, perlūtum*, &c.)
(*nuo*, nod) occurs only in the compounds *adnuo, abnuo, renuo;* but *abnuo* has a part. fut. *abnuiturus.*
congruo, agree ; and *ingruo*, penetrate.
metuo, fear.
pluo (generally impersonal), rain ; the perfect is sometimes *pluvi*, instead of *plui.*
ruo, fall, has a part. fut. *ruĭturus*, and rarely a part. perf. *rŭtus*, though in compounds this is the common form — as *dirŭtus, obrŭtus.*

The following three verbs are irregular : —

fluo,	*fluxi,*	*fluxum,*	flow.
struo,	*struxi,*	*structum,*	build, pile up.
vīvo,	*vixi,*	*victum,*	live.

§ 155. Verbs in which the vowel *i* is inserted in the present after the stem, form the perfect and supine from the pure stem without the *i* — as

căpio,	*cēpi,*	*captum,*	take.
concipio,	*concēpi,*	*conceptum,*	conceive.
făcio,	*fēci.*	*factum,*	make, do. The passive of this

verb is *fio*, and so also in its compounds, except in those compounded with a preposition, which are regular — as *perficio, perfēci, perfectum*, passive *perficior.* *Conficio*, however, has sometimes *conficior*, and sometimes *confio;* and *deficio* both *deficior* and *defio.* See § 177. Some compounds of *facio* follow the first conjugation — as *amplifico, sacrifico;* and others are deponents of the first conjugation — as *gratificor* and *ludificor.*

jacio,   jēci,   jactum.   When *jacio* is compounded with a preposition, the *a* is changed into *i*—as *conjicio, injicio;* and instead
of *ji* we sometimes find *i* alone—as *abicio, inicio,* a contraction
arising from rapid pronunciation.

fŏdio,   fōdi,   fossum,   dig.

(*lacio* occurs only in compound verbs, as)—

allicio,	*allexi.*	*allectum,*	allure; but *elicio* makes
			ēlicui, ēlĭcĭtum.
pario,	*peperi,*	*partum,*	bring forth, get; part.
quatio,	(*quassi* not used),	*quassum,*	shake. [fut. *parĭturus.*
concutio,	*concussi,*	*concussum,*	shake together.

(*specio* or *spicio* only in compounds.)

aspicio,   aspexi,   aspectum.

The following are irregular:—

cŭpio,	*cŭpīvi,*	*cŭpītum,*	desire.
fŭgio,	*fūgi,*	*fūgĭtum,*	flee.

§ 156. Verbs ending in *bo* and *po* form the perfect in *psi,*
and the supine in *ptum,* according to the laws of euphony—as
scribo, scripsi, scriptum; glubo, glupsi, gluptum. (See § 134.)
But the following form exceptions:—

(*cumbo* only in compounds.)

incumbo,	*incubui,*	*incubitum,*	lie upon.
rumpo,	*rūpi,*	*ruptum,*	break.
strĕpo,	*strĕpui,*	*strĕpĭtum,*	make a noise.
bĭbo,	*bĭbi,*	————	drink.
lambo,	*lambi,*	————	lick.
scăbo,	*scābi,*	————	scratch.

§ 157. Verbs ending in *co* (not *sco*), *go, ho, guo, quo,* form
their perfect in *si,* which, combined with the final letter of the
stem, becomes *xi* (*qu* and *gu = c*), and the supine in *tum,* before
which the final consonant of the stem is always *c*—as *dico,
dixi, dictum; tego, texi, tectum; traho, traxi, tractum; exstinguo,
exstinxi, exstinctum; coquo, coxi, coctum.* (Compare § 134.)
The following deviate from this rule; in some of them the
stem increasing in the present, and the simple stem reappearing in the supine:—

fingo,	*finxi,*	*fictum,*	feign.
mingo,	*minxi,*	*mictum,*	make water.
pingo,	*pinxi,*	*pictum,*	paint.
stringo,	*strinxi,*	*strictum,*	press close.
ăgo,	*ēgi,*	*actum,*	do, drive, act. In compounds the *a* is

generally changed into *ĭ*—as *abĭgo, redĭgo;* but *perăgo* and *cir-
cumăgo. Dēgo* is contracted for *deago,* and *cōgo* for *coago,* perf.
coegi, sup. *coactum.*

frango,	*frēgi,*	*fractum,*	break.
ĭco (ĭcio?),	*īci,*	*ĭctum,*	strike.
lĕgo,	*lēgi,*	*lectum,*	gather, read. In compounds the

e is sometimes changed into *i*—as *intelligo, colligo, deligo, eligo.*

linquo,	*līqui,*	*(līctum),*	leave.
vinco,	*vīci,*	*victum,*	conquer
fīgo,	*fixi,*	*fixum,*	fasten.
mergo,	*mersi,*	*mersum,*	dip.
spargo,	*sparsi,*	*sparsum,*	scatter.
tergo,	*tersi,*	*tersum,*	wipe.
vergo,	——	——	incline towards [*parsi.*
parco,	*pĕperci,*	*parsum,*	spare. The perfect sometimes
pungo,	*pŭpŭgi,*	*punctum,*	prick. The compounds make the
			perfect regularly *punxi.*
tango,	*tĕtĭgi,*	*tactum,*	touch. Compounds change the *a*

into *i*—as *attingo, attĭgi, attactum.*

pango, {*panxi,* or *panctum,* or fix in. This verb, in the sense of
{*pēgi,* *pactum,* 'bargain,' makes the perfect
pĕpĭgi, and the supine *pactum.* Compounds regularly have the perfect *pēgi,* and the supine *pactum.*

§ 158. Verbs in *do* form their perfect in *si,* and the supine in *sum,* the *d* being thrown out before these terminations for euphonic reasons—as *claudo, clausi, clausum;* but there are many in which this general rule is not complied with:—

cēdo,	*cessi,*	*cessum,*	move, yield.
accendo,	*accendi,*	*accensum,*	kindle. So also the other com-

pounds of *cando,* which itself is not used.

cūdo,	*cūdi,*	*cūsum*	forge, stamp.
defendo,	*defendi,*	*defensum,*	ward off, defend.
ĕdo,	*ēdi,*	*ēsum,*	eat. For the peculiar conjuga-
fundo,	*fūdi,*	*fūsum,*	pour. [tion of *ĕdo,* see § 172.
mando,	*(mandi),*	*mansum,*	chew.
prehendo,	*prehendi,*	*prehensum,*	sometimes *prendi, prensum,* seize.
scando,	*scandi,*	*scansum,*	climb. Compare *accendo* above.
strīdo,	*strīdi,*	——	whistle, hiss. (Sometimes *strī-*
rŭdo,	{*rudīvi,* and ——		bray. [*deo, stridēre.*)
	{*rudi,*		
findo,	*fĭdi,*	*fissum,*	split.
frendo,	——	{*fressum,* or	gnash.
		{*fresum,*	
pando,	*pandi,*	{*passum,* or	spread open. *Dispando* has only
		{*pansum,*	*dispansum.*
scindo,	*scĭdi,*	*scissum,*	cut.
sīdo,	*sēdi (sīdi),*	*sessum,*	seat myself.
cădo,	*cĕcĭdi,*	*cāsum,*	fall. In compounds there is no

reduplication, and the *ă* is changed into *ĭ*—as *concĭdo, occĭdo, recĭdo.*

caedo,	*cecīdi,*	*caesum,*	cause to fall. In compounds there

is no reduplication, and the *ae* is changed into *ī*—as *concīdo, concīsi, concīsum.* [reduplication.

pendo,	*pĕpendi,*	*pensum,*	weigh. Its compounds have no

tendo,   *tĕtendi,* $\begin{cases} tensum, \text{or} \\ tentum, \end{cases}$ stretch. Its compounds have no reduplication, and usually have
tentum; though some, as *extendo* and *retendo,* have both forms.

tundo,   *tŭtŭdi,* $\begin{cases} tūsum, \text{or} \\ tunsum, \end{cases}$ beat. Its compounds generally have *tūsum.*

crēdo,   *crēdĭdi,*   *crēdĭtum,*   believe, intrust.

do in compounds following the third conjugation—that is, in those compounded with a monosyllabic preposition—make the perfect in *dĭdi,* and supine *dĭtum*—as *addo, addĭdi, addĭtum; condo, condĭdi, condĭtum.* The double compound *abscondo* has usually *abscondi,* and rarely *abscondidi.* Compare § 152.

fīdo,   *fīsus sum,*   trust (a semideponent).

§ 159. Verbs ending in *lo* never form the perfect and supine according to the general rule ; some make them according to the second conjugation, perfect *ui,* supine *tum* or *ĭtum;* and some present other irregularities :—

ălo,   *ălui,* $\begin{cases} ăltum, \text{or} \\ ălĭtum, \end{cases}$ nourish.
cŏlo,   *cŏlui,*   *cultum,*   cultivate, till.
consŭlo,   *consului,*   *consultum,*   give advice, or ask for advice.
occŭlo,   *occului,*   *occultum,*   conceal.
mŏlo,   *molui,*   *molĭtum,*   grind.
antecello,   *antecellui,*   ————   excel. From the obsolete *cello;*
in like manner are conjugated *excello* and *praecello.*
fallo,   *fĕfelli,*   *falsum,*   deceive.
pello,   *pĕpŭli,*   *pulsum,*   thrust. The compounds have no
percello,   *percŭli,*   *perculsum,*   strike down.   [reduplication.
psallo,   *psalli,*   ————   play a stringed instrument.
vello,   *velli(vulsi),*   *vulsum,*   pull or pinch. The compounds
have *velli, vulsum;* but *avello* and *evello* have both *avelli* and *evelli,* and also *avulsi* and *evulsi.*
tollo,   *sustŭli,*   *sublātum,*   lift up. Perfect and supine are
here formed from a different stem, with the preposition *sub.* See § 173.

§ 160. Verbs ending in *mo* make their perfect regularly in *si,* and their supine in *tum ;* but a euphonic *p* is generally inserted before these terminations—as *sumo, sumpsi, sumptum ; como, compsi, comptum.* The following, however, do not comply with this rule :—

frĕmo,   *frĕmui,*   *fremĭtum,*   make a noise.
gĕmo,   *gĕmui,*   *gemĭtum,*   groan.
vŏmo,   *vŏmui,*   *vomĭtum,*   vomit.
trĕmo,   *trĕmui,*   ————   tremble.
ĕmo,   *ēmi,*   *emptum,*   buy. Its compounds, with the
exception of *coëmo,* change *ĕ* into *ĭ*—as *adĭmo, adēmi, ademptum.* So also *exĭmo, interĭmo, perĭmo, redĭmo.*
premo,   *pressi,*   *pressum,*   press.

§ 161. Verbs ending in *no* never follow the general rules for the formation of the perfect and supine, with the exception of *temno* and its compounds, which make the perfect *tempsi* and the supine *temptum* — as *contemno, contempsi, contemptum.* The others must be remembered separately: —

căno,   cĕcĭni,   cantum,   sing.   Among its compounds, *concĭno* and *occĭno* (also *occăno*) make their perfect *concinui* and *occinui,* and the supine *concentum* and *occentum.* The other compounds of *cano* have neither perfect nor supine.
gigno,   gĕnui,   genitum,   beget.
pōno,   pŏsui,   positum,   place.
lĭno,   {*lēvi,* / *livi,*}   *lĭtum,*   {anoint, daub. Another form is *linio,* / *linire.*}
sĭno,   sīvi,   sĭtum,   allow, permit. *Desino,* perf. *desivi,* admits of contraction, *desii, desisti, desiit, desieram,* &c. *Siverim,* &c. is contracted into *sirim, siris, sirit, sirint.*
cerno,   crēvi,   (crētum),   separate, perceive.
sperno,   sprēvi,   sprētum,   despise.
sterno,   strāvi,   strātum,   disdain, slight.

§ 162.   Verbs in *ro* generally form the perfect and supine in an irregular manner, but it must be observed that when *r* is changed into *s,* this cannot be regarded as an irregularity, *s* and *r* being convertible in so many instances: —

gĕro,   gessi,   gestum,   carry.
ūro,   ussi,   ustum,   burn.
curro,   cŭcurri,   cursum,   run, race.
fŭro,   ———   ———   rage.
quaero,   quaesīvi,   quaesītum,   seek, pray. For *quaero* and *quaerimus* we also find the ancient forms *quaeso* and *quaesumus.* See § 184.
sĕro,   sĕrui,   sertum,   twist, arrange.
sĕro,   sēvi,   sătum,   sow. Its compounds make the supine in *ĭtum* instead of *ătum* — as *consĕro, consēvi, consĭtum.*
tĕro,   trīvi,   trītum,   rub.
verro,   verri,   versum,   sweep.

§ 163.   Verbs in *so* (*xo*) usually form their perfect in *ui,* like those of the second conjugation, and in the supine they generally drop the connecting vowel *i* before *tum:* —

vīso,	*vīsi,*	———	visit.
depso,	*depsui,*	*depstum,*	knead.
pinso,	{*pinsui,* or / *pinsi,*}	{*pinsĭtum,* / *pinsum,* / *pistum,*}	pound.
texo,	*texui,*	*textum,*	weave.

Those in *esso* make their perfect in *īvi* and the supine in *ĭtum,* as if they belonged to the fourth conjugation: —

arcesso,   arcessīvi,   arcessītum,   {send for. The passive infinitive
accerso,   accersīvi,   accersītum,   is sometimes *arcessiri.*}
capesso,   capessīvi,   capessītum,   take away.
facesso,   facessīvi,   facessītum,   cause.
lacesso,   lacessīvi,   lacessītum,   provoke.
incesso,   incessīvi,   ———   attack. There is a perfect *incessi,* which, however, may be derived from *incedo* as well as from *incesso.*

§ 164. In many verbs ending in *to* the *t* is only an increase of the stem in the present, and is accordingly thrown out in the perfect and supine, the original stem ending in *c;* as —

flecto,	*flexi,*	*flexum,*	bend.
necto,	{ *nexi,* or { *nexui,*	*nexum,*	tie, knit.
plecto,	——	——	punish, twist; in the latter sense [we find a part. perf. pass. *plexus.*
pecto,	{ *pexi,* and { *pexui,*	*pexum,*	comb.

These four verbs must be considered regular, but the follow ing are not reducible to any rule :—

mĕto,	*messui,*	*messum,*	reap.
mitto,	*mīsi,*	*missum,*	send.
pĕto,	{ *pĕtīvi,* or { *pĕtii,*	*petītum,*	seek, aim at.
sisto,	*stĭti,*	*stătum,*	cause to stand. In its intransitive

meaning, 'I stand,' its perfect is *stĕti* (from *sto, stare*), and the supine *stātum.*

sterto,	*stertui,*	——	snore.
verto,	*verti,*	*versum,*	turn.

§ 165. In verbs ending in *sco,* the *sco* either belongs to the stem, and is consequently retained in conjugation, or *sco* is a derivative syllable, by means of which verbs are derived from verbs, substantives, and adjectives. This class of derivative verbs are called *inchoatives,* and denote actions or conditions as beginning to take place. There are but few verbs in which the *sc* belongs to the stem, and which are not derivatives : —

disco,	*dĭdĭci,*	——	learn.
posco,	*pŏposci,*	——	demand.
glisco,	——	——	increase.

Real inchoatives take the perfect of the verbs from which they are formed — as *incalesco,* perf. *incalui* (from *caleo*)*; ingemisco, ingemui* (from *gemo); deliquesco, delicui* (from *liqueo,* perf. *liqui* or *licui*). Few inchoatives have the supine of the verbs from which they are derived. Some, which are derived from adjectives in *us, a, um,* or *er, a, um,* form a perfect in *ui,* but have no supine — as *maturesco* (grow ripe), perf. *maturui; obmutesco* (grow dumb), *obmutui; percrebresco* (become frequent), *percrebrui;* and so also *evilesco, evilŭi,* though it is derived from the adjective *vilis.* *Irraucesco* (grow hoarse, from *raucus*) makes the perfect irregularly *irrausi.* All others derived from adjectives in *is,* and many of those derived from adjectives in *us,* have neither perfect nor supine.

The following inchoatives have also the supine of their simple verbs:—

coalesco,	coalui,	coalĭtum,	grow together (from *alo*).
concupisco,	concupīvi,	concupītum,	desire strongly (from *cupio*).
convalesco,	convalui,	convalĭtum,	grow well, strong (from *valeo*).
exardesco,	exarsi,	exarsum,	begin to blaze (from *ardeo*).
inveterasco,	inveteravi,	inveteratum,	grow old (from *invetero*).
obdormisco,	obdormīvi,	obdormītum,	fall asleep (from *dormio*).
revivisco,	revixi,	revictum,	revive (from *vivo*).

§ 166. The following verbs, though originally inchoatives, have lost their inchoative meaning, or are derived from simple verbs which are no longer in use, so that they may be regarded as simple verbs:—

adolesco,	adolēvi,	adultum,	grow up,) from the obsolete
exolesco,	exolēvi,	exolētum,	disappear,) [*oleo*, grow.
cresco,	crēvi,	crētum,	grow.
compesco,	compescui,	————	tame, subdue.
dispesco,	dispescui,	————	sever, separate.
hisco,	————	————	yawn.
nosco,	nōvi,	nōtum,	become acquainted. Compare

§ 179. Its compounds make the supine in *ĭtum*—as *agnosco*, *agnĭtum; cognosco*, *cognĭtum;* but *ignosco* (pardon) has *ignōtum.*

pasco,	pāvi,	pastum,	feed, or give food.
quiesco,	quiēvi,	quiētum,	rest.
suesco,	suēvi,	suētum,	accustom myself. [*scīre*).
scisco,	scīvi,	scītum,	ordain, sanction (from *scio*,

§ 167. The following deponent verbs also form their supine, or rather their perfect participle, more or less differently from the general rule. We arrange them in the order observed in regard to the active verbs—namely, according to the final letters of their stem:—

fruor,	{ fruitus, and { fructus sum,	enjoy (part. fut. *fruiturus*).
grădior,	gressus sum,	proceed.
aggrĕdior,	aggressus sum,	attack.
lĭquor,	————	melt.
lŏquor,	lŏcutus sum,	speak.
mŏrior,	mortuus sum,	die (part. fut. *morĭturus*).
nĭtor,	{ nixus, or { nisus sum,	lean upon, strive.
pătior,	passus sum,	suffer.
amplector, and } complector, }	amplexus, and } complexus sum, }	embrace (from *plecto*).
quĕror,	questus sum,	complain.
ringor,	————	gnash the teeth.
ūtor,	ūsus sum,	use. [more common.
ăpiscor,	aptus sum,	obtain; *adipiscor, adeptus sum*, is
defetiscor,	defessus sum,	grow weary.
expergiscor,	experrectus sum,	awake. [adjective, 'angry.'
irascor,	irātus sum,	am angry; *iratus*, however, is an

comminiscor,	*commentus sum,*	devise,	⎱ from *meniscor,* which
reminiscor,	——————	remember,	⎰ [is not used.
nanciscor,	⎧ *nactus,* or	obtain.	
	⎩ *nanctus sum,*		
nascor,	*nātus sum,*	am born (part. fut, *nascĭturus*).	
obliviscor,	*oblītus sum,*	forget.	
paciscor,	*partus sum,*	make a treaty.	
proficiscor,	*profectus sum,*	depart, travel.	
ulciscor,	*ultus sum,*	avenge.	
vescor,	——————	feed on.	
revertor,	*reversus sum,*	return.	
divertor,	——————	turn aside.	

CHAPTER XXVI.

VERBS OF THE FOURTH CONJUGATION FORMING THEIR PERFECT AND
SUPINE DIFFERENTLY FROM THE GENERAL RULE.

§ 168. It should be remembered that verbs of the fourth
conjugation make their perfect by adding to the stem *vi* foɪ
the perfect, and *tum* for the supine ; but the following form
the perfect in *si,* and the supine in *tum,* before which the *i* of
the stem is in many cases omitted :—

farcio,	*farsi,*	⎧ *fartum,* or	stuff. In compounds the *a* is changed
		⎩ *farctum,*	into *e*—as *refercio,refersi,refertum.*
fulcio,	*fulsi,*	*fultum,*	prop.
haurio,	*hausi,*	*haustum,*	draw (part. fut. *hausturus,* or *hausu-*
sancio,	*sanxi,*	⎧ *sanctum,* or	decree. [*rus*).
		⎩ *sancītum,*	
sarcio,	*sarsi,*	*sartum,*	patch.
sentio,	*sensi,*	*sensum,*	feel.
saepio,	*saepsi,*	*saeptum,*	hedge in ; is also spelled *sepio.*
vincio,	*vinxi,*	*vinctum,*	bind.

The following present various irregularities :—

amicio,	——————	*amictum,*	clothe ; the perf. is sometimes *ami-*
cio,	*cīvi,*	*cĭtum,*	summon, call. Comp. §153. [*cīvi.*
eo,	*ivi,*	*ĭtum,*	go. Compare § 175.
ferio,	——————	——————	strike.
ăpĕrio,	*ăpĕrui,*	*ăpertum,*	open.
rĕpĕrio,	*rĕpĕri,*	*rĕpertum,*	find ; the perfect is better spelled
reppĕri.	So also *comperio, compĕri, compertum.*		
sălio,	⎧ *sălui,* or	*saltum,*	leap. In compounds the *a* is changed
	⎩ *sălii,*		into *i*—as *desilio, desilui,* or *de-*
			silii, desultum.
sĕpĕlɪo,	*sĕpĕlīvi,*	*sĕpultum,*	bury. There is also a perfect *sepeli,*
vĕnio,	*vēni,*	*ventum,*	come. [for *sepelivi.*

Desiderative verbs ending in *urio* — that is, derivative verbs denoting a desire to do that which is implied in the simple verb — have neither perfect nor supine — as *dormiturio*, wish to sleep, or am sleepy; *esurio*, want to eat. The same is the case with some derivatives from adjectives — as *caecutio* (from *caecus*), am blind; *ineptio* (from *ineptus*), am silly.

§ 169. There are also some deponents of the fourth conjugation which form their supine, or rather the past participle, differently from the general rule: —

assentior,	*assensus sum*,	assent.
expĕrior,	*expertus sum*,	experience.
mētior,	*mensus sum*,	measure.
oppĕrior,	{ *oppertus*, or *opperĭtus sum*,	wait for.
ordior,	*orsus sum*,	begin. [vum *oriundus*).
orior,	*ortus sum*,	rise (fut. part. *orĭtūrus*, and gerundi-

Note. In the present indicative, *orior* is inflected according to the third conjugation—as *orĕris*, *orĭtur*, *orĭmur;* in the imperfect subjunctive we find both *orērer* and *orīrer*. The same is the case with the compounds *coorior* and *exorior;* but *adorior* entirely follows the fourth conjugation. Poets and some prose writers make *potior* in the present indicative, and the imperfect subjunctive, follow the third instead of the fourth conjugation—as *potĭtur*, *potĭmur*, *potĕrer*, *potĕreris*, &c. instead of the regular forms *potītur*, *potīmur*, *potīrer*, *potīreris*, &c.

CHAPTER XXVII.

IRREGULAR VERBS.

§ 170. Irregular verbs are those which not only form their perfect and supine in an unusual manner, but also differ from the ordinary practice in the manner in which the terminations are added to the stem. Most of these irregularities, however, arise from euphonic change, from syncope and contraction, and lastly, from the fact that different tenses of one verb are formed from different stems, as we have seen in the case of the verb *esse*. (See § 137.) The number of irregular verbs is eleven—*sum, possum, edo, fero, volo, nolo, malo, eo, queo, nequeo,* and *fio*, to which, however, their derivatives and compounds must be added, which are conjugated like the simple verbs.

§ 171. The verb *possum* (I am able, or I can) is a compound of *pot* (from *potis, pote*, able) and *sum*, the *t* before *s* being assimilated to *s* for the sake of euphony, but reappearing wherever *sum* begins with a vowel; in the perfect, and the tenses derived from it, the *f* (of *fuo*) is thrown out. Its conjugation accordingly is as follows: —

INDICATIVE.   SUBJUNCTIVE.

PRESENT.

Sing. *pos-sum*, I am able, I can
     pŏt-ĕs
     pŏt-est.
Plur. *pos-sŭmus*
     pŏt-estis
     pos-sunt.

Sing. *pos-sim*, I may be able
     pos-sīs
     pos-sĭt.
Plur. *pos-sīmus*
     pos-sītis
     pos-sint.

IMPERFECT.

Sing. *pŏt-ĕram*, I was able, or I
     could
     pŏt-ĕrās
     pŏt-ĕrat.
Plur. *pŏt-ĕrāmus*
     pŏt-ĕrātis
     pŏt-ĕrant.

Sing. *pos-sem*, I was, might, or
     should be, able
     pos-sēs
     pos-sĕt.
Plur. *pos-sēmus*
     pos-sētis
     pos-sent.

FUTURE.

Sing. *pŏt-ĕro*, I shall be able
     pot-ĕris
     pot-ĕrit.
Plur. *pot-ĕrĭmus*
     pot-ĕrĭtis
     pot-ĕrunt.

The subjunctive is wanting.

PERFECT.

Sing. *pŏt-ui*, I was, have been,
     able
     pot-uistī
     pot-uit.
Plur. *pot-uimus*
     pot-uistīs
     pot-uĕrunt, or *ēre.*

Sing. *pŏt-uĕrim*, I may have been
     able
     pot-uĕris
     pot-uĕrĭt.
Plur. *pot-uĕrĭmus*
     pot-uĕrĭtis
     pot-uĕrint.

PLUPERFECT.

Sing. *pŏt-uĕram*, I had been able
     pot-uĕrās
     pot-uĕrat.
Plur. *pot-uĕrāmus*
     pot-uĕrātis
     pot-uĕrant.

Sing. *pŏt-uissem*, I had, should
     or might have been able
     pot-uissēs
     pot-uissĕt.
Plur. *pot-uissēmus*
     pot-uissētis
     pot-uissent.

FUTURE PERFECT.

Sing. *pŏt-uĕro*, I shall have been
     able
     pot-uĕris
     pot-uĕrĭt.
Plur. *pot-uĕrĭmus*
     pot-uĕrĭtis
     pot-uĕrint.

The subjunctive is wanting

The imperative is entirely wanting.

INFINITIVE.

Present, *pos-se*, to be able.
Perfect, *pot-uisse*, to have been able.

PARTICIPLE.

Potens, is used only as an adjective, 'powerful.'

Note. In ancient Latin we still find *potis sum, potis es, potis est*, for *possum, potes, potest, potis* being the same in all genders and numbers. In common conversation the Romans also said *pote* for *potest*. The imperfect subjunctive *possem*, and the infinitive *posse*, are formed by syncope for *potessem* and *potesse*, and the latter of these forms actually occurs in early Latin. In the present subjunctive we also find *possiem, possies, possiet*, &c. for *possim*, &c. Compare § 137, note 3.

§ 172. The verb *ĕdo* (I eat) may be conjugated regularly after the third conjugation, perf. *ēdī*, sup. *ēsum*, inf. *ĕdĕre;* but in several of its forms a syncope is sometimes employed, in consequence of which they become like the corresponding tenses of the verb *sum*. The following are the tenses in which this resemblance occurs :—

INDICATIVE.	SUBJUNCTIVE.
PRESENT.	IMPERFECT.
Sing. *edo, edis* or *ēs, edit* or *ēst.*	Sing. *ederem* or *ēssem, ederes* or *ēsses, ederet* or *ēsset.*
Plur. *edimus, editis* or *ēstis, edunt.*	Plur. *ederemus* or *ēssemus, ederetis* or *ēssetis, ederent* or *ēssent.*

IMPERATIVE.	
PRESENT.	FUTURE.
Sing. *ede* or *ēs.*	Sing. *edito* or *ēsto.*
Plur. *edite* or *ēste.*	Plur. *edito* or *ēsto, editote* or *ēstote, edunto.*

INFINITIVE.

ĕdĕre or *ēsse.*

In the passive, the syncope takes place only in *editur, estur*, and *ederetur, ēssetur.*

Note. The same syncope occurs in the compounds of *edo*—as *comedo, comedis = comēs, comedit = comēst, comedĕre = comēsse*, &c. The *e* in all these syncopated forms was pronounced as long by nature, and not by position only.

§ 173. The irregularity of the verb *fĕro* (I bring, or bear), which properly belongs to the third conjugation, consists in its taking its perfect *tŭli* and its supine *lātum* from different words.   The tenses derived from these two forms, however, are perfectly regular ; but in the other tenses an irregularity occasionally occurs, which arises from the omission of the connecting vowel between the stem and termination, as will be seen in the following table :—

ACTIVE VOICE.

INDICATIVE.	SUBJUNCTIVE.

PRESENT.

Sing. *fĕr-o, fer-s, fer-t.* | Sing. *fĕr-am, fĕr-as, fĕr-at.*
Plur. *fĕr-ĭ-mus, fer-tis, fĕr-u-nt.* | Plur. *fĕr-āmus, fĕr-ātis, fĕr-ant.*

IMPERFECT.

Sing. *fer-ē-bam, fer-ē-bas, fer-ē-bat.* | Sing. *fer-rem, fer-res, fer-ret.*
Plur. *fer-ē-bamus, fer-ē-batis, fer-ē-bant.* | Plur. *fer-remus, fer-retis, fer-rent.*

FUTURE.

Sing. *fĕr-am, fĕr-ēs, fĕr-et.* | Sing. *la-turus (a, um) sim, sis, sit.*
Plur. *fĕr-ēmus, fĕr-ētis, fĕr-ent.* | Plur. *la-turi (ae, a) simus, sitis, sint.*

PERFECT.

Sing. *tŭl-i, tŭl-isti, tŭl-it.* | Sing. *tŭl-ĕrim, tŭl-ĕris, tŭl-ĕrit.*
Plur. *tŭl-imus, tŭl-istis, tŭl-ērunt* | Plur. *tŭl-ĕrĭmus, tŭl-ĕrĭtis, tŭl-ĕrint.*
or *ēre.*

PLUPERFECT.

Sing. *tŭl-ĕram, ĕras, ĕrat.* | Sing. *tŭl-issem, isses, isset.*
Plur. *tŭl-ĕrāmus, ĕrātis, ĕrant.* | Plur. *tŭl-issemus, issetis, issent.*

FUTURE PERFECT.

Sing. *tŭl-ĕro, ĕris, ĕrit.* | The subjunctive is wanting.
Plur. *tŭl-ĕrĭmus, ĕrĭtis, ĕrint.* |

IMPERATIVE.

PRESENT.	FUTURE.
Sing. *fer.*	Sing. *fer-to*
	fer-to.
Plur. *fer-te,*	Plur. *fer-tote*
	fer-unto.

INFINITIVE.

Present, *fer-re.*
Perfect, *tŭl-isse.*
Future, *lā-tūrum (am, um) esse.*

GERUND.

fer-endum, fer-endi, fer-endo.

SUPINE.

lā-tum and *lā-tū.*

PARTICIPLES.

Present, *fĕr-e-ns.*
Future, *lā-tūrus, a, um.*

PASSIVE VOICE.

INDICATIVE.   SUBJUNCTIVE.

PRESENT.

Sing. *fĕr-or, fer-ris, fer-tur.* | Sing. *fĕr-ar, āris, ātur.*
Plur. *fĕr-ĭ-mur, fĕr-ĭ-mini, fĕr-* | Plur. *fĕr-āmur, āmini, antur.*
    u-ntur.

IMPERFECT.

Sing. *fĕr-ē-bar bāris,* (or *bāre),* | Sing. *fer-rer, fer-rēris* (or *rēre),*
    bātur. | *fer-rētur.*
Plur. *fĕr-ē-bāmur, bāmini, ban-* | Plur. *fer rēmur, fer-rēmini, fer-*
    tur. | *rentur.*

FUTURE.

Sing. *fĕr-ar, ēris, ētur.*
Plur. *fĕr-ēmur, ēmini, entur.* | The subjunctive is wanting.

PERFECT.

Sing. *lā-tus (a, um) sum, es, est.* | Sing. *lā-tus (a, um) sim, sis, sit.*
Plur. *lā-ti (ae,a) sumus,estis,sunt.* | Plur. *lā-ti (ae, a) simus, sitis, sint.*

PLUPERFECT.

Sing. *lā-tus (a,um) eram,eras,erat.* | Sing. *lā-tus (a, um) essem,* &c.
Plur. *lā-ti (ae, a) eramus, eratis,* | Plur. *lā-ti (ae, a) essemus,* &c.
    erant.

FUTURE PERFECT.

Sing. *lā-tus (a, um) ero,* &c.
Plur. *lā-ti (ae, a) erimus,* &c. | The subjunctive is wanting.

IMPERATIVE.

PRESENT.   FUTURE.

Sing. *fer-re.* | Sing. *fer-tor*
     | *fer-tor.*
Plur. *fĕr-ēmini.* | Plur. *fer-u-ntur.*

140

LATIN GRAMMAR.

INFINITIVE.

Present, *fer-ri.*
Perfect, *lā-tum (am, um) esse.*
Future, *lā-tum iri.*

PARTICIPLES.

Perfect,   *lā-tus, a, um.*
Gerundive,   *fer-e-ndus, a, um.*

Note. Like *fĕro* are conjugated all its compounds; but it must be observed that the final consonant of prepositions with which it may be compounded undergoes certain euphonic changes—as *affero* (from *ad* and *fero*), *attuli, allatum; aufero* (from *ab* and *fero*), *abstuli, ablatum, auferre; offero* (from *ob* and *fero*), *obtuli, oblatum; suffero* (from *sub* and *fero*), *sustuli, sublatum* (used as the perfect and supine of the verb *tollo*); *differo* (from *dis* and *fero*), *distuli, dilatum.* When the preposition ends in a vowel, in *r, m,* or *ns,* no such change occurs- as *defero, detuli, delatum; circumfero, circumtuli, circumlatum; trans fero, transtuli, translatum.*

§ 174. *Vŏlo* (I will) is a simple verb; but *nōlo* (I will not) is composed of *ne* or *non,* and *volo;* and *mălo* (I will rather) of *magis* or *mage,* and *volo,* so that it should properly be *mavŏlo.* They are irregular only in the tenses formed from the present and the infinitive.

INDICATIVE.

PRESENT.

Sing.	*vŏl-o*	*nōl-o*	*māl-o*
	vīs	*non vīs*	*māvīs*
	vul-t	*non vul-t*	*māvul-t.*
Plur.	*vŏl-ŭ-mus*	*nōl-ŭ-mus*	*māl-ŭ-mus*
	vul-tis	*non vul-tis*	*māvul-tis*
	vŏl-u-nt	*nōl-u-nt*	*māl-u-nt.*

IMPERFECT.

| *vŏl-ē-bam, bas, &c.* | *nōl-ē-bam, bas, &c.* | *māl-ē-bam, bas, &c.* |

FUTURE.

| *vŏl-am, es, et, &c.* | *nōl-am, es, et, &c.* | *māl-am, es, &c.* |

PERFECT.

| *vŏl-ui, uisti, &c.* | *nōl-ui, uisti, &c.* | *māl-ui, uisti, &c.* |

PLUPERFECT.

| *vŏl-uĕram, uĕras, &c.* | *nōl-uĕram, uĕras, &c.* | *māl-uĕram, ueras.* |

FUTURE PERFECT.

| *vŏl-uĕro, uĕris, &c.* | *nōl-uĕro, uĕris, &c.* | *māl-uĕro, uĕris.* |

SUBJUNCTIVE.

PRESENT.

Sing.	vĕl-i-m	nōl-i-m	māl-i-m
	vĕl-ī-s	nōl-ī-s	māl-ī-s
	vĕl-i-t	nōl-i-t	māl-i-t.
Plur.	vĕl-ī-mus	nōl-ī-mus	māl-ī-mus
	vĕl-ī-tis	nōl-ī-tis	māl-ī-tis
	vĕl-i-nt	nōl-i-nt	māl-i-nt.

IMPERFECT.

vel-lem, ēs, et, &c.   *nol-lem, es, et, &c.*   *mal-lem, es, et, &c.*

PERFECT.

vŏl-uĕrim, ueris, &c.   *nōl-uĕrim, uĕris, &c.*   *māl-uĕrim, uĕris, &c.*

PLUPERFECT.

vŏl-uissem, uisses, &c.   *māl-uissem, uisses, &c.*   *māl-uissem, uisses, &c.*

IMPERATIVE.

PRESENT.

——————   *nōl-ī, nōl-ītĕ.*   ——————

FUTURE.

nōl-ī-to, nōl-ī-to; nōl-ī-tōte, nōl-u-nto.

INFINITIVE.

Present, *vel-lĕ*,	*nol-lĕ*,	*mal-lĕ*.
Perfect, *vol-uisse*,	*nōl-uisse,*	*māl-uisse.*

PARTICIPLES.

vŏl-e-ns.   *nōl-e-ns.*   ——————

Note. More ancient forms for *vult* and *vultis* are *volt* and *voltis*. The full forms *mavŏlo, mavŏlunt, mavelim,* and *mavolem* or *mavellem,* and others, likewise occur in early writers instead of *malo, malunt, malim,* and *mallem.* So also *nevis, nevult, nevelle,* for *non vis, non vult, nolle.*

§ 175. The verb *eo* (I go) belongs to the fourth conjugation, and is almost quite regular. Its stem consists of a simple *i*, which before *a, o,* and *u,* is changed into *e;* the imperfect indicative is formed without the connecting vowel *e;* and the future ends in *bo* instead of *am.*

INDICATIVE.	SUBJUNCTIVE.
PRESENT.	
Sing. *e-o, ī-s, ĭ-t.*	Sing. *e-am, e-ās, e-at.*
Plur. *ī-mus, ī-tis, e-unt.*	Plur. *e-āmus, e-ātis, e-ant.*

INDICATIVE.   SUBJUNCTIVE.

IMPERFECT.

Sing. *ī-bam, ī-bas, ī-bat,* &c. | Sing. *ī-rem, ī-res, ī-ret,* &c.

FUTURE.

ī-bo, ī-bis, ī-bit, &c. | *ī-tūrus (a, um) sim, sis,* &c.

PERFECT.

i-vī, ī-visti, ī-vit, &c. | *ī-verim, ī-vĕris, ī-vĕrit,* &c.

PLUPERFECT.

ī-vĕram, ī-vĕras, ī-vĕrat, &c. | *ī-vissem, ī-visses, ī-visset,* &c.

FUTURE PERFECT.

ī-vĕro, ī-vĕris, ī-vĕrit, &c. | The subjunctive is wanting.

IMPERATIVE.

PRESENT.   FUTURE.

Sing. *ī.*   Sing. *ī-to*
                                 ī-to.
Plur. *ī-te.*   Plur. *ī-tote*
                                 e-unto.

INFINITIVE.

Present, *ī-re.*
Perfect, *ī-visse.*
Future, *ĭ-tūrum (am, um) esse.*

GERUND.

e-u-ndum, e-u-ndi, e-u-ndo.

SUPINE.

i-tum, ĭ-tu.

PARTICIPLES.

Present, *i-e-ns;* gen. *e-u-ntis.*
Future, *ĭ-tūrus, a, um.*

As *eo* is an intransitive verb, it has a passive only in the third person singular — that is, it has an impersonal passive *ī-tur, ī-bātur, ī-bitur, ĭ-tum est, ĭ-tum erat,* &c. *e-atur, ī-retur,* &c. *e-u-ndum est, ī-ri.*

In like manner are conjugated all the compounds of *eo;* but in the perfect *īvi, ivisti,* &c. the endings are generally contracted into *ii, iisti,* or *isti*—as *abeo,* perf. *abii, abiisti,* or *abisti; redeo,* perf. *redii, rediisti,* or *redisti, redieram, rediissem,* or *redissem,* &c. Some of these compounds have a transitive meaning, and accordingly have a complete passive voice—such as *ïdeo, ineo, praetereo.*

Note 1. Some compounds of *eo* occasionally make their future in *um* instead of *bo*—as *redeam, redies; abies, abiet.* Instead of the gerund *abeundi* we sometimes find *abiendi.*

2. Among the compounds of *eo* two deserve especial notice—*vēneo* (I am sold), *ambio* (I go round). The former, which has a passive meaning, is composed of *venum* and *eo*, which expression is in fact often used, and takes the place of the passive of *vendo* (that is, *venum do*), I sell. It is conjugated like the simple *eo*, except that it sometimes makes its imperfect indicative *veniēbam*, instead of *venībam;* but it has neither imperative, nor gerund, nor participles.

Ambio is conjugated regularly according to the fourth conjugation— as *ambiunt, ambiam, ambiebam* (also *ambibam*), *ambient* (also *ambibunt*), *ambiendum, ambiens,* genitive *ambientis.*

§ 176. The verbs *queo* (I can) and *nequeo* (I cannot) are both conjugated like *eo*—perfect *quīvi* and *nequīvi,* supine *quĭtum* and *nequĭtum,* infinitive *quīre* and *nequīre;* but neither of them have an imperative, a gerund, or a future participle.

Note. In the present indicative we also find *non quis* and *non quit* for *nequis* and *nequit.* In the early language, *queo* and *nequeo* were sometimes used in the passive form, when joined to another passive verb, and such constructions are still found in Plautus, Terence, Lucretius, and Sallust—as *forma nosci non quita est,* 'the form could not be recognised;' *ulcisci nequitur,* 'there is no possibility of taking revenge.' *Queo* and *nequeo* are, on the whole, used much more rarely than *possum* and *non possum;* and *queo* scarcely ever occurs except in negative sentences.

§ 177. *Fio* (I become, or am made) is a verb of the fourth conjugation, and presents but few irregularities, except that its participle perfect, and consequently its compound tenses, are taken from *facio,* to which it supplies the place of a passive. Its stem is *fĭ.*

INDICATIVE.	SUBJUNCTIVE.
PRESENT	
Sing. *fĭ-o, fĭ-s, fĭ-t.*	Sing. *fĭ-am, fĭ-ās, fĭ-at.*
Plur. *fĭ-mus, fĭ-tis, fĭ-u-nt.*	Plur. *fĭ-āmus, fĭ-ātis, fĭ-ant.*
IMPERFECT.	
Sing. *fĭ-ē-bam, fĭ-ē-bās, fĭ-ē-bat.*	Sing. *fĭ-ĕ-rem, fĭ-e-res, fĭ-e-ret.*
Plur. *fĭ-ē-bāmus, fĭ-ē-bātis, fĭ-ē-bant.*	Plur. *fĭ-ĕ-rēmus, fĭ-ĕ-rētis, fĭ-ĕ-rent.*
FUTURE.	
Sing. *fĭ-am, fĭ-ēs, fĭ-et.*	The subjunctive is wanting.
Plur. *fĭ-ēmus, fĭ-ētis, fĭ-ent.*	
PERFECT.	
fac-tus (a, um) sum, es, &c.	*fac-tus (a, um) sim, sis,* &c.

INDICATIVE.	SUBJUNCTIVE.

PLUPERFECT.

fac-tus (*a, um*) *eram, eras,* &c.	*fac-tus* (*a, um*) *essem, esses,* &c.

FUTURE PERFECT.

fac-tus (*a, um*) *ero, eris,* &c.	The subjunctive is wanting.

IMPERATIVE.

PRESENT.	FUTURE.
Sing. *fĭ.*	Is wanting.
Plur. *fĭ-te.*	

INFINITIVE.

Present, *fĭ-ĕrī.*
Perfect, *fac-tum* (*am, um*) *esse.*
Future, *fac-tum, iri.*

PARTICIPLES.

Present is wanting.
Perfect,   *fac-tus, a, um.*
Gerundive, *fac-i-e-ndus.*

Note. The *ī* ın *fĭo* is long throughout, even when followed by another vowel ; but it is short in *fĭt,* in the infinitive present *fĭeri,* and in the imperfect subjunctive *fĭerem, fĭeres,* &c. In regard to the compounds of *fĭo,* see § 155, under *facio. Confĭo* and *defĭo* are used chiefly as impersonal passives—*confĭt, confĭat, confĭeret;* and *defĭo* has only the forms *defĭt, defĭat,* and *defĭunt. Infĭt* is used only in this one form.

CHAPTER XXVIII.

DEFECTIVE VERBS.

§ 178. We have already had occasion to notice many verbs which had either no supine, or no perfect, or neither; and among the irregular verbs there are some which take certain tenses from different words, and of which certain tenses are not used. All such verbs are, strictly speaking, defectives. But we shall here confine ourselves to those which have no present, and of which only certain isolated forms occur in Latin authors—these are *coepī, mĕmĭnī, ōdī, nōvī, ajo, inquam, fārĭ, cĕdo, quaeso;* the imperatives, *ăvē, ăpăgĕ, salvē, vălē,* and *ovāre.*

§ 179. The four verbs *coepī* (I begin), *mĕmĭnī* (I remember), *ōdī* (I hate), *nōvī* (I know), are in reality perfects, the presents of which are not in use, with the exception of *nōvi*, which is derived from *nosco* (I become acquainted). Their presents must have signified the beginning of a state or action, as *nosco* denotes the beginning of knowledge; hence these perfects have the meaning of a present; for *nōvi*, 'I have become acquainted,' is equivalent to 'I know.' These four perfects, then, having the meaning of a present, the pluperfect has that of an ordinary imperfect, and the future perfect that of an ordinary future. They have, of course, with very few exceptions, only those tenses which are derived from the perfect; and their conjugation is quite regular.

INDICATIVE.

PERFECT.

coepī.	*mĕmĭn-ī.*	*ōd-ī.*	*nōv-ī.*
coep-istī.	*mĕmĭn-istī.*	*ōd-istī.*	*nōv-istī.*
coep-it, &c.	*mĕmĭn-it,* &c.	*ōd-it,* &c.	*nōv-it,* &c.

PLUPERFECT.

coep-ĕram.	*mĕmĭn-ĕram.*	*ōd-ĕram.*	*nōv-ĕram.*

FUTURE PERFECT.

coep-ĕro.	*mĕmĭn-ĕro.*	*ōd-ĕro.*	*nōv-ĕro.*

SUBJUNCTIVE.

PERFECT.

coep-ĕrim.	*mĕmĭn-ĕrim.*	*ōd-ĕrim.*	*nōv-ĕrim.*

PLUPERFECT.

coep-issem.	*mĕmĭn-issem.*	*ōd-issem.*	*nōv-issem.*

IMPERATIVE.

FUTURE.

Sing. *mĕmen-to.* | Plur. *mĕmen-tŏte.*

INFINITIVE.

coep-isse.	*mĕmĭn-isse.*	*ōd-isse.*	*nōv-isse.*

PARTICIPLES.

PERFECT.

coep-tus.	———	*ō-sus* (obsolete). (*nō-tus.*)

FUTURE.

coep-tūrus.	———	*ō-sūrus.*	———

Note 1. The obsolete present of *ōdī* was *ōdio*, *odīre*, perf. *ōdīvi*; and of *coepi* it was *coepio*. *Memini* has a reduplication (from *meno*, *meniscor*). *Nōvi* has been included in this list merely because it clearly shows how a verb in the perfect can come to have the meaning of a present; for otherwise *nosco*, *nōvi*, *nōtum*, *noscere*, is quite regular.

2. *Coepi* also has a passive *coeptus* (*a*, *um*) *sum*, which is used in connection with other passive verbs—*domus aedificari coepta est* (the building of the house was commenced). Hence we have the forms *coeptus sum*, *coeptus eram*, *coeptus ero*, *coeptus essem*, *coeptum* (*am*, *um*) *esse*, &c.

3. The obsolete participle *ōsus*, which has an active meaning, 'one who hates,' occurs only in the compounds *exōsus* and *perōsus*. *Notus* is almost exclusively used as an adjective, 'known.'

§ 180. Of *ajo* (I say, say yes, or affirm), only the following forms occur:—

PRESENT INDICATIVE.	PRESENT SUBJUNCTIVE.
Sing. *ajo*, *aïs*, *aït*.	Sing. — *ajas*, *ajat*.
Plur. —— —— *ajunt*.	Plur. — — *ajant*.

IMPERFECT INDICATIVE.	PARTICIPLE PRESENT.
Sing. *ajebam*, *ajebas*, *ajebat*.	*ajens*, affirming.
Plur. *ajebamus*, *ajebatis*, *ajebant*.	

The imperative *ai* is obsolete, and the perfect *ait* is like the present.

Note. The imperfect *ajebam* is sometimes used by comic writers as a word of two syllables—*aibam*. In like manner *ais*, *ait*, and *ain*, (for *aisne*), are used as monosyllables. *Ait* is used only between the words of a quotation.

§ 181. *Inquam* (I say) is very defective, the following forms only occurring:—

INDICATIVE.

PRESENT.	IMPERFECT.
Sing. *inquam*, *inquis*, *inquit*.	Sing. ——— ——— *inquiēbat*.
Plur. *inquĭmus*, *inquĭtis*, *inquiunt*.	Plur. ——— ——— ———
PERFECT.	**FUTURE.**
Sing. ——— *inquisti*, *inquit*.	Sing. ——— *inquiēs*, *inquiet*.

IMPERATIVE.

Present Sing. *inque*.	Future Sing. *inquĭto*.

Note. *Inquam* is, like *ait*, used only between the words of a quotation—as *tum ille*, *nego*, *inquit*, *verum esse*, 'I deny, he then said, that it is true.' The present *inquam* is also used as a perfect, and thus supplies the place of the first person of the perfect, which is wanting.

§ 182. The verb *fārī* (to speak), a deponent of the first conjugation, is defective: there are, however, some compounds—as *affari*, *effari*, *praefari*, and *profari*, which have a few more forms; these we shall distinguish from the others by putting them in parentheses.

<table>
<tr><td align="center">INDICATIVE.</td><td align="center">SUBJUNCTIVE.</td></tr>
<tr><td colspan="2" align="center">PRESENT.</td></tr>
</table>

Sing. ———— ———— *fatur.*
Plur. (*famur, famini*) ———— | The subjunctive is wanting.

IMPERFECT.

(*fabar.*) | (*farer*, &c.)

FUTURE.

fabor (*faberis*), *fabitur.* | The subjunctive is wanting.

PERFECT.

fatus (*a, um*) *sum*, &c. | *fatus* (*a, um*) *sim*, &c.

PLUPERFECT.

fatus (*a, um*) *eram;* &c. | *fatus* (*a, um*) *essem*, &c.

IMPERATIVE.	INFINITIVE.	SUPINE.
Pres. *fare.*	Pres. *fari.*	*fatu.*

PARTICIPLES.

Present, *fantis, fanti, fantem, fante.*
Perfect, *fatus, a, um.*
Gerundive, *fandus, a, um.*

Note. Fari is, generally speaking, a poetical word, and rarely occurs in prose. From it is derived *infans* (infant); that is, 'a child that cannot yet speak.'

§ 183. *Cĕdŏ* is used only as an imperative in the sense of 'give' or 'tell'—as *cedo librum*, 'give up the book;' *cedo quid faciam*, 'tell me what I am to do.' The plural *cette* is obsolete. No other form of this verb occurs.

§ 184. *Quaeso* (I pray) and *quaesumus* (we pray) are only different in form from *quaero* and *quaerimus*. Both *quaeso* and *quaesumus* are, like the English 'pray,' inserted in a sentence —as *dic, quaeso, unde venias*, 'tell me, pray, whence you are coming.'

§ 185. The four imperatives *ăvē, ăpăgĕ, salvē, vălē*, are derived from the verbs *aveo* (I am inclined, desire), the Greek ἀπάγω (Lat. *abigo*), *salveo* (I am safe), and *valeo* (I am well or strong). They deserve to be noticed here, only on account of the peculiar meaning which they have assumed as imperatives :—

ăvē (or *have*), plural *avēte*, and the future imperative *avēto* (sometimes *avēre jubeo*), signify 'be greeted,' or 'good day,' 'I am glad to see you.'

ăpăgĕ is the imperative of the Greek verb ἀπάγω, and was used by the Romans in the sense of 'begone,' or 'be off.' Sometimes the pronoun *te* is added.

salvē, plural *salvēte*, and future *salvēto*, are used in the sense of 'hail!' or 'be welcome.'

vălē or *vălēte* signify 'farewell.'

§ 186. Of *ovare* (to rejoice, or celebrate a kind of triumph) there occur only *ovet, ovaret, ovandi, ovaturus, ovatus, ovandi,* and very frequently *ovans*.

CHAPTER XXIX.

IMPERSONAL VERBS.

§ 187. Impersonal verbs are those which are used only in the third person singular, and can have no substantive or substantive pronoun for their subject. They state only in a general way that something happens or takes place, and their subject in English is the indefinite 'it'—as *pluit*, it rains; *lĭcet*, it is permitted; *oportet*, it is a duty. Some verbs are always, or at least usually, impersonal, while others are used as impersonals only in a peculiar sense, being otherwise personal verbs — as *expĕdit*, it is useful (from *expedio*, I disentangle); *appăret*, it is clear (from *appareo*, I appear); *accĭdit*, it happens (from *accĭdo*, I fall in or upon a thing).

Among those which are always, or at least generally, used as impersonal verbs, are —

1. Those which denote the various states of the weather, as—

pluit, it rains.	*lucescit* and *illucescit*, it dawns.
ningit, it snows.	*fulgŭrat* and *fulmĭnat*, it lightens.
grandĭnat, it hails.	*tŏnat*, it thunders.
lapidat, or *lapidatum est*, stones fall from heaven.	*vesperascit* and *advesperascit*, it grows dark.

Note. Verbs of this kind are sometimes used personally — as *dies illucescit*, 'the day is dawning;' and this is more especially the case with those referring to thunder and lightning — as *tonat, fulgurat, fulminat*, with which we often find the subject *deus* or *Jupiter*, a god being conceived to produce those phenomena. In a figurative sense also these verbs may be used personally—as *tonat orator*, 'the orator thunders.'

2. Those describing certain states of the mind, and requiring the person in whom the state of mind exists in the accusative, as—

mĭsĕret (me), I pity, perf. *miseritum est, misertum est*, or *miseruit*.
pĭget (me), I regret, perf. *piguit*, or *pigitum est*.
poenĭtet (me), I repent, perf. *poenituit*.
pŭdet (me), I am ashamed, perf. *puduit*, or *puditum est*.
taedet (me), I am disgusted, perf. *pertaesum est*, and rarely *taeduit*.
oportet (me), it is necessary for me, I must, perf. *oportuit*.

Note. These verbs are always used impersonally, and have a whole clause or an infinitive for their subject — as ' I am ashamed that you have done this,' *pudet me te hoc fecisse;* for here *te hoc fecisse* forms the subject of *pudet.* Sometimes, however, we find a neuter pronoun in the singular as their subject, though never with *miseret, taedet,* and *oportet*—as *hoc me pudet,* ' I am ashamed of this ;' *quod poenitet me,* ' what makes me repent.' Instead of the impersonal *miseret* we may also use the personal *misereor,* which latter itself, however, is sometimes used impersonally — as *miseretur me tui,* ' I pity thee.'

3. Those which have no personal subject, but may have a substantive for their subject, and are also used in the third person plural with a neuter plural for their subject : —

dĕcet (me), it becomes me, perf. *dĕcuit*.
dĕdĕcet (me), it does not become me, *dĕdĕcuit*.
lĭbet or *lubet (mihi)*, I like, choose, perf. *lĭbuit*, or *lĭbĭtum est*.
lĭcet (mihi), I am permitted, perf. *lĭcuit*, or *lĭcĭtum est*.
lĭquet, it is obvious, perf. *licuit*.

Note. We may accordingly say, for example, *hic color eum decet,* this colour is becoming to him ;' *parva parvum decent,* ' small things are becoming a small man ;' *multa* or *omnia licent,* ' many or all things are permitted.'

§ 188. The second class of impersonal verbs contains those which in the third person singular assume a meaning, differing from that which they have in the other persons. They are accordingly personal verbs, and impersonal only in a peculiar sense. The most common among them are —

interest and *rēfert*, it is of importance to.
accĭdit ēvēnit, contingit, or *fit*, it happens.
accēdit, it is added to, or in addition to.
attĭnet and *pertĭnet (ad)*, it concerns or pertains to.
condūcit, it is conducive.
convĕnit, it suits.
constat, it is known or established.
expĕdit, it is expedient.

dēlectat and *jŭvat (me)*, it delights me.
fallit, fŭgit, and *praeterit (me)*, it escapes me.
plăcet, it pleases, perf. *plăcuit*, or *plăcitum est*.
praestat, it is better.
restat, it remains.
vacat, it is wanting.
est, in the sense of *licet*, it is permitted.

Impersonal verbs, as such, generally cannot have an impe-rative, a supine, or participle; but a participle perfect passive in the neuter gender often occurs, as we have seen above. *Libet, licet, poenĭtet,* and *pŭdet,* however, have participles, though with a somewhat altered meaning. *Libens* signifies 'willing;' *licens,* 'free' or 'unbridled;' *licĭtus,* 'permitted' or 'allowed' (also *licĭturum,* 'a thing which will be permitted'); *poenĭtens,* 'repentful;' *poenĭtendus,* 'to be repented;' *pŭdendus,* 'one to be ashamed of' (also the gerunds *poenĭtendum* and *pŭdendo*). Instead of the imperative, the subjunctive is used — as *pŭdeat te,* 'be ashamed!'

§ 189. The third person singular passive is very often used impersonally, especially of intransitive verbs, which other-wise have no passive. This mode of speaking, which can scarcely be imitated in English, is employed to indicate gene-rally that an action takes place, without attributing it to any definite person or persons — as *currĭtur,* 'running is going on,' or 'people run;' *vivĭtur,* 'people live;' *ventum est,* 'people came,' or 'have come;' *dormĭtur,* 'sleeping is going on,' or 'people sleep.' The compound tenses of such passives have the participle only in the neuter — as *ventum est;* and in like manner the gerundive occurs only in the neuter in connection with *esse* — as *pugnandum est,* 'there is a necessity for fight-ing;' *veniendum est,* 'there is a necessity for coming.' (See §§ 125 and 129, 3.)

CHAPTER XXX.

ADVERBS.

§ 190. Adverbs are indeclinable words qualifying the notions expressed by adjectives, verbs, or other adverbs, to which, accordingly, they stand in the same relation as adjectives stand to substantives — as *valde strenuus,* 'very energetic;' *bene loquitur,* 'he speaks well;' *epistola male scripta,* 'a badly-written letter;' *satis bene scriptum,* 'tolerably well written.' All adverbs, as far as their form is concerned, may be divided into three classes: — 1. Primitive adverbs — as *saepe,* often, *nunc,* now; to which may be added prepositions when used as adverbs — as *ante,* before; *post,* after. 2. Adverbs derived from adjectives by the terminations *ē, ō, ter* (answering to the English *ly*) — as *docte,* learnedly; *merito,* deservedly; *for-*

titer, bravely; or the adjective in its neuter form — as *facile* (from *facilis*), easily. 3. Adverbs which are in reality particular cases or forms of substantives, pronouns, or adjectives — as *noctu* (an old ablative), by night; *partim* (an old accusative for *partem*), partly; *hic*, here; *qua*, where; *ibi* (from *is*), there; *ubi* (from *qui*), where. In regard to meaning, they chiefly express circumstances of place, time, manner, order, or degree.

§ 191. The only inflection of which adverbs are capable is that of comparison; that is, they may have the degrees of the comparative and superlative. But even this inflection is limited almost to those which are derived from adjectives. The general rule for these is, that the neuter singular of the comparative of an adjective is at the same time its adverb; and the superlative of an adjective is changed into an adverb by changing the termination *us* into *ē* — as *doctus*, adverb *docte;* comparative *doctior*, neuter *doctius*, which is also an adverb; *doctissime* is the adverb formed from the superlative *doctissimus*.

Note 1. It hardly requires to be stated, that when an adjective forms its degrees of comparison irregularly, or has no such degrees, its adverb presents the same irregularity — as *melius* and *optime* (from *bonus); pejus* and *pessime* (from *malus); but instead of *majus*, the adverb is *magis*. *Tutus* and *meritus* make their adverbs in the superlatives oftener in *o* than *e* — as *tutissimo* and *meritissimo;* and *primus* has both *primum* (accusative) and *primo* (ablative). *Validus* makes its adverb *valde* (contracted for *valide*), but in the comparative it is *validius*, and in the superlative *validissime*.

2. Adverbs of place, from which adjectives are formed in the comparative and superlative (compare § 97), have the same degrees as the adjectives — as *prope* (near), *propius, proxime; intra* (within), *interius, intime; ultra* (beyond), *ulterius, ultimum*, and *ultimo; extra* (without), *exterius, extremum*, and *extremo; supra* (above), *superius, supremum*, and *supremo; post* (after), *posterius, postremum*, and *postremo; citra* (this side), *citerius; infra* (below), *inferius;* the last two have no superlative.

§ 192. Primitive adverbs, and those formed from substantives and pronouns, have no degrees of comparison, excepting the following six : —

diū (long)	*diutiūs,*	*diūtissimē.*
saepĕ (often),	*saepius,*	*saepissimē.*
sĕcus (otherwise),	*sēcius,*	—————
tempĕrī (in time),	*tempĕrius,*	—————
nūper (lately),	—————	*nuperrimē.*
sătĭs (enough, or sufficient),	*sătius,*	—————

CHAPTER XXXI.

PREPOSITIONS.

§ 193. Prepositions are not capable of any inflection whatever, and denote in what relation or connection a person, thing, or action, stands to another; *e.g.*, Rome is a town *in* Italy; I travel *through* England; Nero lived *in* the first century after Christ; we come *from* the lakes. Many of the relations and connections which we express in English by prepositions, are expressed in Latin by certain cases of nouns without a preposition, whereby the Latin language has the advantage of brevity and conciseness—as *domo,* 'from home;' *hoc modo,* 'in this manner;' *illo tempore,* 'at that time;' *eo regnante,* 'in his reign;' *me ducente,* 'under my guidance.'

§ 194. Prepositions are always connected with a noun upon which they exercise an influence, which is called government, and whereby it becomes necessary that the noun should be in a particular case. According to the cases which they govern, prepositions are divided into three classes —

1. Prepositions governing the accusative are twenty-six in number : —

ad, to, up to, near, or nearly.	*juxtā,* near to or beside.
adversus or *adversum,* opposite,	*ob,* against or on account of.
antĕ, before. [against.	*pĕnĕs,* in the power of.
ăpud, near, with.	*per,* through.
circa or *circum,* around, about.	*pōnĕ,* behind.
circĭter, about (in regard to time or	*post,* after.
number).	*praeter,* besides, excepting.
cis or *citra,* on this side of.	*propter,* on account of, close by.
contrā, against.	*sĕcundum,* next after, in accord-
ergā, towards.	ance with.
extrā, without (opposite of within).	*suprā,* above,
infrā, below, beneath.	*trans,* on the other side of, beyond.
inter, between, among.	*ultrā,* beyond.
intrā, within.	*versus,* towards (a place).

2. The following eleven prepositions govern the ablative : —

a, ab, or *abs,* from.	*prae,* before, in consequence of.
absquĕ, without (wanting).	*prō,* before, instead of.
cōrām, in the presence of.	*pălam,* with the knowledge of.
cum, with.	*sĭne,* without (that is, not with).
dē, from, concerning.	*tĕnus,* up to, as far as.
e or *ex,* out of, of	

3. The following four prepositions sometimes govern the accusative, and sometimes the ablative : the former, when they denote motion towards ; and the latter, when they denote rest, or being in a place : —

With the Accusative.		*With the Ablative.*
in,	into, against.	in.
sub,	under, about, towards.	under.
super,	above, over.	upon, concerning.
subter,	under, beneath ; generally with the accusative in either sense, rarely with the ablative.	

Note 1. Nearly all prepositions in their primary meaning express the notion of place, but secondarily they also express time and other relations — as *ante januam*, ' before the door ;' and *ante Christum natum*, ' before the birth of Christ.' Prepositions are often used as adverbs — as in English, ' my friend came *before* I was ready ;' and in this case prepositions cannot govern any case. On the other hand, it sometimes happens that words, which are in reality adverbs, are used as prepositions, and, as such, govern a certain case — as *prŏpĕ* (near), *sĕcus* (otherwise), are found with an accusative ; while *clam* (without the knowledge of), *prŏcul* (at a distance), and *sĭmul* (at the same time with), occur with the ablative, and *clam* also with the accusative.

2. Prepositions are generally put before the case they govern, but *versus* and *tenus* are always placed after it. *Ante, contra, inter,* and *propter* may be put after their case when it is a relative pronoun—as *quos contra* for *contra quos;* and when the substantive governed by them is accompanied by an adjective, they are often put between the adjective and the substantive—as *probos inter cives.* The same is the case with the following monosyllabic prepositions, *ob, post, de, ex,* and *in*—as *magna ex parte, qua in re, quam ob causam.* The preposition *cum* is always suffixed to the ablative of the personal pronouns — as *mecum, tecum, secum, nobiscum, vobiscum;* and frequently also to relative pronouns — as *quocum, quacum, quibuscum.* Some writers, and especially poets, take great liberty in placing the prepositions.

3. Wherever, in the above lists, two or more forms are given of the same preposition, they are, generally speaking, used indifferently. But the following exceptions must be observed :—*a* is used only before consonants ; *ab* before vowels, and all consonants except *m* and *v; abs* is used only in connection with *te*—as *abs te*, for which, however, we may also say *a te.* The form *e* is used only before consonants, and *ex* before vowels, and the consonants *c, p, q, s,* and *t.*

§ 195. Prepositions are very frequently compounded with other words, and if the latter begin with a consonant, the preposition in many cases undergoes a change for the sake of euphony. The following cases are of most common occurrence :—

1. *A* is used before words beginning with *m* or *v*—as *amoveo, aveho; ab* before vowels, and most other consonants — as *abeo, abjicio, abripio, abnego, ablego; abs* is used only before

c and *t* — *abscondo, abstineo.* In *aufero* and *aufugio* the *b* is changed into *u* (that is, *v*).

2. *Ad* remains unchanged before vowels, and *d, j, m,* and *v* — as *adeo, adoro, adjicio, admoveo, adventus ;* before other consonants it assimilates itself to them — as *attero, attingo, alloquor, affero, appono ;* and before *q* the *d* becomes *c* — as *acquiro, acquiesco.*

3. *Cum* in compound words is changed into *com, con,* or *co.* *Com* is used before *b, m,* and *p* — as *comburo, commoveo, comparo ;* before *l, n, r,* it assimilates itself to them — as *colloco, conniveo, corrodo.* Before vowels and *h* the *m* is generally dropped—as *coire, cohaereo, cogo* (for *coago*); but it is retained in *comeo, comitor, comitium,* and *comedo.* Before all other letters *con* is used, but before *r* and *l* the *n* assimilates itself to them — as *corripio, collabor.*

4. *Ex* is retained before vowels, and the consonants *c, p, q, s,* and *t* — as *exitus, exoro, excipio, expeto, exquiro, exsilium,* or *exilium* (the *s* after *x* being generally dropped), *extendo, extraho.* Exceptions are — *escendo* and *epoto.* Before *f* the *x* assimilates itself — as *effero.* Before all other consonants *e* is used, except the word *exlex* — as *eligo, emineo, edico, egredior, enisus.*

5. *In* changes its *n* into *m* befor *b* and *p* — as *imbibo, impono ;* and assimilates it to *l* and *r* — as *illusio, irruo.* Before *gn* the *n* is dropped altogether — as *ignoro, ignarus.* In all other cases *in* remains unchanged — as *ineptus, inutilis, inopinatus, indoctus, incautus.*

6. *Ob* assimilates its *b* to *c, f, g,* and *p* — as *occurro, offero, oggannio, oppono ;* but before all other letters it remains unchanged.

7. *Pro* always remains unchanged ; but when the word with which it is compounded begins with a vowel, a *d* is introduced between them, to prevent the hiatus — as *prodesse, prodeo, prodigus.* Compare § 137, note 2. But still there is *proavus* and *prohibeo.* In a few cases the *r* is transposed— as in *porrigo* and *portendo* for *prorigo* and *protendo.*

8. *Sub* assimilates its *b* to *c, f, g, m, p,* and *r* — as *succedo, sufficit, suggero, summoveo, suppono, surripio.* Before *sp* the *b* is dropped—as *suspiro, suspicio ;* but before all other letters *sub* remains unchanged.

9. *Per* remains unchanged except in the words *pellicio* (for *perlicio*) and *pejero* (for *perjero*—that is, *perjuro*). *Post* also remains unchanged except in *pomoerium* and *pomeridianus,* where *st* is thrown out. *Trans* is frequently changed into

tra in the words *trado, traduco, trajicio;* but in all other cases it remains unchanged.

Of the remaining prepositions none undergoes any change in composition.

Note. We may here notice certain particles which are never used by themselves, and are found only in composition with other words, whence they are called inseparable particles, or inseparable prepositions. They are *amb, dis, re,* and *se.*

Amb (the Greek ἀμφι) denotes 'around'—as in *ambio, ambigo, ambiguus;* before *p* the *b* is dropped—as in *amplector;* before other consonants *amb* is changed into *an*—as *anceps, anquiro, anfractus*—but before vowels it remains unchanged.

Dis denotes separation, and remains unchanged before *c, p, q, s,* and *t*—as *discepto, disputo, disquisitio, dissero, distraho;* before other consonants, and *sp* and *st,* it is changed into *dī*—as *dimoveo, diripio, dispergo, distinguo;* before *j* we find both *dis* and *dī*—as *disjudico* and *dijudico, disjungo* and *dijungo.* Before *f* the *s* assimilates itself to it—as *differo, difficilis.*

Rĕ signifies 'back,' or 'again.' When prefixed to a word beginning with a vowel or *h,* a *d* is inserted—as *redeo, reditus, redigo, redarguo, redhibeo;* before all other consonants it remains unchanged.

Sē signifies 'aside,' or 'without;' undergoes no change in composition—as *seduco, separo, sejungo.* In *seditio* (from *se* and *itio*) a *d* is inserted; *sobrius* is a contraction for *seebrius*—that is, *non ebrius; socors* is only another form for *secors;* and *sursum* is a contraction of *seorsum*—that is, *sevorsum,* 'turned to one side.'

CHAPTER XXXII.

CONJUNCTIONS.

§ 196. Conjunctions are indeclinable words, whose function is to connect sentences or clauses, and show the connection or relation existing between them. As regards their form, conjunctions are either simple—as *et, āc, at, sĕd, vĕl, aut, nam;* or compound—as, *atquĕ, namquĕ, ĭtăque, quamvīs, attămĕn, ĕnimvērō, quamquam.*

Note. Some words, which may be classed among adverbs, were originally words of a different kind—as *cēterum* (an accusative, 'as for the rest'), *vērum* ('it is true,' or 'true'), *vērō* ('in truth'), *lĭcet* ('it is permitted'), *quamvīs* (*quam* and *vis,* from *volo,* 'as you wish' or 'like'), *quārē* ('for which thing' or 'reason'). Of the same class are *idcircō, quamobrem, deindĕ, postrēmum, mŏdŏ, ubi, inde, quandō,* and others.

§ 197. In regard to their meaning, all conjunctions may be divided into ten classes:—

1. Copulative conjunctions, whereby clauses are put in the relation of equality to one another, or are merely placed in juxtaposition. Conjunctions of this kind are *ĕt, quĕ* (Greek καί), *ăc* and *atquĕ* (and), *nĕquĕ* or *nĕc* (and not or nor), *nĕc non,* or *nĕquĕ non* (equivalent to *et,* and), *quoque* (also), *neque-neque,* or *nec-nec* (neither-nor), *vĕl-vĕl, sīvĕ-sīvĕ, aut-aut* (either-or), *mŏdo-mŏdo,* or *nunc-nunc* (sometimes-sometimes), *quum-tum* (both-and).

Note. *Etiam* (even, also) is sometimes classed with these conjunctions, but its meaning is different from that of *quoque; etiam* denotes that that which follows is something new, and of more or less importance than what precedes, while *quoque* merely adds something, and intimates that it is something of the same kind as the preceding.

Quĕ is an enclitic which never occurs by itself, but is always suffixed to a word—as *audio videoque,* 'I hear and see.'

ăc is never used before vowels ; *atque,* on the other hand, is used before vowels as well as consonants.

It is one of the great peculiarities of the ancient languages by means of particles to point out the relations and connections in which clauses stand to one another, where the English language merely puts them side by side, without connecting them by any particle. An instance of this tendency appears in the frequent connection of two clauses by means of *et-et, et-que, que-et,* and in poetry by *que-que,* which we may render by 'as well-as,' or 'both-and;' but sometimes we are obliged to leave out the first *et* (or *que*) altogether, and translate only the second as usual by 'and.'

Nĕquĕ is a compound of the negative *ne* and *que,* and accordingly signifies 'and not;' and *neque-neque,* 'both not-and not,' *neque-et,* 'both one thing not-and the other;' so that in reality two things, one negative, and the other affirmative, are connected by *que(et)-et.* In like manner an affirmative clause is connected with a negative one by *et-neque.*

Sīvĕ—that is, *si vis* (if you please)—when followed by another *sive,* leaves it doubtful as to which of two things is to be done. *Aut-aut* denotes an opposition between two things, one of which excludes the other ; whereas *vel-vel* does not denote that one thing excludes the other.

2. Comparative conjunctions:—*ŭt, ŭtī, sīcŭt, vĕlŭt, prout, praeut,* and *ceu,* signify 'as' or 'like ;' *quam,* 'than ;' *tamquam, quasi, ut si, ac si,* 'as if.' Also *ăc* and *atque* in the sense of 'as' and 'than.'

3. Conjunctions denoting concession ; all of them are rendered in English by 'although,' 'though,' and 'even if'—as *etsī, ĕtiamsī, tămetsī,* or *tămenetsī, quamquam, quamvīs, quantumvīs, quamlībĕt, līcĕt,* and sometimes *quum; quĭdem,* or *equĭdem* signifies 'indeed.'

4. Conditional conjunctions:—*sī* (if) ; *sin* (if however) ; *quodsī* (if therefore) ; *nĭsī,* or *nī* (if not) ; *sĭmŏdŏ, dummŏdŏ, dum, mŏdŏ* (if only, if but) ; *dummŏdŏ ne, modo nĕ,* or *dumnĕ* (if but not).

5. Inferential conjunctions with the meaning of 'therefore'—as *ergō, ĭgĭtur, ĭtăquĕ, eō, ĭdeō, idcircō, proinde, proptereā;* to which may be added *quāpropter, quārē, quamobrem, quōcircā* (wherefore); and *unde* (whence, or for which reason).

6. Conjunctions denoting reason or cause. The following are rendered in English by 'for:'—*nam, namque, ĕnim, ĕtĕnim; quĭă, quod, quŏniam,* signify 'because;' and *quippe, quum, quandō, quandōquidem,* and *sĭquĭdem,* 'since,' or 'as.'

7. Conjunctions denoting a purpose or object:—*ŭt,* or *ŭti* (in order that); *quō* (in order that thereby); *nē,* or *ŭt nē* (in order that not); *nēvĕ,* or *neu* (and in order that not); *quĭn* (that not); *quōmĭnŭs* (in order that not).

8. Adversative conjunctions, all of which answer more or less to the English 'but,' or 'however:'—*sĕd, autem, vērum, vērō, ăt, ăt ĕnĭm, atquē, tămĕn, attămĕn, sedtămĕn, vērumtămĕn, at vērō, ĕnimvērō, vērum ĕnimvērō, cētĕrum.*

9. Conjunctions denoting time:—*quum, ŭt, ŭbĭ, quandō* (when); *quum prīmum, ut prīmum, ŭbĭ prīmum, sĭmŭlăc, sĭmŭlatque,* or *sĭmŭl* (as soon as); *postquam* (after); *antĕquam, priusquam* (before); *dum, usque dum, dōnĕc, quoad* (until, as long as).

10. Interrogative conjunctions, also called interrogative particles—*num, utrum, ăn;* the suffix *nĕ (nonnĕ, annon) necnĕ* (or not); and the prefixes *ec* and *en.*

Note 1. These interrogative particles are generally untranslatable into English, since with us the interrogative nature of a clause is indicated by the position of the words.

Num, and the prefixes *ec* and *en,* introduce a question to which we expect a negative answer; *ec* and *en* occur only in *ecquis, ecquid, ecquando,* and *enunquam.*

Utrum is properly the neuter of *uter?* (which of two?) and accordingly introduces a double question, the second of which begins with *an* (or)—as *utrum patrem an matrem pluris facis?* 'dost thou value thy father or thy mother more highly?' Sometimes *ne* is used in the first question for *utrum,* or in the second instead of *an.* The parts of double questions may be connected with each other in four ways : --

utrum (utrumne)	——	*an*
————————	——	*an (anne)*
ne ———————	——	*an*
————————	——	*ne*

It frequently happens in Latin, as in English, that the first part of a double question is omitted, and the second only is expressed by *an.*

The enclitic *ne* is always suffixed to the first word of an interrogative clause, and simply characterises the clause as an interrogative one—as *videsne fratrem tuum?* 'do you see your brother ?'

2. Conjunctions are generally placed at the beginning of the clause which they introduce ; but *enim, autem, vero,* are always put after the first word of a clause, or after the second when the first two belong

together, and cannot be separated. *Quidem* and *quoque* always follow the word which has the principal emphasis, whatever may be its place in the clause. *Itaque* and *igitur* have the same meaning, but *itaque* usually stands at the beginning of a clause, while *igitur* is generally inserted after the first or second word of a clause. *Tamen* (yet) may be put at the beginning, or after the first word of a clause.

CHAPTER XXXIII.

INTERJECTIONS.

§ 198. Interjections are indeclinable words or sounds uttered to express some strong emotion. Such sounds expressing the emotions of joy, grief, wonder, surprise, &c. are very nearly the same in all nations, but may at the same time vary according to the peculiarities of individuals; we must, therefore, here confine ourselves to those interjections which are found written in ancient authors.

io, iu, ha (ha), he,	are expressive	of joy and delight.
hei, heu, ēheu, păpae, ō,	... ...	of grief (alas!)
ō, prō, or *prōh, ătăt,* *hem, ehem, en, eccĕ,*	... ...	of astonishment and surprise.
hui, phui, vah, vae,	... ...	of contempt and disgust.
heus, ō, ehō, ehodum,	... ...	of calling attention to something.
eiă, eugĕ,	... ...	of praise (well done! bravo!)
ēvoe, evax,	... ...	of triumphant joy.

§ 199. Interjections are thrown in between the parts of a sentence or clause without exercising any influence upon it. In Latin, as well as in English, it often happens that words which belong to other parts of speech are thrown in between the parts of a sentence, and thus become interjections. The most common among them are—

Nouns.—*pax !* peace! be still! — *infandum !* shame! — *miserum !* wretched! — *mactĕ !* (voc. sing.), *mactī !* (voc. plur.), or *mactĕ virtute !* admirable! bravo!

Verbs.—*age! agite !* come! or quick! — *cedo !* give up! — *sodes ! (si audes)* if you dare!

Advs.—*belle !* excellent! bravo! — *bene !* very well! — *cito !* quick!

All kinds of invocations of the gods may be regarded as interjections—as *per deos !* 'by the gods!'—*per deos immortales!* 'by the immortal gods!'—*mehercule, mehercle, hercle !* 'by Hercules!' Such exclamations are sometimes accompanied by real interjections—as *proh* or *pro Jupiter !*—*pro dii immortales !*

CHAPTER XXXIV.

ETYMOLOGY IN GENERAL.

§ 200. The words of a language are either *simple, derivative,* or *compound.* That which forms the basis of both simple and derivative words is called the stem. A stem by itself does not convey any distinct meaning, but acquires it by the addition of certain suffixes, whereby it becomes a noun, a verb, adverb, &c. Thus the stem *duc,* by the addition of *s,* becomes the substantive *ducs = dux* (leader), and by the addition of *o* it becomes the verb *duco* (I lead); from the stem *prob* we form by the suffix *ē* the adverb *probe.* Words thus formed from a stem, by simply adding a suffix to give to the stem a definite meaning, are called simple words.

Note 1. A stem, it was said, conveys no distinct meaning; but at the same time it contains an idea which only requires development to acquire a distinct meaning. The most common idea implied in a stem is that of action or condition, so that by adding the ending of a verb, we at once obtain a verb: thus *leg* becomes *lego; ama* becomes *amao,* or contracted *amo; scrib* becomes *scribo,* &c. Sometimes nouns are formed with equal facility — as *duc, dux; leg, lex.* The general process, however, is that from a stem is formed a verb, from the verb the noun, &c.; so that, for example, we say *amo* is formed from the stem *ama,* and *amator* from *amo,* although we can with equal propriety refer both *amo* and *amator* to the stem *ama.*

2. Sometimes the stem becomes a distinct word by a simple euphonic change without the addition of a suffix; thus the stem *flor* becomes *flos* (a flower); *mur* becomes *mus* (a mouse). In some cases the addition of the suffix produces a euphonic change in the stem: thus *frons* and *laus* are formed from the stems *frond* and *laud,* euphony requiring the *d* to be dropped before the *s.* Sometimes, again, the stem, on becoming a distinct word, undergoes more violent changes; it is curtailed, *e.g.,* in *leo* from *leon,* in *sum* from *esum* (*es* being the stem); it is extended in *frango* from the stem *frag,* and in *tango* from the stem *tag.* It may be observed here that, in the simple verbs of the second conjugation, the *ē,* properly speaking, does not belong to the stem, although, for the sake of convenience, we have treated it as such. The only verbs in which the *ē* does belong to the stem are those which retain the *ē* in the perfect and supine — as *deleo, delevi, deletum; fleo, flevi, fletum;* and others.

3. It is well known that there exists the greatest affinity not only between the Latin and Greek languages, but between the Latin and nearly all the languages of Europe. In many cases the affinity shows itself in the identity of suffixes and terminations, but it is most striking in the stems of these languages. Hence, in comparing two lan-

11   G 2

guages, we should first of all compare their stems, and not the words as they are in actual use. It must further be observed, that it is impossible to trace every Latin word to its stem without having recourse to other languages, and even then it is often impracticable.

§ 201. Derivative words may, like simple ones, be traced at once to the stem, but it is customary to trace them only to the simple ones; for a simple word conveys distinctly the idea of what was indistinctly contained in the stem, whereas a derivative word gives us a modification of the idea conveyed by the simple word — as *ama*, verb *amo*, I love; from *amo*, is formed *amabilis*, loveable; *amabilitas*, loveableness; and *amator*, lover. Derivative words are formed from simple ones by derivative syllables (derivative suffixes, also called simply suffixes), as in the above example, *bilis*, *bilitas*, and *tor*. The same derivative suffix generally modifies in the same way the meaning of all words to which it is added.

Note 1. All derivative suffixes themselves consist of a stem and a suffix indicating the class of words to which the word which receives them must belong. Thus in the above-mentioned derivative suffixes *bilis*, *bilitas*, and *tor*, the stem is *bil*, *bilitat*, and *tor*.

2. There are in Latin many words with derivative suffixes without it being possible for us to point out their stem; other derivative suffixes occur only in isolated instances; and others, again, are so common, that it is impossible to say in what manner they modify the meaning of the simple word or stem — as in the case of *a* (the ending of feminine nouns of the first declension), and *us*, *a*, *um* (the endings of the three genders of a certain class of adjectives). Sometimes, moreover, there are two derivative suffixes modifying the meaning of a word in quite the same manner—as *tas* and *tudo;* in which case it is customary in some words to use the one suffix, and in others the other.

§ 202. 1. Derivative suffixes are generally appended to the stem of a word, such as it appears when divested of those simple suffixes by which it becomes a distinct word—as from *miles* (stem *milit*) are derived *militaris*, *militia; frango* (stem *frag*, *fragilis*, *fragor; semen* (stem *semin*), *seminarium.* In substantives of the first, second, and fourth declensions, the final vowels of the stem *a* and *u(s)* are usually thrown out — as *filia*, *filiola; luna*, *lunula; hortus*, *hortulus.*

Note. There are, however, many exceptions to this rule—as *aqua, aquarius; epistola, epistolaris;* from *semen* is formed *sementis;* but these will be explained more fully hereafter.

2. Verbs of the first and second conjugations generally drop the *ā* and *ē* before those derivative suffixes which begin with a vowel—as *amo* (stem *ama*), *amor; palleo* (stem *palle*), *pallor; opinor* (stem *opina*), *opinio.* The *e* in verbs of the second

conjugation is dropped also before consonants, except in those
which make their perfect in *vi*.

When the stem ends in a consonant, and the derivative
suffix begins with a consonant, it often happens that a connecting vowel (*ĭ* or *ŭ*) is inserted between them, or that one
of the consonants is thrown out—as in *fulmen* (from *fulgeo*,
stem *fulg*). The latter is the case especially when the stem
ends in *v*—as *mōtus, mōbilis* (from *moveo*, stem *mov*); *adjutor*
and *adjumentum* (from *juvo*).

3. When the stem of a verb ends in *a, e, i,* or *u,* these vowels are generally lengthened before the derivative suffix—as
velāmen, complēmentum, molīmen, volūmen.

4. In forming derivative nouns from verbs by suffixes beginning with *t,* the stem undergoes the same change as in the
formation of the supine ending in *tum;* hence we may say
that they are formed from the supine—as *amator* (from *amo,
amatum*), *lector* (from *lego, lectum*). Compare §§ 135 and 203, 2.

CHAPTER XXXV.

DERIVATION OF SUBSTANTIVES FROM VERBS, SUBSTANTIVES, AND ADJECTIVES.

§ 203. It has been observed that in general the most natural
way is to form the stem into a verb, and to make from that
verb all other derivatives. We shall therefore enumerate the
different suffixes by means of which substantives are derived
from verbs, substantives, and adjectives:—

Note. Sometimes it is not the verb that is nearest to the stem, but
the substantive ; e.g. in those cases where the stem itself with a slight
euphonic change becomes a substantive—as *flos* (from *flor*), *mus* (from
mur), *honos* or *honor* (from *honor*), *corpus* (from *corpor*). § 200, note 2.
In many cases, moreover, no verb can be formed from a stem, whereas
the stem either is, or may easily be changed into, a substantive—as
sol (the sun), *frons* (foliage, from *frond*). In cases like these we must
reverse the usual custom, and derive, where possible, the verb from
the substantive—as *frondēre*, from *frons; florēre*, from *flos*.

1. Substantives are derived from verbs (chiefly intransitives
of the first three conjugations) by adding the suffix *or* to
the pure stem (that is, after the *a* and *e* of the first and
second conjugations are dropped); and such substantives

express the action or condition substantively—as *amor, error, clamor, favor, pallor, furor, fragor,* from *amo, erro, clamo, faveo, palleo, furo, frango.*

Note. There are some substantives in *or* which are not derived from any known verb, and must therefore be regarded as simple nouns, from which others may be derived—as *honor, labor (honos, labos),* from which are derived the verbs *honoro* and *laboro.*

2. Substantives are formed from verbs by adding *or* to the stem as it appears in the supine—that is, by changing *um* into *or* (§ 202, 4). Such substantives denote a male person performing the action implied in the verb — as *amator,* a lover; *adjutor,* a helper; *monitor,* an adviser; *victor,* a conqueror; *cursor,* a runner; *petītor,* a seeker; *audītor,* a hearer. From many of these substantives in *tor,* feminines may be formed by changing *tor* into *trix* — as *victor, victrix; fautor, fautrix; adjutor, adjutrix.* Those in *sor* sometimes make feminines in *strix* — as *tonsor, tonstrix; defensor, defenstrix;* but *expulsor* makes *expultrix,* throwing out the *s.*

Note. Similar substantives denoting persons are sometimes formed from substantives of the first and second declensions—as *viātor* (traveller), *gladiātor* (gladiator), *funditor* (a slinger), from *via, gladius, funda;* so also *janitor* (gatekeeper), from *janua,* and *vinitor* (vinedresser), from *vinea.* Substantives ending in *a, o,* or *us,* denoting persons, are likewise sometimes derived from verbs, though more rarely than those in *or*—as *scriba* (scribe), *conviva* (guest), *advĕna* (a comer), from *scribo, vivo,* and *venio; erro* (a wanderer), from *errāre; coquus* (a cook), from *coquo.*

3. Substantives denoting abstractedly the action or condition expressed by a verb are formed from the supine by changing the termination *um* into *io,* gen. *iōnis* — as *tractatio* (from *tracto, tractatum*), *cautio* (from *caveo, cautum*), *divisio* (from *divido, divisum*), *actio* (from *ago, actum*).

Note. There are cases, though they occur more rarely, in which the ending *io* is added to the stem of the verb—as *obsidio,* from *obsideo; contagio,* from *tango* (stem *tag*); *opinio,* from *opinor; oblivio,* from *obliviscor* (the real stem being *obliv*); *legio,* from *lego;* though we also have *lectio,* from *lectum; condicio,* from *condico.*

4. Substantives with the termination *us* (fourth declension) are likewise formed from verbs by changing the supine ending *um* into *us.* Their meaning is very nearly the same as that of substantives in *io,* and in some cases the same verb admits the formation of substantives both in *io* and in *us* — as *contemptio, contemptus; concursio, concursus; consensio, consensus; motio, motus; potio, potus.* In some words of this kind in *io,* the abstract idea of what is implied

in the verb is lost—as in *legio*, a legion; *coenatio*, a dining-room; *regio*, a district.

Note. In regard to use, these forms are almost entirely arbitrary, one writer preferring the one, and another the other, without there appearing to be any difference in meaning. In some, however, there is a difference—as *auditio*, the act of hearing; and *auditus*, the power or faculty of hearing. As a third class of verbal substantives with the same meaning, we may mention those in *ūra*, formed likewise from the supine—as *conjectura, pictura, cultura, mercatura*. There are also a few verbs from which all the three kinds of substantives may be formed—as *positio, positus*, and *positura* (from *pono*); *censio, census*, and *censura* (from *censeo*). In some words, the ending *ēla*, attached either to the stem of the verb or to that of the supine, conveys the same meaning as the endings *io, us*, or *ura*—as *querēla* (from *queror*); *corruptēla* (from *corrumpo, corruptum*). Very nearly the same meaning is conveyed by some substantives ending in *ium*, in which the *ium* is suffixed to the stem of the verb—as *judicium* (from *judico*), *odium* (from *odi*), *gaudium* (from *gaudeo*), *studium* (from *studeo*), *refugium* (from *refugio*), *colloquium* (from *colloquor*).

5. There are a few verbs from which substantives in *īgo* are formed, denoting an action, or a condition which is the result of that action — as *orīgo*, origin (from *orior*); *vertīgo*, turning or whirl (from *verto*); *tentīgo*, stretching (from *tendo*); *robīgo*, a blight; *petīgo* and *impetīgo*, scab; *prurīgo*, itch; *porrīgo*, scurf.

Note. To these may be added substantives in *īdo*—as *cupīdo*, desire (from *cupio*); *formīdo*, fear (from *formido*); *libīdo*, lust (from *libet*).

6. Substantives in *men* (gen. *mĭnis*) derived from verbs, denote the thing performing the action or serving the purpose expressed by the verb. In some cases *men* is affixed to the stem — as *flumen* (a river, from *fluo*), *velamen* (a cover, from *velo*), *lumen* (a light, from *luceo*, the *c* being thrown out). In others, a connecting vowel (*i* or *u*) is introduced between the stem and *men* — as *regĭmen* (from *rego*), *specĭmen* (from *specio*); *tegmen, tegĭmen*, or *tegŭmen* (a covering, from *tego*). In many cases the suffix *men* is lengthened by the addition of *tum*, without producing any change of meaning — as *velamen, velamentum; tegŭmen, tegŭmentum*. The termination *mentum*, however, occurs more frequently in words which have no form in *men*—as *ornamentum, complementum, instrumentum, alimentum, condimentum, monumentum, documentum, adjumentum* (from *juvo*, the *v* being thrown out), *tormentum* (from *torqueo*, the *qu* being thrown out).

Note. Some substantives in *mentum* are derived from nouns of the second declension—as *atramentum* (blacking or ink from *ater*), *ferra-*

mentum (iron-work, from *ferrum*), *calceamentum* (covering for the feet, from *calceus*), *capillamentum* (a wig, from *capillus*). In all these words the ending *mentum* is preceded by *a*, as if they were derived from verbs of the first conjugation; but this *a* must be looked upon as a connecting vowel.

7. Substantives ending in *culum* (contracted *clum*) or *bulum* are derived from the stem of verbs, sometimes with, and sometimes without, a connecting vowel; they denote the instrument, and sometimes the place, of the action expressed by the verb—as *gubernaculum* (rudder, from *guberno*), *coenaculum* (dining-room, from *coeno*), *ferculum* (bier, from *fero*), *operculum* (from *operio*), *vehiculum* (from *veho*), *everriculum* (from *everro*), *vocabulum* (from *voco*), *pabulum* (from *pasco, pavi*), *stabulum* (from *sto, stare*), *latibulum* (from *lateo*), *infundibulum* (from *infundo*). If the stem of the verb ends in *c* or *g*, the termination is *ulum*—as *cingulum* (from *cingo*), *vinculum* (from *vincio*).

Note 1. Instead of *culum* or *clum*, the suffix *crum* is appended when one of the two preceding syllables contains an *l*—as *sepulcrum* (from *sepelio*), *fulcrum* (from *fulcio*), *simulacrum* (from *simulo*), *lavacrum* (from *lavo*). In like manner *bulum* is changed into *brum* when the preceding syllable contains an *l* — as *flabrum* (from *flo*), *ventilabrum* (from *ventilo*). There are also some feminines in *bra* formed in the same manner—as *dolābra, latēbra, vertĕbra*.

2. Some substantives take the termination *trum* with the same meaning as *culum*, and if the stem of the verb ends in *d*, this letter is changed before *trum* into *s*—as *aratum* (from *aro*), *claustrum* (from *claudo*), *rostrum* (from *rodo*), *castrum* (from *cado*), *rastrum* (from *rado*). Some substantives in *bulum* and *brum* are derived from other substantives—as *candēlabrum* (from *candēla*), *turibulum* (from *tus*, incense).

§ 204. 1. Substantives are derived from other substantives in a variety of ways: a very common process is to form feminine substantives from masculines. This is the case especially with names of animals ending in *er* or *us*, from which feminines are formed by adding *a* to the stem of the word instead of the masculine termination—as *asinus, asina; equus, equa; caper, capra; cervus, cerva; magister, magistra*: so also *deus, dea; dominus, domina; filius, filia; herus, hera; servus, serva*. Respecting the feminine substantives in *trix* formed from masculines in *tor*, see § 203, 2.

Note. There are some more irregular modes of forming feminines from masculines — as *regīna* (from *rex*), *gallīna* (from *gallus*), *leaena* (from *leo*), *neptis* (from *nepos*), *avia* (from *avis*), *socrus* (from *socer*). Compare § 46. It occurs but rarely that a substantive of the third declension admits the formation of a feminine by the mere addition of *a* to the stem — as in *clienta* (from *cliens*), *hospita* (from *hospĕs*), *tibīcĭna* (from *tibīcen*), *antistita* (from *antistes*).

2. By the terminations *lus* (*la, lum*) and *culus* (*cula, culum*), diminutives are formed from other substantives. Such diminutives denote primarily a small thing, but are used also as endearing terms, and to express contempt — as *hortulus*, a small garden; *filiolus*, dear little son; *homunculus*, a contemptible little man. All diminutives are of the same gender as the substantives from which they are formed, so that if the primitive is a masculine, the diminutive must end in *lus* or *culus*; if a feminine, in *la* or *cula*; and if neuter, in *lum* or *culum*.

Regarding the manner in which the diminutive terminations are appended to the primitive word, the following rules must be observed:—

(*a*). *lus* (*la, lum*) is used in words of the first and second (and a few of the third declension, in which the stem ends in *t*, *c*, or *g*); the terminations (*q* or *us*) are dropped, and the termination *lus* is connected with the stem by means of the connecting vowel *ŭ* — as *arca, arcŭla; cera, cerŭla; littera, litterŭla; luna, lunŭla; virga, virgŭla; servus, servŭlus; hortus, hortŭlus; puer, puerŭlus; oppidum, oppidŭlum; vox, vocŭla; rex, regŭlus; caput, capitŭlum; aestas, aestatŭla; adolescens, adolescentŭlus.* If the stem of words of the first and second declensions ends in a vowel, the connecting vowel *ŏ* is inserted instead of *ŭ* — as *filius, filiŏlus; filia, filiŏla; ingenium, ingeniŏlum; linea, lineŏla; gloria, gloriŏla.*

(*b*). Words of the first and second declensions, whose stem ends in *ul, r* (with a consonant before it), or *n*, the termination *lus* (*la, lum*) is affixed to the stem without a connecting vowel; but the *r* and *n* become assimilated to *l*. The vowels of the stem *u* and *i* are changed into *e*; and in the case of *r*, preceded by a consonant, an *e* is inserted between that consonant and *r* — as *tabula, tabella; fabula, fabella; catulus, catellus; populus, popellus; libra, libella; ager, agellus; liber, libellus; labrum, labellum; lamina, lamella; pagina, pagella; asinus, asellus; catina, catella; corona, corolla; puera, puella; opera, opella.*

Note. By means of this termination, diminutives are sometimes formed from other diminutives—as *cista, cistula,* and *cistella; puella, puellula;* from *cistella* we have even a third diminutive—*cistellula.* A few words make their diminutives in *illus* instead of *ellus* — as *baculum, bacillum; pugnus, pugillus; signum, sigillum; tignum, tigillum; pulvinus, pulvillus;* and on the same principle some are formed from substantives of the third declension—as *codex, codicillus; lapis, lapillus; anguis, anguilla.*

(*c*). The diminutive termination *culus* (*a, um*) is applied in forming derivatives from substantives of the third, fourth, and fifth declensions. When the stem of words of the third declension ends in *l, r, s* (equivalent to *r*), *culus* (*a, um*) is affixed to the nominative of the word — as *animal, animalculum ; frater, fraterculus ; mater, matercula ; tuber, tuberculum ; uxor, uxorcula ; cor, corculum ; flos, flosculus ; os, osculum ; opus, opusculum ; munus, munusculum ; vas, vasculum.*

Note. There are a few exceptions to this rule ; for *rumor* makes *rumusculus; arbor, arbuscula;* and in the same manner diminutives are formed from many comparatives of adjectives—as *major, majusculus; grandior, grandiusculus.* (Compare § 90, note.) *Venter* makes *ventriculus;* and *os* (*ossis*), *ossiculum.*

(*d*). Substantives ending in *o*, and making their genitive in *on-is* or *in-is*, change *on* and *in* into *un* before adding the termination *culus*—as *homo, homunculus ; sermo, sermunculus ; virgo, virguncula ; ratio, ratiuncula.*

Note. Upon the same principle are formed irregularly some diminutives from substantives of the first and second declensions—as *avunculus,* from *avus; ranunculus,* from *rana* (the change of the gender is here not to be overlooked); and also *furunculus,* from *fur.*

(*e*). Substantives ending in *es* (genitive *is* or *ei*) and *is* (genitive *is*) make diminutives by suffixing *culus* to their stem, after the nominative termination *s* is thrown off — as *nubes, nubecula; dies, diecula; piscis, pisciculus; aedes* (or *aedis*), *aedicula.* Words ending in *e* change this vowel into *i* — as *rete, reticulum.*

(*f*). In words of the third declension, in which the *s* of the nominative is preceded by a consonant, *culus* is suffixed to the stem by means of a connecting *i* — as *pons, ponticulus; pars, particula; cos, coticula.* In words of the fourth declension, *culus* is likewise joined to the pure stem by means of the connecting vowel *i* — as *cornu, corniculum; versus, versiculus.*

Note. It has already been observed above (§ 204, 2 (*a*) that, if the stem of words of the third declension ends in *c* or *g*, diminutives are formed by the suffix *lus*—as *rex, regulus. Equus* makes *eculeus,* and *acus* (fem.) *aculeus* (masc.), *qu* being equivalent to *c.* *Homo* has also a diminutive *homuncio.*

3. The termination *ium*, when added to the stem of substantives denoting persons, expresses an assemblage or a relation of persons to one another—as *collega* (a colleague); *collegium,* an assembly of persons who are colleagues ; *sacerdos, sacerdotium ; conviva, convivium ; minister, ministerium ; exul, exilium.* When *ium* is added to verbal substantives in *tor,* it

denotes the place where the action is going on—as *auditor*, *auditorium ; conditor, conditorium.*

4. The termination *atus*, suffixed to words denoting persons, expresses a position or office—as *consul, consulatus ; tribunus, tribunatus.* The same thing is sometimes expressed by the suffix *ŭra* being added to the stem — as *dictator, dictatura ; censor, censura ; praetor, praetura.*

5. Substantives derived from others by the suffix *ārius* denote persons pursuing as a trade that which is implied in the primitive — as *aqua, aquarius ; sica, ·sicarius ; argentum, argentarius ; mensa, mensarius.* Those derived from others by the termination *ārium* denote a place where the things expressed by the primary word are collected and kept—that is, a receptacle—as *granum, granarium ; semen, seminarium ; armamenta, armamentarium ; vivus, vivarium ; planta, plantarium.*

6. The termination *ētum*, suffixed to the stem of names of plants, denotes the place where they grow—as *oliva, olivētum ; myrtus, myrtētum ; frutex, fruticētum ; quercus, quercētum ; arundo, arundinētum.*

Note. Some nouns of this class are formed in a somewhat different way—as *salix, salictum; carex, carectum; arbor, arbustum; virga* or *virgula, virgultum.*

7. The termination *īle*, when added to names of animals, denotes the place in which they are kept—as *ovis, ovīle ; bos, bovīle ; equus, equīle ; caper, caprīle.* In like manner are formed *cubīle* (a place for lying), and *sedīle* (a place for sitting), from *cubo* and *sedeo.*

8. The termination *īna*, when added to names of persons, denotes a business, pursuit, or the place where it is carried on — as *medicus, medicīna ; sutor, sutrīna ; doctor, doctrīna ; discipulus, disciplīna :* so also *officīna,* from *officium ; textrīnum, pistrīnum ; ruīna* (from *ruo*), *aurifodīna* (from *fodio*), *rapīna* (from *rapio*).

9. Some substantives are derived from others by the ending *io,* and denote persons occupying themselves with that which is expressed by the primitive — as *restis* (rope), *restio* (rope-maker); *centurio,* from *centuria ; pellis* (skin), *pellio* (skinner); *ludus* (play), *ludio* (player)..

10. A few substantives denoting a condition or quality are derived from names of persons by adding *tus* to the stem—as *vir, virtus ; senex, senectus ; juvenis, juventus ; servus, servitus.*

11. In the Greek language it is customary to derive from

the names of male persons other names, to designate their sons, daughters, and other descendants. Such derivatives are called patronymics, and are frequently made use of by the Latin poets; but in prose they occur only in the case of the most illustrious Greek heroes—as *Priamĭdes*, a son or descendant of Priam; *Tantalis*, a daughter of Tantalus.

Note. Masculine patronymics commonly terminate in 'ĭdes, which is added to the stem of the proper name—as *Priamĭdes*, *Cecropĭdes* (from *Cecrops*). But names in *eus* and *cles* make their patronymics in ĭdes (ειδης)—as *Atrīdes* (from *Atreus*), *Pelīdes* (from *Peleus*), *Heraclīdes* (from *Heracles*). Names of the first declension in *as* make patronymics in *ădes*—as *Aeneădes* (from *Aeneas*); those in *ius* make *iădes* —as *Thestiădes* (from *Thestius*); and this termination is also used in forming patronymics from other names, because it is very convenient in hexameter verse—as *Abantiădes* (from *Abas*), *Atlantiădes* (from *Atlas*), *Laërtiădes* (from *Laërtes*).

Feminine patronymics mostly end in *is* — as *Tantalis*; but those which have the masculine in ĭdes make the feminine in ēis — as *Nerēis* (from *Nereus*); and those which make the masculine in *iădes* have the feminine in *ias*—as *Thestias* (from *Thestius*). Aeneas, however, has the feminine patronymic *Aenēis*.

§ 205. Substantives denoting quality are formed from adjectives by the following terminations :—

1. *tas* added to the stem of the adjective, together with the connecting vowel ĭ, produces substantives denoting a quality abstractedly — as *bonus, bonĭtas; asper, asperĭtas; crudelis, crudelĭtas; atrox, atrocĭtas; celer, celerĭtas; alacer, alacrĭtas.* Adjectives ending in *ius* take the connecting vowel ĕ — as *pius, piĕtas; varius, variĕtas; ebrius, ebriĕtas;* and those in *stus* take no connecting vowel at all—as *honestus, honestas; venustus, venustas; vetustus, vetustas.* In these last cases one *t* is dropped, as no consonant can be doubled when preceded by another.

Note. The following also are formed without a connecting vowel : —*libertas*, from *liber; paupertas;* from *pauper; facultas* (but also *facilitas* in a different sense), from *facilis; difficultas*, from *difficilis;* and in like manner *voluntas* (from the verb *volo*) and *potestas* (from the verb *possum*).

2. *ia* added to the stem is principally used to form substantives from adjectives and participles of one termination for all genders — as *audax, audacia; concors, concordia; clemens, clementia; elegans, elegantia; abundans, abundantia; demens, dementia.* But the same termination is also used to form substantives from adjectives ending in *cundus*—as *facundus, facundia; iracundus, iracundia; verecundus, verecundia,* though *jucundus* makes *jucunditas.* In like manner *miser* and *perfidus* make *miseria* and *perfidia.*

3. *tia*, with the connecting vowel *ĭ*, serves to form substantives from a few adjectives, the stem of which ends in *t* or *r*—as *justus, justĭtia; laetus, laetĭtia; moestus, moestĭtia; avarus, avarĭtia; piger, pigrĭtia;* but we also have *pudicitia* and *tristitia,* from *pudicus* and *tristis.*

4. *tūdo*, with the connecting vowel *ĭ*, is employed to form substantives from adjectives of two and three terminations— as *altus, altĭtūdo; beatus, beatĭtūdo; aeger, aegrĭtūdo; similis, similĭtūdo; longus, longĭtūdo.* Some adjectives, the stem of which ends in *t*, require no connecting vowel—as *consuetus, consuetūdo; sollicitus, sollicitūdo.*

Note. In some cases substantives in *tas* and *tūdo* are formed from the same adjective, without any material difference in meaning; but in such cases the substantive in *tūdo* is more rarely used than the one ending in *tas*—as *clarus, clarĭtas,* and *clarĭtūdo; firmus, firmĭtas,* and *firmĭtūdo.* (Compare § 201, note 2.) Some adjectives, on the other hand, form substantives with different terminations, which at the same time have different meanings—as *dulcis* (sweet), *dulcēdo* (charm, agreeableness), and *dulcĭtūdo* (sweetness); *gravis* (heavy), *gravĭtas* (heaviness, weight), and *gravēdo* (heaviness in the head, or a cold). Other substantives in *ēdo* are *torpēdo,* from *torpeo; pinguēdo,* from *pinguis,* instead of *pinguitudo; putrēdo,* from *putresco.*

5. *mōnia*, preceded by the connecting vowel *ĭ*, occurs only in a few substantives — as *sanctus, sanctimōnia; castus, castimonia; acer, acrimonia; parsimonia* (for *parcimonia*), from the verb *parco;* and *querimonia,* from *queror.*

CHAPTER XXXVI.

DERIVATION OF ADJECTIVES FROM VERBS, SUBSTANTIVES, AND PROPER NAMES.

§ 206. Adjectives are derived from verbs and substantives —proper and common; a few are also formed from other adjectives and adverbs. [We shall not here take into account the formation of participles from verbs, this subject having been treated of in another part of this grammar. Chap. xvii.] Adjectives are derived from verbs by means of the following suffixes :—

1. *dus*, preceded by the connecting vowel *ĭ*, added to the pure stem of verbs of the second conjugation, produces adjectives denoting the condition or quality implied in the verb—as *caleo, calĭdus; frigeo, frigĭdus; tepeo, tepĭdus; humeo, humĭ-*

dus; areo, arĭdus; madeo, madĭdus; timeo, timĭdus; but we also have *rapĭdus,* from *rapio.*

2. *lis,* preceded by the connecting vowel *ĭ,* added to stems of verbs ending in a consonant, denotes the capability of enduring the action implied in the verb — as *frango, fragĭlis; facio, facĭlis; utor, utĭlis; doceo, docĭlis.* The same meaning is still more frequently produced by the suffix *bĭlis,* which is sometimes preceded by the connecting vowel *ĭ* — as *amo, amabĭlis; probo, probabĭlis; fleo, flēbĭlis; deleo, delēbĭlis; volvo, volubĭlis; credo, credibĭlis; moveo, mōbĭlis; novi, nōbĭlis,* in which two cases the *v* is thrown out.

Note 1. The meaning of such adjectives is generally passive, but some have an active sense—as *terribĭlis,* creating terror ; *penetrabilis,* penetrating ; *horribilis,* creating horror ; *fertilis,* bringing forth, fertile.

2. Some adjectives in *lis* are not formed from the stem of a verb, but from the stem as it appears modified in the supine—as *findo, fissilis; verso, versatilis; fingo, fictilis; coquo, coctilis; alo, altilis;* so also *comprehendo, comprehensibilis; plaudo, plausibilis.*

3. *ax,* added to the stem of a verb, produces adjectives denoting an inclination or propensity, and in most cases a censurable one — as *pugno, pugnax; audeo, audax; edo, edax; loquor, loquax; rapio, rapax.* Sometimes the suffix *ax* gives to the verb merely the meaning of a present participle—as *minor, minax = minans; fallo, fallax = fallens. Capax* signifies that which can hold or contain.

4. *cundus* is less frequently employed to derive adjectives denoting capability, inclination, or approximation—as *iracundus,* of an angry disposition (from *irascor); facundus,* eloquent (from *facio); verēcundus,* inclined to be bashful (from *vereor); rubĭcundus,* reddish, approaching to redness (from *rubeo); jucundus,* helping on, agreeable (from *juvo).*

5. *lus,* with the connecting vowel *ŭ* added to the stem of verbs, produces adjectives either simply denoting an action or the inclination to it — as *patet, patulus* (being open) ; *queror, querulus,* inclined to complain ; *credo, credulus,* inclined to believe, credulous ; *garrio, garrulus,* inclined to talk or gossip, garrulous.

6. *uus* forms adjectives of a passive meaning from transitive verbs—as *conspicuus, individuus;* and others of an active meaning from intransitives—as *congruus, innocuus, assiduus.*

§ 207. Adjectives are formed from substantives by a great variety of terminations, some of which present scarcely any difference in meaning, and cannot therefore be clearly defined in every instance.

1. *eus*, added to the stem of substantives, produces adjectives denoting the material of which a thing consists or is made — as *lignum, ligneus; aurum, aureus; argentum, argenteus; cinis, cinereus; ignis, igneus; vimen, vimineus*. Sometimes, especially in poetry, adjectives with the suffix *eus* denote mere resemblance — as *virgineus*, virgin-like; *roseus*, rosy, or rose-like; *arundineus*, like a reed.

Note. Adjectives denoting the kind of wood of which a thing consists or is made, usually have the suffix *neus* or *nus*—as *ilex, iligneus*, or *ilignus; quercus, querneus*, or *quernus; populus, populneus*, or *populnus*. From *fagus* and *cedrus*, however, we have *faginus* and *cedrinus*, in which the *ĭ* is the connecting vowel. In like manner we have *eburneus*, and *eburnus*, from *ebur; coccinus* and *coccineus*, from *coccum;* and *adamantinus*, from *adamas*. The suffix *nus* also indicates that something belongs to, or originates with, that implied in the substantive — as *paternus, maternus, fraternus, vernus*, from *pater, mater, frater, ver*. In like manner we have *infernus* and *supernus*, from *inferi* and *superi*, and *hibernus*, from *hiems*.

2. *cius*, preceded by the connecting vowel *ĭ*, added to the stem of a substantive, produces adjectives denoting that a thing consists of what is implied in the substantive or belongs to it — as *later, latericius; caementum, caementicius; tribunus, tribunicius; aedilis, aedilicius; gentilis, gentilicius*. Sometimes adjectives are formed by the suffix *icius* from the supine of verbs — as *commentum, commenticius; collatum, collaticius; subditum, subditicius; adventum, adventicius; suppositum, supposititius*. So also *novicius*, from *novus*.

3. *āceus* forms adjectives almost exclusively from substantives of the first declension, denoting a substance or a resemblance to it — as *argilla, argillaceus; charta, chartaceus; rosa, rosaceus; ampulla, ampullaceus; gallina, gallinaceus*. With the exception of the last, these adjectives are not often used by the best writers.

4. *cus*, preceded by the connecting vowel *ĭ*, forms adjectives which denote belonging or relating to a thing — as *civis, civicus; bellum, bellicus; hostis, hosticus*. Sometimes the suffix *ticus* is employed in the same way — as *rus, rusticus; aqua, aquaticus; domus, domesticus*.

Note. For *civicus* and *hosticus* we more commonly find *civilis* and *hostilis*, though the former are common in certain expressions—as *corona civica*, 'a civic crown.' These adjectives in *ĭcus* must not be confounded with those ending in *īcus*, which are formed from verbs and prepositions — as *amicus* and *inimicus* (from *amo*), *pudicus* (from *pudet*), *anticus* (from *ante*), *posticus* (from *post*). *Apricus* is of uncertain origin.

5. *ilis*, appended to the stem of substantives, produces adjectives denoting what is in accordance with, like, or becoming to that which is expressed by the substantive — as *civis,*

*civīlis; hostis, hostīlis; vir, virīlis; puer, puerīlis; anus,
anīlis; scurra, scurrīlis; herus, herīlis; gens, gentīlis; sextus, Sextīlis; quintus, Quintīlis;* but from *tribus* we have
tribūlis, and from *fides, fidēlis; humus* makes *humĭlis,* and
par, parĭlis. Subtīlis is of uncertain origin.

6. *ālis* serves to form adjectives of the same meaning as those
ending in *īlis,* but is employed much more frequently — as
*annus, annālis; conviva, convivālis; natura, naturālis; pes,
pedālis; rex, regālis; virgo, virginālis.* When the stem of
the substantive ends in *l,* or its last syllable begins with *l,*
ālis becomes *āris* — as *populus, populāris; miles, militaris;
palma, palmaris; pluvia,* however, makes *pluviālis,* and
fluvius, fluviālis. These terminations appear curtailed in
many English adjectives derived from the Latin, or formed
according to its analogy — as natural, regal, popular, military, regular, singular, &c.

Note. A lengthened suffix *ătĭlis* makes adjectives which denote
belonging to, living in, or arranged for—as *aquatilis,* belonging to or
living in water ; *fluviatilis,* belonging to a river ; *umbratilis,* arranged
to give shade.

7. *ius* forms adjectives denoting suitableness, belonging or
peculiar to the idea expressed by the substantive — as *rex,
regius; pater, patrius; praetor, praetorius; soror, sororius;
uxor, uxorius; imperator, imperatorius; amator, amatorius.*
It must be observed that this suffix is appended only to substantives denoting persons ; and that those words in *or,*
which do not denote persons, form adjectives by simply
adding *us* to the nominative — as *odor, odōrus; decor, de-
cōrus; honor, honōrus* (less frequently used than *honestus*).

8. *īnus* makes adjectives, especially from names of animals,
denoting what belongs to, or is derived from, that expressed
by the substantives, most commonly the flesh of the animals
—as *divus, divīnus; mare, marīnus; libertus, libertīnus; pere-
grīnus,* from *peregre; fera, ferīnus; equus, equīnus; canis,
canīnus; agnus, agnīnus; anas, anatīnus;* but from *bos, ovis*
and *sus,* we have *bubulus, ovillus,* and *suillus.*

Note. To these may be added *clandestīnus* (from *clam*), and *intes-
tīnus* (from *intra*). From these adjectives must be distinguished
those in *ĭnus* (in which *ĭ* is merely the connecting vowel), derived
from names of substances and trees. (See § 207, note.) We must
further distinguish those in *tĭnus* which denote time — as *diutĭnus,*
from *diu; annotĭnus,* from *annus; hernotĭnus,* from *heri; pristĭnus,*
from *prius.* The following, however, have a long *ī—matutīnus, re-
pentīnus,* and *vespertīnus.*

9. *ānus,* added to the stem of substantives, makes adjectives
denoting a resemblance, or belonging to what is expressed

by the substantive — as *urbs, urbānus; mons, montānus; homo, humānus.* So also *rusticānus,* from *rusticus.* In like manner are formed adjectives from ordinary numerals, to denote that which belongs to the number implied—as *quartana febris,* a fever lasting for four days; *primanus,* belonging to the first legion; *quartanus,* belonging to the fourth legion. (Compare § 105, note 3.)

10. *ārius,* added to the stem of substantives, makes adjectives signifying that something belongs, or has reference, to what is implied in the substantive—as *legio, legionārius* (belonging to a legion); *grex, gregārius,* belonging to a flock. (Compare § 204, 5.) *ārius* also makes adjectives from distributive numerals, to denote the quality of having a certain number of units — as *deni, denarius* (a coin containing ten units — that is, ases); *septuagenarius,* a man who has lived seventy years; *numerus ternarius,* the number three — that is, containing three units.

11. *ivus,* added to the stem of substantives, forms adjectives denoting that which belongs to, or is fit for, the thing expressed by the substantive — as *furtum, furtivus; festum, festivus; votum, votivus;* but *aestas* makes *aestivus,* and *tempestas, tempestivus.* When added to the stem of participles, it denotes the manner in which a thing has arisen—as *natus, nativus; satus, sativus; captus, captivus.*

12. *ōsus,* added to the stem of substantives, produces adjectives denoting fulness of what is expressed by the substantive or bringing it about — as *calamitas, calamitōsus; lapis, lapidōsus; damnum, damnōsus; periculum, periculōsus; saltus, saltuōsus; vinum, vinōsus.* Sometimes the connecting vowel *ĭ* is introduced — as *artifex, artificiōsus; bellicōsus* is formed from *bellicus;* and on the same model is formed *tenebricosus* (from *tenebrae*).

13. *lentus,* with the connecting vowel *ŭ* or *ŏ* added to the stem, denotes fulness or manner — as *fraus, fraudŭlentus; turba, turbŭlentus; sanguis, sanguinŏlentus; vis, viŏlentus.*

14. *ātus,* added to the stem of a substantive, forms numerous adjectives denoting possession of what is expressed by the substantive—as *ansa, ansātus: barba, barbātus; calceus, calceātus; dens, dentātus; falx, falcātus; virga, virgātus; aurum, aurātus; toga, togātus.*

Note 1. Adjectives of the same meaning are formed from substantives in *is* (genitive *is*) by the suffix *itus* — as *auris, auritus; turris, turritus; crinis, crinitus;* so also *mel, mellitus; galerus, galeritus.* Words of the fourth declension form a few adjectives in *ūtus* — as *cornu, cornūtus; astu, astūtus;* but *arcus* makes *arcuātus;* and *nasus,* though belonging to the second declension, makes *nasūtus.*

2. Some, again, ending in *us* or *ur* (equivalent to a stem in *ur* or *er*) make adjectives in *tus*—as *onus, onustus; robur, robustus; venus, venustus; funus, funestus; scelus, scelestus;* and so also *honos, honestus; modus, modestus.*

15. The following suffixes occur only in a very limited number of words:—

(a). *tĭmus,* with the connecting vowel *ĭ,* in *legĭtĭmus, finĭtĭmus,* and *marĭtĭmus,* from *lex, finis,* and *mare.*

(b). *nus,* in *paternus, fraternus, maternus, infernus,* and *externus,* from *pater, frater, mater, infra,* and *extra.* (§ 207, note.)

(c). *ernus* and *urnus* make adjectives denoting belonging to the time expressed by the substantive—as *ver, vernus; hiems, hibernus; heri (hester), hesternus; aevum, aeternus* (for *aeviternus*); *dies, diurnus; nox, nocturnus.*

(d). *ensis* makes adjectives denoting belonging to the place expressed by the substantive—as *forum, forensis; castra, castrensis.*

(e). *ester* occurs in *campester, equester,* from *campus* and *equus.*

(f). *āneus,* in adjectives derived from verbs and other adjectives, approaching in meaning to a participle present, or to the adjective from which they are formed—as *consentāneus* (from *consentio*), *subitāneus* (from *subeo*), *supervacāneus* (from *supervacuus*); so also *mediterrāneus,* from *terra.*

16. Many adjectives also admit the formation of diminutives, which are made on the same principle on which diminutive substantives are formed from other substantives (see § 204, 2)—as *parvus, parvulus; aureus, aureolus; pulcher, pulchellus; miser, misellus; pauper, pauperculus; levis, leviculus; bellus* is irregularly formed from *bonus, novellus* from *novus,* and *paullum* from *parvus,* though we also have *parvulus.*

§ 208. Adjectives are formed from proper names far more frequently in Latin than in English; and we must therefore frequently have recourse to circumlocution, where in Latin a single adjective suffices. We shall, for the sake of convenience, divide all proper names into names of persons, towns, and countries, to show in what manner adjectives are formed from each of these three classes.

1. The Roman Gentile names ending in *ius*—as *Fabius, Cornelius*—are in reality adjectives, and are used as such to designate the works of persons bearing those names—as *lex Cornelia, lex Julia, via Appia, circus Flaminius.* Other adjectives in *ānus,* however, are formed from these names to denote things which have reference to a member of a family or gens, and are named after him—as *jus Flavianum*

from *Flavius*), *classis Pompeiana* (from *Pompeius*), *bellum Marianum* (from *Marius*).

2. From Roman surnames (cognomen) are formed adjectives ending in *ānus*, sometimes with the connecting vowel *i*, and sometimes without it, and with the same meaning as those in *ānus* derived from Gentile names — as *Cicero*, *Ciceronianus; Caesar, Caesarianus; Sulla, Sullanus; Gracchus, Gracchanus; Lepidus, Lepidanus*, and *Lepidianus; Lucullus, Lucullianus*. The termination *īnus* is more rare—as *Verres, Verrīnus; Jugurtha, Jugurthīnus; Messala, Messalīnus; Drusus, Drusīnus*.

Note. Some surnames are themselves occasionally used as adjectives—as *domus Augusta, portus Trajanus;* the same may likewise form the basis of new adjectives—as *Augustānus*. Poets and the later writers also make adjectives in *eus* from Roman names — as *Caesareus, Romuleus*—though this termination is properly Greek; for in the latter language it is customary to form adjectives from proper names by the terminations *ēus* or *īus* (ειος), and *īcus* — as *Aristotelīus, Epicurēus, Platonīcus, Demosthenīcus*.

§ 209. Adjectives are formed from names of towns by the suffixes *ānus, īnus, as*, and *ensis;* they denote belonging to the place from which they are derived, and are therefore used as names for the inhabitants. Adjectives of this kind are formed not only from towns in Italy, but from many towns in Greece and other countries.

1. *ānus* forms adjectives from names of towns ending in *a, ae, um*, and *i* — as *Roma, Romānus; Sora, Sorānus; Formiae, Formiānus; Tusculum, Tusculānus; Fundi, Fundānus; Troja, Trojānus; Syracusae, Syracusānus; Thebae, Thebānus; Tralles*, according to the Greek, makes *Tralliānus*.

Note. Greek towns forming the names of their inhabitants in *ītes* (ίτης), admit the formation of Latin adjectives in *itānus* — as *Panormus, Panormitānus; Tyndaris, Tyndaritānus; Neapolis, Neapolitānus;* so also *Gades, Gaditānus*.

2. *īnus* makes adjectives from names of towns ending in *ia, ium* — as *Ameria, Amerīnus; Lanuvium, Lanuvīnus; Arretium, Arretīnus;* but *Praeneste* and *Reate* also make *Praenestīnus, Reatīnus*. Some names of Greek towns make adjectives by the same suffix — as *Tarentum, Tarentīnus; Agrigentum, Agrigentīnus; Centuripa, Centuripīnus; Saguntum, Saguntīnus*.

3. *as* (gen. *ātis*) forms adjectives from some names of towns ending in *a, ae*, and *um* — as *Capena, Capenas; Fidenae, Fidenas; Arpinum, Arpinas; Antium, Antias*. This suffix
12

is never used to form adjectives from names of Greek towns.

4. *ensis* is employed to derive adjectives from names of towns ending in *o*, and from some ending in *a*, *ae*, or *um* — as *Narbo*, *Narbonensis*; *Tarraco*, *Tarraconensis*; *Sulmo*, *Sulmonensis*; *Bononia*, *Bononiensis*; *Cannae*, *Cannensis*; *Athenae*, *Atheniensis*; *Ariminum*, *Ariminensis*; *Carthago*, *Carthaginiensis*; *Laodicea*, *Laodiciensis*; *Nicomedea*, *Nicomedensis*.

Note. In Greek names which make adjectives in *eus* (εὺς), the Latins commonly substitute *ensis*; but in some cases *eus* also was adopted by Latin writers—as *Cittium*, *Cittieus*; *Halicarnassus*, *Halicarnasseus*, as well as *Halicarnassensis*. Some Latin names also make their adjectives in an irregular manner — as *Veii*, *Veiens*; *Caere*, *Caeres*; *Tibur*, *Tiburs* (gen. *Tiburtis*).

5. *ius* makes adjectives from Greek names of towns and islands in *us*, *um*, *ōn*, and some others, and answers to the Greek ιος—as *Corinthus*, *Corinthius*; *Byzantium*, *Byzantius*; *Rhodus*, *Rhodius*; *Lacedaemon*, *Lacedaemonius*; *Clazomenae*, *Clazomenius*; *Aegyptus*, *Aegyptius*. The Greek terminations ηνος (*ēnus*) and αιος (*aeus*) are likewise retained in Latin in some instances — as *Cyzicus*, *Cyzicenus*; *Smyrna*, *Smyrnaeus*; *Erythrae*, *Erythraeus*; *Cuma*, *Cumaeus* in poetry, but in prose *Cumanus*.

Note. The names of the inhabitants of a place often terminate in Greek in της — as in *ātes*, *ītes*, *ōtes*; and these endings are often retained by Latin writers — as *Abdera*, *Abderītes*; *Sparta*, *Spartiātes*; *Tegea*, *Tegeātes*; *Heraclea*, *Heracleōtes*; but sometimes the Greek ending *tes* is changed into the Latin *ta*.

§ 210. Of the names of nations, some are real adjectives, and are used as such — as *Latinus*, *Romanus*, *Sabinus*, *Oscus*, *Volscus*, *Etruscus*, *Graecus*; e.g., *lingua Latina*, 'the Latin language;' *nomen Romanum*, 'the Roman name.' Others are real substantives, and from them are formed adjectives by means of the termination *icus*—as *Gallus*, *Gallicus*; *Arabs*, *Arabicus*; *Macedo*, *Macedonicus*; *Marsus*, *Marsicus*; *Italus*, *Italicus*; *Britannus*, *Britannicus*; or by the ending *ius* — as *Syrus*, *Syrius*; *Thrax*, *Thracius*; *Cilix*, *Cilicius*. When persons are spoken of, the adjective is not used, but the substantive, which stands in apposition to the name of the person — as *miles Gallus*, 'a Gallic soldier;' *servus Thrax*, 'a Thracian slave.'

Note 1. Poets sometimes use even those names of nations which are real substantives, as if they were adjectives—as *orae Italae*, 'the Italian coasts;' *aper Marsus*, 'a Marsic boar;' *flumen Medum*, 'the Median river ;' *Colcha venena,* 'Colchian poisons.' Nay, sometimes they treat in the same way names of rivers and seas, which, as if adjectives, they make agree with other nouns — as *flumen Metaurum* for *Metaurus; flumen Rhenum* for *Rhenus; mare oceanum* for *oceanus.*

2. The Greek names of female inhabitants of towns and countries ending in *is* and *as* (genitive *ĭdos, ădos*) are also used by Latin poets as adjectives (see § 70) ; and in like manner they employ, both as substantives and adjectives, those Greek feminine names of nations which end in *ssa*—as *Cilissa, Cressa, Libyssa, Phoenissa, Threissa,* or *Thressa.*

§ 211. Names of countries ending in *ia,* and formed from the names of nations, sometimes admit of the formation of adjectives, to denote that which belongs to, or comes from, them — as *pecunia Siciliensis,* 'money derived from the country of Sicily,' not from the inhabitants ; *exercitus Hispaniensis,* 'a Roman army stationed in Spain,' and not an army consisting of Spaniards. So also *Africanus, Asiaticus, Italicus.*

Note. Some names of people do not admit the formation of names of countries ; but serve themselves as the name of the country or town — as *Aequi, Sabini, Sequani,* and *Leontini,* 'the town of the Leontini.' This mode of using the name of the people for that of the country is adopted even in cases where there exists a distinct name for the country — as *Lucani* for *Lucania; Bruttii* for *Bruttium;* and many others.

CHAPTER XXXVII.

DERIVATION OF VERBS FROM SUBSTANTIVES, ADJECTIVES, AND
OTHER VERBS.

§ 212. The number of verbs derived from substantives and adjectives is not very great. As a general rule, it may be observed that intransitive verbs formed from nouns follow the second conjugation — as *flos, florēre* (flourish) ; *albus, albēre* (to be white) ; whereas transitive verbs follow the first conjugation—as *fraus, fraudare* (to deceive); *honor, honorare* (honour); *laus, laudare* (praise) ; *albus, albare* (whitewash); *vulnus, vulnerare* (wound); *celeber, celebrare* (celebrate); *maturus, maturare* (make ripe); *lēvis, lēvare* (make smooth); *memor, memorare* (mention). There are a few verbs of the fourth conjugation formed from substantives in *is* — as *finis, finire* (end); *vestis, vestire* (clothe).

Note. Verbs in *āre* and *īre* derived from nouns are very rarely intransitive, as is the case with *germinare* (from *germen*), germinate ;

and *servire* (from *servus*), to be a servant. In some cases a preposition is prefixed when a verb is formed from a noun, and the verb without the preposition either does not occur at all, or only in poetry — as *agger, exaggerare* (accumulate); *stirps, exstirpare* (root out); *hilaris, exhilarare* (exhilarate); *acervus, coacervare* (pile up).

§ 213. A great many deponents of the first conjugation are derived from substantives and adjectives, and most of them have an intransitive meaning — as *philosophus, philosophor* (I am a philosopher); *Graecus, Graecor* (I conduct myself like a Greek); *aqua, aquor* (I fetch water); *piscis, piscor* (I fish); *negotium, negotior* (I carry on a business); *laetus, laetor* (I am joyful). They have more rarely a transitive meaning — as *fur, furor* (I steal); *osculum, osculor* (I kiss). A few deponents formed from nouns follow the fourth conjugation — as *pars, partior* (divide); *sors, sortior* (obtain by chance).

§ 214. Derivative verbs are much more frequently formed from simple verbs by means of certain suffixes which modify their meaning, than from substantives and adjectives:—

1. By means of the suffix *ĭto* (in deponents, *ĭtor*) are formed what are called frequentative verbs—that is, such as denote frequent repetition of an action. All frequentative verbs belong to the first conjugation. In verbs of the first conjugation this suffix is appended to the real stem of the word —as *clamo, clamĭto ; rogo, rogĭto ; volo, volĭto ; minor, minĭtor.* In verbs of the third conjugation, and in those of the second and fourth which make their supine in the same manner as those of the third, the suffix *ĭto* is appended to the stem such as it appears in the supine — as *lego, lectĭto ; dico, dictĭto ; jacio, jactĭto ; curro, cursĭto ; haereo, haesĭto ; venio, ventĭto.*

2. Another class of frequentative verbs, with quite the same meaning, are formed by adding the termination of the first conjugation to the stem of simple verbs, as it appears in the supine — as *curro, curso, cursare ; mergo, merso, mersare ; adjuvo, adjuto, adjutare ; tueor, tutor, tutari ; amplector, amplexor, amplexari ; eo, ĭto, ĭtare.* In this manner some verbs have two frequentatives — as *curro, curso,* and *cursĭto ; dico, dicto,* and *dictito ; defendo, defenso,* and *defensito.*

Note 1. It must be observed, however, that many of these frequentative verbs do not simply denote a repetition of the action they express. They sometimes express a somewhat different idea from that contained in the primitive, along with a repetition of the action denoted by the primitive — as *dicto,* I dictate; *pulso* (from *pello*), I strike ; *quasso* (from *quatio*), I dash to pieces ; *tracto* (from *traho*), I treat ; *salto* (from *salio*). I dance. Sometimes there is scarcely any difference of meaning between the simple verb and the frequentative —as *canto* and *cano,* I sing ; *gero* and *gesto,* I carry.

2. Some verbs form their frequentatives on a different principle from those laid down in the above rules—as *ago, agito; quaero, quaerito; nosco, noscito; cogo, cogito; lateo, latito; paveo, pavito; polliceor, pollicitor; habeo, habito; liceor, licitor.*

§ 215. Inchoative verbs — that is, such as denote the beginning of the action implied in the primitive verb — are formed by means of the suffix *sco.* This suffix is appended to the stem of the verb, as it appears in the infinitive after removing the termination *re ;* but in the third conjugation, the connecting vowel *i* is inserted between the stem and the suffix. · All inchoatives follow the third conjugation : — *labo, labasco,* I begin to waver ; *caleo, calesco,* I begin to be warm ; *caleo, incalesco ; ardeo, exardesco ; floreo, effloresco ; gemo, ingemisco ; dormio, obdormisco.*

Many inchoatives are derived from substantives and adjectives—as *puer, puerasco ; silva, silvesco ; ignis, ignesco ; maturus, maturesco ; niger, nigresco ; mitis, mitesco.*

Note. Many verbs in *sco,* which were originally inchoatives, have lost their inchoative meaning. Respecting the manner in which they form their perfect and supine, see §§ 165 and 166.

§ 216. Desiderative verbs—that is, such as denote a desire to do that which is implied in the primitive verb—are formed by the suffix *ŭrio* appended to the stem, as it appears in the supine — as *edo, esŭrio,* I want to eat, or am hungry ; *emo, emptŭrio,* I want to buy ; *pario, partŭrio,* I want or try to bring forth. The number of real desideratives is very small, and all follow the fourth conjugation.

Note. There are some verbs in *ŭrio* which are not desideratives—as *ligūrio, scatūrio, prūrio.*

§ 217. Diminutive verbs are formed by the suffix *illo* being appended to the stem. The number of such verbs is not great, and all follow the first conjugation — as *canto, cantillo,* I sing in an under voice, or shake ; *conscribo,* and *conscribillo,* I scribble ; *sorbeo, sorbillo,* I sip.

§ 218. There are a number of intransitive verbs from which transitives are formed by changing the conjugation to which they belong, and sometimes also by changing the quantity of the vowel contained in the stem, as —

fugio, I flee.	*fugo, āre,* put to flight.
jaceo, I lie.	*jacio, ĕre,* throw.
pendeo, I hang.	*pendo, ĕre,* weigh, or suspend.
liqueo, I am clear, or fluid.	*liquo, āre,* clear.
cădo, I fall.	*caedo,* fell, or cause to fall.
sĕdeo, I sit.	*sēdo,* appease, or cause to sit still.

CHAPTER XXXVIII.

DERIVATION OF ADVERBS.

§ 219. Adverbs are derived from adjectives (participles), numerals, substantives, pronouns, verbs, and sometimes also from other adverbs and prepositions.

1. Adverbs are formed from adjectives and participles by the suffixes *ē*, *ō*, and *tĕr*.

(*a*). Adverbs in *ē* are formed from adjectives and participles belonging to the second and first declensions—that is, from those ending in *us*, *a*, *um*, and *er*, *a*, *um* — as *altus*, *altē*; *longus*, *longē*; *probus*, *probē*; *doctus*, *doctē*; *amatus*, *amatē*; *liber*, *liberē*; *aeger*, *aegrē*; *pulcher*, *pulchrē*; *validus*, *valdē* (for *validē*).

Note. *Bonus* makes its adverb irregularly *bĕnĕ*, and *malus* makes *mălĕ*; and these two are the only adverbs of this class in which the *e* is short. There are, however, three other adverbs—*inferne*, *superne*, and *interne*, which are sometimes used by poets with the *e* short.

(*b*). A limited number of adjectives of the second and first declensions form adverbs by adding the suffix *ō* to the stem — as *tutus*, *tutō*; *creber*, *crebrō*; *necessarius*, *necessariō*; *consultus*, *consultō*. These adverbs are in reality the ablative singular of the neuter gender. The following are those most commonly in use : — *arcano*, *secreto*, *cito*, *continuo*, *falso*, *gratuito*, *liquido*, *manifesto*, *perpetuo*, *precario*, *serio*, *sero*, *auspicato*, *directo*, *festinato*, *necopinato*, *improviso*, *merito*, *optato*, *sortito*, *primo*, *secundo*, &c.

Note. In some cases two adverbs in *ē* as well as in *ō* are formed from the same adjective, and generally without any difference in meaning; but there are some in which there is a slight difference— namely, *raro* signifies 'rarely' or 'seldom,' but *rare* 'thinly scattered ;' *certo* and *certe* both signify ' certainly,' but *certe* alone is used in the sense of ' at least ;' *vere* and *vero* both mean ' truly' or ' in truth,' but *vero* is more commonly used as a conjunction in the sense of ' however' or ' but.' There are a few other adverbs in *o* not derived from adjectives of the first and second declensions—as *extemplo*, immediately ; *oppido*, very ; *omnino*, in general, on the whole, or thoroughly ; *profecto* (probably *pro facto*), truly.

2. All adjectives and participles belonging to the third declension make their adverbs by adding the suffix *tĕr* to the

stem : between the two, however, the connecting vowel ĭ is commonly inserted—as *gravis, graviter; acer, acriter; felix, feliciter; audax, audaciter,* but more commonly *audacter.* When the stem of an adjective ends in *t*, the connecting vowel is not used, and one *t* is thrown out—as *sapiens, sapienter; prudens, prudenter; amans, amanter.*

Note. The adjective *hilarus* or *hilaris* has the adverb *hilariter;* and *opulens* or *opulentus* also has *opulente* and *opulenter.* There are some adjectives in *us, a, um,* which have adverbs both in *ē* and in *ter* — as *humanus, humane,* and *humaniter; firmus, firme,* and *firmiter; largus, large,* and *largiter; durus, dure,* and *duriter.* Those in *lentus* generally have both forms — as *luculentus, luculente,* and *luculenter;* and some of them — as *violentus, fraudulentus,* and *temulentus* — have only adverbs in *ter.* *Alius* also makes *aliter; propter* is the adverb from *prope* (near), instead of *propiter.*

3. There is a number of adjectives from which no regular adverbs are formed, and in which the neuter (in the accusative singular) supplies the place — as *facilis, facile; difficilis, difficile* (also *difficulter); recens, recens* (recently); *sublimis, sublime; multus, multum; plurimus, plurimum;* so also *paulum, nimium, quantum, tantum, ceterum, plerumque, potissimum,* and all the ordinal numerals—as *primum, postremum, ultimum,* &c. See § 109, note 1.

Note. The poets frequently use the neuter of an adjective as an adverb, although the regular adverb also exists. Respecting the numeral adverbs, see § 109.

§ 220. By means of the suffix *ĭtus,* adverbs are formed from some substantives to denote origin from the thing implied by the substantive — as *coelum, coelĭtus,* from heaven; *fundus, fundĭtus,* from the foundation, completely; *radix, radicĭtus,* from or with the root, radically. So also *primĭtus, medullĭtus, antiquĭtus, divinĭtus.*

§ 221. A considerable number of adverbs are formed from the supine of verbs by means of the suffix *im;* they generally denote manner — as *caesim,* by way of cutting down; *punctim, conjunctim, carptim, separatim, cursim, passim* (from *pando), praesertim* (from *prae* and *sero), privatim, raptim, sensim, statim.*

In a similar manner adverbs are formed from nouns by the termination *ātim*—as *caterva, catervatim; grex, gregatim; vicus, vicatim; gradus, gradatim; singuli, singulatim; oppidum, oppidatim; paulum, paulatim.*

Note. The following are formed in a peculiar manner — *vir, virītim; tribus, tribūtim; fur, furtim; uber, ubertim;* and to these we may add *olim* (from *ollus* — that is, *ille); interim,* from *inter.*

§ 222. Some adverbs in *o* are formed from prepositions to denote motion towards a place — as *citro, ultro, intro, porro,* (for *proro*), *retro* (from the inseparable particle *re*). These are formed on the same principle as those derived from pronouns, such as *eo, quo*.

§ 223. There is a considerable number of words which are used as adverbs, but are in reality the ablative or accusative of nouns used in the sense of adverbs — as *noctu*, by night; *vesperi*, in the evening; *mane*, in the morning; *tempore, tempori*, at a time; *diu* and its compounds are derived from *dies*; *modo*, in a manner; *partim* (for *partem*); *forte* (from *fors*); *aliās*, elsewhere; *repente* (from *repens*); *foris* and *foras; sponte, gratis* (that is, *gratiis*), *vulgo, frustrā*, and many others.

§ 224. Lastly, a large number of adverbs are formed by composition of two or more words belonging to different parts of speech—as *quamdiu, tamdiu, interdiu, aliquamdiu, hodie* (*hoc die*), *quotidie, postridie, pridie, perendie, nudius tertius* (*nunc dies tertius*), *nudius quartus, nudius quintus*, &c. *propediem, imprimis* (*in primis*), *cumprimis, protinus* or *protenus, postmodo, interdum, cummaxime, tummaxime, denuo* (*de novo*), *ilicet* (*ire licet*), *illico* (*in loco*), *extemplo, intereā, praetereā, insuper, obviam, comminus* or *cominus* (*cum* and *manus*), *eminus* (*e* and *manus*); *hāctenus, eātenus*, and *quātenus*, contain ablatives governed by *tenus; nimirum, scilicet* (*scire licet*), *videlicet* (*videre licet*), *utpote, dumtaxat, praeterquam, admodum, quemadmodum, quomodo, quamobrem, quapropter, quantopere, tantopere, quantumvis, quamvis, alioqui* and *alioquin, ceteroqui* and *ceteroquin*, and a considerable number of adverbs compounded with the participle *versus* — as *horsum* (*hoc versum*), *quorsum* (*quo versum*), *aliorsum* (*alio versum*), *aliquoversum, quoquoversus, prorsus* and *prorsum* (*pro versus* and *versum*), *rursum, rursus* (*re versus*), *retrorsum* (*retro versum*), *introrsum, sursum,* (*sub versum*), *deorsum, seorsum, dextrorsum, sinistrorsum*.

Note. The *ā* in *posteā* and *praetereā* is long, either because the original forms were *posteam* and *praeteream*, to which *rem* is to be understood; or, what is more probable, we must believe that in early times, before the language became fixed, the prepositions *post, praeter*, and others, governed the ablative as well as the accusative, and that accordingly such forms, as *posteā, praetereā, intereā, posthāc, quāpropter*, are remnants of the early language.

CHAPTER XXXIX.

FORMATION OF COMPOUND WORDS.

§ 225. Compound words are those which consist of two or more words, each of which by itself conveys a distinct idea. A compound word, nevertheless, expresses only one idea, made up of those contained in the separate words of which it consists. Thus from *de* and *scribo*, we make the compound *describo;* and from *pater* and *familia*, we make *paterfamilias.* The class of words to which a compound belongs, is determined by the last of the words of which it consists — that is, if the last is a substantive, the whole compound is a substantive; if the last is a verb, the whole is a verb; and if the last is an adjective, the whole is an adjective.

Note. There are some compound words which, although they express only one idea, are yet treated as two distinct words (for example, in declension), and even admit of other words being inserted between them—as *respublica, resquepublica; jus jurandum, jusve jurandum; senatusconsultum, unusquisque, alteruter*, and some others. These may be termed spurious compounds. But there are some genuine compounds, especially verbs compounded with a preposition, which in poetry are sometimes separated from each other by the insertion of some particle — as for *et illigatus*, we find *inque ligatus;* for *insalutatusque*, we find *inque salutatus.* The same is now and then the case with the compound adverbs *hactenus, eatenus, quadamtenus;* as in Horace—*quadam prodire tenus.* Adjectives compounded with *per* are sometimes separated even by prose writers—as *per mihi mirum visum est* for *permiram mihi visum est.* The same is also the case with *quicunque, qualiscunque*, and *quilibet.* Compare § 119.

§ 226. The first part of a compound word is either a noun (substantive, adjective, or numeral), or an adverb, or a preposition, and in a very few cases a verb. There are, besides, a number of inseparable particles which have a distinct meaning, and are found only prefixed to other words — namely, *amb* (about, around); *rĕ*, sometimes *red* (back again); *sē* (aside); *dis* (in different directions, the English *dis* in distribute); and the negatives *in* (the English *in* or *un*, as in infallible, unjust) and *ve.* (§ 195, note.)

Note. In occurs only in adjectives (including a few participles) and adverbs—as *injustus, inimicus, incultus, indoctus;* and of course in substantives formed from such adjectives as *injustitia, inimicitia.* It is also used in forming adjectives from substantives—as *forma, informis.* Before consonants, it undergoes the same changes as the preposition *in.* See § 195, 5. In some compounds the negative *ne (nec)* is used instead of *in*—as *nequeo, nefas, negotium* (from *otium*), *neco pinatus.*

H 2

Ve has likewise a negative meaning, but occurs very rarely—as in *vecors, vegrandis,* and *vesanus.*

§ 227. When the first word of a compound is a noun, the second is usually appended to the stem of the first; and the vowels *a* and *u,* if the noun belongs to the first, second, or fourth declension, are omitted. When the second word begins with a consonant, an *i* is usually inserted between the two as a connecting vowel — as *causidicus* (from *causa* and *dico*), *magnanimus* (from *magnus* and *animus*), *corniger* (from *cornu* and *gero*), *auriger* (*auris* and *gero*), *aedifico* (*aedes* and *facio*), *lucifer* (*lux* and *fero*), *coelicola* (*coelum* and *colo*); *naufragus* (*navis* and *frango*) requires no connecting vowel, *v* being equal to *u.*

Note. In some compounds no connecting vowel is used — as in *puerpera* (from *puer* and *pario*), *muscipula* (*mus* and *capio*). In some such cases it is necessary to drop the final consonant of the stem of the first word, in order to avoid a disagreeable sound—as *lapicida* for *lapidcida,* *homicida* for *homincida.* From *opus* and *facio* we have the irregular *opifex.* In a few instances *o* or *u* is used as the connecting vowel—as *Ahenobarbus, Trojugena.*

When adverbs formed from adjectives are compounded with other words, the adverbs take the stem of the adjective from which they are formed—as *magniloquus, suaviloquus;* but *bene* and *male* remain unchanged—as *benedico, maleficus.*

§ 228. When the first word of a compound is a preposition or the negative *in,* the vowel of the second word (*ă, ĕ,* or *ae*) is very often changed — as *amicus, inimicus; arma, inermis; barba, imberbis; calco, inculco; habeo, perhibeo; sedeo, assideo; frango, perfringo. Maneo,* however, makes *permaneo; traho, contraho; fremo, perfremo; haereo, inhaereo; cavus, concavus.*

Note. The same change also takes place in many compounds where the first word is a substantive — as *tubicen* (*tuba, cano*), *opifex* (*opus, facio*), *lapicida* (*lapis, caedo*), *stillicidium* (*stilla, cado*); and in like manner *triennium, biennium, biduum, triduum* (from *annus* and *dies*).

§ 229. It sometimes happens that a compound word belongs to a different class of words from the last part or element, and in this case the last receives a suitable termination to mark the class of words to which the whole belongs — as the adjective *maledicus,* from *male* and *dico; opifex,* from *opus* and *facio; beneficus,* from *bene* and *facio; biformis,* from *bis* and *forma.* Sometimes, however, the addition of such a termination is unnecessary — as in *crassipes,* from *crassus* and *pes; discolor,* from *dis* and *color.*

Sometimes the last word in a compound assumes a derivative suffix, without which it cannot form a compound — as *exardesco,* from *ex* and *ardeo; latifundium,* from *latus* and *fundus; Cisalpinus,* from *Cis* and *Alpes.*

SYNTAX.

§ 230. Syntax is that part of grammar which teaches us how to combine the various words and their forms in such a manner as to make sentences, conveying clearly and correctly the thoughts or sentiments which we mean to express. All the forms of words with which we have hitherto become acquainted are necessary under certain circumstances; and it is the part of syntax to teach us under what circumstances we have to employ this or that form of a word.

The rules of syntax may be divided into two departments: —1. The rules of concord or agreement; 2. The rules of government or dependence.

In modern languages, the order in which words must follow one another, for the purpose of forming sentences, is more or less fixed by custom; and it is chiefly in poetry that we find deviations from the established rules. In the Latin language the case is different; for, generally speaking, the words of a sentence may follow one another in any succession without creating ambiguity; which arises from the fact, that each word, by its peculiar termination, sufficiently shows what part it performs in the construction of the sentence. We must not, however, believe that the Romans acted in an arbitrary manner in composing their sentences; for by the liberty which they enjoyed in this respect, they were enabled to arrange the words of a sentence in such a manner that each was most likely to produce the desired effect. They were further guided by euphony—that is, their ear was allowed to decide whether one arrangement of words was more pleasing than another. These and other considerations guided the ancients; and it requires a careful study of their works to feel and appreciate the beautiful harmony of liberty and of law which regulates the construction of their sentences.

CHAPTER XL.

THE RULES OF CONCORD OR AGREEMENT BETWEEN SUBSTANTIVES AND
WORDS WHICH QUALIFY THEM — APPOSITION.

§ 231. Concord or agreement presupposes one thing which does agree and another with which it agrees. The latter is fixed and established, and the former must accommodate itself to it. A substantive may be qualified by adjectives (including participles), pronouns, numerals; and the substantive. being regarded as the fixed point, adjectives, pronouns, and numerals must accommodate themselves to the substantive to which they belong—that is, they take such terminations as may be required by the nature of the substantive.

1. Adjectives, pronouns, and declinable numerals, if they qualify or belong to a substantive or a substantive pronoun in the same clause, must agree with it in gender, number, and case—that is, the qualifying word must be put in the same gender, number, and case as the word qualified—as,

pater bonus, a good father.
mater cara, the dear mother.
librum utilem (accusative), a use-, ful book.
duae arbores, two trees.
domus mea, my house.

templum splendidum, a splendid temple.
templa splendida, splendid temples.
consul primus, the first consul.
tria bella, three wars.   [selves.
fratres ipsi, the brothers them-

2. When one adjective (participle or pronoun) belongs to two or more substantives, it either agrees only with the one nearest to it, or the adjective is repeated before each — as *omnes agri et maria*, or *omnes agri et omnia maria*.

Note. If several adjectives belong to one substantive, so as to denote more than one thing, the adjectives are in the singular, but the substantive is in the plural — as *prima et decima legiones; Cneius et Lucius Scipiones*.

3. When the adjective, pronoun, and numerals occur in a different clause from that in which the substantive or substantive pronoun exists, they can agree with it only in gender and number, the case being dependent on the nature of the clause in which they occur, as —

Amicus adest, sed eum non video, the friend is there, but I do not see him.

Est quidem bonus orator, sed meliorem jam audivi, he is indeed a good orator, but I have already heard a better one.

Omnibus virtutibus praeditus est, quae vitam ornant, he is endowed with all the virtues which adorn life.

§ 232. This is the case more especially with relative pronouns, which generally occur in a different clause from that containing the substantive to which they refer, and accordingly agree with it only in gender and number; but when the relative is joined to its substantive, it agrees with it also in case, like every other pronominal adjective — as *quo die veneram,* on which day I had come; that is, on the day on which I had come.

1. When a relative pronoun refers to more than one substantive, it is usually put in the plural. If the substantives denote living beings, and are of different genders, the relative takes the gender of the masculine, if there is a masculine among them. If there is no masculine, but only feminines and neuters, the relative takes the feminine — as *matres et parvuli liberi, quorum utrorumque aetas misericordiam requirit;* mothers and little children, the age of both of whom demands our pity. When substantives are names of inanimate objects, the relative is usually in the neuter plural — as *otium atque divitiae, quae prima mortales putant;* ease and riches, which mortals regard as the principal things.

Note 1. Sometimes, however, the relative agrees in number and gender only with the last of several substantives—that is, with the one nearest to it—as *eae fruges atque fructus, quos terra gignit,* where the *quos* agrees only with *fructus.* Sometimes several names of inanimate things may be of the same gender; and the relative, instead of taking their gender in the plural, appears in the neuter plural—as *inconstantia et temeritas, quae digna certe non sunt deo.*

*2. When a relative refers to a common noun joined to a proper name, it may agree either with the former or with the latter — as *flumen Rhenus, qui fluit,* and *flumen Rhenus, quod fluit.*

2. When a relative refers to a whole clause, and not to a single word, the neuter singular is used, before which the pronoun *id* is frequently added, the clause being treated as a neuter substantive — as *sapientes contenti sunt rebus suis, quod est summum bonum; si a vobis deserar, id quod non spero.*

3. When a relative pronoun refers to a substantive, which is explained by another in a clause containing the verb *sum,* or a verb of *naming,* the relative may agree either with the preceding substantive or with the explanatory one which follows—as *animal, quod homo vocatur,* or *qui homo vocatur; veni ad locum, quem Pylas vocant,* or *quas Pylas vocant*

Thebae, quae caput est Boeotiae, or *quod caput est Boeotiae.* There is, however, a nice difference of meaning between these two modes of speaking, for the noun with which the relative agrees is generally the one to which attention is more especially directed.

Note. Sometimes the relative pronoun is in the plural, though the substantive to which it refers is in the singular; this is the case when the substantive is a collective noun, such as *exercitus, equitatus, peditatus, nobilitas, plebs, populus,* and the like — e.g., *exercitum mittit, qui videant,* he sends the army, that they (the soldiers) may see; *unus ex eo numero, qui parati erant,* one of that number (of men) who were prepared.

4. Relative, as well as other pronouns, are often used without a substantive or substantive pronoun to which they refer, and in such cases it must be ascertained first of all whether human beings or things are spoken of. In the former case the pronouns are put in the masculine gender, either in the singular or plural; and in the latter in the neuter gender, likewise either in the singular or plural — as *ii qui virtutem amant,* those (men) who love virtue; *qui voluptatibus se dedunt,* those (men) who give themselves up to pleasures; *ea quae vitanda sunt,* those (things) which are to be avoided; *quaecunque facienda sunt,* whatever (things) are to be done; *quod bonum est, inutile esse non potest,* what is good, cannot be useless.

Note. What is here said of relative and other pronouns also applies to adjectives and participles when they are used without a substantive to which they belong—that is, when they themselves supply the place of a substantive. When they denote men, they take the masculine gender; and when things, the neuter—as *omnes boni amant virtutem,* all good (men) love virtue; *amisit omnia bona,* he has lost all goods (good things), or property; *vel doctissimus quaedam nescit,* even the most learned (man) is ignorant of some things. Instead of the neuter plural, however, which denotes things, the Latins may, like the English, use the word *res*—as *res bonae*—that is, *bona;* and this is done more especially where the cases of the neuter do not differ from the cases of the other genders, as in the genitive, dative, and ablative of both the singular and plural. Thus we can say *amor boni,* 'the love of what is good,' when it is clear from the context that *boni* is not masculine; but *amor utilis,* 'love of the useful,' can hardly be said.

§ 233. When one substantive is qualified by another which denotes the same person or thing, but at the same time contains an explanation or qualification of the former, the latter substantive stands in the relation of apposition, and must agree with the former in case—as *Cicero, magnus orator, interfectus est,* where *magnus orator* is in apposition to *Cicero;* *Hannibal, dux Carthaginiensium, in Africam trajecit,* where *dux Carthaginiensium* is in apposition to *Hannibal.*

If the substantive which stands in apposition has two genders, it generally takes the gender of the substantive which it explains—as *aquila regina avium*, the eagle, the king of birds, because *aquila* is feminine; *philosophia, magistra vitae*, philosophy is the instructor of life. In other cases the apposition cannot of course agree in gender or number with the substantive to be explained — as *Tullia, deliciae meae*, Tullia, my delight; *Cneius et Publius Scipiones, duo fulmina belli.* When plural names of places are explained by such words as *urbs, oppidum, civitas, caput*, the latter are always in the singular—as *Athenae, urbs Graeciae; Thebae, caput Boeotiae; Leontini, urbs Siciliae.*

Note. In Latin, one noun is sometimes put in apposition to another, to describe its state or condition during, or at the time of, the action spoken of; and in this case the apposition is often accompanied in English by the word 'as,' which cannot be rendered in Latin; e.g., *Cicero praetor legem Maniliam suasit*, Cicero, as praetor, or in his praetorship, recommended the Manilian bill; *Cicero consul conjurationem Catilinae oppressit*, Cicero as consul, or in his consulship, suppressed the Catilinarian conspiracy; *hic liber mihi puero valde placuit*, this book pleased me much as a boy, or when I was a boy. But when the 'as' means the same as 'as if,' it must be rendered in Latin by *tamquam, quasi*, or *ut*.

CHAPTER XLI.

AGREEMENT BETWEEN SUBJECT AND PREDICATE.

§ 234. Every sentence consists of two parts: the *subject*—that is, the person or thing spoken of; and the *predicate*, or that which is said of it. As, however, the Latin verb, in ordinary circumstances, does not require the addition of a personal pronoun, a sentence sometimes consists of a single word—as *dormio*, I am sleeping; *eo*, I go; *sedet*, he is sitting; *dicunt, ferunt*, they (people) say.

Note 1. With impersonal verbs no subject is used, nor is it always possible to conceive a definite subject—as *pluit*, 'it rains.' Here it is merely stated that an action is going on, without its being assigned to any definite subject. The same is the case with the passive of intransitive verbs — as *curritur*, 'running is going on,' a mode of expression which is often employed in Latin.

2. The personal pronouns are expressed in Latin only when they are emphatic—that is, when stress is laid upon the person in speaking — as *ego feci, non ille*, I have done it, not he.

§ 235. The subject of a sentence, when it is expressed, is generally a substantive, an adjective, or a pronoun: the two latter, however, must be regarded as representing substantives — *pater amat filium; ego curro ; isti morantur ; boni.virtutem colunt.* Any word which is used as a substantive may, however, be made the subject of a sentence, as is most frequently the case with the infinitive of a verb — as *errare humanum est,* where *errare* is the subject; *in errore perseverare turpe est,* where the expression *in errore perseverare* is the subject; *vides habet duas syllabas* (the word *vides* has two syllables), where *vides* is the subject.

Note. It may even happen that a whole clause is the subject of a sentence — as *quod hunc librum legisti, gratum mihi est,* where the subject consists of the clause *quod hunc librum legisti; civem pro patria mori honestum est,* where the clause *civem pro patria mori* forms the subject.

§ 236. The subject of a sentence is generally in the nominative case ; but when the verb is in the infinitive, the subject is always in the accusative — as *credo eum bonum esse virum ;* here the first sentence consists of the word *credo,* and the subject of the infinitive *esse* is *eum,* which is accordingly in the accusative ; *fratrem meum ad te venisse mihi gaudio est,* where *fratrem meum* is the subject of the infinitive *venisse.*

§ 237. The predicate consists either of a verb or of a noun (adjective or substantive) joined to the subject by means of the verb *esse*—as *arbor crescit,* the tree is growing ; *aqua fluit,* the water flows ; *arma capiuntur,* the arms are taken up ; *urbs est splendida,* the town is splendid ; *liber est utilis,* the book is useful ; *Deus est creator mundi,* God is the creator of the world ; *mors non est calamitas,* death is not a misfortune.

Note 1. The neuter of a demonstrative or relative pronoun is used as a predicate when it refers to a preceding adjective or substantive, either of which may denote a person—as *ille non erat sapiens; quis enim hoc fuit?*—where *hoc* refers to *sapiens. Quod ego semper fui, id tu hodie es,* where *quod* and *id* refer to some noun denoting a person which is understood.

2. Sometimes the predicate consists of an adverb joined to a substantive by the verb *esse* — as *recte sunt omnia,* all things are right, or in a right condition ; *inceptum frustra fuit,* the undertaking was useless ; *hostes prope erant,* the enemy was near. So also we frequently find *sic est,* or *ita est,* so it is.

§ 238. The predicate, when a noun, is sometimes connected with its subject by verbs expressing a modification of the idea contained in *esse*—as *fio* and *evado* (I become—that is, I come to be, or begin to be); *maneo* (I remain—that is, I continue to be) ; and the passive of verbs denoting to call, to make, elect, create, consider, think, &c.—as *nominor, creor, dicor, habeor,* which in the active voice govern two accusatives (see below, §§ 247 and 252) ; e.g., *frater meus evadit* (or *fit*) *sapiens,* my brother becomes wise; *tu quidem pauper manebis*, you indeed will remain poor; *Cicero consul creatus est; Aristides justissimus habebatur; Sulla dictator dictus est.*

§ 239. When the predicate is a verb, it agrees with its subject in number and person. Every substantive in the singular represents the third person singular, and every substantive in the plural the third person plural; e.g., *pater aegrotat*, the father is ill; *patres aegrotant*, the fathers are ill; *ego valeo*, I am well; *tu dormis*, thou sleepest; *nos dolemus*, we grieve; *vos scribitis*, you are writing.

(*a*). When there are several subjects of different persons, one of which is a first person, the verb, the predicate, is put in the first person plural; if there is among them no subject of the first person, but one of the second, the predicate is put in the second person plural; and when all the subjects belong to the third person, in the third person plural, precisely as in the English language — as *ego et pater meus ambulamus*, I and my father (we) are taking a walk; *tu et uxor tua estis in periculo*, thou and thy wife (you) are in danger; *feminae, liberi et senes interfecti sunt*, women, children, and old men (they) were killed.

Note. When two subjects of different persons have the same verb for their predicate, but in such a manner that it belongs to each in a different way, so that the one sentence consists in reality of two, the verb agrees only with the subject nearest to it—as *tu librum legis, ille epistolam.* This is sometimes the case also when two subjects are connected by *et-et* (both-and)—as *et ego et Cicero flagitabit*, both I and Cicero (we) shall demand. Sometimes also the verb is put after the first of several subjects, and agrees with it alone—as *et ego hoc video et vos et illi*, I see this as well as you and they.

(*b*). When there are several subjects of the third person, the predicate is in the plural, when the plurality of subjects is to be set forth, as is usually the case when the subjects are names of persons — as *Romulus et Remus urbem Romam condiderunt; coitio consulum et Pompeius obsunt.* If, however, the several subjects may be conceived as forming only one whole—that is, one body of persons and things— the predicate is generally put in the singular — as *senatus populusque Romanus intelligit*, where the people and senate form only one body of people; *tempus necessitasque coëgit*, where time and necessity are regarded as forming together one thing which compels.

Note. It often happens that the subject consists of several names of persons, and yet the verb is in the singular, either because the attention is to be directed to one subject in particular, or merely because the verb agrees with the subject nearest to it, as in Caesar— *Orgetorigis filia et unus e filiis captus est; et proavus L. Murenae et avus praetor fuit.* This is more commonly the case when the several subjects consist of names of inanimate things.

(*c*). When of several subjects one is in the plural, the predicate is generally in the plural; but if the one nearest the predicate is in the singular, and is of particular importance, the predicate may agree with this subject alone—as *prodigia et eorum procuratio consules Romae* (at Rome) *tenuerunt; et Peripatetici et vetus Academia concedit,* where *concedit* agrees with the nearest subject; *ad corporum sanationem multum ipsa corpora et natura valet,* where *valet* agrees only with *natura,* which is the more important of the two subjects.

Note 1. When two subjects are connected by the disjunctive conjunction *aut,* the predicate may be either in the singular or in the plural — as *si Socrates aut Antisthenes diceret; siquid Socrates aut Aristippus locuti sint.* When two subjects are connected by *aut-aut* (either-or), *vel-vel* (either-or), or *neque-neque* (neither-nor), the predicate generally agrees with the subject nearest to it; but when the subjects are of different persons, the plural is preferable — as *Haec neque tu neque ego fecimus.*

2. When the several subjects are enumerated without being connected by conjunctions, so that each forms a sentence by itself, the predicate generally agrees with the nearest; but the plural also may be used—as *nihil libri, nihil literae, nihil doctrina prodest; quid ista conjunctio, quid ager Campanus, quid effusio pecuniae significant?*

⁄ § 240. When the predicate consists of an adjective or participle, it agrees with the subject in gender, number, and case — as *miles est fortis; milites sunt fortes; femina est timida; feminae sunt timidae; templum est splendidum; templa sunt splendida; hic liber est meus; hi libri sunt mei.*

Note. It sometimes happens that the predicate is in the neuter gender, while the subject is either masculine or feminine—as *lupus est triste stabulis; varium et semper mutabile femina; turpitudo pejus est quam dolor.* In all such cases the neuter adjective in the predicate must be regarded as a substantive, and must be rendered, *e.g.,* in the first sentence by 'a sad thing,' in the second by 'a varying and changeable thing,' and in the last by 'a worse thing,' or 'something worse.'

(*a*). When there are several subjects of the same gender, the predicate is either put in the plural in the same gender as that of the subjects, or it attaches itself more particularly to the one nearest to it, and remains in the singular. (§ 239, *b.*)

Note. Sometimes, when the subjects are names of inanimate objects and of the same gender, the predicate is put in the neuter plural—as *ira et avaritia imperio potentiora sunt; nox atque praeda hostes remo-rata sunt.*

(*b*). When the subjects are of different genders, the predicate may agree with the subject nearest to it, or it may be put in the plural: but in the latter case there are two ways, for if the subjects are names of persons, the predicate is commonly put in the plural of the masculine gender; if they are names of inanimate things, the predicate is commonly in the neuter plural—as *uxor mea et filius mortui sunt; imperia, honores, victoriae fortuita sunt.*

, *Note.* This rule is very often disregarded, for sometimes the predicate agrees only with the subject nearest to it, whether the subjects denote persons or things ; and if the nearest happens to be a plural, the predicate sometimes agrees with it alone in gender and number —as *visae sunt faces ardorque coeli; brachia atque humeri liberi ab aqua erant.*

'*c*). When the subjects consist of names of persons mixed with names of inanimate objects, the predicate may either agree in the plural with the gender of the names of persons, or may be put in the neuter plural — as *rex et regia classis profecti sunt; Romani regem regnumque Macedoniae sua futura sciunt.* But in these cases, too, the predicate often agrees only with the subject nearest to it.

§ 241. When the predicate consists of a substantive, it cannot, generally speaking, agree with the subject either in gender or in number — as *Maecenas est dulce decus meum;* but when both the subject and predicate denote persons or living beings, and when the substantive, used as a predicate, has two genders, it agrees with its subject like an adjective—as *aquila est regina avium; philosophia est magistra vitae.* Compare § 233.

Note. It often happens that when the predicate consists of a substantive, the verbs *sum, fio, evado,* and others (§ 228) agree with the substantive forming the predicate—as *amantium, irae amoris integratio est; hic honos ignominia putanda est.*

§ 242. When the subject is accompanied by an apposition, the predicate generally agrees with the subject — as *Tullia, deliciae nostrae, tuum munusculum flagitat.* But when plural names of places have the apposition *urbs, oppidum,* or *civitas,* the predicate agrees with the latter—as *Athenae, urbs nobilissima Graeciae, a Sullae militibus direpta est.* All other cases in which the predicate is found to agree with the apposition must be regarded as exceptions to the rule.

Note 1. A subject in the plural is often referred to by such words as *alter-alter, alius-alius,* or *quisque,* which stand in apposition to it, and having a partitive meaning, remain in the singular, though the predicate is in the plural—as *ambo exercitus, Vegens Tarquiniensisque, suas quisque abeunt domos; decemviri perturbati alius in aliam partem castrorum discurrunt.* Sometimes the plural substantive, to which such adjectives stand in apposition, is omitted, but must be supplied by the mind, to account for the plural of the predicate—as *cum alius alii subsidium ferrent,* as one brought succour to the other; that is, when they (the soldiers) brought succour to one another. There are a few instances of this kind in which the predicate agrees with the apposition *alter, alius,* and *quisque*—as *pictores et poetae suum quisque opus considerari vult.*

2. When several subjects are connected by *quam (tantum, quantum)* or *nisi,* the predicate generally agrees with the subject nearest to it —as *magis pedes quam arma eos tutata sunt; quis illum consulem nisi latrones putant?*

§ 243. When the subject consists of an indeclinable word, or of a whole clause, it is regarded as a neuter noun in the singular, and the predicate accommodates itself to it — as *pro patria mori honestum est,* where the subject consists of the clause *pro patria mori; errare humanum est, in errore perseverare turpe est.* Compare § 235, note.

Note. If, however, in such a case the predicate consists of a substantive, *esse* and similar verbs sometimes agree with the predicate —as *contentum rebus suis esse maximae sunt certissimaeque divitiae,* where the subject consists of the clause *contentum rebus suis esse.*

§ 244. It is a peculiarity common to all languages, that the real nature and meaning of the subject of a sentence is often more attended to than its grammatical form; the most common phenomena of this kind are that —

1. Collective nouns — as *pars, vis, multitudo, uterque, quisque,* and others, when they are used as subjects — have the predicate in the plural, agreeing in gender with the beings understood — as *pars perexigua Romam inermes delati sunt; missi sunt honoratissimus quique.* This, however, is the case chiefly when persons are spoken of, and even then only when the plurality is to be set forth more prominently than the oneness of the body of men, whence we rarely find the predicate in the plural with such subjects as *exercitus, classis, populus, senatus,* because each of them denotes a body of men which is to be regarded as one whole. Compare § 239, *b.*

2 When male beings are expressed figuratively by feminine or neuter substantives, the predicate sometimes follows the natural rather than the grammatical gender of the words used — as *capita conjurationis virgis caesi ac securibus percussi sunt.* The same is often the case with the numeral substantive *millia*—as *millia triginta servilium capitum capti sunt.*

3. A subject in the singular, connected with another by the preposition *cum*, usually has the predicate in the plural—as *ipse dux cum aliquot principibus capiuntur; Ilia cum Lauso de Numitore sati.* The singular, however, may be used when the subjects are not conceived as performing an action or enduring it in common—as *Tu cum Sexto scire velim quid cogites*, where the main point is to know what thou (*tu*) art thinking, and not what the two together are thinking.

§ 245. Adjectives in the masculine and neuter gender are often used as the subjects of sentences, without their referring to distinct persons or things mentioned in a preceding sentence. In this case they are said in grammar to be used substantively: the masculine gender denoting human beings, *homo* or *homines* being understood—as *sapientes virtutem colunt; iners laborem fugit;* and the neuter, either in the singular or plural, denoting things — as *omne malum vitandum est; mala fortunae fortiter ferenda sunt.* Compare § 232, 4.

CHAPTER XLII.

RELATION OF THE NOMINATIVE AND ACCUSATIVE CASE.

§ 246. The nominative is the case which names the subject of a proposition — that is, the person or thing of which anything is said. Hence the subject of a sentence or clause is in the nominative case; and as the predicate must agree with the subject, the predicate also is in the nominative, if it consists of a declinable word, and is connected with the subject by means of the verb *esse*, or one of those verbs which express only modifications of the idea contained in *esse*—as *fio*, I become; *evado*, I become; *maneo*, I remain; *videor*, I appear or seem—as *Cicero fuit magnus orator; Appius captator aurae popularis evasit; Cicero fit consul; haec causa mala videtur*, or *mala esse videtur*.

Note. The only case in which both the subject and predicate appear in the accusative is in the construction of the accusative with the infinitive. The verb *videor* is rarely used impersonally, like the English ' it seems,' or ' it appears'—as *videtur mihi virtutem satis posse*, instead of which it is better to say *virtus mihi videtur satis posse.*

§ 247. The passive verbs *dicor, vocor, nominor, appellor, nuncupor, scribor, ducor, habeor, judicor, existimor, numeror, putor, intelligor, agnoscor, reperior, invenior, reddor, creor, deligor, designor, declaror, renuntior*, and some others, are accompanied by a noun as a predicate, which must, accordingly like the subject, be in the nominative case—as *Numa rex creatus est; Aristides habitus est justissimus ; Sulla dictator dictus est.* Compare § 238.

§ 248. The accusative denotes the object of transitive verbs —that is, the person or thing affected by the action expressed by a transitive verb in its active form. The object of a transitive verb in the active voice is therefore always expressed by the accusative — as *pater amat filium ; Caesar vicit Pompeium; frater emit librum.*

Every sentence containing a transitive verb and an object (accusative) may be changed into the passive form by changing the accusative into the nominative (the object into the subject), and changing the nominative into the ablative with the preposition *a* or *ab* before it — as *Pompeius a Caesare victus est; filius a patre amatur ; liber emitur a fratre.* The preposition *a* or *ab* in such cases denotes the quarter from which the action proceeds.

Note 1. We have here used the term transitive verb in the common acceptation of verbs with an active form, and having their object in the accusative. It must, however, be observed, that there are many transitive verbs which do not govern the accusative, but the dative or ablative — as *obedio* and *obtempero*, I obey ; *egeo*, I want ; and many deponents also are transitive in meaning, but govern either the dative, as *adulor*, or the ablative, as *utor.* Transitives which have their object in any other case than the accusative, cannot be changed into the passive in the manner above described, but the case governed by the verb in the active remains the same in the passive, which is of an impersonal nature—as *ego legibus obtempero;* passive, *legibus a me obtemperatur.* Deponents of course cannot be changed into the passive at all. It must further be observed that some verbs in Latin are transitive — that is, have their object in the accusative — while in English they govern a different case, or are followed by a preposition ; and other verbs are transitive in English without their Latin correspondents being the same—as *persuadere alicui*, to persuade a person ; *parare bellum*, to prepare (one's self) for war ; *effugere periculum*, to escape from the danger ; *excusare morbum*, to bring forward illness as an excuse.

2. The Latin passive in many verbs supplies the place of the Greek middle voice, and has a reflective meaning—as *fallor*, I am deceived, or deceive myself; *lavor*, I am washed, or wash myself; *moveor*, I am moved, or move myself; *crucior*, I am tormented, or torment myself. Others have this reflective meaning even in the active voice —as *verto*, I turn myself; *muto*, I change myself; *remitto*, I give way (or send myself back), *me* being understood in each case. Compare § 125, note 2, and § 126.

§ 249. As to whether a verb is transitive depends entirely upon its meaning, so that the same verb may in one sense be transitive, while in another it is intransitive — as *consulo aliquem,* I consult a person ; *consulo alicui,* I give a person

advice, or take care of a person; *animadverto aliquid,* ʻI observe a thing; *animadverto in aliquem,* I punish a person; *ardeo,*
I burn; *ardeo aliquid* or *aliquem,* I love a thing or a person
ardently.

Note 1. In this manner a great many verbs, which are properly intransitives, may acquire a transitive meaning, and govern the accusative. This is especially the case in poetry; but the following are
common even in prose : — *doleo* and *lugeo aliquid,* I grieve at, and I
mourn over a thing; *horreo aliquid,* I am horrified at a thing; *miror
aliquid,* I wonder at a thing; *queror aliquid,* I complain of a thing; so
also *gemo, lacrimo, lamentor, fleo, ploro, rideo; maneo* (I await); *crepo*
(am in the habit of talking of); *depereo* (I love desperately); *navigo
mare* (I sail on the sea); *salto aliquem* (I represent a person in dancing). Peculiarities of this kind must be learned by observation.

2. The verbs *olere* and *redolere,* ʻto smell of a thing,' and *sapere*
and *resipere,* ʻto taste of a thing,' are likewise used in Latin as transitives, with an accusative of the thing of which anything smells or
tastes — as *olere vinum,* to smell of wine. In like manner we find
such expressions—as *sitire sanguinem,* to be bloodthirsty, or have a
thirst of blood; *vox hominem sonat,* the voice sounds like that of a
man; *anhelat scelus,* he is panting for a crime. Poets take very great
liberties with intransitive verbs, and even form passives of them; but
their example should not be followed in prose—as *gentes triumphatae,*
instead of *gentes de quibus triumphatum est.*

3. Many verbs which are otherwise intransitive, and never govern
the accusative, are sometimes accompanied by the accusative of a substantive of the same root, or at least of the same or a similar meaning ;
in this case, however, the substantive in the accusative is commonly
qualified by an adjective, and in reality supplies the place of an adverb
—as *vitam tutiorem vivere,* ʻto lead a safer life,' is the same as *tutius
vivere; justam servitutem servire*—that is, *juste servire*—ʻto be a regular slave ;' *haec pugna pugnata est,* ʻthis battle has been fought ;' so
also *gaudium gaudere, risum ridere, ludum ludere, preces precari,* and
others.

4. Lastly, many intransitive verbs·are accompanied by a neuter pronoun in the accusative, denoting the thing in reference to which an
action is performed or a feeling is manifested—as *illud tibi assentior,*
I agree with you in reference to that thing; *omnes unum student,* all are
anxious in reference to one thing ; *non idem glorior,* I do not boast in
reference (or of) the same thing ; *hoc gaudeo,* I rejoice at this ; *utrumque
laetor,* I am delighted with both things. Compare § 253, 3, note.

§ 250. Many intransitive verbs denoting motion may, by
being compounded with prepositions, and by thus being
modified in their meaning, become transitive, and accordingly
govern the accusative. The prepositions chiefly used in forming such compounds are *circum, per, praeter, trans, super,
subter, ad, cum,* and *in* — as *circumeo, circumvenio, circumvehor,
percurro, pervagor, praetereo, praetergredior, praetervehor, transeo,
transilio, supergredior, subterfugio, subterlabor, adeo, aggredior,
adorior, convenio, ineo,* and others ; e.g., *exercitus flumen transiit,*

the army crossed the river; *locum periculosum praetervehor*, I
ride by a dangerous place.

Note 1. The same is the case with some verbs compounded with the
prepositions *prae* and *ob*—as *praecedo, praegredior, praefluo, praevenio*
(*praecurro* is joined with the dative as well as with the accusative);
obeo (as *mortem, negotium, regionem*), *obambulo, obequito, oberro*, in the
sense of I walk, ride, wander through, or over a thing; but they govern
the dative when *ob* signifies 'in front of,' or 'towards'—as *obequitare
portis*, to ride towards the gates. *Subire*, 'to go under,' or 'to ap-
proach,' is commonly construed with the accusative—as *muros subire;*
but also with the dative or the preposition *ad*—as *subire ad muros*, or
subire muris. In the sense 'it occurs to me,' *mihi subit*, it always takes
the dative. *Supervenio* (I come upon, I am added to) is construed
with the dative—as *pugnae supervenit*, he came upon the battle; that
is, he came while the battle was going on, or during the battle.

2. Sometimes the preposition with which such a verb is compounded
is repeated before the accusative — *adire ad aliquem*, to go to a person; *accedere ad arma*, to go to arms. Verbs compounded with *ad*,
and retaining their primitive meaning, are rarely found with the accusative alone, except in poetry. Most verbs compounded with *ob*,
however, govern the dative.

3. Some intransitive verbs denoting rest in a place, as *jacēre, stare*,
and *sedere*, may acquire a transitive meaning by being compounded
with prepositions, especially with *circum*—as *insidere locum*, to occupy
a place; *insistere viam* or *iter*, to enter upon a journey; *multa me pe-
ricula circumstant*, many dangers surround me; *silva totum campum
circumjacet*, a forest surrounds the whole plain; *exercitus urbem obsi-
det*, the army besieges the town.

4. The verbs *excedo* and *egredior*, in the sense of 'transgress,' govern the accusative; but when they denote 'to go' or 'come out of,'
they, like other compounds with *ex*, generally repeat the preposition
e or *ex*—as *fines excessit*, he transgressed the boundaries; but *ex urbe
egreditur*, he goes out of the city. *Excello*, however, is construed
with the dative or the preposition *inter* — as *ceteris excellit*, or *inter
ceteros excellit*.

5. The verbs compounded with *ante, antevenio,* and *antegredior* (I
go, or step before) are construed with the accusative; but those denoting to 'excel' or 'surpass' are more often found with the dative
than with the accusative — such as *antecedo, anteeo, antecello*, and
praesto. For *excello*, see note 4.

§ 251. Transitive verbs, compounded with the preposition
trans — as *traducio, trajicio, transporto*—have two accusatives,
one of the object, and the other dependent upon the preposition,
which is, in fact, sometimes repeated before it — as *Hannibal
copias Iberum traduxit* (where *Iberum* is governed by *trans*);
milites flumen transportat; copias trans Rhenum trajecit.

Note. Sometimes, though very rarely, we find the ablative instead
of the accusative governed by the preposition — as *exercitum Pado
trajicere;* but here the ablative denotes either the place *where* the
action took place, or the means by which it was accomplished.
The verb *adigo* is sometimes construed like those compounded with

trans—as *adigere milites jusjurandum*, or *ad jusjurandum*, or *jurejurando*, to put the soldiers to their oath.

§ 252. The impersonal verbs *piget* (I am vexed), *pudet* (I am ashamed), *poenitet* (I repent), *taedet* (I am disgusted), and *miseret* (I pity), govern an accusative of the person in whom these feelings exist, and the genitive of the thing which causes them — as *pudet me facti*, I am ashamed of the deed; *miseret nos hominis*, we pity the man; *piget puerum negligentiae*, the boy is vexed at his carelessness.

Decet (it is becoming) and its compounds *dedecet, condecet,* and *indecet*, likewise govern the accusative of the person to whom anything is or is not becoming. So also *latet*, it is concealed from, or unknown to.

Note. Some of the five first of these impersonals also have an impersonal passive—as *pertaesum est, puditum est,* which are construed in the same manner as the active forms. *Veritum est* is used by Cicero in the same manner—as *hos non est veritum,* they were not afraid.

Decet and *latet* are sometimes found with the dative, the former especially in the early writers.

When the thing causing the feeling expressed by these impersonal verbs is expressed by a verb, it is always in the infinitive — as *pudet me confiteri; taedet me enumerare.*

§ 253. Many transitive verbs, conveying only an incomplete idea, govern, besides the accusative of the object, another which stands to the object in the relation of a predicate or apposition, and completes the idea contained in the verb. Verbs of this kind are those of naming, making, creating, electing, having, showing, and the like—as *dico, voco, appello, nomino, nuncupo, scribo* and *inscribo, duco, habeo, judico, existimo, numero, puto, arbitror, intelligo, agnosco, reperio, renuntio, invenio, facio, reddo, instituo, constituo, creo, deligo, designo, declaro* (*me*), *praebeo* (*me*), *praesto,* and others. These same verbs, when in the passive, are accompanied by two nominatives, one being the subject, and the other the predicate or apposition to it. See § 238. e.g., *Romulus urbem Romam vocavit; avaritia homines coecos reddit; populus Numam regem creavit; Socrates se incolam et civem totius mundi arbitrabatur; Appius Claudius libertinorum filios senatores legit; Tiberius Druso Seianum dedit adjutorem; rex se clementem praebebit; praesta te virum; senatus Antonium hostem judicavit; Cicero librum aliquem Catonem inscripsit.*

Note. In the case of the verb *habeo*, the object is in English often expressed by the preposition 'in'—as *hunc egregium ducem habemus,* in him we have an excellent leader. The verbs *habere, putare,* and *ducere,* are sometimes followed by *pro*, with the ablative instead of the accusative of the predicate—as *habere aliquem pro hoste,* to con·

sider a person as an enemy, or in the light of an enemy ; *id pro nihilo puto*, I consider this as nothing. The same meaning is sometimes conveyed by such expressions as *aliquem in hostium numero habere*, to consider a person as an enemy ; *parentis loco* (*in loco*) *aliquem habere*, or *ducere*, to look upon a person as a parent.

§ 254. Some transitive verbs, which have the name of a person for their object, govern a second accusative of the thing which may be regarded as a second object. Such verbs are —

1. *doceo* and *edoceo*, I teach ; *dedoceo*, I cause to unlearn ; *celo*, I conceal or keep in ignorance of ; e.g., *docere puellam litteras*, to teach a girl the letters ; *Catilina juventutem mala facinora edocebat*, Catiline taught the young evil deeds ; *non celavi te sermonem hominum*, I did not conceal from you what people say. Sometimes, however, the preposition *de* with the ablative is used instead of the accusative of the thing — *docere aliquem de aliqua re*, to inform a person of a thing ; *matrem celabat de veneno*, he kept his mother in ignorance regarding the poison.

Note. When verbs of this kind are changed into the passive, the accusative of the first or personal object as usual becomes the subject, but the accusative of the thing may remain unchanged—as *legiones militiam edoctae sunt;* but it is more common, especially with *celor*, to use the preposition *de* with the ablative, except when the thing is expressed by the neuter of a pronoun—*hoc nos celati sumus*, this has been concealed from us. When the thing taught is expressed by a verb, the infinitive is used—as *doceo te Latine loqui*, or *scribere*, I teach you to speak or write Latin. The participle *doctus* is found also with the ablative alone, as *doctus literis Graecis*, learned in Greek literature.

2. The verbs *posco*, *reposco*, and *flagito* (I demand), *oro* (I pray), *rogo* (I ask), *interrogo* and *percontor* (I ask or question); e.g., *pacem te poscimus*, we demand peace of you ; *Caesar frumentum Aeduos flagitabat*, Caesar demanded corn of the Aedui ; *tribunus me sententiam rogavit*, the tribune asked me my opinion. With these verbs the accusative of the thing remains unchanged when the verb is made passive—as *interrogatus sum sententiam*, I was asked for my opinion.

Note. The accusative of the thing with these verbs is most common when it is expressed by the neuter of a pronoun or an adjective—as *id te oro; quod me rogas; nihil aliud te oro atque obsecro*. The verbs *posco* and *flagito* are also construed with the accusative of the thing, the person being expressed by the preposition *a* or *ab* with the ablative—as *illud a te posco* or *flagito*, 'I demand this of you.' This is the usual construction of the verbs *peto* (ask), *quaero* (ask), and *postulo* (demand).

3. The verbs *moneo*, *admoneo*, and *hortor* (I admonish), and *cogo* (I compel), when the thing is expressed by the neuter

of a pronoun or adjective — as *te id unum moneo,* this one thing I give you as my advice; *pauca milites hortatus est,* he gave the soldiers a few words of admonition. The accusative of the thing with these verbs also remains unchanged when the verb becomes passive — as *multa monemur,* many admonitions are given to us : *si consules aliquid cogi possunt,* if the consuls can be compelled to anything.

Note. There are a great many intransitive verbs, which may be accompanied by a neuter pronoun in the accusative, denoting not the object, but the thing in reference to which, or in regard to which the action expressed by the verb is performed. Such verbs are *laetor, glorior, irascor, succenseo, assentior, dubito, studeo,* and many others —as *illud glorior,* I boast in regard to that, or of that ; *utrumque laetor,* I rejoice at both things ; *id dubito,* I am in doubt regarding this thing ; *siquid te offendi,* if I have offended you in anything ; hence also the passive *siquid offensum est,* if offence has been given in anything. If with these verbs the thing in reference to which the action takes place is expressed by a substantive, it is either put in the ablative or takes some preposition — as *glorior hac victoria,* I rejoice at this victory. Compare § 249, note 4.

§ 255. The following prepositions always govern the accusative : — *ad, adversus* or *adversum, ante, apud, circa* or *circum, circiter, cis* or *citra, contra, erga, extra, infra, inter, intra, juxta, ob, penes, per, pone, post, praeter, propter, secundum, supra, trans, ultra, versus.* Compare § 194.

Note 1. The words *pridie* and *postridie,* in connection with the days of the months, are like prepositions followed by the accusative —as *pridie Calendas, postridie Nonas, pridie Idus,* which depends upon the preposition *ante* understood.

2. From *prope* are derived the adverbs *propius* and *proxime,* which are, like *prope,* commonly construed with the accusative, and rarely with the dative ; even the adjectives *propior* and *proximus* are sometimes found with the accusative, though they are more common with the dative.

Praeter, in the sense of 'except,' is sometimes used as a mere adverb governing no case at all—as *ceteris licebat ab armis discedere praeter rerum capitalium damnatis,* the rest were allowed to depart except those found guilty of capital offences.

Ante and *post,* when they are real prepositions, are put before the case they govern ; but they are also used as adverbs, and then they are put after their case, which becomes the ablative instead of the accusative — as *ante multos annos,* before many years ; but *multis annis ante,* many years before ; *post tres dies,* after three days ; but *tribus diebus post,* three days after. Compare § 194, note 2.

The following four, which sometimes govern the accusative and sometimes the ablative, deserve more special attention :—

1. *In* governs the accusative when it answers to the English 'into ;' that is, when it denotes motion towards the inte-

rior of anything — as *in urbem ire, in Galliam proficisci, in civitatem recipere, in mare projicere.* Also, in a secondary sense, when it denotes activity directed towards something, or in general the tendency or direction towards something — as *scamnum habet sex pedes in longitudinem; oratio in Catilinam* (a speech directed against Catiline); *amor in patriam* (love directed towards one's country); *consistere in orbem* (to stand together so as to form a circle); *multa dixit in eam sententiam* (he said much in the direction of this opinion — that is, he said much to the same effect); *commeatus in tres annos* (provisions for three years); *indies* (from day to day — that is, daily).

In governs the ablative when it denotes being in a place, answering to the English 'in' — as *in urbe esse, in horto ambulari, in flumine navigare, in campo currere;* and also in all derivative meanings, where no motion towards anything is expressed — as *in morbo,* in or during the disease; *in hoc homine,* in this man, or in the case of this man.

Note 1. *In* joined to the name of a person must often be rendered in English by 'in the case of' — as *hoc facere in eo consuerunt,* they were accustomed to do this in the case of that man; *hoc dici in servo non potest,* this cannot be said in the case of a slave.

There are a few cases in which *in* is joined with the accusative, although no motion is expressed — as *habere in potestatem* (for *potestate*); *in amicitiam ditionemque populi Romani esse;* but these are mere irregularities of speech. The verbs *pono, loco, colloco, statuo, constituo,* on the other hand, although they denote motion, are yet regularly construed with *in* and the ablative — as *Epicurus ponit summum bonum in voluptate.* The compounds *impono, repono,* and *expono,* however, are sometimes found with *in,* and the accusative.

2. After some verbs compounded with *in,* this preposition may be repeated either with the accusative or the ablative — as *incidere aliquid in tabulam,* or *in tabula,* to inscribe a thing on a table. Sometimes they are joined with the dative — as *nomen inscribere saxis,* to inscribe the name on the rocks. In some cases there is a slight difference of meaning — as *furem in carcerem includit* (he takes the thief to the prison and locks him up there); *furem in carcere includit* (he locks the thief up in the prison); and *furem carcere includit* (he locks up the thief by means of a prison).

2. *Sub* governs the accusative when it denotes motion towards under a thing — as *venire sub oculos; sub scalas se conjicere.* It also governs the accusative when it refers to time, and signifies 'about' — as *sub idem tempus,* about the same time; *sub noctem,* towards night; *sub Hannibalis adventum,* about the time of Hannibal's arrival.

It governs the ablative when it denotes being under anything — as *sub muro, sub oculis;* sometimes, though very rarely, it is construed with the ablative, when it denotes time—as *sub ipsa profectione*, about the very time of departure.

3. *Super* is joined in good prose with the ablative only when it denotes 'about' or 'concerning' — as *super hac re ad te scribam*, I shall write to you about this matter. In all other cases it governs the accusative, though poets sometimes use it with the ablative—as *super foco*, over or on the hearth.

4. *Subter* is generally construed with the accusative, and rarely with the ablative, except in poetry.

§ 256. Verbs, adjectives, and adverbs, denoting extent of time or space, govern the accusative of the noun describing the extent. Adjectives of this kind are *longus, latus, altus, crassus;* e.g., *hasta sex pedes longa*, a lance six feet long; *fossa decem pedes alta*, a ditch ten feet deep; *fines Helvetiorum patebant in longitudinem ducenta quadraginta millia passuum; laborare dies noctesque; Troja decem annos oppugnata est; tres annos mecum habitavit.*

Note 1. Instead of the accusative denoting extent or duration of time, we sometimes, especially in later writers, find the ablative — as *Panaetius vixit triginta annis*, instead of *annos.* Sometimes the accusative is accompanied by the preposition *per* — as *per tres annos mecum habitavit;* but this preposition suggests that the writer or speaker regards the extent of time as a long one.

2. When the distance between two places is indicated, the measure of the distance may be expressed either by the accusative or the ablative, though the former is preferable—as *abest tridui iter*, it is three days' journey distant; or *abest tridui itinere; castra locat mille passus ab hoste; magnum spatium abesse* (to be at a great distance), or *magno spatio abesse.* Sometimes, however, the distance is indicated by the words *spatium* or *intervallum*, which are always put in the ablative—as *quindecim milium spatio castra ab Tarento posuit*, he pitched his camp at a distance of fifteen miles from Tarentum. When the place from which the distance is calculated is not mentioned, the preposition *a* or *ab* is sometimes put before the words describing the distance; as in Caesar — *a millibus passuum duobus castra posuerunt*, they pitched their camp at a distance of two thousand paces.

3. In like manner the participle *natus*, in the sense of 'old,' is joined with the accusative of the number of years which a person has lived—as *viginti annos natus est*, he is twenty years old; *sex annos natus;* six years old.

§ 257. Names of towns and small islands are put in the accusative without any preposition to express motion towards them in answer to the question whither?—as *Romam profectus est*, he has gone to Rome; *legatos Athenas misit*, he sent ambassadors to Athens; *Corinthum abiit*, he went away to Corinth ; *Delum navigavit*, he has sailed to Delos.

Note 1. The preposition *ad*, with names of towns, always signifies 'near' or 'in the neighbourhood of,' and is equivalent to *apud*—as *ad Capuam profectus est*, he has gone to the neighbourhood of Capua; *haec ad Geronium gesta sunt*, these things were done near Geronium. *Ad* is further used when the distance between two places is stated— as *omnis ora a Salōnis ad Oricum*.

2. When the substantive *urbs* or *oppidum* is put before the name of a town, motion to it is expressed by the preposition *in*—as *consul pervenit in oppidum Cirtam*, the consul arrived in the town of Cirta. When *urbs* or *oppidum*, accompanied by an adjective, is added as apposition to the name of a town, the apposition likewise usually takes the preposition *in* — as *Demaratus se contulit Tarquinios, in urbem Etruriae florentissimam*.

3. Motion to large islands and countries is generally expressed by *in* with the accusative, but sometimes the preposition is omitted, and poets, in particular, are very free in their use of the accusative alone to express motion or direction towards a place; hence we find *Cyprum venit*, as well as *in Cyprum venit; Italiam venit; Aegyptum profectus est; verba non pervenientia aures* (for *ad aures*); *Dido et dux Trojanus speluncam eandem* (for *in speluncam eandem*) *deveniunt*.

4. The words *domus* (house) and *rus* (country) are always put in the accusative without a preposition to express the place whither?— as *domum revertor*, I return home; *domos redierunt*, they returned home—that is, each to his own house; *rus ire*, to go into the country. The same construction remains when *domus* is joined by a possessive pronoun or a genitive—as *domum meam venit*, he came to my house; *domum Pompeii venisti*, thou camest to the house of Pompey; so also *domum alienam*, to another man's house; *domum regiam*, to a royal house; but when *domus* is accompanied by an adjective, it is more common to add the preposition *in*. The accusative *domum* is retained also with verbal substantives denoting motion towards—as *reditio domum*, the return home; *reditus Romam*, the return to Rome.

§ 258. In exclamations of wonder or grief at the state or condition of a person or a thing, the name of the person or thing is put in the accusative either with or without an interjection—as *heu me miserum!* or *me miserum!*—Oh, I, wretched man! *O, fallacem hominum spem!*—Oh, the deceitful hope of men! *Hanc audaciam!*—Oh, this audacity!

Note 1. The accusative in these and similar expressions may be explained by supplying some suitable verb, such as 'behold' or 'look at,' *aspice* or *aspicite*.

2. In connection with interjections the vocative also may be used - as *O magna vis veritatis! O fortunate adolescens! Pro, dii immortales! Pro, sancte Jupiter!* The interjections *hei* and *vae* are usually joined with the dative—as *hei mihi! vae misero mihi! En* and *ecce*, which direct attention to something present, are usually construed with the nominative — as *ecce tuae literae!* lo (behold) your letter! *En ego!* here I am! They are rarely found with the accusative, as in the expression *ecce me!* and in the contracted forms *eccum* for *ecce eum, eccos* for *ecce eos, eccillum* for *ecce illum, eccillam* for *ecce illam,* and *eccistam* for *ecce istam.* Compare § 115, note 4.

§ 259. We have already remarked several cases in which poets are more free in the use of the accusative than prose writers, though the latter sometimes also make use of similar expressions. The following cases deserve especial notice :—

1. The participle perfect passive (like the Greek perfect passive or middle) sometimes denotes, in a reflective sense, a person having done something to himself, and accordingly governs an accusative like an active verb — as *Dido Sidoniam picto chlamydem circumdata limbo* (Virg.)—that is, *quae sibi circumdederat ; pueri laevo suspensi loculos tabulamque lacerto* (Hor.); *Juno nondum antiquum saturata Dolorem* (Virg.). In the same manner the passive of the verbs *cingo* (I gird), *accingo, induo* (I clothe), *exuo* (I undress or put off), *induco* (I cover), sometimes has a reflective meaning, and is joined with an accusative — as *galeam induitur,* he puts on (himself) a helmet ; *Priamus ferrum cingitur,* Priam is girded (girds himself) with the sword. Sometimes, however, the passive participle retains its genuine passive meaning — as in *per pedes trajectus lora tumentes,* a person through whose feet thongs were drawn ; *victima inducta cornibus aurum,* a victim whose horns are (have been covered) covered with gold.

Note. In prose it is usual to say *induo vestem,* I put on a garment ; and *induo aliquem veste,* I dress some one with a garment. On the analogy of what was said above, we also find *censeri magnum agri modum,* to enter a large amount of land in the census lists ; *moveri Cyclopa,* to dance the Cyclops, or imitate the Cyclops in dancing.

2. The accusative is often used with passive and intransitive verbs, to denote the part to which the attribute contained in the verb is limited. Such an accusative may fitly be termed an accusative of reference or limitation — as *os humerosque deo similis,* resembling a god in regard to his face and shoulders — the resemblance being here limited to the face and shoulders ; *qui genus estis?* who are you in regard to your descent? *capita Phrygio velamur amictu,* we are covered as far as our heads are concerned ; *ictus adversum femur,* struck in front of the thigh ; *saucius pedes,* wounded in his feet.

Note 1. With the exception of the words denoting ' wounded,' which generally are accompanied by an accusative expressing the part which is wounded, it is more common in prose to use the ablative — as *ore humeroque similis deo,* resembling a god in face and shoulders. The accusative is, in fact, an imitation of the Greek language, in which it is of very common occurrence.

2. There are some instances in which even in prose such an accusative, in the sense of an adverb, is quite common — as in the ex-

pressions *magnam* or *maximam partem* (for *magna* or *maxima parte*), 'in a great measure,' or 'for the most part;' *vicem meam, tuam, suam,* &c. in my, thy, his place, &c. ; e.g., *tuam vicem saepe doleo,* I am often grieved for you. So also *ceterum* and *cetera,* 'in other respects,' or 'as for the rest.'

§ 260. There are certain expressions in which the accusative, especially of neuter pronouns, stands for the genitive or ablative — as *id temporis,* at that moment of time, for *eo tempore; id* or *illud aetatis* for *ejus* or *illius aetatis,* of that age — as *homo id aetatis; id* or *hoc genus* for *ejus* or *hujus generis,* of that kind — as *id genus alia,* other things of this kind.

Note. We may here also notice the accusative in elliptical expressions, in which it must be explained by supplying some verb — as *quo mihi fortunam, si non conceditur uti?* what am I to do with my fortune, if I am not allowed to use it ? where *fortunam* may be explained by supplying *habeam; unde mihi lapidem (sumam)?* whence shall I get the stone ?

CHAPTER XLIII.

USE OF THE DATIVE CASE.

§ 261. The dative generally expresses the person or thing for which, or in regard to which, something is or is done, and may therefore be termed the remoter object. The English language usually expresses this relation by the prepositions 'to' or 'for' — as *Solon leges Atheniensibus scripsit,* Solon wrote laws for the Athenians ; *non scholae sed vitae discimus,* we learn not for the school, but for life ; *orabo nato filiam,* I shall ask his daughter for my son ; *domus pulchra dominis aedificatur, non muribus,* a beautiful house is built for its owners, not for mice.

Note 1. When the English preposition 'for' signifies 'instead of,' or 'in defence of,' the relation is never expressed by the dative, but always by *pro* with the ablative—as *pro me locutus est,* he has spoken for (instead of) me, or on my behalf, in my defence ; *pro patria mori,* to die for (in the defence of) one's country.

2. The dative is generally connected with the predicate of a clause, but it may also belong to an entire clause, and take the place of the genitive or some preposition with another case — as *is finis populationibus fuit,* where *populationibus* depends on the clause *is finis fuit,* and where, instead of the dative, *populationum* might be used,

which genitive would then depend upon *finis; Quis huic rei testis est?* who is witness to this affair? where the genitive *hujus rei* would be dependent upon *testis; Aduatici locum sibi domicilio delegerunt,* where the dative *domicilio* is dependent upon the clause *locum delegerunt.* Poets take greater license in the use of the dative—as in Virgil, *Dissimulant, quae sit rebus causa novandis,* where in prose we should say *causa rerum novandarum;* and in Tacitus, *longo bello materia,* 'fuel for a long war,' where the common expression would be *longi belli materia.*

§ 262. The dative accordingly is used with transitive verbs, when, besides their object, a person or thing is mentioned to which or for which the action is performed — as *exercitum collegae tradidit,* he surrendered the army to his colleague; *viam tibi monstro,* I show you the way; *pater librum mihi dedit,* the father has given me a book ; *salus militum duci mandata est,* the wellbeing of the soldiers was intrusted to their leader.

Note 1. In a great many cases the transitive verb and its object together constitute, as it were, only one idea, and express that something is done to or in reference to some one or something. Such expressions are always joined with the dative—as *finem bello imponere,* where *finem imponere* is only a paraphrase for *finire; praecludere aditum hosti,* where likewise *praecludere aditum* must be taken together as expressing only one idea ; *morem gerere alicui; nullus locus poenitentiae relictus est.* If, however, the person or thing to which, or in reference to which, anything is done, is regarded as connected with the object rather than with the verb and the object conjointly, the genitive must be used — as *finem faciam dicendi,* I shall finish, or leave off speaking.

2. Some phrases of this kind admit of a different mode of expression with a difference in meaning — as *dare puero litteras,* to give a letter to the boy, that he may forward it ; *dare litteras ad puerum,* to write a letter to the boy, or to give some one a letter to be delivered to the boy ; *mittere alicui librum,* to send a book to some one, that he may have it and use it ; but *mittere librum ad aliquem,* 'to send a book to some one,' without its being implied that it is for his use ; *scribere alicui,* to communicate something to a person by letter; *scribere ad aliquem,* to address a letter to some one ; *dicere populo,* to tell to the people ; *dicere ad populum,* to speak before the people. There are a great many other instances of the same kind, but these are sufficient to show the principle.

§ 263. Many transitive verbs compounded with the prepositions *ad, ante, circum, cum, ex, in, inter, ob, post, prae,* and *sub,* have, besides their real object, some other noun, the relation to which is indicated by the prepositions; and this other noun is put in the dative both with the active and passive of such compound verbs — as *haec res mihi magnum commodum affert,* this affair gives me a great advantage; *milites consuli circumfundebantur,* the soldiers were crowding

around the consul; *circumdare moenia urbi,* to put walls
around the city, or surround the city with walls; *magnum
mihi imposuit negotium,* he has imposed upon me a serious
business; *se alterius potestati subjicere,* to submit to another
man's power.

If, however, by such compound verbs, the idea of place
contained in the prepositions is to be expressed more emphatically than the mere action contained in the verb, the preposition with its proper case must be repeated — as *signa inferre
in hostes,* to carry the standards against the enemy; *eripere
aliquem e periculo,* to rescue a person from (or out of) danger;
inscribere in tabula, to write upon a tablet.

Note 1. This rule is not always strictly observed, for some verbs,
compounded with *ad,* especially *addo, adjicio, adjungo,* are found
more frequently with the preposition repeated than with the dative,
although the idea of place is not to be set forth with any degree of
prominence—as *applico me ad philosophiam, ad virtutem,* I apply myself to philosophy, to virtue; but *adjungo mihi amicum,* I gain a
friend for myself. *Subjicio* and *subjungo* admit of both constructions
—as *subjicio aliquid oculis,* and *sub oculos.*

2. Verbs compounded with *cum* (*con*) repeat the preposition in most
cases, but the dative also occurs — as *comparare Graecos cum Roma-
nis; parva componere magnis;* but after *communicare* the preposition
is always repeated. The verbs *socio, jungo,* and *continuo,* also are
sometimes joined with the dative, their meaning being similar to that
of verbs compounded with *cum*—as *sapientia juncta eloquentiae; continuo laborem diurnûm nocturno.*

3. In the later times of the Latin language it became more and
more customary not to repeat the preposition, but to use the dative.

4. The verbs *adspergo* and *circumdo* admit of a different construction from that pointed out above; for instead of *moenia urbi circumdare,* we may also say *urbem circumdare moenibus* (ablative, 'with
walls'), and *adspergere alicui maculam,* or *adspergere aliquem macula*
(ablative, 'with a stain'). Compare below, § 290.

§ 264. The dative is joined with many intransitive verbs,
such as those which denote benefiting, pleasing, injuring, and
others. The principal verbs of this kind are—*prosum, obsum,
noceo, incommodo, expedit, conducit; adversor, obtrecto, officio,
cedo, suffragor, refragor, intercedo, gratificor; faveo, studeo,
ignosco, indulgeo, invideo, insidior; auxilior, opitulor, patro-
cinor, consulo, prospicio, medeor, parco; placeo, displiceo; impero,
obedio, obsequor, obtempero, pareo, servio, famulor; assentior,
adulor, blandior, irascor, succenseo, convicior, maledico, minor;
suadeo, persuadeo; credo, fido, confido, diffido; desum, nûbo,
propinquo, appropinquo, supplico, videor* (seem or appear); *accidit, contingit, evenit; libet, licet; obviam eo, praesto sum, dicto
audiens sum.*

Note 1. Many of these verbs are in fact transitives, which have their object in the dative case, for which reason they have only an impersonal passive—as *mihi invidetur*, I am envied; *nemini parcitur*, no one is spared; *legibus parendum est*, laws must be obeyed. Such verbs require particular attention on the part of the learner, because in many cases their English equivalents are real transitives governing the objective case or accusative. Sometimes an accusative of the object is added, even in Latin, to the dative—as *credo tibi hanc rem; imperavit provinciae tributum*, or *milites; hoc mihi persuadet; mihi minatus est mortem; invideo alicui aliquam rem;* and the like.

2. Some verbs of this kind are sometimes construed with the dative and sometimes with the accusative, according to their meaning—as *consulo alicui*, I give advice to some one, or take care of some one; but *consulo aliquem*, I ask a person for advice, or consult him; *metuo* and *timeo aliquem*, I dread or fear a person; but *timeo* and *metuo alicui*, I am in fear for some one, lest any harm should be done to him; *caveo aliquem*, I am on my guard against a person, but *caveo alicui*, I am cautious for, or on behalf of, a person; *prospicio* and *provideo aliquid*, I foresee a thing, but with the dative, 'I provide for;' *moderor*, with the accusative, 'I arrange, regulate,' with the dative, 'I moderate;' *tempero*, with the accusative, 'I arrange' or 'mix,' but with the dative, 'I moderate.'

3. Others, again, are joined with the dative or accusative without any perceptible difference of meaning—as *adūlor* (mostly with the accusative), *aemūlor* (nearly always with the accusative), *comitor, despero,* and *praestolor.*

4. It sometimes, though rarely, happens that a substantive derived from a verb governing the dative is itself joined with that case—as *obtemperatio legibus*, obedience to the laws; *insidiae consuli*, snares laid for the consul.

§ 265. Intransitive verbs compounded with the prepositions *ad, ante, cum, in, inter, ob, post, prae, (re), sub,* and *super,* follow the same rule as the compound transitives mentioned in § 263; e.g., *adesse amicis*, to succour one's friends; *antecellere omnibus*, to surpass all; *indormire causae*, to fall asleep over a thing; *occurrere hostibus*, to rush against the enemy; *praeesse equitibus*, to command the cavalry; *interesse proelio*, to take part in a battle; *resistitur audaciae hostium*, resistance is made against the audacity of the enemy; *egentibus subveniendum est*, the needy must be assisted. But, on the other hand, *navis adhaeret ad scopulum*, the boat sticks to the rock; *inhaeret sententia in animo*, the opinion is fixed in my mind; *severitas inest in vultu*, there is severity in his countenance; *congressum est cum hoste*, the attack was made upon the enemy.

Note. Sometimes a different preposition is used from that with which the verb is compounded—as *obrepit in animum*, it comes over my mind; *obversari ante oculos*, to float before one's eyes. So also *incumbo in* or *ad aliquid; acquiesco in aliqua re.* In the case of the verbs *adjaceo*, *adsto*, and *assideo*, we generally find the dative rarely the accusative, and never the preposition repeated.

§ 266. The verb *esse* governs the dative in the sense of ' to be,' or ' to exist for a person's use,' when it must be rendered in English by the verb ' to have'—as *mihi sunt multi libri*, I have many books; *homini cum deo similitudo est*, man has a resemblance to God; *controversia mihi est cum fratre*, I have a controversy with my brother; *mihi nomen est*, I have a name, or I am called.

Note. In the last-mentioned instance, when the name is added, it may either be put in the nominative, so as to stand in apposition to *nomen*—as *nomen ipsi erat Romulus*—or the name may be a sort of attraction to the dative *ipsi*, and be put in the dative—as *nomen ipsi erat Romulo*. Sometimes the name itself is put in the genitive, as in English, being governed by *nomen* — as *nomen ipsi erat Romuli*. These variations occur not only when *esse* is the verb to *nomen*, but also when we have such expressions as *nomen dare, nomen manet, nomen inditum est*, and others.

§ 267. Adjectives generally govern the dative when it is to be expressed that the qualities which they denote exist for some person or thing; e.g., *pax reipublicae utilis erat*, the peace was useful to the republic ; *res tibi facilis, ceteris difficilis*, the thing easy for you, difficult for others ; *haec res mihi et omnibus.meis gratissima erat*, this thing was most agreeable to me and mine.

But in particular the dative is joined with such adjectives as denote a certain relation to something or somebody, as those expressing a kindly or unkindly disposition, similarity, proximity ; e.g., *amicus, inimicus, aequus, iniquus, propitius, infensus, infestus, obnoxius ; par, impar, dispar, similis, dissimilis, consentaneus, contrarius, aequalis, propinquus, propior, proximus, vicinus, finitimus, conterminus, affinis, cognatus ;* e.g., *hic locus urbi propinquus est*, this place is near the city; *omnia mihi invisa atque infesta erant*, all things were opposed to me and hostile *; dii nobis propitii erunt*, the gods will be propitious to us.

Note 1. Respecting *propior* and *proximus* with the accusative, see above, § 254, note 2. Some of these adjectives—as *amicus, inimicus, familiaris, aequalis, cognatus, propinquus*, and others, are often used as substantives, and as such govern the genitive ; the same is sometimes the case even when they are in the superlative—as *amicissimus nostrorum hominum*.

2. The adjectives *similis, dissimilis*, and *par*, govern the dative when an outward resemblance is to be indicated—as *canis lupo similis est ;* but when a resemblance in character is to be expressed, they usually govern the genitive. *Ajacis similis*, accordingly, is, ' similar to Ajax in character and disposition.' *Diversus*, in the sense of *dissimilis*, is

found in poetry with the dative, though it is commonly followed by the preposition *a* or *ab*. *Affinis*, in the sense of 'partaking' or 'accomplice,' may be construed either with the genitive or the dative— as *affinis huic turpitudini*, or *hujus turpitudinis*. The dative·occurs in poetry also with the verbs *discrepo*, *differo*, *disto*, *dissideo*, instead of the ablative with *a* or *ab*.

3. Adjectives denoting aptness, fitness, or unfitness for anything— such as *aptus*, *utilis*, *habilis*, *idoneus*, *accommodatus* — are more frequently construed with *ad* and the accusative than with the dative— as *homo ad nullam rem utilis*, *aptus*, *idoneus*, a man useful or fit for nothing. *Superstes* (surviving) in early Latinity was joined with the dative, but afterwards more commonly with the genitive.

4. The following adverbs also are usually construed with the dative : *convenienter*, *congruenter*, *constanter*, and *obsequenter;* e.g., *vivere convenienter naturae*, to live consistently with nature. Poets now and then, in imitation of the Greek language, join the pronoun *idem* (ὁ αὐτός) with the dative — as *idem facit occidenti*, he does the same thing as one who kills.

§ 268. Names of towns and small islands are put in the dative, to denote the place where anything is or happens—as *Romae*, at Rome ; *Capuae*, at Capua ; *Athenis*, at Athens. When the name belongs to the. second or third declension, it takes the termination *i*—e.g., *Corinthi*, at Corinth ; *Tarenti*, at Tarentum ; *Carthagini*, at Carthage ; *Auxuri*, at Auxur ; *Lacedaemoni*, at Lacedaemon.

Note 1. That the dative of the second declension in Latin should at one time have ended in *i* cannot be surprising, since the same is the case in Greek ; and many Latin words continued in the best age of the language to make their dative in *i*—as *ulli*, *nulli*, *alii*, *neutri*, &c. In words of the third declension we sometimes find the termination *e*, whence it is usually said that names of towns of the third declension are put in the ablative, to denote the place where ? but the *e* is only a softer form for *i* — as in *here* for *heri*. The termination *i*, to denote place where (the Sanscrit locative), occurs also in the adverbs *ibi*, *ubi*, *hic* (that is, *hi-ce*), *illic* (*illi-ce*).

2. If a name of a town is accompanied by an apposition, the latter usually takes the preposition *in* with the ablative — as *milites Albae constiterunt, in urbe opportuna*, &c. ; but sometimes the ablative is used without a preposition—as *Corinthi, Achaiae urbe*, at Corinth, a town of Achaia. When the word *urbs* or *oppidum* precedes the name of a town, the preposition *in* is always used—as *in urbe Roma*, in the city of Rome ; *in insula Samo*, in the island of Samos ; so also *in ipsa Alexandria*.

3. The termination *i* is also used to denote place where in the words *domi*, at home ; *humi*, on the ground ; *belli*, in war ; *militiae* (for *militiai*), in war. *Domi* may be joined by a possessive pronoun or a genitive—as *domi suae*, in his house ; *domi Caesaris*, in the house of Caesar ; but when any other adjective is added, the preposition *in* with the ablative must be used — as *in domo celebri*, in a celebrated house. Instead of *humi*, poets sometimes use *humo* or *in humo*. A similar use of this locative case in *i* occurs in *animi*, in certain phrases de-

noting doubt or fear — as *te angis animi* (also *animo*) you torment yourself in your mind ; *pendemus animi*, we are doubtful in our minds.

§ 269. The datives of the personal pronouns *mihi, tibi, sibi,* and *nobis*, are frequently used in expressions of astonishment and censure, and in questions, denoting a certain vivacity of feeling and familiarity for which there is nothing equivalent in our language. This kind of dative, which occurs still more frequently in Greek, is called the *Ethical Dative ;* e.g., *Hic mihi quisquam misericordiam nominat !* Let any one here talk to me of mercy ! *Quid ait nobis Sannio?* What does Sannio say ? or what does our Sannio say ? *Quid tibi vis?* What do you want ? *Quid sibi volunt haec verba?* What do these words mean ?

§ 270. The dative is used to denote the purpose which anything serves, or the effect it produces. This is the case especially with *esse* in the sense of 'to redound to,' or ' to serve the purpose of '), *do, habeo, mitto, venio, pono, duco, verto, tribuo.* It not unfrequently happens that such verbs are also accompanied by their ordinary dative — as *cui bono est?* to whom is it (does it) any good ?—*est mihi et honori et utilitati*, it does me honour and is useful to me ; *hoc est argumento, documento, testimonio*, this serves as an argument, a proof, a testimony ; *pater filio id culpae dedit*, the father considered this to be the fault of the son ; *hoc mihi superbiae tribuit*, he put this to my pride ; *hunc librum mihi muneri dedit*, he gave me this book as a present ; *eum ludibrio habuit*, he made a laughing-stock of him ; *Caesar legiones duas castris praesidio reliquit*, Caesar left behind two legions as a protection for the camp ; so also *receptui canere*, to sound a retreat.

Note. Sometimes, however, instead of the dative denoting the purpose, the accusative is used in apposition to another noun—as *librum mihi donum dedit*, he gave the book to me as a present ; but the dative is much more common. When, in addition to the name of an officer, the object of his office is mentioned, the latter is generally expressed by the dative of a substantive joined by a gerundivum—as *decemviri legibus scribendis creati sunt*, decemvirs were created for the purpose of drawing up a code of laws ; *triumviri agris dividendis, rei publicae constituendae.*

§ 271. With passive verbs the agent is sometimes expressed by the dative instead of the ablative with the preposition *a* or *ab*. This, however, is done more frequently in poetry than in prose, and oftener with the compound tenses of the passive than with the simple ones — as *quidquid mihi* (for *a me*) *susceptum est*, whatever has been undertaken by me ; *non intelligor ulli* (*ab ullo*), I am not understood by any one ; *carmina quae scribuntur aquae potoribus* (*a potoribus*), poems which are written by water-drinkers.

The gerundive is regularly construed with the dative instead of the preposition *a* or *ab*—as *hoc mihi faciendum est,* this must be done by me; *non omnibus eadem facienda sunt,* not all men must do the same things.

Note. Here it may be observed that poets sometimes express motion towards with the dative—as *coelo,* towards heaven; *spolia conjiciunt igni,* they throw the spoils into the fire, where in prose we should say *in coelum* and *in ignem.*

CHAPTER XLIV.

USE OF THE GENITIVE CASE.

§ 272. The genitive principally serves to denote that relation between two substantives by which the two conjointly express only one idea, the genitive supplying the place of an adjective—as *castra hostium,* the camp of the enemy—that is, the hostile camp; *domus patris,* the house of the father—that is, the paternal house. The genitive, however, is sometimes also governed by verbs and adjectives.

Note 1. The genitive is often called the possessive case, because it denotes possession, connection, or origin — as *filius Ciceronis,* the son of Cicero; *dominus servi,* the master of the slave; *horti Sallustii,* the gardens of Sallust; *libri Ciceronis,* the books of Cicero (either written by him, or belonging to him). The relation of the genitive is expressed in English by the termination *s*—as my father's house; or more commonly by prepositions, especially *of.*

2. A substantive governing the genitive may be omitted when it is mentioned in a preceding part of the sentence, and can thus be easily supplied by the mind — as *meo judicio stare malo quam omnium reliquorum,* I will rather take my stand on my own judgment than (on the judgment) of all the rest; *flebat pater de filii morte, de patris filius,* the father wept over the death of his son, the son over (the death) of his father. Sometimes, though rarely, the place of the substantive governing the genitive is supplied by the pronoun *hic* or *ille*—as *nullam virtus aliam mercedem desiderat praeter hanc laudis et gloriae,* virtue desires no other reward except that of praise and honour (which I have already mentioned). Sometimes, when the substantive governing the genitive is omitted, the word which should be in the genitive is put in the case of the omitted substantive—as *oratio captivorum convenit cum perfugis* (that is, *cum oratione perfugarum*), the words of the captives agreed with those of the deserters; *ingenia nostrorum hominum multum ceteris hominibus praestiterunt,* the genius of our countrymen has greatly surpassed that of all other men (for

multum ceterorum hominum ingeniis). But such expressions are anomalies which should not be imitated.

3. In speaking of the temple of a god, the words *aedes* and *templum* are often omitted, especially after the prepositions *ad* and *ab* — as *ad Opis* (*aedes*), near the temple of Ops ; *ad Vestae*, near the temple of Vesta. Sometimes also the words *filius*, *uxor*, and *servus*, are omitted — as *Verania Pisonis*, Verania, the wife of Piso ; *Hasdrubal Gisgonis*, Hasdrubal, the son of Gisgo ; *Flaccus Claudii*, Flaccus, the slave of Claudius.

§ 273. Substantives which are derived from transitive verbs, and have an active meaning, govern, like all other substantives, a genitive ; but this genitive may be of a twofold nature — namely, *objective*, when it denotes the person or thing affected by the action implied in the substantive — as *amor patriae*, love for one's country ; *accusatio sceleratorum*, the accusation of criminals ; *timor hostium*, the fear of one's enemies ; — or *subjective*, when it denotes the person or thing from which the action implied in the governing substantive proceeds — as *amor parentum*, the love which parents entertain (*e.g.*, for their children) ; *odium hominum*, the hatred which men bear (to one another) ; *Romanorum res gestae*, the things done by the Romans, or the deeds of the Romans.

Note 1. Sometimes it may be uncertain whether a genitive is subjective or objective—as *amor Dei* may be ' the love which we feel for God' (objective), and 'the love which God feels towards us' (subjective); so also *timor hostium* and *odium hominum*. The real meaning is usually clear from the context ; but where the genitive would produce a decided ambiguity, its use must be avoided.

2. Substantives expressing a state of feeling, either friendly or hostile, often take a preposition instead of the genitive, whereby all ambiguity is avoided — as *odium mulierum* and *odium in mulieres; Meum erga te studium*, my zeal for thee ; *reverentia adversus homines*, reverence for men. When the governing word itself is in the genitive, the preposition is almost necessary—as *siquid amoris erga me in te residet*, if there is any particle of love for me in you. A preposition must be used when the governing substantive expresses motion—as *iter in Italiam, iter ex Hispania*.

3. The objective genitive with such verbal substantives, therefore, expresses the same thing which with the verb would be expressed by the accusative. But the objective genitive occurs also with substantives which are not derived from verbs governing the accusative, and it then denotes a sort of remoter object to which the action implied in the verb tends — as *incitamentum periculorum*, the incitement to brave dangers ; *aditus laudis*, the access to praise ; *amicitia est omnium divinarum humanarumque rerum consensio*, friendship is the agreement on all affairs human and divine ; *fiducia virium*, confidence in one's strength ; *victoria belli civilis*, the victory in the civil war ; *contentio honorum*, the contest for honours ; *dux belli*, the commander in the war.

4. As a possessive pronoun supplies the place of a genitive, we can say both *vestri causam ago* and *vestram causam ago*, I conduct your

case; *ipse fuit suus* (or *sui*) *accusator*, he was his own accuser; *fiducia tua* or *tui*, confidence in thee; *rationem habet suam* or *sui*, he takes notice of himself. For the same reason a possessive pronoun is sometimes followed by a genitive, which stands in apposition to it—as in Horace, *quum mea nemo scripta legat, vulgo recitare timentis*, where *timentis* stands in apposition to *mea*, which involves the idea of the genitive *mei*.

§ 274. One substantive is sometimes followed by another in the genitive, which contains in reality the same idea, and gives only a more specific explanation of it — as *arbor fici*, a fig-tree; *arbor abietis*, a fir-tree; *nomen regis*, the name of king (but it may also be 'the name of the king'); *verbum monendi*, the word *monere*; *vitium ignorantiae*, the fault of ignorance; *remedium ignis*, a remedy consisting of fire; *verbum dubitandi*, a verb of doubting. In cases of this kind, the genitive is little more than a noun in apposition to another.

Note 1. The genitive of the gerund is thus always used like the genitive of a substantive; but in some cases of this kind, instead of the genitive, the infinitive may be used, which stands as a kind of apposition to the substantive—as *tempus est abire* for *abeundi*.

2. When names of towns are preceded by the generic terms *urbs, oppidum*, or *civitas*, the name is treated as standing in apposition to the generic term, whereas in English we use the preposition of — as *urbs Roma*, the city of Rome; *oppidum Praeneste*, the town of Praeneste — on the same principle on which we say *rex Tullius, flumen Rhenus, mons Vesuvius, terra Italia*, &c. In a few instances, however, and especially in poetry, the Latins, on the same principle as the English, put the proper name in the genitive — as *urbs Buthroti*, the town of Buthrotum; *promontorium Pachyni*, the promontory of Pachynum; *tellus Ausoniae*, the land of Ausonia; *oppidum Antiochiae*, the town of Antioch.

3. There are many cases in which a substantive, instead of being followed by a genitive, takes a preposition—as *pugna ad Alliam, pugna ad Cannas, liber de officiis, victoria de Hannibale, templum de marmore, accusator de plebe, iter ex Hispania, tua erga me voluntas.* (See § 273, note 2.) In many cases of this kind the preposition must be explained by some verb understood.

§ 275. The genitive denotes the whole of which anything is a part, and is governed by the noun which expresses the part—as *magnus numerus militum*, a large number of soldiers; *magna vis auri*, a great quantity of gold; *tria millia equitum*, three thousand soldiers. Such a partitive genitive is governed by all nouns denoting part of a whole: —

(*a*). By the nominative or accusative neuter singular of adjectives denoting quantity — as *multum, plurimum, amplius, minus, minimum, tantum, quantum, tantundem, nimium, exiguum;* and by the neuter of a pronoun (demonstrative, relative, or indefinite) and *nihil* — as *multum temporis*, a considerable time; *minus laboris*, less labour; *tantum otii*,

K

so much leisure; *id negotii*, this (or this part of the) business; *hoc praemii*, this reward; *nihil virium*, no strength;
quod roboris erat, whatever strength there was; *quid mihi
consilii datis?* what kind of advice do you give me?
Wherever the partitive character is not to be expressed,
the adjectives regularly agree with their substantives — as
tantum studium, so great zeal; whereas *tantum studii* would
mean 'so much of zeal.' *Plus*, which is never used as an
adjective, is always followed by the genitive—as *plus pecuniae*, more money; *plus diligentiae*, more diligence.

Note 1. The genitive in connection with such adjectives and pronouns used substantively, may be that of the neuter of an adjective
of the second declension—as *quid novi? aliquid boni; nihil pulchri;
tantum mali.* But we may also say *aliquid bonum; nihil magnificum.*
Adjectives of the third declension are never so used, on account of
the ambiguity which would thereby be created, whence we must
always say *aliquid utile, nihil suave, nihil dulce.*
2. The above-mentioned neuter adjectives and pronouns are not
followed by a genitive when they are governed by a preposition—as
ad tantum malum, not *ad tantum mali.* There are, however, some
cases in which this rule is not observed — as *ad multum diei* for *ad
multum diem*, to a late part of the day; *ad id loci*, and *ad id locorum*,
up to this point of time or place.
3. The following expressions must be particularly noticed — *nihil
reliqui facere*, not to leave or omit anything; *nihil pensi habere*, to
have nothing weighed, or not to care about a thing.

(*b.*) By the adverbs *satis, abunde, affatim, nimis, nimium, parum*,
which in the nominative and accusative are used as substantives, though never with a preposition — as *satis sapientiae*, enough of wisdom; *parum prudentiae*, too little prudence; *nimium laboris*, too much labour.

(*c*). By all words which denote a part of a whole, whether
they be substantives, adjectives, numerals, or pronouns,
but especially by the superlative of adjectives — as *magna
pars civium*, a great part of the citizens; *duo genera militum*,
two kinds of soldiers; *multi civium*, many of the citizens;
tertius regum Romanorum, the third of the Roman kings;
alter imperatorum, the one of the two generals; *solus omnium*, he the only one among all; *fortissimus Graecorum*,
the bravest of the Greeks; *doctissimus Romanorum*, the
most learned of the Romans; *plerumque Italiae*, the greater
part of Italy.

Note 1. Instead of the genitive partitive in some of the cases enumerated under *c*, we frequently find the prepositions *ex* or *de*, and
sometimes even *inter* or *in*—as *fortissimus e* or *de Graecis* and *inter
Graecos; multi de* or *e civibus; aliquis de heredibus.* A partitive substantive, however, is never followed by a preposition, whence we
cannot say *pars e militibus* for *pars militum.*

2. The word *uterque* is joined only with the genitive of pronouns— as *uterque eorum*, each of them ; *uterque nostrum*, each of us ; but when accompanying a substantive, it generally agrees with it as an adjective — as *uterque legatus, uterque consul*, and we rarely meet with such expressions as *uterque legatorum*. *Partim* is construed both with a genitive and with a preposition — as *partim eorum ficta sunt*, and *partim e nobis timidi sunt*.

3. The neuter of any adjective, both in the singular and plural, is often used as a substantive, and accordingly followed by a genitive, especially in poetry and late prose writers, but rarely in Cicero and the earlier authors — as *medium noctis*, for which Cicero would say *media nox; ad ultimum inopiae* — that is, *ad ultimam inopiam; plana urbis* — that is, *plana urbis loca*.

4. In English, the adjectives *many, few, all, none*, are often followed by *of*, without their denoting a part of a whole, but comprising all the persons or things which make up the whole. In this case the Latins can neither use the genitive nor a preposition, but make the adjectives agree with their nouns — as *amicis, quos multos habet*, his friends, of whom he has many — that is, whom he has in great numbers ; *hominibus opus est eruditis, qui adhuc nostri nulli fuerunt*, there is need of learned men, of whom there have as yet been few among us.

5. Pronominal adverbs of place—as *hic, huc, eo, eodem, quoad, ibi, ubi, ubicunque, quo*, and others, are often joined with the genitive of a noun—as *hic loci*, in this place ; *huc dementiae processit*, he went to that pitch of madness ; *eo insolentiae*, to that point of insolence ; *quoad ejus fieri potest*, as far as it can be done ; *ubi terrarum, gentium* or *locorum?* where on earth?—*nusquam gentium*, nowhere in the world ; *postea loci*, afterwards ; *interea loci*, in the meantime ; *adhuc locorum*, up to this point (of time). In like manner the ablative of pronouns, *hoc, eo, eodem, quo*, are sometimes used substantively, and followed by a genitive—as *eo loci, hoc loci*, for *eo loco* and *hoc loco*, in that place.

§ 276. When the nature, quality, size, or extent of anything is described by a substantive accompanied by an adjective (numeral, participle, or pronoun), the latter is put in the genitive (genitive of quality) which is governed by the substantive they explain — as *vir magni ingenii*, a man of great talent ; *homo insignis prudentiae*, a man of extraordinary prudence ; *res magni laboris*, an undertaking of great labour ; *classis ducentarum navium*, a fleet of two hundred ships ; *exilium trium annorum*, an exile of three years ; *vir ordinis equestris*, a man of equestrian order. Such a genitive of quality cannot be used when the substantive is not accompanied by an adjective ; we cannot therefore translate 'a man of talent' by *homo ingenii*, but must use the adjective, *ingeniosus homo*.

Note 1. When the verbs *esse, fieri*, or *haberi*, occur in such sentences as *est, habetur vir magni ingenii; classis fuit trecentarum navium*, the genitive is not dependent upon these verbs, but upon the substantive of which the quality is stated, and that substantive must in many cases be supplied a second time by the mind — as *haec classis fuit (classis) trecentarum navium; Caesar diversarum partium (vir) habe-*

batur, Caesar was considered to be (a man) of the opposite party; *Di me finxerunt (hominem) animi pusilli*, the gods have made me (a man) of little courage.

2. The word *modi*, in conjunction with a pronoun, occurs very frequently as a genitive of quality — as *res hujusmodi, ejusmodi, illiusmodi, istiusmodi, cujusmodi*, &c.

3. Sometimes the ablative is used in the same manner to express a quality—as *moneo te, praestanti prudentia virum*, I admonish you, a man of unusual prudence; but there is this difference between the genitive and ablative of quality, that the former indicates more the essential nature and character of a thing, while the latter expresses the quality merely as a special or accessory property or quality of a thing. Hence, when outward peculiarities of a person or a thing are stated, it is done by the ablative, and not by the genitive—as *Britanni sunt capillo promisso*, the Britons are persons with floating hair. Observe also the difference between *bono animo esse*, to be of good courage, and *homo maximi animi*, a man of a very great mind — the ablative denoting a particular disposition, and the genitive the real nature or character of the man.

4. Sometimes one substantive may govern two genitives, or one substantive in the genitive may govern another; but as ambiguity may often arise from such a construction, it requires great caution and attention. Caesar, *e.g.*, says, *superiorum dierum Sabini cunctatio*, the delay of Sabinus during the preceding days; and Cicero, *Scaevolae dicendi elegantia*, the elegance of Scaevola in speaking; and *haec fuit causa intermissionis litterarum*, this was the cause of the interruption in our correspondence. When such a construction would occasion ambiguity, it must be altered either by means of a preposition or otherwise.

§ 277. The genitive is governed by several adjectives denoting a quality existing in reference to certain things—that is, by relative adjectives, the meaning of which is not complete without the thing being added in regard to which this quality exists. Adjectives of this kind are—

1. All present participles of transitive verbs, when used as real adjectives, and all adjectives ending in *ax*, which are derived from transitive verbs—as *amans patriae; amantissimus republicae; patiens laboris et frigoris; appetens gloriae; tenax propositi; capax aquae; tempus edax rerum.*

Note. When such participles retain their character as participles—that is, when they express an action performed at a certain time—they govern the case which they require as verbs.

2. Adjectives denoting desire, knowledge, experience, remembering, and their opposites — as *avarus, avidus, cupidus, studiosus, conscius, inscius, nescius, gnarus, ignarus, peritus, imperitus, prudens, rudis, insolens, insuetus, memor, immemor*, and others; and sometimes also those which denote foresight and want of care — as *providus, diligens, curiosus, incuriosus;* e.g., *cupidus gloriae*, desirous of **fame;**

peritus belli, experienced in war; *ignarus omnium rerum,* ignorant of all things; *memor beneficii,* remembering an act of kindness; *studiosus sapientiae,* desirous of, or anxious about, wisdom.

Note 1. Poets and late prose writers use the genitive also with many other adjectives, especially with those which denote any mental emotion—as *ambiguus, anxius, certus, dubius, impiger, laetus, modicus, ferox,* and others.

2. *Consultus* (experienced) is construed both with the genitive and the ablative—as *juris consultus* and *jure consultus.* The comparative of *certus* in the phrase *certiorem aliquem facere,* is construed with the genitive and also with the preposition *de*—as *certiorem me fecit consilii sui,* and *certiorem me fecit de consilio suo. Conscius* is commonly construed with the genitive of the thing which one knows, and with the dative of the person with whom one knows a thing—as *conscius sibi tanti sceleris,* he was conscious (to himself) of so great a crime; but sometimes also the thing of which a person is conscious is expressed by the dative, and the person by the genitive—as *conscius facinori, conscius mendacio alicujus. Rudis* and *prudens* are also used with *in* and the ablative instead of the genitive—as *prudens* or *rudis in jure civili. Rudis* and *insuetus,* moreover, are construed with *ad,* denoting the thing in regard to which the qualities exist—as *rudis ad pedestre certamen,* unskilful in regard to fighting on foot.

3. Adjectives denoting power over a thing, or the contrary, as *compos, impos, potens,* and *impotens*—as *compos mentis,* in possession of one's mind; *impotens equi regendi,* unable to control the horse; *diva potens Cypri,* the goddess who has power or rules over Cyprus.

4. Adjectives denoting participation, or the contrary, as *particeps, expers, consors, exsors, reus, affinis, insons* — as *particeps consilii,* partaking in a plan or design; *expers periculorum,* not sharing the dangers; *reus furti,* accused of theft; *insons probri,* innocent of a crime; *affinis rei capitalis,* an accomplice in a capital offence.

5. Adjectives denoting abundance, fulness, or want, may govern either the genitive or the ablative; but *inops* (poor) is construed only with the genitive, and *plenus* more commonly with the genitive than with the ablative.

Note. Pauper is always construed with the genitive, and commonly also *egenus, indigus,* and *sterilis.* The following adjectives also are often found with the genitive : —*prodigus, profusus, liberalis,* and *parcus ;* and poets also construe adjectives and participles denoting 'free from' with the genitive, such as *liber, purus, vacuus*—as *liber curarum ; purus sceleris, vacuus operum,* though it is more common to construe them with the ablative.

6. The adjectives *similis* and *dissimilis* are joined both with the genitive and dative (see § 267, note 2); the same is the case with *proprius,* though the neuter in the sense of 'pro-

perty' or 'peculiarity' is generally joined with the genitive
—as *proprium est oratoris*, it is peculiar to an orator ; but
tempus agendi mihi fuit proprium, the time of action was
convenient to me.

Note 1. *Communis* also takes both the genitive and dative—as *memoria communis est multarum artium ; omni aetati mors est communis;* but with personal pronouns *communis* always takes the dative—as *commune mihi, tibi, sibi*, &c.

2. Poets and late prose writers, such as Tacitus, join the genitive
to many other adjectives to express certain relations which are more
commonly expressed either by the ablative alone, or by the prepositions *de* and *in*—as *integer vitae, lassus maris, atrox odii, modicus
voluptatis, ambiguus futuri, dubius viae.* Adjectives denoting a disposition of the mind—as *aeger, anxius, laetus, ingens*, and others,
are often joined with the genitive of *animus*.

§ 278. The verbs *sum* and *fio*, when they connect two substantives, and signify 'to belong to' and 'to come to belong
to,' govern the genitive of' the person to whom anything
belongs—as *domus est patris*, the house belongs to the father ;
ego totus Pompeii sum, I belong wholly to Pompey ; *omnia
viri fiunt*, all things come to belong to the man ; *Thebae
populi Romani factae sunt*, Thebes came to belong to the
Roman people.

Note. In like manner *facio* (the active of *fio*), in the sense of ' to
make a thing a person's property,' governs the genitive of the person
who is made the proprietor—as *non faciam laborem illorum*, I shall
not make labour their property — that is, I shall not devolve the
labour upon them. Similar expressions are—*hoc est mei judicii*, this
is a matter of my judgment—that is, I have a right to judge of this
matter ; *facio hanc terram meae ditionis, meae potestatis* or *mei arbi-
trii*, I bring this country under my control or supremacy.

§ 279. The genitive with *sum* often denotes the person or
thing to which anything belongs, is proper or becoming, or
whose duty anything is—as *ista oratio non est hujus temporis*,
that speech is not suited to this time ; *non est mearum virium*,
it is not proper for my strength—that is, I have not strength
enough ; *oratoris est*, it is becoming to an orator ; *petulantia
magis est adolescentium quam senum*, petulence is more fit for
young than for old men. When the person to whom anything
is a duty or becoming is expressed in English by a personal
pronoun, the Latins must use the neuter of the possessive—as
meum est pro republica pugnare, it is becoming to me to fight
for the republic ; *tuum est deum colere*, it is your duty to
worship God.

Note. In like manner we find *tempori cedere semper sapientis habitum
est*, to yield to circumstances has always been considered the duty
of a wise man. Sometimes the word *officium* or *munus* (duty) is

added to the genitive, but it does not follow that such a substantive is to be supplied where it is not expressed, for the genitive depends upon the word *sum.* In the expression *moris est* (it is the custom), the genitive *moris* is a kind of partitive genitive dependent upon *est.* There are, however, cases in which the genitive after *sum* depends upon a preceding noun, which is to be understood a second time—as *unum genus est eorum* (there is one class of men), where *eorum* depends upon the word *genus,* as if it were *unum genus est genus eorum.* So also *captivorum numerus fuit (numerus) septem millium ac ducentorum.* In this case the verb *sum* may often be rendered by 'to consist of'—as *major pars Atheniensium erat,* the greater part consisted of Athenians.

§ 280. The verbs of remembering, forgetting, and reminding — as *memini, reminiscor (recordor,* rarely), *obliviscor, admoneo, commoneo,* and *commonefacio,* govern the genitive of the person or thing which we remember, forget, or of which we remind a person—as *semper hujus diei et loci meminero,* I shall always remember this day and place ; *obliti sunt pristinae virtutis,* they have forgotten their former valour ; *reminiscor beneficii tui,* I remember your kindness ; *admonuit eos matris sororumque,* he reminded them of their mother and sisters ; *omnes tui sceleris commonefiunt,* all are reminded of your crime.

Note 1. The verbs of remembering and forgetting, especially *memini,* are often joined with the accusative — as *memini numeros, obliviscor causam, amicum meum bene meministi.* This is the case especially when the object of these verbs is a neuter adjective or pronoun used substantively. *Recordor* is more generally construed with the accusative than with the genitive.

2. The verbs of reminding are very often found with the accusative of the thing of which you remind a person, especially when the thing is expressed by the neuter of a pronoun or adjective — as *illud te admoneo, unum te admoneo;* and such an accusative also remains with the verb in the passive — as *illud admoneor.* (See above, § 254. 3.) Sometimes also the preposition *de* is used—as *de avaritia tua commonemur,* we are reminded of your avarice. As the expression *venit mihi in mentem,* 'it occurs to my mind,' is in meaning equivalent to *reminiscor,* is is sometimes, like *reminiscor,* construed with the genitive—as *venit mihi Platonis in mentem,* I am reminded of Plato ; but the thing which occurs to the mind is more commonly expressed by the nominative as the subject of *venit* — as *pugna Cannensis venit mihi in mentem,* the battle of Cannae occurs to my mind.

§ 281. The verb *misereor (miseresco),* I pity, and the impersonal verbs *miseret, (miserescit, miseretur), piget, poenitet, pudet, taedet, pertaesum est,* are accompanied by the genitive of the thing exciting the feelings expressed by these verbs, and govern the accusative of the person in whom the feelings exist (compare § 252) ; e. g., *misereor (miseresco* or *miseret me), amici mei,* I pity my friend ; *poenitet me consilii,* I repent of my plan ; *pudet me negligentiae meae,* I am ashamed of my carelessness; *pudet hunc hominem insolentiae,* this man is ashamed of his insolence.

Note. When the thing producing the feeling denoted by these verbs is expressed by a verb, it may be introduced by the conjunction *quod,* or it may be expressed by the infinitive — as *non poenitet me vixisse,* or *non poenitet me quod vixi,* I do not regret having lived; *pudet me pecasse,* or *pudet me quod peccavi,* I am ashamed of having sinned. The verbs *piget, poenitet,* and *pudet,* are sometimes used personally with a neuter pronoun for their subject — as *non te haec pudent,* these things cause you no shame. The participle *pertaesus* is generally construed with the accusative — as *pertaesus ignaviam suam,* disgusted with his own idleness, though it also occurs with the genitive. The verbs *miseror* and *commiseror* (I pity or lament) are construed only with the accusative.

§ 282. Verbs of charging, accusing, convicting, condemning, and acquitting, govern the accusative of the person and the genitive of the thing with which any one is charged, and of which he is accused, convicted, acquitted, &c. Such verbs are *accuso, incuso, insimulo, arcesso* (I summon before a court of justice); *postulo, ago cum aliquo* (I begin a lawsuit with a person); *arguo, coarguo, convinco, damno, condemno, absolvo;* e. g., *accusavit Titum furti,* he accused Titus of theft; *damnatus est repetundarum,* he was condemned for extortion; *proditionis absolvit ducem,* he acquitted the general of treachery.

Note 1. The genitive governed by these verbs is commonly said to be governed by the substantive *crimine* or *nomine* understood; but there is no necessity for assuming such an ellipsis, although these words are occasionally added to the genitive. Besides the above-mentioned verbs, there are a few adjectives of similar meaning, which, in legal phraseology, are joined with the genitive — as *reus, noxius, innoxius, insons,* and *manifestus, compertus* (convicted), and also *interrogare* (to bring an action against) — as *nullius probri compertus; interrogavit eum ambitus.*

2. Instead of the genitive we sometimes find the preposition *de* with the verbs *accusare, postulare,* and *damnare* — as *accusare de vi, de veneno.* The verbs *damno* and *condemno* are frequently joined with the genitive or ablative of the punishment — as *damnari capitis* or *capite,* to be condemned to death; so also *damnare mortis* or *morte, multae* or *multa, pecuniae* or *pecunia.* When a fixed sum of money (fine) is mentioned, the ablative is always used.

§ 283. When the price or value of a thing is stated in a general way, it is always done by the genitives *magni, permagni, tanti, tantidem, quanti, quantivis, quanticunque, pluris, plurimi, maximi, parvi, minoris, minimi.* This is the case especially with the verbs of estimating and valuing—as *duco, facio, habeo, pendo, puto, taxo;* e. g., *domum tanti ducit quanti ducenda est,* he values the house at as much as it should be valued; *sapiens voluptatem non tanti facit quanti virtutem,* a wise man values pleasure not so much as virtue. Verbs of selling and purchasing, however, are joined with the ablatives *magno, parvo, minimo, nihilo, nonnihilo.* (Compare § 294.) The verb *aestimo* may be joined either with the genitive or the ablative—as *magni* or *magno virtutem aestimo,* I value virtue highly.

Note 1. Verbs of valuing are joined in conversational discourse with the genitives *flocci, nauci, assis, teruncii,* generally with a negative, to denote that a thing is worth nothing—as *judices rempublicam flocci non faciunt.* In like manner we also find the genitive *nihili* or the ablative *pro nihilo,* 'worth nothing.' *Hujus non facio* is a comic phrase, signifying 'I do not care *that* for it.' We must further notice the phrases *aequi bonique* or *boni facio,* and *boni consulo,* I take a thing in good part, or am satisfied.

2. *Tanti est* properly signifies 'it is worth so much,' but also · it is worth while,' or contemptuously with a snap of the finger, 'so much,' as in Cic. *in Catil.* i. 2.

§ 284. The impersonal verbs *interest* and *rēfert* (it is of importance, or interest to) are joined with the genitive of the person to whom anything is of interest or importance; but when the person is expressed in English by a personal pronoun, the Latins use the possessive forms *mea, tua, sua, nostra, vestra* — as *patris interest* or *refert,* it is of interest to the father; *Clodii intererat Milonem perire,* it was of interest to Clodius that Milo should perish; *mea interest* or `refert,* it is of interest to me; *vestra interest,* it is of interest to you.

Note 1. The genitive with these verbs must be explained by an ellipsis. In the case of interest we have to supply *commoda*—as *est inter patris* or *mea commoda,* so that here the possessives are neuter plurals. *Rēfert* is probably a compound of *rem* and *fert,* whence the *rē* is long. The possessive forms with this verb have the *ā* long, whence they cannot be neuter plurals. If the etymology of *rēfert* here given be correct, the perfect phrase would be *rem fert patris* and *rem fert meam,* and the possessives *meā, tuā, suā,* &c. would be abridged forms of the accusative feminine singular *meam, tuam, suam,* &c.

2. The thing which is of importance or interest may be expressed by a neuter pronoun — as *hoc interest reipublicae,* or, as is the case most frequently, by a clause in the accusative with the infinitive, or by the conjunction *ut* and the subjunctive—as *mea interest te hodie venire,* or *mea interest ut hodie venias.* When it is stated of how much importance a thing is, it is expressed either by the genitives *magni, parvi, quanti, tanti,* &c. (see § 283), or more commonly by the adverbs *multum, plurimum, nihil, magnopere, vehementer.*

§ 285. As a possessive pronoun is the representative of a noun in the genitive, it frequently occurs that a substantive standing in apposition to the person implied in the possessive
15

pronoun is put in the genitive — as *mea scripta timentis*, my writings who (I) fear—that is, the writings of me who fear; *tuum, hominis simplicis, pectus vidimus*, we have seen your heart, who are a single-minded man; *mea unius opera respublica salva est*, through my exertion alone the republic is safe; *vestrā ipsorum causā*, for your own sake; *ad vestram omnium caedem restiterunt*, they have remained behind for the purpose of murdering you all.

Note. The genitives *nostrum* and *vestrum* are frequently joined to *omnium*, being in apposition to it, instead of their being joined as adjectives to a substantive; e.g., *voluntati vestrum omnium parui* for *voluntati vestrae omnium parui*, I have complied with the will of you all; *patria est communis omnium nostrum parens* (instead of *communis nostra omnium parens*), the fatherland is the common mother of us all.

§ 286. Sometimes the genitive of the personal pronoun is used instead of a possessive pronoun; and this is the case chiefly with substantives containing the meaning of an active verb, so that the genitive of the personal pronoun is an objective genitive—as *accusator tui* for *accusator tuus*, your accuser (the man who accuses you); *laudator tui* for *laudator tuus*, the man who praises you. Sometimes, however, there is a difference of meaning—as *imago mea*, my image, or the image belonging to me; but *imago mei*, an image of me, or a portrait of me; *meum desiderium*, my desire, or the desire which I have; but *desiderium mei*, a desire of me, which some one has of me.

§ 287. The genitives *nostrum* and *vestrum* are used only in a partitive sense, when a number of persons is spoken of—as *magna pars nostrum*, a great many of us; *multi vestrum*, many of you; *uterque nostrum*, each of us two; *quis vestrum?* which of you? But when a part of one thing (the human body) is spoken of, the genitives *nostri, vestri, mei, tui*, and *sui*, must be used—as *nostri melior pars animus est*, the better part of us is our mind.

Note. It was remarked in § 286, that the genitives *mei, tui, sui, nostri, vestri*, are used as objective genitives instead of possessive pronouns; the same is the case, though very rarely, with the genitives *nostrum* and *vestrum*—as *cupidus vestrum*, desirous of you; *custos vestrum*, a guardian of you, or your guardian.

CHAPTER XLV.

USE OF THE ABLATIVE CASE.

§ 288. The ablative, which is peculiar to the Latin language, expresses a variety of relations necessary to define and modify the predicate—that is, those relations which in English are expressed by the prepositions *by*, *with*, *from*, *in*, or *at*. It is used partly with and partly without prepositions.

§ 289. The ablative is used to denote the part of a person or thing, or the point to which the statement contained in the predicate is limited ; e. g., *aeger est pedibus*, he is suffering in his feet; *eloquentia insignis est*, he is distinguished in eloquence; *claudus altero pede*, lame in one foot; *natione Gallus*, a Gaul by birth ; *centum numero erant*, they were one hundred in number; *sunt quidam homines non re, sed nomine*, some are men not in reality, but only in name; *specie urbs libera est*, in appearance the city is free; *tu temporibus errasti*, you were mistaken in regard to the times.

Note. When the predicate is an adjective, the extraneous thing in regard to which the adjective is predicated is generally expressed by the preposition *ad*—as *accusare multos sordidum est ad famam*, to accuse many is a bad thing for one's reputation ; *utilis ad legendum ; pulchrum ad rationem solertiamque*. When the quarter is indicated from which the action or condition implied in the predicate proceeds, the preposition *ab* is used—as *Caesar metuebat, ne a re frumentaria laboraret*, Caesar feared lest he should suffer from (want of) corn.

§ 290. The ablative is used to express the means or instrument by which anything is done or brought about—as *manu aliquem ducere*, to lead a person by the hand ; *securi aliquem percutere*, to strike a person with an axe ; *amorem moribus conciliare*, to win affection by one's manners ; *respublica mea cura et opera servata est*, the republic has been saved by my care and exertion ; *veneno maritum interfecit*, she killed her husband by poison ; *Britanni lacte et carne vivunt*, the Britons live on milk and meat ; *Lycurgus leges suas auctoritate Apollinis Delphici confirmavit*, Lycurgus got his laws sanctioned by the authority of the Delphian Apollo ; *lege Cornelia de vi damnatus est*, he was condemned by the Cornelian law concerning violence.

Note 1. Instead of the ablative of the instrument, we sometimes find with passive verbs the preposition *a* or *ab* with the ablative; but this is the case only when the thing which is the instrument is conceived as an agent or as a personification—as *vincitur a voluptate*, he is overcome by the love of pleasure; *eo a natura ipsa deducimur*, to this we are led by nature herself. Poets sometimes use the preposition *a* or *ab* even where the thing is not regarded as the agent, but simply as an instrument, as in *Tibullus*, i. 5, 4.

2. When a person is employed as the means or instrument through which anything is done, the ablative cannot be used; but instead of it we must take the preposition *per* with the accusative—as *litteras tibi misi per servum*, I sent you the letter by a slave; *provinciam per legatos administrat*. Sometimes a paraphrase is used by means of *operā* (by means of) —as *operā legatorum*, by means of lieutenants. Instead of the accusative with *per*, however, the instrumentality of a person may be expressed by the ablative alone, when persons are named instead of a thing connected with them, and when they are treated as things and mere instruments—as *testibus* (by witnesses); that is, *dictis testium*, or *testimonio; terrere hostem sagittariis et funditoribus*, to terrify the enemy by means of archers and slingers. *Per*, on the other hand, is joined with names of things to denote instrumentality, when a concomitant circumstance is to be expressed rather than the real instrument—as *per vim mihi bona eripuit*, he robbed me of my property in a violent manner; *per simulationem*, in a deceitful manner; *per scelus*, in a criminal manner; *per causam*, under the pretext.

3. An instrumental ablative is usually connected·with some verb or adjective, but there are a few cases in which it is connected with a substantive—as *interitus ferro, fame, frigore, pestilentia*, destruction by the sword, by hunger, by cold, by a pestilence.

§ 291. The ablative denotes the moving cause by which, or through the influence of which, anything is done—as *ardere studio*, to burn with zeal; *exsultare gaudio*, to exult with delight; *hoc odio factum est*, this has been done from hatred; *Servius Tullius regnavit non jussu, sed voluntate atque concessu civium*, Servius Tullius reigned not by the command, but by the wish and with the consent of the citizens; *ipsius rogatu*, by his request; *legibus in exilium mitti non potest*, by the laws he cannot be sent into exile.

Note 1. The ablative of cause is used most frequently with intransitive and passive verbs, denoting a mental emotion, and especially with their participles, such as *ardens, commotus, incitatus, incensus.* In some cases the preposition *a* or *ab* is added to express the origin more emphatically—as *ab ira, ab odio*, from anger, from hatred. When the cause is to be described as preventing anything, the preposition *prae* is added to the ablative—as *prae lacrimis loqui non potest*, he cannot speak on account of his tears; *prae moerore*, in consequence of grief.

2. We must further notice the ablatives *mea sententia*, in my opinion; *meo judicio*, according to my judgment; and the like, where the ablative expresses that in consequence of which we think or judge. The English expressions 'in consequence of,' 'in accordance with,' are sometimes given in Latin by the preposition *ex;* e. g., *coloniae ex*

foedere milites dare debebant, the colonies, according to treaty, were bound to furnish soldiers.

§ 292. The ablatives *causā* and *gratiā* (for the sake of, on account of) are in reality ablatives of cause, and are joined with a genitive or a possessive pronoun. When joined with a genitive, they usually stand after it—as *patris causa* or *gratia*, on the father's account; *regis causa* or *gratia*, for the sake of the king; *tua causa huc veni*, I have come hither for thy sake; *dolorum effugiendorum causa*, for the sake of avoiding pains.

Note. A motive is not expressed by the ablative, but by the prepositions *ob*, *propter*, or by the words *causā* and *gratiā*, which have assumed the character of prepositions. There are, however, instances in which the ablative is used instead of these prepositions, which then becomes a kind of instrumental ablative, as in Caesar—*levitate armorum et quotidiana exercitatione nihil hostibus noceri poterat.* When *gratia* and *causa* are not accompanied by a genitive or possessive pronoun, it is more common to use the preposition *de* or *ob* than the ablative—as *ea de causa*, or *eam ob causam* (for this reason,) is more common than *eā causā.*

§ 293. A substantive accompanied by an adjective, pronoun, or participle, is put in the ablative to express the manner or concomitant circumstance of the predicate—as *summa aequitate rempublicam constituit*, he settled the affairs of the republic with the greatest fairness; *deos pura et incorrupta mente venerari debemus*, we must worship the gods with a pure and sincere mind; *hoc nullo modo fieri potest*, this cannot be done in any way; *summa vi hostibus restitere*, they opposed the enemy with the greatest effort. Substantives denoting manner—as *modus, mos, ratio, ritus*, and *consuetudo*, may be used in the ablative without being accompanied by an adjective, participle, or pronoun, if they are followed by a genitive—as *latronis modo*, in the manner of a highwayman; *more majorum*, according to the custom of our ancestors; *ritu festinantis*, in the manner of one who hastens; *consuetudine Romanorum*, according to the custom of the Romans.

Note 1. Sometimes, however, the Latins use the preposition *cum* to express a concomitant circumstance, when this circumstance is something external, and is regarded as something quite distinct from the idea contained in the predicate—as *magno cum studio aderat*, he was present with great zeal (that is, and displayed great zeal); *moliri aliquid cum molesto labore*, to attempt something with laborious exertion (that is, and to spend laborious exertion upon it). So also *magno gaudio* and *magno cum gaudio aliquid facere; magno comitatu venire* and *magno cum comitatu venire.* But *cum* can never be used with words denoting manner, intention, a state of mind, or a condition—as *hac mente scripsi, hoc consilio vos convocavi, aequo animo aliquid ferre, hac conditione, hac lege.* Nor can *cum* be used when a part of the human body is mentioned to denote a concomitant circumstance — as *promisso capillo incessit*, she walked along with floating hair ; *capite involuto*, with her head wrapt up.

2. When the substantive used to express a concomitant circumstance or manner is not accompanied by an adjective, participle, or pronoun, the preposition *cum* must be used—as *cum cura aliquid facere*, to do a thing with care ; *cum fide exponere*, to explain faithfully ; but in most cases of this kind it is preferable to use an adverb instead of the ablative with *cum*. There are, however, some ablatives of substantives which are used alone in the sense of adverbs—as *omnes ordine profecti sunt*, all set out in order. Ablatives of this kind are—*ratione, ordine, via et ratione, more, jure, injuria, clamore, silentio, dolo, vi*. Sometimes also the preposition *per* is used to denote the manner in which anything is done—as *per vim*, by force ; *per simulationem*, under the pretence. Compare above, § 290, note 2.

3. When it is to be expressed that while anything is done a thing is in the hands or possession of a person, it must, under all circumstances, be expressed by *cum*, to avoid ambiguity—as *milites capti sunt cum armis*, the soldiers were taken with their arms—that is, while in the possession of their arms. *Cum*, moreover, sometimes denotes the result or consequence accompanying an action—as *Verres venit Lampsacum cum magna calamitate et prope pernicie civitatis*, Verres came to Lampsacus, and the consequence was a great calamity and almost the ruin of the state.

§ 294. With verbs of buying, selling, estimating, and the like, the price or value, if stated by a distinct sum or amount, is expressed by the ablative—as *emere aliquid denario*, to purchase a thing for a denarius ; *orationem vendidit viginti talentis*, he sold a speech for twenty talents ; *vitam auro vendere*, to sell one's life for gold ; *victoria Poenis multo sanguine stetit*, the victory cost the Punians much blood ; *tritici modius erat ternis sestertiis*, the bushel of wheat cost three sesterces.

Note. Respecting the manner in which the price or value is expressed when stated in a general way, see above, § 283. The verbs *mutare* and *commutare* are generally construed like the verbs of selling and buying —as *fidem et religionem pecunia mutare*, to sell one's faith and religion for money ; but sometimes the construction is reversed, the thing which we receive being put in the accusative, and the one we give in the ablative—as *valle Sabina permuto divitias*, I give the Sabine valley in exchange for riches. Sometimes the preposition *cum* is added to the ablative—as *mortem cum vita commutare*, to exchange life for death.

§ 295. The ablative is used with a variety of verbs both transitive and intransitive, to denote that in which, or in regard to which, the action or condition implied in the verb manifests itself. Verbs of this kind are those denoting plenty, abundance, filling, conferring on, or providing with—as *affluere divitiis*, to abound in wealth ; *manare cruore*, to drip with blood ; *Germania rivis fluminibusque abundat*, Germany abounds in streams and rivers ; *afficere aliquem honore*, to confer honour on a person ; *mente eximia praeditus est*, he is endowed with an extraordinary mind. Verbs of this kind are—*abundo, redundo, affluo, scateo, compleo, expleo, impleo, refercio, cumulo, stipo, instruo, afficio, imbuo, conspergo, dignor,* and many others.

Note 1. In some cases the ablative with these verbs may be regarded as an ablative of the instrument. There are some verbs which are used in this way only in a particular meaning—as *pluit sanguine, lapidibus,* it rains stones, blood. The verbs *impleo* and *compleo* are sometimes, especially in poetry, construed with the genitive instead of the ablative—as *ollam denariorum implere,* to fill the vessel with denarii ; *hostes formidinis implere,* to fill the enemies with fear.

2. Some verbs of this kind admit of a twofold construction ; either the one stated in the general rule, or instead of the ablative they take the accusative, putting that which before was their object (accusative) in the dative—as *donare aliquem libro* (to present a person with a book), or *donare librum alicui* (to give a book to some one). Verbs of this kind are—*dono,circumdo (urbem muris* or *urbi muros), adspergo (aliquem ignominia,* or *alicui ignominiam), inuro, misceo,* (also *misceo aliquid cum aliqua re), admisceo,* and some other compounds with *in* and *ad.* The verb *induo* (I put on) is construed in the same manner—as *induo puerum veste* and *induo puero vestem,* and in the passive also it may be *induor vestem* and *induor veste* (compare § 259, 1), while the other verbs cannot retain the accusative in the passive—as *urbs circumdata muris,* or *urbs cui murus circumdatur.*

§ 296. Verbs, both transitive and intransitive, which denote want or depriving, are accompanied by an ablative of the thing of which any one is in want or is deprived. Such verbs are —*careo, egeo, indigeo, vaco ; orbo, privo, spolio, fraudo, nudo ;* e. g., *carere consuetudine amicorum,* to be without the intercourse of friends ; *egere auxilio,* to be in want of assistance ; *vacare culpa,* to be free from guilt ; *hostes armis spoliare,* to strip the enemy of their arms ; *nudare turrem defensoribus,* to deprive the tower of its defenders ; *auctoritate orbari,* to be deprived of influence.

Note 1. The verb *egeo,* and especially the compound *indigeo,* is often construed with the genitive instead of the ablative—as *custodis eges,* thou art in want of a guardian ; *indiget celeritatis,* it requires quickness.

2. The verbs *invideo* (I envy) and *interdico* (I forbid), which take their personal object in the accusative, are generally followed by the ablative of the thing—as *tibi hac re invideo,* I envy you this thing ; *exuli aqua et igni interdixit,* he forbade the exile (the use of) water and fire ; but sometimes, though more rarely, the thing is expressed by the accusative, *laudem tibi invideo, interdicit feminis usum purpurae.* *Invideo* is also construed with the dative of the thing and the genitive of the person—as *Ciceronis laudi invidebat,* he envied the praise of Cicero. *Abdico* (I abdicate), lastly, has likewise two modes of construction ; either, e. g., *me magistratu abdico,* or *abdico magistratum.*

§ 297. The ablative is joined with verbs of abstaining, renouncing, freeing, delivering,·and excluding—such as *abstineo,*

desisto, solvo, exsolvo, levo, exonero, arceo, prohibeo, excludo;
e. g., *abstineo maledictis,* I abstain from calumny ; *levavi ami-*
cum onere, I have released my friend from his burden ; *liberare*
hominem catenis, to free a man from chains ; *prohibebat agrum*
populationibus, he prevented the field from being ravaged.
The verbs of abstaining, preventing, and excluding, however,
often take the preposition *a* or *ab*—as *abstinere a vitiis,* to
abstain from vices ; *milites a pugna prohibuit,* he kept his
soldiers from fighting ; and the preposition must always be
used when the ablative is the name of a person—as *arcere*
hostes a civibus, to keep the enemy away from the citizens ;
tu me prohibuisti a praedonibus, you have protected me from
robbers.

Note 1. The verbs *levo, exonero,* and *exsolvo,* never take the preposition *a* or *ab,* and *libero* but rarely ; in a few instances *libero* is joined
with *ex*—as *liberare ex incommodis. Intercludo* has a threefold construction—*alicui aliquam rem, aliquem aliqua re,* and *aliquem ab aliqua re.*
2. Poets and some late writers join *absterreo, deterreo, secerno,* and
separo, as well as some verbs compounded with *dis* (as *disto, dis-*
tinguo) , with the ablative alone ; but it is preferable to use the preposition *a.* There are, moreover, instances in which poets join verbs of
abstaining, freeing, &c. with the genitive—as *abstinere irarum,* to abstain from anger or passions ; *desine querelarum,* cease your complaints ;
solutus operum, freed from work.

§ 298. Verbs denoting a forcible removal of some one from
a place may be construed with the ablative alone, to denote
such place, but it is more common to use the prepositions *ab,*
ex, or *de*—as *movere* or *pellere aliquem loco,* to remove or expel
a person from a place ; *hostes depellere loco, urbe,* to drive the
enemy from a post, from the city ; *deturbare aliquem muris,*
to hurl a person from the walls ; *spe dejectus,* driven from
hope (that is, deprived of hope). In like manner the ablative alone is sometimes used with the verbs *cedo, excedo,* and
decedo — as *vita, de* or *e vita cedere ; decedere Italia* or *ex*
Italia.

Note 1. The verbs *exeo, egredior, ejicio,* are rarely used with the
ablative alone, except when a name of a town is the place from which
the removal takes place. See below, § 307, 3.
2. Verbs denoting ' to include,' ' comprehend,' ' keep,' and ' receive,' are sometimes followed by the ablative of the place or space in
which anything is included, comprehended, &c.—as *aliquem carcere*
(also *in carcerem* and *in carcere*) *includere ; recipere aliquem tecto* (*in*
domo and *in domum*); *tenere se castris* and *in castris.* The verb *consto*
(I consist of) is generally followed by *ex,* but sometimes also by *in* with
the ablative, or by the ablative alone.

§ 299. The verbs *gaudeo, laetor, glorior, delector, doleo, maereo,*
fido, and *confido,* are followed by the ablative to denote the

thing at which you rejoice or grieve, and in which you trust—
as *gaudeo tua felicitate,* I rejoice at your happiness; *doleo patris
morte,* I grieve at the death of my father; *confido natura loci,*
I trust in the nature of the locality. The ablative in these
cases is in reality the ablative of the moving cause. Compare
§ 291.

Note. The verbs *fido* and *confido* are also construed with the dative,
and *diffido* nearly always. *Doleo* occurs also with the accusative—as
casum meum illi doluerunt, they grieved over my fall. *Glorior* also
takes the preposition *de* or *in. Nitor* (I lean upon) is followed either
by the ablative alone, or the ablative with *in.*

§ 300. The verbs *utor, abutor, fruor, perfruor, fungor, defun-
gor, perfungor, potior, vescor,* have their object in the ablative—
as *carne utuntur,* they use meat; *fruor suavi otio,* I enjoy
delightful ease; *functus est munere praetoris,* he has held the
office of praetor; *hostes urbe potiti sunt,* the enemy took possession of the city; *patre optimo usus est,* he had a most excellent
father.

Note. These verbs are in meaning transitive, and it is a somewhat
unaccountable phenomenon that they have their object in the ablative
instead of the accusative. In the early poets, however, and in some
prose writers, they are sometimes joined with the accusative as real
transitives, and their gerundivum is very often used like that of transitive verbs—as in *munere fungendo,* in performing the duties of the
office; *dare alicui vestem utendam,* to give to a person clothing to use
it. *Potior* is construed also with the genitive, especially in the expression *rerum potiri,* to occupy the highest power in the state, where
the ablative is never used. *Pascor* (I feed or graze) is joined both with
the ablative and the accusative.

§ 301. The expression *opus est* (there is need, it is necessary)
is either treated as an impersonal verb, and then takes the
thing of which there is need in the ablative, or *opus* is treated
as an indeclinable adjective, and then the thing which is
needed is expressed by the nominative—as *praesidio opus est,*
there is need of a garrison; *quid opus est verbis?* why are words
needed? and *dux et auctor opus est,* a leader and adviser are
needed; *exempla nobis opus sunt,* we need examples. The person to whom anything is needful is expressed in each case by
the dative.

Note 1. The expression *usus est* (there is need) is occasionally construed in the same manner as *opus est*—as *viginti usus est minis,* twenty
minae are wanted. When the thing needed is expressed by a verb,
opus est is followed by the infinitive—as *id te scire opus est,* you must
know this; *opus est epistolam scribere,* it is necessary to write the letter.
Sometimes, however, we find the ablative of a neuter participle or of a
participle joined to a substantive—as *maturato opus est,* it is necessary
to hasten; *opus fuit Hirtio convento,* it was necessary to meet Hirtius.

K 2

2. The verbs *assuesco* and *assuefacio* are likewise construed with the ablative of the thing, and more rarely with the dative—as *assuetus labore, assuetus militiae.*   *Sto* (I stand by, or persevere in) is generally construed with the ablative alone, but sometimes also *in* is added—as *stare in promissis, conditionibus, suo judicio.*   *Fio* and *facio* are joined with the ablative, to denote that something is to be made or become out of something—as *quid facies hoc homine?* what will you make of this man? *quid fiet nave?* what is to become of the ship?   But in the same sense *facio* and *fio* are also construed with the dative—as *quid facies huic homini?* or with *de*—as *quid fiet de militibus?* what is to be done with the soldiers?

§ 302. The adjectives conveying the same ideas as the verbs enumerated in §§ 295, 296, and 297 — that is, those denoting plenty, abundance, want of and freedom from, govern the ablative.   Such adjectives are—*praeditus, onustus, plenus, fertilis, dives; inanis, orbus, vacuus, liber, immunis, purus, alienus;* also *dignus, indignus, contentus, anxius, laetus, moestus, superbus, fretus,* and others of a similar meaning—as *onustus praeda,* laden with booty; *dives agris,* rich in landed possessions; *dignus laude,* worthy of praise; *orbus rebus omnibus,* deprived of all things; *animus cura liber,* a mind free from care; *natura parvo cultu contenta est,* nature is satisfied with little care; *fretus virtute sua,* trusting to his virtue.

Note 1. The adjectives *plenus, fertilis, dives,* and *inanis,* are also construed with the genitive, and *plenus* even more commonly than with the ablative—as *Gallia plena bonorum civium.*   The participles *refertus* and *completus* likewise are often joined with the genitive when that of which anything is full are human beings—as *carcer plenus sceleratorum, urbs referta mercatorum.*   The other adjectives of this kind occur with the genitive only in poetry—as *liber curarum,* free from cares; *purus sceleris, vacuus operum.*   Like *dignus* is construed *dignor* (I think worthy).   Respecting the construction of *dignus* and *indignus,* when that of which a person is worthy or unworthy is expressed by a verb, see the chapter on the subjunctive.

2. *Liber* is always followed by *a* or *ab* when persons are mentioned —as *locus liber ab arbitris,* a place free from witnesses.   *Alienus* in a few instances is joined with the genitive; in the sense of 'unfavourable,' with the dative; and in that of 'disinclined to,' with *a* and the ablative—as *locus exercitui alienus,* a place unfavourable to the army; *alienus a litteris,* not inclined to literary pursuits.

3. The word *macte* is used either alone or in conjunction with an imperative of *sum (este, esto)* with the ablative of the thing for which we congratulate a person—as *macte virtute,* or *macte virtute esto,* I congratulate you on account of your valour; *juberem te macte virtute esse,* I would congratulate you for your valour.   *Macte* is commonly considered as the vocative of *mactus*—that is, *magis auctus;* but this is a doubtful etymology.

4. *Conjunctus* (joined to or with) is often followed by the ablative alone, instead of the ablative with *cum;* but when it is joined with the dative, it generally signifies 'bordering upon'—as *talis simulatio conjuncta est vanitati,* such a pretence is bordering upon vanity.

§ 303. The participles denoting birth or origin (*natus, ortus, genitus, satus, editus*) are joined with the ablative denoting the parents of whom, or the station in which, a person is born—as *nobili patre natus*, born of a noble father ; *humili genere natus*, born of a humble family ; *equestri loco ortus*, born in the station of an eques.

Note. When a person's real parents are mentioned, the preposition *ex* or *de* is sometimes used ; e. g., *ex fratre et sorore nati sunt.* But when remoter ancestors are spoken of, the preposition *ab* is commonly employed—as *Belgae orti sunt a Germanis; Cato Uticensis a Censorio ortus erat.*

§ 304. With comparatives the ablative denotes the amount of difference existing between two things which are compared —as *Romani duobus millibus plures erant quam Sabini*, there were two thousand more Romans than Sabines ; *uno digito plus habere*, to have one finger more ; *Germani multo plures erant*, the Germans were much more numerous ; *multis partibus major*, many times larger. In like manner the ablative with the adverbs *ante* and *post* denotes how much one thing is earlier or later than another—as *tribus annis ante*, three years before or earlier ; *decem annis post*, ten years after or later.

Note 1. In this manner comparatives and words containing the idea of a comparative, such as *aliter*, and *secus* (otherwise), are frequently joined by the ablative of a neuter pronoun or adjective which denotes how much more or less—as *multo secus*, very differently ; *quo sapientior, eo betior*, the wiser, the happier ; *multo major*, much (by much) greater ; *tanto facilius*, so much more easy ; *quanto magis*, how much more. Sometimes adverbs are used instead of such ablatives—as *longe aliter, longe major*, far otherwise, far greater ; and in poetry and late prose writers, it is very common to use the accusative of the neuter instead of the ablative—as *multum injucundior, aliquantum inferior.* The ablative *multo* is used in the same manner with superlatives— as *multo* (or *longe*) *audacissimus*, by far the most daring.
2. The same ablative of adjectives and pronouns is used with verbs containing the idea of a comparative, such as *malo, praesto, supero, antecello*, and others—as *multo malo*, I wish much rather ; *multo praestat*, it is much better ; *tanto antecellit*, he excels so much. These verbs, with the exception of *malo*, are also found with the accusative neuter, as *tantum* and *multum praestat.*
3. *Abhinc*, which is usually construed with the accusative, is found also with the ablative—as *tribus abhinc annis*, three years ago, or before this time. It must be remembered that when *ante* and *post* are used as prepositions, they govern the accusative—*ante decem annos*, ten years ago, or before. See § 255, note 2.

§ 305. The ablative is often used with comparatives to express the person or thing surpassed by another, which is commonly expressed by *quam*—as *filia matre pulchrior*—that is, *filia pulchrior quam mater*—a daughter more beautiful than her mother ; *major fuit Scipione*—that is, *major fuit quam Scipio*, he was greater than Scipio. This mode of speaking, however, can be used only when the things compared with each other are either in the nominative or accusative.

Note 1. This ablative with a comparative seems to be a sort of instrumental ablative, denoting that one of the things compared is set forth more prominently by comparison with or by means of the other. In the best prose writers the ablative is used most commonly when the things compared are in the nominative, or in accusative, which is the subject of an infinitive, though it is also used in place of the accusative of the object—as *vitat cautius olivum sanguine viperino*, he shuns the olive more cautiously than the blood of a viper ; *hoc* (ablative) *nihil mihi gratius facere poteris*, you cannot do anything more agreeable to me than this. The relative pronoun, when accompanied by a negative, is likewise used in the ablative after a comparative—as *Phidiae simulacra, quibus nihil perfectius videmus*, the statues of Phidias, than which we see nothing more perfect—that is, which are the most perfect we see ; *Punicum bellum, quo nullum majus Romani gessere*, the Punic war, than which the Romans have not carried on a greater— that is, the greatest which the Romans have carried on. In such sentences the ablative is necessary, and *quam* cannot be used.

2. The ablatives *spe, expectatione, opinione, justo, solito, aequo*, and *necessario*, are frequently joined to a superlative to denote that a thing surpasses our hope, expectation, belief, &c. ; e. g., *Caesar celerius omnium opinione venit*, Caesar came more quickly than any one had believed ; *amnis solito citatior*, a river more rapid than usual ; *tardior necessario*, slower than necessary.

3. It occurs very rarely that the ablative after a comparative is used instead of any other case than the nominative and accusative—as in Horace : *Pane egeo, jam mellitis potiore placentis* for *quam mellitae placentae*. Poets use this ablative also after *alius*—as *ne putes alium sapiente bonoque beatum*, for *quam sapientem bonumque*.

4. When the size or measure is indicated by a substantive or numeral, the *quam* may be omitted after the comparatives *plus, amplius*, and *minus*, without the nominative or accusative being changed into the ablative, though the ablative also may be used—as *plus quam trecenti milites, plus trecenti milites*, and *plus trecentis militibus*. It must further be observed, that when *amplius, plus*, or *minus*, joined with a plural, either with or without *quam*, is the subject of a clause, the verb is always in the plural—as *amplius quam sex menses sunt* and *amplius sex menses sunt*.

§ 306. The ablative of a substantive joined by an adjective participle, or pronoun, is frequently used, both with and without the verb *sum*, to describe the nature or quality of anything —as *Agesilaus fuit corpore exiguo*, Agesilaus was a man of a small body ; *Herodotus magna est eloquentia*, Herodotus possesses great eloquence ; *orator summo ingenio*, an orator of the highest genius ; *flumen difficili transitu*, a river difficult to cross. Respecting the genitive used in a similar way, see § 276. It must be observed that neither the genitive nor the ablative of quality can be used, unless the substantive is accompanied by an adjective, participle, or pronoun; 'a man of genius,' therefore, cannot be rendered either by *homo ingenii* nor by *homo ingenio*, but must be changed into *homo ingeniosus*. Compare § 276, note 3.

Note. When the size or outward form of a thing is to be described, the place of the adjective may be supplied by a genitive—as *clavi ferrei digiti magnitudine*, iron nails of the thickness of a finger, where *digiti* qualifies the word *magnitudine*, just as the adjective *eximia* might do.

§ 307. The relations of place *where?* and *whence?* are generally expressed in Latin by the prepositions *in, ab, ex*, or *de;* but there are many cases in which these relations are expressed by the mere ablative without any preposition.

1. Place where? is expressed by the ablative alone in the case of the word *locus*, when accompanied by an adjective or pronoun; *dextrā* (on the right-hand side), *laevā* (on the left-hand side), *terrā marique* (by land and by sea), and sometimes *medio* (in the midst or middle), and *numero* (in the place of); e. g., *hoc loco*, in this place; *illo loco*, in that place; *aequo loco*, in a favourable place; *opportunis locis*, in opportune places; *medio aedium*, in the centre of the house.

Note 1. When *locus* is used in a figurative sense, it scarcely ever takes the preposition *in*—as *meliore loco*, in a better condition ; *secundo loco*, in the second rank ; *parentis loco aliquem habere*, to consider a person as one's parent ; but in this case *in* is sometimes added—as *in parentis loco*, or *in filii loco aliquem habere*. When *locus* signifies ' the right' or ' proper place,' it almost always takes *in* when it is not accompanied by an adjective—as *desipere in loco*, to be foolish in its proper place ; but when an adjective is added, the *in* may be omitted—as *suo loco*, in his own (proper) place. In referring to a book, we may say both *in libro* and *libro*, with this difference, that *libro* refers to the whole, and *in libro* only to a part of the book.

2. Poets use the ablative of words to denote place where ? with great freedom, provided always 'that it does not create obscurity or ambiguity—as *lucis opacis*, in shady groves ; *vestibulo*, in the vestibule ; *silvisque agrisque*, both in forests and fields.

2. The ablative of place where? is very frequently used without a preposition when a substantive denoting place is accompanied by the adjective *totus* or *omnis*, and when the meaning is ' throughout a place'—as *totā Italiā*, in all Italy or throughout Italy ; *tota urbe*, throughout the city ; *tota Asia*, in all Asia ; *tota mari*, throughout the extent of the sea ; *omni Gallia*, throughout all Gaul. The preposition *in*, however, may be added when the idea of ' throughout' is not to be emphatically stated—as *in tota Sicilia*, in all Sicily.

3. Place whence? is expressed by the ablative alone in the case of names of towns and small islands—as *Roma profi-cisci*, to set out from Rome ; *discedere Athenis*, to go away from Athens ; *Delo Rhodum navigare*, to sail from Delos to Rhodes. In the same manner are used *domo*, from home ; *rure*, from the country ; and sometimes *humo*, from the ground.

Note 1. The preposition *ab* is used in these cases when the move-ment is to be described as proceeding only from the neighbourhood of a town, or in the direction from it—as *Caesar a Gergovia discessit*, Caesar departed from the neighbourhood of Gergovia. When the name of a town is preceded by the noun *urbs* or *oppidum*, a preposition must be used—as *ab urbe Roma, ex oppido Gergovia*. When *urbs* or *oppidum* follows after the name of the town, the preposition is put be-fore *urbs* or *oppidum*—as *Tusculo, ex clarissimo oppido*, from Tuscu-lum, a very celebrated town.

2. Poets make very free use of the ablative alone to denote place whence—as *labi equo*, to glide from a horse ; *descendere coelo*, to de-scend from heaven.

3. The ablative to denote place whence occurs not only with verbs expressing motion, but also with substantives derived from them—as *qui Narbone reditus!* what a return from Narbo ! A person's native place is sometimes added in the ablative to his name—as *Cn. Magius Cremonā*, Cn. Magius of Cremona ; but it is more common to form an adjective from the name of the place—as *Cn. Magius Cremonensis; Miltiades Atheniensis.* When the name of his tribe is added to the name of a Roman, it is always in the ablative—as *Ser. Sulpicius Le-moniā*, Ser. Sulpicius of the Lemonian tribe.

4. The ablative alone is also used to express the line along or by which anything is done—as *profectus est viā Latinā*, he travelled along the Latin road ; *recta linea fertur*, it is carried along in a straight line ; *Pado frumentum subvehere*, to convey provisions by the river Po.

§ 308. The ablative of words denoting time is used to express the time when, at which, or within which anything happens— as *tertio anno bellum confecit*, in the third year he concluded the war ; *hoc die*, on this day ; *horā octavā*, at the eighth hour ; *eadem nocte*, in the same night ; *eodem die*, on the same day ; *initio aestatis*, in the beginning of summer ; *Roscius Romam multis annis non venit*, Roscius did not come to Rome for many (within the space of many) years ; *his viginti annis*, within these (the last) twenty years. So also *hieme*, in winter ; *aestate*, in summer ; *vere*, in the spring ; *nocte*, at or by night ; *luce*, by day-light, or in daytime.

Note 1. In some expressions the preposition *in* is added to express the time when anything is done, as, for example, when anything is stated which happens at all times—as *in omni aetate*, in all ages ; *in omni aeternitate*, in all eternity ; *in omni puncto temporis*, at every point of time. *In tempore*, or simply *tempore*, signifies ' at the right' or ' proper time,' which may also be expressed by *ad tempus*. *In gra-vissimis temporibus*, in the most serious circumstances.

2. Some substantives not denoting time, are used in the ablative without a preposition, to indicate the time at which anything occurred. Such words are, particularly, *adventu*, on the arrival; *discessu*, at the departure—as *adventu Caesaris in Galliam; discessu consulis.* In like manner are used *comitiis*, at or during the comitia; *ludis*, at or during the games; *pace*, in time of peace ; *bello*, in time of war (whereas *in bello* means 'in the war' or 'in war') ; *bello Punico primo*, in the time of the first Punic war. In stating any of the stages of human life the preposition *in* is used—as *in pueritia;* but when an adjective is added, the *in* may be omitted—as *primā*, or *extremā pueritiā*. 'At the beginning' may be expressed by *initio, principio*, or *in initio, in principio.*

3. The time within which anything is done is sometimes expressed by the ablative with *in*, especially when it is to be stated how often a thing is done, or how much within a certain time—as *bis in die*, twice every day ; *ter in anno*, thrice every year ; *Lucilius in hora saepe ducentos versus dictabat*, Lucilius often recited two hundred verses within an hour. But we also find the ablative alone in such cases—as *septies die*, seven times a day. *In* is further sometimes added to express the time within which anything happens, in cases when the calculation is made from a certain point—as *in diebus proximis decem*, within the next ten days (reckoning from the present moment) though the ablative alone is equally good—as *his annis quadringentis*, within these four hundred years—that is, less than four hundred years from the present time.

4. Instead of the adverbs *ante* and *post* with the ablative, we may, without altering the sense, use them as prepositions with 'the accusative—as *tribus diebus post* and *post tres dies, tribus ante diebus* and *ante tres dies;* the same meaning is also expressed by *tertio die post*, and *post tertium diem.*

§ 309. It was remarked above (§ 308, note 2) that substantives not denoting time may be used in the ablative to express the time at which, or the circumstances under which, anything happens. To this we may here add, that any substantive (or personal pronoun) accompanied by an adjective, participle, or another substantive standing in apposition, may be put in the ablative to describe the time or circumstances under which anything happens. This ablative, usually called the ablative absolute (because it is not dependent upon anything), may always be resolved into a distinct clause, and may therefore be defined as a clause put in the ablative to express time and circumstances ; e.g., *hoc factum est rege vivo*, this was done while the king was alive ; *hae res gestae sunt rege duce*, these things were done under the guidance of the king; *urbem cepit me adjutore* or *adjuvante*, he took the city with my assistance, or I assisting him ; *Pythagoras Tarquinio regnante in Italiam venit*, Pythagoras came to Italy in the reign of Tarquinius ; *Cicerone et Antonio consulibus conjuratio Catulinae erupit*, in the consulship of Cicero and Antony the conspiracy of Cataline broke out; *regibus expulsis consules creari cocpti sunt*, after the expulsion of the kings consuls began to be elected ; *hoc factum est me ig-*

naro, this was done without my knowledge; *Lex Cassia lata est Scipione auctore*, the Cassian Law was passed on the advice of Scipio; *quo auctore id fecisti?* by whose advice did you do this? *moribus simillimis figura saepe dissimilis est*, the appearance (of men) is often unlike, their manners being perfectly like; *haec fieri solent te non invito*, these things usually happen not against your will; *quid hoc populo obtineri potest?* what can be gained with this people?—that is, so long as this people is what it is.

Note 1. Such an ablative absolute may either qualify a particular word (usually the predicate) or an entire clause. In English we sometimes use the nominative as an absolute case, but not so frequently as in Latin, *e.g.*, 'the work being done, the boy went to play, where the clause ' the work being done' is the nominative absolute, answering to the Latin ablative *opere perfecto.* More of this ablative see in the chapter on the participles.

2. There are some cases in which such an ablative absolute consists of a single word—as *sereno* (namely, *coelo*), the sky being bright; *austro*, during a south wind.

§ 310. The following prepositions always govern the ablative:—*a, ab* (*abs*), *absque, clam, coram, palam, cum, de, ex*, or *e, prae, pro, sine, tenus. In* and *sub* govern the ablative when they denote place where? *Subter* may be joined with either the accusative or the ablative, and *super* takes the ablative in the sense of ' about' or 'concerning.' Compare § 194, 2 and 3.

Note. The verbs *pono, loco, colloco, statuo, constituo,* and *consido,* although they express motion, are yet generally followed by *in* with the ablative. The compounds of *pono*—as *impono, repono*—however, are construed with *in* and the accusative, as well as with *in* and the ablative. There are a few remnants of the ancient Latin language in which *in*, though no motion is expressed, is yet joined with the accusative—as *esse* or *habere in potestatem; in custodiam haberi; in carcerem asservari.* These irregularities can be explained only by supposing that two different ideas have coalesced into one: first that of motion towards a place; and secondly, the result of the first—namely, the being in the place.

CHAPTER XLVI.

USE OF THE VOCATIVE CASE.

§ 311. The vocative is used to address a person, and is inserted in clauses without affecting their construction in any way. The vocative, like the nominative, is a *casus rectus*, not being governed by any other word. A vocative, however, may consist of a word which, when qualified by others, exercises its influence upon them as a word, but as a vocative it exercises none ; e.g., *vos, o amici !* you, my friends ! *primā dicte mihi, summā dicende camenā, Maecenas!* Maecenas, praised by me in my first, and to be praised in my last poem !

Note. In poetry and early writers the nominative is often used instead of the vocative—as *almae filius Maiae! aures mihi, Memmius, adhibe! vos, o Pompilius sanguis! audi tu, populus Albanus!* Any word in apposition to a vocative should of course be in the vocative, but sometimes the apposition is in the nominative ; sometimes, on the other hand, the vocative of a participle or adjective is used, though it stands in apposition to a nominative, as in Virgil, *Aen.* ii. 283, ix. 485.

CHAPTER XLVII.

PECULIARITIES IN THE USE OF ADJECTIVES.

§ 312. An adjective is used in Latin not merely as a simple attribute and predicate, but frequently stands in apposition to a substantive or pronoun, and then expresses the condition in which a person or thing is during an action, where we generally use adverbs or abverbial combinations of words—as *multi eos, quos vivos coluerunt, mortuos contumelia afficiunt,* many treat persons after their death (*mortuos*) with contumely, whom during their lifetime (*vivos*) they have honoured ; *naturā ipsā de immortalitate animorum tacitā judicat,* nature herself silently (*tacita*) expresses her opinion of the immortality of the soul.

This is the case especially with adjectives denoting order (ordinal numerals) or succession—as *Hispania postrema perdo mita est,* Spain was subdued last, or was the last country that was subdued ; *Dubito, quid primum, quid medium, quid extremum ponam,* I doubt what I shall put first, what in the middle, and what last ; *Sicilia omnium terrarum prima provincia facta est,* Sicily was the first of all countries that was made a province.

Note 1. In this manner are often used *totus, solus, diversus, sublimus, frequens, proximus, medius*—as *nos totos philosophiae tradimus,* we give ourselves wholly up to philosophy ; *soli hoc contingit sapienti,* this happens to the wise alone, or only ; *avis sublimis abiit,* the bird flew away high in the air ; *Roscius erat Romae frequens,* Roscius was frequently at Rome. Poets also use adjectives denoting relations of time and place in the same manner—as *Aeneas matutinus* (that is, *mane*) *se agebat; vespertinus* (that is, *vespere*) *pete lectum; domesticus* (that is, *domi*) *otior.*

2. Proper names in Latin cannot take any other adjectives than

16   J.

those which are used to distinguish several persons or things from one another—as *Cato major, Africanus minor, Scipio Asiaticus;* and such as denote a person's native country—as *Livius Patavinus, Hannibal Carthaginiensis.* In all other cases a common noun must be added to the proper name as an apposition, and then this apposition may take any adjective—as *Plato, vir sapiens,* the wise Plato; *Capua, urbs opulentissima,* wealthy Capua. Poets, however, do not always comply with this practice.

§ 313. Adjectives (and pronouns) are frequently used as substantives to denote persons or things of a certain kind or class.

(*a*). When *persons* of a certain class are to be indicated, the masculine plural of an adjective is used—as *boni,* the good; *sapientes,* the wise; *omnes fortes,* all brave men. Sometimes the word *homines* is added. The masculine singular is more rarely used in this way, and only in cases where there can be no ambiguity—as *sapiens omnia virtuti postponit,* a wise man considers everything inferior to virtue; *est prudentis sustinere impetum benevolentiae,* it is the duty of a prudent man to check the fervour of his benevolence; *illi fortes sunt,* those men are brave. Compare § 232, 4.

Note. An adjective thus used substantively is sometimes accompanied by another adjective which qualifies it—as *insipiens fortunatus,* a fool favoured by fortune; *nobilius indoctus,* an uneducated nobleman.

(*b*). When *things* of a certain class or kind are to be designated, the Latins use the neuter plural of an adjective, though they may also use the substantive *res* in the same way as is done in English—as *bona,* good things or property; *mala,* bad things or evils; *multa memorabilia* (or *multae res memorabiles*), many memorable things; *omnia pulchra,* all beautiful things; *haec vitanda sunt,* these things are to be shunned. The neuter singular of an adjective is used when an individual thing is to be indicated—as *bonum,* a good thing; *malum,* an evil or a bad thing; and when the abstract idea is to be expressed—as *verum,* the truth; *justum,* justice. Compare § 232, note.

Note 1. Care must be taken in the use of such adjectives to avoid ambiguity, since some cases of the neuter plural do not differ in their endings from the masculine and feminine. For this reason adjectives of the third declension are generally used as substantives only in the nominative and accusative, though there are a few instances in which the other cases also are so used—as *potior utilis quam honesti cura,* greater care for that which is useful than for that which is virtuous.

2. Neuter adjectives used substantively are sometimes joined with prepositions, and thereby acquire the force of adverbs—as *de integro,* anew, afresh; *in integrum,* to the full possession of a thing; *in integro,* in the full possession of a thing; *de* or *ex improviso,* unforeseen; *ex*

facili, easily ; *ex affluenti*, abundantly. But such expressions occur only in particular phrases.

(*c*). Some adjectives have so completely acquired the meaning of substantives, that they are almost invariably used as such —as *amicus*, a male friend ; *amica*, a female friend ; *inimicus*, *inimica*, a male and female enemy ; *adversarius*, an opponent ; *ludicrum*, a play on the stage ; *simile*, a simile, and so also *bonum* and *malum*. Some adjectives are used as substantives with an ellipsis of some substantive which determines the gender—as *patria* (viz. *terra*, *urbs* or *civitas*), native country or city ; *fera* (viz. *bestia*), a wild beast ; *cani* (viz. *capilli*), gray hair ; *dextra* (viz. *manus*), the right hand ; *hiberna* (viz. *castra*), winter quarters ; *stativa* (viz. *castra*), a stationary camp ; *praetexta* (viz. *toga*), the toga praetexta. So also *frigidam*, *calidam* (viz. *aquam*), *primae*, *secundae*, *tertiae* (viz. *partes*).

Note 1. Sometimes, though mostly in poetry, a substantive is treated as an adjective or participle, and is accordingly accompanied by an adverb instead of an adjective — as *populus late rex* (that is, *regnans*) a people ruling far and wide ; *minime largitor dux*, a commander by no means liberal.

2. Poets frequently use the neuter of an adjective in the sense of an adverb—as *perfidum ridere*, to smile perfidiously ; *acerba tuens*, looking fiercely ; *turbidum laetari*, to rejoice riotously, and many others. Compare § 219, note.

§ 314. The comparative of both adjectives and adverbs is frequently used to denote a higher degree than usual, or than it should be, where we generally employ the word ' rather'— as *senectus est naturā loquacior*, old age is naturally rather loquacious ; *liberius vivebat*, he lived too freely ; which, however, may also be expressed by *nimis libere*. Compare § 89, note.

Note 1. If it is to be expressed that a thing possesses a quality in too great a proportion for something else, the latter is introduced by *pro* —as *proelium atrocius quam pro numero pugnantium*, a battle more fierce than could have been expected from the number of the combatants. ' Too great for a thing' is always expressed by the comparative followed by an ablative—as *ampliores humano fastigio honores*— that is, *honores humanum fastigium excedentes*. When the English ' too great' is followed by an infinitive with ' to,' the Latins use *quam qui* with the subjunctive after it—as *major est quam cui nocere possis*, he is too great for you to hurt him.

2. Sometimes the comparatives *magis* or *potius* are omitted before *quam*, so that *quam* has no comparative to refer to (as in Sallust, *Catil.* 8.) ; or *potius* or *magis* is added pleonastically to a comparative ; or lastly, a positive is joined with a comparative—as *quanto inopina* (for *magis inopina*), *tanto majora;* but these are anomalies which should not be imitated.

§ 315. The superlative often does not indicate absolutely the highest degree of a quality, but only a very high degree—that is, the highest degree in comparison with some, but not with all. In this case we may render the Latin superlative in English either by 'very' with the positive, or with the positive alone—as *Sulla, qui est vir fortissimus et clarissimus*, Sulla, who is a very brave and illustrious man; *optime valeo*, I am very well; *es tu quidem mihi carissimus, sed multo eris carior, si bonis praeceptis laetabere*, you are indeed very dear to me, but you will be still dearer if you will take a pleasure in good precepts. Whether a superlative has its real meaning, or the one here pointed out, can always be seen from the context. Compare § 89, note.

Note 1. Such a superlative is only an exaggerated mode of speaking, which is more natural to southern nations than to us, and is especially used in complimentary addresses, applying to the persons spoken to or to persons spoken of, when the speaker wishes either to compliment them or the reverse.

2. The meaning of a superlative may be strengthened by the adverbs *quam, longe, multo*, by *omnium* or *unus omnium*—as *quam diligentissime*, as diligently as possible; *longe* or *multo diligentissimus*, by far the most diligent; *unus diligentissimus*, or *unus omnium diligentissimus*, the one most diligent of all. A superlative is often joined with the pronoun *quisque*, which gives to it a general meaning answering to the suffix *cunque* in certain pronouns—as *optimus quisque*, the best whoever he may be, or all good persons.

§ 316. It is a peculiarity of the Latin language, that a considerable number of superlatives which denote order, succession, time, and place, are often joined to a substantive, although in reality they qualify only a part of the thing expressed by the substantive. Such superlatives are *primus, postremus, ultimus, novissimus, summus, infimus, imus, intimus, extremus*, and *medius*; e.g., *primo vere* — that is, *prima parte veris*, at the beginning of spring; *in summo monte* — that is, *in summa parte montis*, on the top of a mountain; *extremo anno* — that is, *extrema parte anni*, at the end of the year; *in media urbe*, in the centre of the city; *per medium mare*, through the midst of the sea. In like manner are also used *reliqua* and *cetera* — as *reliqua Graecia*, the remaining part of Greece; *cetera multitudo*, the other part of the multitude.

Note. Medius, which is in meaning equivalent to a superlative, is for this reason sometimes joined with a partitive genitive like other superlatives, as in Caesar: *locum medium regionum earum delegerant*, they had chosen a place in the centre of those districts. Otherwise, *medius* is usually followed by the preposition *inter*.

CHAPTER XLVIII.

DIFFERENT KINDS OF CLAUSES, AND THEIR RELATIONS TO ONE ANOTHER.

§ 317. Every clause is either an independent or leading clause, or it is merely subordinate or explanatory. The former simply states a fact by itself, in the form of an assertion or a question—as *miles dormit*, the soldier sleeps; *fratremne vidisti?* have you seen the brother? A subordinate sentence is usually of such a structure that it cannot stand by itself, and can be understood only when viewed in connection with another — as *miles dormit, ut vires reficiat*, the soldier sleeps, that he may restore his strength. Sometimes, however, an independent clause also remains unintelligible unless some subordinate clause be added — as *miles fortior est quam expectaveram*, the soldier is braver than I had anticipated, where *miles fortior est* is not complete without the accessory clause. Two clauses thus combined form a compound sentence, and always convey a distinct meaning.

§ 318. Subordinate clauses are connected with the leading clause by conjunctions, relative pronouns, or by an interrogative particle — as *te non laudo, quoniam mihi non obtemperasti*, I do not praise you, because you did not obey me; *omnes qui adfuerunt hoc sciunt*, all who were present know this; *ex me quaesivit, unde haec scirem*, he asked me whence I knew this. Often subordinate clauses are expressed in a peculiar way by the construction called the accusative with the infinitive — as *scio eum esse bonum hominem*, I know him to be a good man, or I know that he is a good man.

Note. A subordinate clause serves either to qualify and explain the whole sentiment contained in the leading clause, or it belongs only to a particular word of the leading clause. Clauses introduced by a relative pronoun always contain an explanation of either a part or the whole of the leading clause. Other subordinate clauses stand to the leading one either in the relation of subject—as *quod ad me venisti, gratum mihi est*, it is agreeable to me that you have come to me, where *quod ad me venisti* forms the subject to the clause *gratum mihi est;*— or in the relation of object—as *video te scribere*, I see that you are writing, where *te scribere* is the object of the verb *video;* or they express certain circumstances, such as intention, result, or consequence, cause, time, and others, which are indicated by conjunctions. When, of two clauses, one begins with a conjunction denoting time, cause, concession, or a condition, this one is termed the protăsis (antecedent), and the other the apodŏsis (consequent)—as *si ad me venisses* (protăsis), *librum tibi dedissem* (apodŏsis).

§ 319. Two or more clauses may be joined together in such a manner by copulative or adversative conjunctions, that none of them is subordinate to another. Such clauses are termed co-ordinate. Co-ordinate clauses may be all leading or all accessory clauses of one and the same sentence — as *haec res mihi valde placet, et pater eam vehementer probat,* this thing pleases me very much, and my father greatly approves of it ; *mihi haec res placet, sed pater eam improbat,* I am pleased with this thing, but my father disapproves of it ; *neque cur tu hoc consilium tam vehementer probes, neque cur pater tantopere improbet, intelligo,* I do not understand either why you so greatly approve of this plan, or why your father so much disapproves of it.

Note. In Latin it occurs more frequently than in English, that co-ordinate clauses are joined together without any conjunction at all. This deserves to be especially attended to when *autem* or *vero* is omitted, a custom which cannot always be imitated in English—as *neminem oportet esse tam stulte arrogantem, ut in se rationem et mentem putet inesse, in coelo mundoque* (autem) *non putet.*

§ 320. In clauses introduced by a relative pronoun, the substantive to which the pronoun refers is often drawn into the relative clause, so that the demonstrative clause follows after the relative one — as *quae cupiditates a natura proficiscuntur, facile explentur sine injuria*—that is, *eae cupiditates, quae a natura,* &c. those desires which proceed from nature are easily satisfied without injury.

Note. Poets adopt this mode of speaking even when the relative clause follows after the demonstrative—as *illi scripta quibus comoedia prisca viris est* for *illi viri quibus prisca comoedia scripta est.* Still more irregular is the passage in Virgil : *urbem quam statuo, vestra est,* for *urbs quam statuo vestra est.*

§ 321. When a substantive is followed by another substantive which stands in apposition to it, and is explained by a relative clause, the apposition is almost invariably drawn into the relative clause — as *frumentum, quae sola alimenta ex insperato fortuna dedit, ab ore rapitur,* the corn, the only food which fortune afforded unexpectedly, is torn away from the mouth ; *Santones non longe a Tolosatium finibus absunt, quae civitas est in provincia,* the Santones are not far from the territory of Tolosa, a city which is in our province.

Note. When a relative clause is added to a superlative, to state to what extent the superlative is to be understood, the superlative is usually drawn into the relative clause—as *misit de servis suis, quem habuit fidelissimum*—that is, *misit fidelissimum e servis suis quem habuit,* he sent the most faithful of his slaves he had. The same is done also with adjectives (in all degrees) belonging to a substantive—as *ex amicis suis quos multos habebat* for *e multis suis amicis quos habebat,* out of the many friends he had.

§ 322. Relative clauses do not always contain a mere explanation, but very often stand to the leading clause in a relation which is commonly expressed by conjunctions denoting intention, cause, and the like. Such clauses require to be expressed in Latin by the subjunctive mood, respecting which see Chapter LI.

§ 323. It is a practice of the Latin language to connect sentences as much as possible with one another, and to show in form also the concatenation of ideas which exists in the mind. One means of effecting this consists in the use of relative pronouns where the English and most other modern languages use demonstrative pronouns, so that *qui* becomes equivalent to *et is*. This, however, can be done only in cases where the demonstrative pronoun is not intended to be emphatic. A sentence, e.g. often begins with *qui quum*, which is equivalent to *et quum is ;* *quae quum*, equivalent to *et quum ea.* In like manner the Latins use the relative adverbs *quare, quamobrem, quapropter, quocirca,* and others, where we must substitute demonstrative forms, as 'therefore,' 'for this reason,' and the like ; e.g., *Caesar equitatum omnem mittit, qui videant, quas in partes hostes iter faciant. Qui* (these) *cupidius novissimum agmen insecuti, alieno loco cum eo proelium committunt.*

Note 1. A relative pronoun cannot be joined in Latin with an adversative (*sed, autem, vero*) or inferential particle (*igitur, ideo itaque*), except when something is mentioned in opposition to a preceding adjective — as *est vir bonus, sed qui omnia negligenter agat,* he is a good man, but one who does everything carelessly. But if a compound sentence begins with the relative pronoun, the conjunction belonging to the leading clause is introduced in the relative one — as *quae vero cupiditates a natura proficiscuntur, facile explentur.*

2. A relative clause may be qualified by another subordinate clause, and in this case the former stands to the latter in the relation of a leading clause—as *ignava animalia quae jacent torpentque, si cibum iis suggeras.*

CHAPTER XLIX.

THE MOODS IN GENERAL.

§ 324. The sentiment contained in a sentence is expressed either in the form of a simple statement (indicative mood) — as *pater me in Graeciam misit ;* or in the form of a wish or command of the speaker (imperative mood) — as *confer te in Graeciam ;* or as a mere conception of the mind (subjunctive mood) as *in Graeciam profectus est, ut philosophos audiret.* In the last sentence, the words *ut philosophos audiret* do not state the fact that he heard, but only his intention to hear. These different modes of stating anything is expressed in Latin by the three moods — indicative, imperative, and subjunctive. Subordinate clauses are mostly expressed by the subjunctive, but sometimes they have the verb in the infinitive — as *opinor eum justissimum esse hominem,* I believe him to be a most just man—that is, that he is a most just man.

Note. A participle is a verb in the form of an adjective, whereby the predicate of a subordinate or explanatory clause is made to agree as an adjective with the subject or any other part of the leading clause—as *milites fortiter pugnantes ceciderunt,* the soldiers fell while they were bravely fighting ; *milites fortiter pugnantes timor repente invasit,* fear suddenly overcame the soldiers while they were bravely fighting.

§ 325. Co-ordinate clauses, whether they be leading or subordinate, usually have the same mood, though the verbs may be in different tenses ; but there are cases in which even co-ordinate sentences are conceived in such a way that they require different moods — as *pugiles ingemiscunt non quod doleant, sed quia omne corpus intenditur,* boxers sigh, not because (as one might imagine) they feel pain, but because every part of their body is on the stretch (a fact).

Note. The latter is the case especially in those co-ordinate sentences, one of which contains the statement of a fact, and must be expressed by the indicative ; while the other, containing a doubt, a supposition, or a concession, requires the subjunctive — as *neque nego, neque affirmare ausim,* I neither deny, nor should I like to venture to affirm.

CHAPTER L.

THE INDICATIVE MOOD AND ITS TENSES.

§ 326. The indicative mood is used to make a simple statement of a fact, either affirmatively or negatively, and to put a question in a direct manner—that is, in such a way that the clause containing the question is not in the relation of a dependent or subordinate clause to any other—as *hunc librum legi,* I have read this book ; *illum librum non legam,* that book I shall not read ; *quando ad me venies?* when will you come to me? *num pater veniet?* will the father come ? *quod non ex urbe profectus es, mihi pergratum est,* the fact that you have not gone out of town is very agreeable to me.

§ 327. The indicative is used in Latin in conditional clauses, beginning with *si, nisi, etiamsi, etsi,* and *sive,* when it is to be intimated that the supposition is really true, so that *si* is equivalent to *quum* (as or since), or that, for the sake of argument, we assume that the supposition is true, or, when negatively expressed, is not true—as *si nihil aliud fecerunt, satis praemii habent,* if (or as) they have done nothing else, they are sufficiently rewarded; *mors plane est negligenda, si extinguit animum,* death must be altogether treated with indifference, if it annihilates the soul; *ista veritas, etiamsi jucunda non est, mihi tamen grata est,* that truth, although it is not agreeable to me, is yet welcome to me; *hoc loco libentissime utor, sive quid mecum ipse cogito, sive aliquid scribo aut lego,* I like this place best, whether I am engaged in meditation, or in writing or reading anything.

Note. In all cases of the latter kind the speaker himself does not intimate any opinion of his own, as to the truth or falsehood of the supposition, but only assumes its truth for the sake of argument; and the first of the above sentences may accordingly be equivalent to, 'I assume the fact that they have done nothing else, and on this supposition they are sufficiently rewarded.' Respecting the further use of the indicative in hypothetical clauses, see § 333, note 2, and especially § 346.

§ 328. Certain tenses of the indicative are used in Latin where we should expect the subjunctive, especially in the case of the verbs *oportet, necesse est, debeo, convenit, possum, licet,* and in the expressions *par, fas, aequum, justum, consentaneum, satis, satius, melius, aequius est.* The imperfect indicative of these verbs and expressions is used when we wish to express that at some past time something should or ought to have been done, but at the same time intimate that the time for doing it is not yet passed, or that it is not yet too late; e.g., *ad mortem te duci jam pridem oportebat,* 'you ought to have been put to death long ago,' suggesting that it is not too late yet, and that it may still be done. The perfect and pluperfect indicative of the same expressions is used when we wish to intimate that something should or ought to have been done, but that the time for it is now passed, and that it is too late — as *Volumnia debuit in te officiosior esse,* 'Volumnia ought to have been more attentive to you,' suggesting that the time is now past, and that it is too late to make amends for her neglect. So also *longe utilius fuit,* it would have been far more useful.

Note. There are, however, sentences of this kind where the subjunctive is used instead of the indicative — as *dedendi fuissent,* they ought to have been given up, for *dedendi erant.*

§ 329. The indicative is commonly used (if there be no special reason for the subjunctive) after doubled relatives, and those having the suffix *cunque* — as *quisquis, quotquot, quicunque, quantuscunque, utut, utcunque,* because in all such cases a simple fact is implied, the uncertainty consisting merely in the extent, amount, manner, &c.; e.g., *quidquid id est,* whatever this may be; *utcunque sese res habet,* however the matter stands; *quicunque is est,* whoever he may be.

Note. It must, however, be observed that less accurate writers, especially later ones, often join the subjunctive with such general relatives.

§ 330. The tenses of the indicative in Latin answer, with few exceptions, to the same tenses in English. Any action or condition is either simply stated as past, present, or future, or as in relation to another action in reference to which it is past, present, or future. In this manner we have three absolute tenses (present, perfect, and future), and three relative tenses (imperfect, pluperfect, and future perfect). Besides these six tenses, there are the six tenses of what is called the *conjugatio, periphrastica,* describing an action as future either in present, or past, or future time. See § 339.

§ 331. The present expresses that which is going on at the time we are speaking, and the Latin language has only one form for our 'I write' and 'I am writing' — *scribo.* The present tense is further used to express that which happens at all times — as *Deus mundum gubernat,* God governs the world; and to state the remarks or opinions of others recorded in books, though the authors may have lived in past ages — as *Plato aliter de hac re judicat,* Plato judges differently of this; *Cicero in primo De Officiis dicit,* Cicero says in the first book On Duties.

Note 1. We may here remark that the whole of the English paraphrastic conjugation by means of a participle present (ending in *ing*) does not exist in Latin, and that in it the English has an advantage which the Latin does not possess.

2. An action which has been going on for some time, and is still going on, is in Latin, as in English, generally expressed by the perfect; but in Latin the present also is used to express the same idea — as *jamdiu ignoro,* I have already for a long time been ignorant; *annum jam audis Cratippum,* you have already been hearing Cratippus for one year.

§ 332. In animated narrative, past events are frequently related by the present tense, as if they were going on before our eyes. This present is termed the historical present. Examples are very numerous, and occur in all languages, especially in poetry.

Note. Dum in the sense of 'while,' when two things are described as occurring simultaneously, is commonly construed with the present, though the action may belong to the past — as *dum haec in colloquio geruntur, equites Ariovisti propius accedunt; mulier dum pauca mancipia retinere vult, fortunas omnes perdidit.* The tenses of the past (imperfect and perfect), however, may likewise be used with *dum* in describing past occurrences. In the sense of ' as long as' or ' until,' *dum* is not construed with the present unless it really refers to present time.

§ 333. The Latin perfect has two distinct meanings—

1. It is used, like the past tense in English, to relate the events of the past — as *Caesar Galliam subegit*, Caesar subdued Gaul; *illo anno multae res memorabiles acciderunt*, many memorable events occurred in that year. The perfect in this sense is called the historical perfect, it being the tense by which past or historical events are simply related as facts.

2. It is used to describe an action as completed and past, but with reference to present time, and thus completely answers to the English perfect — as *pater jam vēnit*, the father has already come; *is mos usque ad hoc tempus permansit*, this custom has continued to the present time; *scripsi epistolam*, I have written the letter; *fuimus Troes, fuit Ilium*, we have been Trojans, Troy has been (implying that now it is no more). The perfect in this sense may be termed the present perfect.

Note 1. As to whether in any given sentence the perfect is a historical or present perfect must be determined by the context, and there can never be any difficulty in this.

2. When anything which usually or always happens is expressed by the perfect in a subordinate sentence denoting time, place, or a supposition, the perfect is used if the action of the subordinate sentence must be conceived as preceding that of the leading clause. This is the case especially after the conjunctions *quum* (' whenever,' denoting purely time), *quoties, simulac, si, ubi, ut* (when), and *postquam* — as *quum ad villam veni, hoc ipsum, nihil agere, me delectat*, whenever I go (not went) to my villa, this very idleness is a pleasure to me ; *si ad luxuriam intemperantia accessit, duplex malum est*, whenever intemperance is joined to luxury, the evil is twofold. If, however, the verb of the leading clause is in a past tense, the subordinate clause takes the pluperfect. Compare § 336, note.

3. The perfect is often used in poetry in the sense of the present, and commonly denotes, like the Greek aorist, that a thing usually or always happens—as in Horace, *collegisse juvat* for *colligere juvat*, *posuisse gaudet* for *ponere gaudet*. Respecting the use of the present for the historical perfect, see § 332.

§ 334. The conjunctions *postquam, posteaquam* (after); *ubi, ut* (when); *simul, simulatque, ut primum*, and *quum primum* (as soon as), are followed in Latin by the perfect, when it is to be expressed that two actions follow one another in immediate succession. The two actions are thus represented simply as past, without their relation to each other being indicated in any way except by the conjunctions — as *postquam victoria parta est, hostes refugerunt,* after the victory had been ‑ gained, the enemy fled back; *ut equitatum suum pulsum vidit, acie excessit,* when he saw his cavalry beaten, he withdrew from the battle.

Note 1. This rule must be particularly attended to by beginners, because the English language sometimes uses the pluperfect and sometimes the simple past after these conjunctions.

2. *Postquam* is construed with the pluperfect indicative when it is to be intimated that the action introduced by it took place a considerable time before the other—as *Hannibal anno tertio postquam domo profu ‑ gerat, in Africam venit; post diem quintum quam barbari pugnaverant, legati a Boccho veniunt. Postquam* is very rarely joined with the pluperfect subjunctive; but sometimes we find it construed with the imperfect indicative, to denote that an action had commenced to take place or used to take place—as *postquam Eros explodebatur,* after Eros began to be hissed at, or whenever Eros was hissed at.

3. When *ubi* and *simulac* introduce a repeated action, they are joined with the pluperfect. See § 336, note.

4. All the conjunctions mentioned in the above rule may also be followed by the historical present, if the action is conceived as still going on at the time when the action of the leading clause takes place —as *postquam perfugae murum arietibus feriri vident, aurum atque argentum domum regiam comportant,* where the action of *videre* is conceived as still going on, while that of *comportare* is taking place.

5. The conjunctions *antequam* and *priusquam* (before), and *dum,* in the sense of ‘until,’ are generally joined with the perfect indicative, and not with the pluperfect—as *antequam legi tuas litteras,* before I had read your letter; *dum rediit Marcellus,* until Marcellus returned. (Compare § 337, note 1.) In conclusion, it may be observed that all the conjunctions here mentioned may be joined with the subjunctive, if the peculiar nature of the clauses they introduce requires it. See the following chapter.

§ 335. The imperfect describes a past action as in progress and not complete, and is therefore used in descriptions of things which in past time were in a certain condition, or of past events which are represented as going on. The imperfect is further used to relate events which used to occur or repeatedly occurred — as *etiam tum Athenae gloriā literarum et artium florebant,* ‘even at that time Athens was flourishing for its reputation in literature and the arts.’ Here the flourishing of Athens is described as then in progress, whereas the perfect would state the same thing only as a historical fact. *Quum Verres ad aliquod oppidum venerat, eādem lecticā usque in cubiculum deferebatur,* ‘whenever Verres came to any town, he was (always) carried in the same lectica to his sleeping apartment.’ Here *deferebatur* states a repeated action, or something which was done on every occasion. *In Graecia musici floruerunt, discebantque id omnes,* ‘musicians flourished (a historical fact) in Greece, and all persons used to learn music.'   In the latter clause the imperfect describes a custom, or what used to be done.   *Hortensius dicebat melius quam scripsit*, 'Hortensius used to speak better than he wrote or has written,' with reference to his works still existing.

Note 1. It often depends upon the writer or speaker himself, as to whether he wishes to state a custom or a repeated action as a mere historical fact by the perfect, or whether he wishes to describe it as a custom or as a repeated action : we must be guided by judgment and taste as to which of the two is preferable in any given sentence.

2. The imperfect is sometimes used to state merely the beginning of an action, or an attempted action, which was not carried into full effect — as *curiam relinquebat*, which is almost equivalent to *curiam relinquere tentabat*, and intimates that he did not actually leave the curia.   An action which at a certain time was about to take place, is sometimes expressed in Latin by the imperfect, as if it had already commenced and were going on — as *hujus deditionis, qui dedebatur, suasor et auctor fuit*, where *qui dedebatur* signifies ' the one who was about to be delivered up.'

§ 336. The pluperfect states an action of past time which was completed before another action, at present likewise completed, began — as *dixerat judex, quum puer nuntiavit*, ' the judge had spoken when the boy gave information.'   Here the speaking of the judge was over when the boy's action (which is now likewise past) began.

Note. When anything which used to happen is expressed in a leading sentence by the imperfect, the subordinate sentence takes the pluperfect in those cases in which we should use the perfect, if the leading clause had the verb in the perfect — as *Alcibiades, simulac se remiserat, luxuriosus, libidinosus, intemperans reperiebatur.*   Compare § 334, note 3.

§ 337. The future denotes an action or condition which is to take place at a future time in general, or at a particular moment in future time — as *hostes venient*, the enemy will come ; *proximo anno ad te veniam*, next year I shall come to you.

Note. Beginners must pay particular attention to the use of the future in subordinate clauses, because in English we generally substitute the present for it — as *si sequemur naturam ducem*, if (in future) we follow nature as our guide ; *dum erimus in terris*, so long as we are (or shall be) on earth ; *qui adipisci veram gloriam volet, justitiae fungatur officiis*, ' let him who wishes to gain a true reputation discharge the duties of justice,' where the idea of futurity is suggested by the exhortation ' let him discharge.'   There are, however, instances where, even in Latin, the present is found in cases where we should expect the future, as in questions addressed to one's self — as *quid arbitramur ?* what shall we believe ? after *dum* in the sense of ' until ' — as *expecto dum ille venit*, I wait until he comes ; and after *antequam* and *priusquam*, when it is stated that one action will take place before another — as *antequam pro Murena dicere instituo, pro me ipso pauca dicam*, before speaking for Murena, I shall say a few things concerning myself.   But in this case we also find the future — as *antequam dicam.* Before anything *has* happened' is expressed by the future perfect.

§ 338. The future perfect describes a future act as completed at a certain future time — as *quum tu haec leges, ego illum fortasse convenero,* when you (will) read this, I shall perhaps have spoken with him; *quum istuc venero, rem tibi exponam,* when I (shall have) come thither, I shall explain the matter to you.

Note 1. The beginner must pay especial attention to the use of this tense, for in consequence of its cumbrous formation the English language seldom employs it, especially in subordinate clauses, where we generally use the present instead of the future perfect — as ' when I come to Rome, I shall explain the matter to you,' must be rendered in Latin by *quum venero,* because the act of coming must be completed before the explanation can be given. There are, however, instances where even in Latin a subordinate clause is expressed by the present, the verb of the leading clause being in the future; but then the act, which is the condition of something future, is conceived as occurring at the present moment — as *moriere virgis, nisi signum traditur,* you shall be scourged to death unless the statue is given up (this moment).

2. Sometimes the verb of the protăsis, as well as that of the apodŏsis, is in the future perfect, and then the meaning is, that both actions will be completed in future at the same time — as *pergratum mihi feceris, si de amicitia disputaris,* ' you will do me a great favour if you will discuss friendship' — that is, when the discussion is completed, my pleasure also will be completed. The English language here treats both actions simply as future.

3. There are cases in which the future perfect is almost equivalent to the future — as *si voluero, potuero, licuerit, placuerit,* for *si volam, potero, licebit, placebit.* This is the case especially when a future result is stated—as *multum ad ea tua ista explicatio profecerit,* that explanation of thine will greatly contribute to those things ; or when it is to be intimated that something will be done quickly or speedily while something else is going on — as *tu invita mulieres, ego accivero pueros,* do you invite the women, I shall in the meantime summon (or shall have summoned) the boys. *Videro, is, it,* &c. is used in this way especially when anything is deferred to another time, or when a thing is left to the consideration of some one — as *quae causa fuerit, mox videro,* what has been the cause, I shall soon see (for I shall soon have seen); *sed de hoc tu ipse videris,* but concerning this you will consider yourself (there will be a time when you yourself will have considered this). Poets, and especially the comic writers, go still further in using the future perfect, where we should expect the future.

§ 339. The tenses of the periphrastic conjugation are, on the whole, used in the same way as those of the ordinary conjugation; but the action expressed by the participle future is in all tenses a future one — as *scripturus sum, scripturus eram, scripturus ero, scripturus fui, scripturus fueram, scripturus fuero.* (Compare § 149.) The following peculiarities must be noticed separately : —

1. The present must be used when the condition of a necessary action is stated — as *me igitur ames oportet, si veri amici futuri sumus*, you must therefore love me, if we are to be true friends.

2. There is little difference between the imperfect (*scripturus eram*) and the pluperfect (*scripturus fueram*), and the poets especially use both forms indiscriminately; but the pluperfect may nevertheless denote an action which was on the point of happening previous to a certain point in past time. Compare § 346, 1.

§ 340. The epistolary style in Latin has this peculiarity—that the writer, transferring himself to the time at which the letter is in the hands of the person addressed, relates what he is doing in writing the letter either by the perfect or imperfect, as the case may be — as *nihil habebam quod scriberem*, I had nothing to write; *haec ad te scripsi ante lucem*, I write this to you before daylight. In the course of his narrative, however, the writer frequently reverts to *his own* actual position, and uses the present tense, as we do in English.

CHAPTER LI.

THE SUBJUNCTIVE MOOD.

§ 341. A verb in the subjunctive expresses an action or condition as a mere conception of the mind, in the form of a wish, a possibility, an intention, a supposition, a concession, and the like, so that the speaker does not treat it as a fact; e.g., *scribo ut scias*, I write that you may know; *quae si ita sint*, if these things be so; *facile aliquis dicat*, a person may easily say.

Note 1. There are, however, certain kinds of subordinate clauses, which, although their verb is in the subjunctive, yet state a fact as much as any other clause — as *pugnabat tam fortiter, ut nemo ei resistere posset*, where the impossibility of resistance is as much a fact as his fighting bravely; but it is expressed in a subordinate clause, which is connected with the leading one in such a manner as to be indispensable to its completeness in point of form.

2. What the Latin language expresses by its subjunctive mood, is expressed in English either by the indicative, or recourse must be had to such auxiliary verbs as *I may, might, should, would*, or *could* — as *ad me venit, ut libros meos videret*, he has come to me that he might see my books. If, however, these auxiliaries retain their own peculiar meaning, they must be rendered in Latin by *possum, licet, debeo, volo*, or *oportet*.

§ 342. The subjunctive is used both in leading and in subordinate clauses, though more especially in the latter. In leading clauses the subjunctive is of a fourfold nature — expressing a supposition or hypothesis (*hypothetical clauses*), a possibility (when it is termed the *potential mood*), a wish or desire (the *optative mood*), and a concession (*concessive mood*). We shall accordingly treat of these four kinds of sentences first : —

§ 343. Every *hypothetical sentence* consists of two clauses — the one, which states the condition or supposition (beginning with *si, nisi, ni, si non, etiamsi, tametsi*), is called the protasis ; and the other, which contains the conclusion or inference, is called the apodosis. (Compare § 318, note 1.) The protasis is sometimes not expressed, being either implied in something which precedes, or supplied by the mind of the hearer or reader — *illo tempore aliter sensisses*, ' at that time you would have thought differently' — namely, ' if you had looked at the matter,' or, ' if you had lived ;' *id ego non facerem*, ' I should not do so' — namely, ' if I were in his place.'

§ 344. The present subjunctive is used both in the protasis and apodosis, to denote that the supposition is possible, and may be true, but at the same time to intimate that it is not true ; and accordingly, that the apodosis likewise is possible, but not true — as *me dies deficiat, si hoc nunc dicere velim*, the day would not suffice for me, if I wished to say this now. Here it is intimated that I might possibly say, but at the same time that it is not my intention. Respecting the indicative in hypothetical clauses, see § 327.

Note. In animated or rhetorical style we sometimes find the present subjunctive, both in the protasis and apodosis, where we should have expected the imperfect subjunctive, it being implied that the supposition is not true, and that, accordingly, the inference cannot be true — as *haec si patria tecum loquatur, nonne impetrare debeat ?* supposing (for a moment) your country were speaking to you about these matters, ought she not to obtain her end ? *Tu si hic sis, aliter sentias*, supposing (for a moment) you were here, you would think differently. (Compare § 345.) Poets use this present subjunctive even in speaking of things which would have happened in past time, where we should have expected the pluperfect, as in Virgil, *Aen.* v. 325 ; — *spatia si plura supersint* for *si superfuissent*.

§ 345. The imperfect subjunctive is used in the protasis and apodosis, to denote that the supposition is not or cannot be true, and that accordingly the inference also is not true. The time expressed in such sentences is the present — as *si pecuniam haberem, ad te venirem*, ' if I (now) had money, I should come to you,' implying that I have no money, and accordingly cannot come to you. The pluperfect subjunctive is used in both clauses, if the supposition as well as the inference belong to past time — as *si pecuniam habuissem, ad te venissem*, if I had had money (which was not the case), I should have come to you (which, under the circumstances, was a matter of impossibility). Sometimes the imperfect and pluperfect are united in the same sentence—as *si sibi cavere potuisset, viveret*, if he had been able to be on his guard, he would (now) be living; *necassem jam te, nisi iratus essem*, I should have killed you already, if I were not angry.

Note. There are many instances in which, although both the protasis and apodosis belong to past time, and where, accordingly, the pluperfect should be used, yet the imperfect is employed, either in both clauses or in the protasis only, or, though very rarely, in the apodosis alone—as *Cur igitur et Camillus doleret* (for *doluisset*), *si haec post trecentos fere et quinquaginta annos eventura putaret* (for *putasset*)? *Non tam facile opes Carthaginis concidissent, nisi illud receptaculum classibus nostris pateret* (for *patuisset*); *esset* (for *fuisset*) *Antonio serviendum, si Caesar ab eo regni insigne accipere voluisset.* Such an imperfect in the protasis indicates that the action expressed by it is conceived as simultaneous with that expressed in the apodosis, and not as preceding it. The imperfect in the leading or in both clauses frequently implies a repetition of the action, or an action in progress.

§ 346. Sometimes the verb of the apodosis is in the indicative, while that of the protasis is in the subjunctive, and implies that the supposition is not true. This is a grammatical irregularity, arising either from an elliptical mode of speaking or from rhetorical animation, whereby the clause containing the conclusion is conceived as independent of that containing the supposition. Examples of this kind occur in the following cases :—

1. The apodosis is expressed by the perfect or pluperfect indicative of the periphrastic conjugation, to denote that which a person at one time was on the point or ready to do, but did not carry into effect in consequence of circumstances — as *Si tribuni me triumphare prohiberent, Turium et Aemilium testes citaturus fui*, I was on the point of calling in Turius and Aemilius as my witnesses, in case the tribunes should refuse me a triumph; *Illi aratores relicturi omnes agros erant, nisi ad eos Metellus litteras misisset*, they were on the point of leaving, had not Metellus, &c. In like manner the apodosis is expressed by the verb in the imperfect or perfect indicative of the ordinary conjugation, when it is to be stated that something was actually commenced, and would of necessity have happened, had not something prevented it—as *Pons sublicius iter paene hostibus dedit, ni unus vir fuisset; deleri totus exercitus potuit, si perseculi victores essent.*

17   L 2

2. The indicative is used in the apodosis to bring before the reader in a vivid manner that which would have happened had not something prevented it. In such cases the rhetorical or poetical style represents as real that which was only possible — as *me truncus illapsus cerebro sustulit, nisi Faunus ictum levasset.* Sometimes the future is used in the apodosis, thus representing as actually future that which in reality is only a possible consequence — as *dies deficiet, si velim paupertatis causam defendere.*

Note 1. Sometimes there are conditional clauses (protases) which are not connected with any expressed apodosis, or at least the apodosis is treated as a clause quite independent of the protasis — as *non dubito mori, si ita melius sit,* I do not hesitate to die, if it be better so ; *Caesar munitiones prohibere non poterat, nisi praelio decertare vellet.* In such cases the protasis usually contains a supposition, referring not to the whole apodosis, but only to a particular word in it. The protasis and apodosis, therefore, are independent of each other, and the apodosis may assume almost any form, according as it may express a wish, a command, a question, &c.—as *si stare non possunt, corruant,* if they cannot stand, let them fall ; *si me audire non vis, cur me rogas ?* if you will not listen to me, why do you ask me ? — *si scio, ne vivam,* I will be hanged if I know it.

2. In animated discourse it sometimes happens that the clause which should be the protasis is expressed as an independent sentence. In such cases, that sentence is expressed by the indicative, when something is mentioned which occasionally occurs—as *de paupertate agitur; multi patientes pauperes commemorantur,* the question is about poverty (that is, if the question is about poverty) ; many patient poor are mentioned. When, on the other hand, something is stated merely as a supposition, or as a fictitious supposition, the subjunctive is used — as *roges me, nihil fortasse respondebo,* if you ask me (that is, supposing you were asking me), I shall perhaps not give you an answer. Poets now and then omit the conjunction *si* in real hypothetical clauses — as *sineret dolor* for *si sineret dolor.* In prose, on the other hand, the conjunction *si* is sometimes implied in the relative pronoun — as *qui videret* (that is, *si quis videret*), *urbem captam diceret.*

§ 347. The subjunctive, as a *potential mood,* is used to express that which does not really exist, but may or might exist, and is conceived as possible. The subject of such clauses is usually an indefinite or an interrogative pronoun — as *dicat aliquis* or *quispiam,* some one may say ; *dixerit aliquis,* some one might say ; *quis credat?* who would believe it? *quem metuat?* whom should he fear? *quis neget?* who would deny? It must be re marked that things which are possible at the present time are expressed by the present or the perfect subjunctive, while a past possibility is expressed by the imperfect—as *quis eum redargueret?* who would have refuted him?

Note. This potential subjunctive is used especially when an indefinite person is addressed — that is, a person not really existing, but merely supposed to exist for the purpose of stating something — as *conservare non possis,* you (or any one) cannot preserve ; *dicas fortasse,* you (or any one) may perhaps say ; *canes venaticos diceres,* you (or any one) would have called them hounds. If in such cases a definite person were addressed, the indicative would be used — as *dicis* or *dicit fortasse.*

§ 348. The potential subjunctive is also used with definite subjects for the purpose of expressing an opinion in a modest manner, and this occurs most frequently in the first person of the perfect, when the speaker expresses his own opinion with a certain degree of modesty or hesitation — as *haud facile dixerim,* I would not easily say; *hoc sine dubitatione confirmaverim,* I feel inclined to assert this without hesitation; *Themistocles nihil dixerit, in quo Areopagum adjuverit,* Themistocles is not likely to have said anything, &c.

Note. This mode of speaking is particularly common in the case of the subjunctives *velim, nolim,* and *malim,* to express a modest wish—as *velim dicas,* please to say ; *velim ex te audire,* I should like to hear from you. If a wish is to be expressed with the intimation that it cannot be realised, it is done by the imperfective subjunctive—as *vellem, mallem, nollem ; vellem adesse posses,* ' I wish you could be present,' implying that it is impossible. The conjunction *forsitan* (perhaps, it may be that) is construed by the best writers with the subjunctive — as *forsitan aliquis fecerit,* it may be that some one has done it. Other particles signifying ' perhaps' are joined with the indicative.

§ 349. The potential subjunctive is used in doubtful questions containing a negative sense — as *quid faciam ?* what shall I do? equivalent to, ' I do not know what I shall do.' *Cur non confitear ?* why should I not confess ? *quid hoc homine facialis ?* what are you to do with this man ? *cur plura commemorem ?* why should I mention more? In like manner the potential subjunctive is used in questions expressive of disapproval — as *hos cives patria desideret ?* is the country to long for such citizens ? the implied answer being ' assuredly not.'

Note. Questions implying something inconceivable are expressed by *ut* and the subjunctive, which is properly an elliptical mode of speak-ing—*fierine potest ?* or a similar expression being understood—as *egone ut te interpellem ?* ' is it possible that I should interrupt you ?' equivalent to, *fierine potest ut ego te interpellem ? Tu ut unquam te corrigas ?* equivalent to, *fierine potest, ut tu unquam te corrigas ?*

§ 350. The subjunctive, as an *optative mood,* is used to express a wish or desire — as *valeas,* fare well ; *valeant cives,* may my fellow-citizens fare well ; *beati sint,* may they be happy ; *inteream, si valeo stare,* I will perish if I am able to stand ; *imitemur majores nostros,* let us imitate our ancestors. The optative is often used in the sense of the imperative, respecting which see § 368.

Note 1. The negative with the optative subjunctive is always *ne,* and not *non ;* it is only in poetry that sometimes *non* occurs in a

negative wish for *ne*—as *non sint sine lege capilli*, in Ovid. A wish is
sometimes expressed more emphatically by the addition of *utinam*
(would that), and *utinam ne* or *non* (would that not)—as *utinam essem
Romae*, would that I were at Rome; *utinam ne id tibi in mentem
venisset*, would this had not come into your mind; *quod utinam non fecis-
sem*, would I had not done this. The *non* after *utinam* is more unusual
than *ne*. A wish is sometimes expressed by *O si* (oh, if)—as *O si illi
anni redire possint!* oh if those years could come back! (namely, I
should feel happy)

2. The particles *dum, dummodo* or *modo* (if but), *dum ne, dummodo
ne*, and *modo ne* (if but not), express a wish or desire containing a limitation—as *oderint, dum (dummodo) metuant*, they may hate if they do
but fear (which I wish they may do); *omnia postposui, dummodo praeceptis patris parerem*, I have disregarded everything, only to obey the
precepts of my father.

3. The imperfect and pluperfect subjunctive (optative) are also used
to denote that which at a certain time ought to have been done—as
potius diceret, he should rather have said; *saltem aliquid de pondere
detraxisset*, he ought at least to have deducted something from the
weight. Lastly, in the *oratio obliqua*, the subjunctive is used in sentences in which in the *oratio recta* the imperative would be employed.
See § 370.

§ 351. The subjunctive is used to express a concession or
permission, in which sense it is sometimes termed the *concessive mood*. It usually denotes that that which we concede
is not true, or at least is left undecided, but that we grant it
for the sake of argument—as *sint haec falsa, invidiosa certe
non sunt*, granting that these things are false, invidious they
certainly are not; *sit sane dolor gravis, malum non est*,
granting that (or although) pain is severe, it is not an evil.
The conjunction *ut* (in the sense of ' granting that') is often
added to a concessive subjunctive—as *ut sit infelix*, granting
that he is unhappy; and in negative clauses *ne* must be added
— as *ne sint in senectute vires*, granting that there is no strength
in old age.

§ 352. All dependent or subordinate clauses introduced by
the conjunctions *ut* (that, in order that, so that, although),
ne or *ut ne* (that not, or in order that not), *ut non* (so that
not), *quin* (that not), *quominus* (that not), and *quo* (in the
sense of *ut eo*, in order that thereby), have the verb in the
subjunctive—as *sol efficit ut omnia floreant*, the sun makes
(that) all things flourish; *virtutem colere debetis, ut beati esse
possitis*, you must cultivate virtue, that (in order that) you
may be able to be happy; *precor, ne me deseras*, I pray that
you may not desert me; *haec ad te scribo, ne putes me in hortis
esse*, I write these things to you, that you may not believe
me to be on my estate; *Verres Siciliam ita vexavit, ut restitui
non possit*, Verres has so ravaged Sicily that it cannot be restored; *vix me contineo, quin aggrediar illum*, I can scarcely

refrain myself so as not to attack him; *multa possunt obsistere quominus illa perficiantur*, many things may be in the way so that those things cannot be accomplished; *ager aratur, quo meliores fetus possit edere*, the field is ploughed, that thereby it may bring forth better fruits; *ut desint vires, tamen est laudanda voluntas*, although (or granting that, § 351) the strength is wanting, still the will deserves praise.

Note 1. The conjunction *ut* expresses—1. Intention (that, in order that, and sometimes ' to' with the infinitive); 2. A result, effect, or consequence (that, so that); 3. A concession (granting that, or although), and is accordingly used in clauses denoting intention, result, or consequence, and concession. Sometimes the conjunction *ut* is omitted, especially when it denotes concession, and after verbs denoting a wish or desire (*volo, nolo, malo, cupio, placet*), advice, request, persuasion; further after *licet, oportet, necesse est, fac*, and *faxo*. Some verbs of this kind—as *moneo* and *cogo*, are sometimes followed by an infinitive, or by a clause in the accusative with the infinitive instead of *ut*, though there is generally some difference in meaning. *Quid vis me facere* and *quid vis faciam* express the same meaning; but *effecit ut animus hominis immortalis sit* (he has made the soul of man such as to be immortal), and *effecit animum hominis esse immortalem*, he has proved that the soul of man is immortal. *Ut* is also used after verbs and expressions denoting in general that anything is or happens—such as *fit, futurum est, accidit, contingit, evenit, usu venit, est, sequitur, restat, reliquum est, relinquitur, superest, proximum est, extremum est, prope est, longe absum, tantum est*, though some of them are also followed by the infinitive — as *non cuivis homini contingit adire Corinthum. Accidit* is followed either by *ut* and the subjunctive, or by *quod* and the indicative. *Ut*, lastly, sometimes introduces a clause which is only an explanation (epexegesis) of some general expression which precedes—as *est hoc commune vitium in magnis liberisque civitatibus, ut invidia gloriae comes sit*, where the clause beginning with *ut* is only an explanation of the words *hoc commune vitium; fuit hoc in Marco Crasso, ut existimari vellet nostrorum hominum prudentiam Graecis anteferre*. Such is the case frequently after the expressions *mos est, cultus est optimus, aequum est, justum est, optimum est*, though they are also followed by the infinitive.

2. *Ne* expresses—1. A negative wish or intention (in order that not); sometimes its meaning is strengthened by the addition of *ut*, so that *ut* indicates the intention in general, and *ne* its specific negative nature —as *tibi haec dico ne ignores*, I tell you this, that you may not be ignorant of it; *sed ut hic, qui intervenit, ne ignoret*, but in order that he who came in between, may not be ignorant. *Neve* stands in the same relation to *ne* as *neque* to *non*, so that *neve* is equivalent to *et ne* or *vel ne*. 2. *Ne* is used after verbs of preventing or resisting, the action of which has the tendency that something should not be done—as *Pythagoreis interdictum est, ne faba vescerentur; impedior dolore, ne plura dicam; caveo, ne cui suspicionem dem. Impedio* and *prohibeo, recuso*, and *caveo*, however, are sometimes construed with the infinitive. 3. After verbs and expressions denoting fear, *ne* is used when it is implied that we do not wish the thing to happen — as *vereor ne veniat*, ' I fear lest he should come,' it being implied that I do not wish him to come. But *ut* is used when we mean to say that we wish the thing to happen— as *vereor ut veniat*, ' I am afraid he will not come,' it being implied

that I wish him to come, and that the object of my fear is his not coming. When the object of my fear is expressed by a simple verb, the latter is put in the infinitive—as *metuo recitare*, I am afraid to recite.

3. *Ut non* denotes a result or consequence, signifying 'so that not,' and care must be taken by the beginner not to confound it with *ne*. It is, however, also used in sentences expressing an intention, provided the negative does not belong to the whole clause, but only to a particular word in it — as *dedi tibi pecuniam ut non vinum emeres sed panem*, where the negative *non* qualifies only the word *vinum*, and not the whole clause beginning with *ut*. Sometimes, however, *ut ne*, or simply *ne*, is used for *ut non*, when *ita* precedes; but it then denotes a care, a desire, or wish—as *ita rem auxit, ut ne quid deperderet*, he increased his property in such a manner (with that caution or wish) that he did not lose anything. *Ut non* is further used after a negative sentence to express a necessary consequence—as *ruere illa non possunt, ut haec non eodem labefacta motu concidant*, those things cannot fall without these things being shaken by the same movement and falling to the ground. The same thing is also expressed by *quin*.

4. *Quin* is equivalent to the relative pronoun in all its cases joined with the negative *non*, so that it may stand for *qui non, quae non, quod non, quorum non, quarum non, quibus non*, &c. It is used after negative clauses, or such interrogative clauses as imply a negative—as *quis credat?* who should believe it?—namely, no one; or *quis ignorat?* who does not know?—namely, no one; e.g., *nihil est quin (quod non) possit depravari*, there is nothing that cannot be depraved; *nullus est cibus tam gravis, quin (qui non) concoquatur*, no food is so heavy that it cannot be digested; *Hortensius nullum patiebatur esse diem, quin (quo non) aut diceret aut meditaretur*, Hortensius allowed no day to pass by on which he did not speak or meditate. The place of the negative in the preceding clause is sometimes supplied by such words as *parum, perpauci*, and *aegre*, which are almost equivalent to a negative — as *pulum abfuit, quin Fabius Varum interficeret*, Fabius almost killed Varus. *Quin* is also used after verbs and expressions implying prevention, opposition, omission, and the like, as well as after *dubito* and *dubium est* — as *vix me contineo, quin illum aggrediar*, I scarcely restrain myself from attacking him; *Agamemnon non dubitat, quin brevi sit Troja peritura*, Agamemnon does not doubt that Troy will shortly perish; *non dubium erat, quin Helvetii plurimum possent*, there was no doubt that the Helvetians were the most powerful. In regard to *dubitare* it must be observed, that if it is not accompanied by a negative, it is always followed by an interrogative clause with *num*—as *dubito num ita sit*, I doubt whether it is so. After *non dubito* we usually find *quin*, but also (though rarely) the accusative with the infinitive. *Non dubito* with an infinitive after it signifies 'I do not hesitate,' though even in this sense it is sometimes followed by *quin*. Instead of *quin* after *non dubito* we sometimes find *quin non*, when the dependent clause is to have a really negative meaning, the negative contained in *quin* having lost its power. In such cases we may translate *non dubito quin* by 'I believe'—as *non dubito quin offensionem vitare non possim*, I believe that I cannot avoid giving offence. Lastly, in questions, *quin* means 'why not' (*qui non*), and is construed with the indicative — as *quin taces?* why are you not silent? *quin imus?* why do we not go?

5. *Quominus* is equivalent to *ut eo minus* (in order that thereby less or not), and accordingly requires the subjunctive, in consequence of

its containing the notion of *ut* or of intention. It is used after verbs denoting a hindrance, such as *impedio, prohibeo, officio, obsto, obsisto, deterreo, per me fit, per me stat* (I am the cause) — as *hiems adhuc prohibuit, quominus de te certum aliquid haberemus*, winter has hitherto prevented us from having any certain news about you; *Cimon nunquam in hortis custodem imposuit, nequis impediretur, quominus ejus rebus, quibus quisque vellet, frueretur.* It has already been remarked above, that these same verbs are sometimes followed by *quin* or an infinitive instead of *quominus*.

6. *Quo* is equivalent to *ut eo;* it denotes intention, 'in order that thereby,' and is usually followed by a comparative — as *ager aratur, quo (ut eo) meliores fetus possit edere.* *Non quo* (or *non quod*) signifies 'not that,' or 'not as if,' while *non quin* signifies 'not as if not.'

§ 353. All questions expressed in the form of a subordinate clause—that is, indirect questions, have the verb in the subjunctive — as *quaero, quid facturus sis*, I ask what you are going to do. Here the direct question would be, *quid facturus es?* but this question being put in the form of a subordinate clause to *quaero*, becomes indirect. *Quaesivi, quid faceret, ubi fuisset*, I asked what he was doing, where he had been; *omnes novisse debemus, quae res valetudini nostrae prodesse soleant aut obesse*, we all ought to know what things are conducive or injurious to our health.

Note 1. All the interrogative pronouns and adverbs which are used in direct questions occur also in indirect questions—as *quis, quae, quid; qui, quae, quod; quot, qualis, quantus, quam, ut* (how?), *ubi, unde, quo* (whither?), *quare, cur, uter, quomodo, num, utrum, an,* and the suffix *ne.* The beginner must be on his guard not to confound relative clauses with indirect questions. The relative always has an antecedent either expressed or understood, but the interrogative pronoun has not — as *dicam, quae sentio*, I shall say what I think — that is, *dicam ea, quae sentio*, and *quae* accordingly is a relative pronoun; but *dic mihi, quid sentias*, tell me what you think; here *quid* has no antecedent, the meaning being, what do you think — tell me?

2. The earliest Latin poets, as Plautus and Terence, sometimes have the verb in an indirect question in the indicative; in Horace, Virgil, and the later poets, this practice occurs more rarely, and in prose not at all. Often, however, it depends upon the writer or speaker whether, after certain expressions, he will use a direct or indirect question—as *dic mihi, num te illa terrent*, and *dic mihi num te illa terreant* The interrogative expressions *nescio quis, nescio quem, quam, quod, quos, quas, quae, quomodo, &c.* are often introduced as a mere parenthesis to explain some word or expression, and exercise no influence whatever upon the mood of the verb.

3. The interrogative nature of a sentence is indicated in English by the position of the words; but as there is no such fixed position of the words in a Latin sentence, certain interrogative particles are necessary to indicate the interrogative nature of a sentence, except in those cases where an interrogative pronoun or adverb introduces the question. Such particles are *ne (nonne), num, utrum (utrumne), an,* and *anne.* *Ne* is appended to the first word of an interrogative sentence,

and introduces a question in a general way, without indicating as to whether we expect an affirmative or negative answer—as *videtisne, quam fortes milites fuerint?* do you see how brave the soldiers have been? But with *non (nonne)* the question intimates that we expect an affirmative answer—as *canis nonne similis lupo?* is the dog not like a wolf? *Num* in direct questions almost invariably intimates that a negative answer is expected; but in indirect questions it only marks the interrogatory nature of a sentence without any further intimation. *Numne* expresses a doubtful question, and *numquid* is often only a strengthened *num*, the pronoun *quid* being the accusative, signifying ' in any respect.' Sometimes, however, questions are introduced without any particle at all, especially when they are expressed with a certain vehemence and impatience.

4. Disjunctive or double questions are introduced both when direct and when indirect, by the particles *utrum* (whether or which of two) and *an* (or). The first of two such questions is generally introduced by *utrum* or *utrumne*, and sometimes by the suffix *ne,* and sometimes without any interrogative particle at all. The second is introduced by *an (anne),* or by the suffix *ne.* The English ' or not' is expressed in Latin by *annon* or *nec ne.* It frequently happens in all languages that the first part of a double question is not expressed, but left to be supplied by the mind of the hearer or reader. In such cases the question begins in English with ' or' which must be rendered in Latin by *an* — as *me valde dementem putas, an me fraudes tuas non perspicere arbitraris?* you consider me to be very senseless, or (that is, do you really think so? or) do you believe that I do not see through your deceptions? Compare § 187, 10, note 1.

§ 354. Subordinate sentences introduced by the conjunctions *quod, quia, quoniam, quando* (because, since), usually have the verb in the indicative when the writer or speaker states his own view of a case; but the subjunctive must be used when he states the reason of another person, intimating that he merely quotes the opinion of another, without assenting to it or dissenting from it — as *Aristides expulsus est patriā, quod praeter modum justus esset.* Here the indicative *erat* would indicate that it was the writer's own opinion that Aristides was too just, whereas *esses* intimates that it was the reason assigned by his enemies; *Socrates accusatus est, quod corrumperet juventutem et novas superstitiones introduceret,* Socrates was accused, because (as his enemies said) he corrupted the young, and introduced new superstitions. The indicative *corrumpebat* and *introducebat* would state the charge as the writer's own opinion.

Note 1. The subjunctive after these conjunctions sometimes also intimates that the reason assigned is not the true reason—as *nemo oratorem admiratus est, quod Latine loqueretur,* no one has admired an orator for speaking Latin. This is the case especially after *non quod (non eo quod,* or *non ideo quod),* or *non quo* (sometimes *non quin*), after which the true reason is introduced by *sed quod* or *sed quia* with the incative — as *pugiles in jactandis cestibus ingemiscunt, non quod doleant animove succumbant, sed quia profundenda voce omne corpus intenditur venitque plaga vehementior.*

2. Sometimes the writer or speaker may treat his own opinion as if it were that of another man, and accordingly expresses it by the subjunctive, if he wishes to intimate that at a certain time this was his opinion, without suggesting what his opinion now is, as in Cic. *Tuscul.* ii. 3.

3. *Quod* is sometimes followed by the subjunctive of a verb denoting ' to say' or ' think,' although it is not meant that some one else said or thought something, but that the substance of what is said or thought is stated as the reason, and, as it were, as another man's opinion — as *in castra rediit, quod se oblitum aliquid diceret*, he returned to the camp, because (as he said) he had forgotten something.

§ 355. The conjunction *quum* or *cum*, when it denotes cause, and signifies ' as' or ' since,' is always construed with the subjunctive — as *cum vita brevis sit, summa diligentia adhibenda est, ut ea bene utamur*, as life is short, we must take the greatest care to make good use of it. In historical narrative, where a preceding event may be looked upon as the cause of a subsequent one, *quum* is always construed with the subjunctive, even when we translate it by ' when,' as if it denoted time; e.g., *Epaminondas quum vicisset Lacedaemonios, atque ipse gravi vulnere exanimari se videret, quaesivit salvusne esset clypeus.* If, on the other hand, *quum* expresses purely time, and is equivalent to *tum quum* (then or at the time when), it is construed with the indicative — as *qui injuriam non propulsat, quum* (that is, *tum quum*) *potest, injuste facit*, he who does not repel an injury when he can, acts wrongly; *quum in Galliam Caesar venit*, at the time when Caesar came to Gaul; *jam in conspectu erat, quum hostes sustulere clamorem*, he was already in sight, when (at that moment when) the enemy raised a shout.

Note 1. There are some cases in which *quum*, although denoting cause, is yet construed with the indicative; this is the case especially after the verbs *laudo, gratulor, gratias ago*, and *gratia est*, where *quum* with the indicative has quite the same meaning as *quod* — as *gratulor tibi quum* (that is, *quod) tantum vales apud Dolabellam*, I congratulate you, because you have so much influence with Dolabella.

2. *Quum* is also construed with the subjunctive in the sense of ' although,' and in this case it is, like *quamvis* and *quamquam*, followed by *tamen* (still or yet). *Quum-tum* (' in general' and ' in particular') is commonly followed by the indicative; but *quum* may at the same time imply a cause, and is then construed with the subjunctive — as *quum multae res in philosophia nequaquam satis adhuc explicatae sint, tum perdifficilis et perobscura quaestio est de natura deorum.* The subjunctive, moreover, is generally used even after such expressions as *tempus est, tempus fuit, tempus erit*—as *illucescet aliquando dies, quum desideres*, the day will come when you shall miss; *fuit, quum id justum arbitrarer*, there was a time when I believed this to be just.

M

3. When a repeated action is expressed by *quum*, or by any other conjunction or pronoun, such as *ubi, postquam, quoties, si, quicunque, ubicunque, quocunque, in quamcunque partem, ut quisque*, either in the imperfect or pluperfect, the best writers usually employ the indicative, but others prefer the subjunctive — as *quum ver esse coeperat*, whenever the spring commenced ; *quamcunque in partem impetum fecerant*, against whatever part they had made the attack ; but also *quum debitorem in jus duci vidissent*, whenever they saw the debtor taken to a court of justice ; *id ubi fetialis dixisset*, whenever the fetialis had said this.

§ 356. The conjunctions *dum, donec*, and *quoad*, in the sense of 'as long as,' are construed with the indicative. In the sense of 'until' they take the indicative, if the event is conceived as one that really happened or happens — as *non desinam, donec perfecero*, I shall not cease until I have accomplished it ; *Milo adfuit, quoad senatus dimissus est*, Milo was present until the senate broke up ; but if the event is conceived as merely possible, and if an intention or purpose is implied, they have the verb in the subjunctive — as *iratis subtrahendi sunt ii, in quos impetum conantur facere, dum se ipsi colligant*, we must withdraw from angry persons those on whom they attempt an attack, until they recover themselves (that is, 'until they can recover themselves ;' and at the same time the intention is implied ' that they may recover themselves').

Note. Respecting the present indicative with *dum*, see above, § 332, note. Some writers, and especially Tacitus, use *donec* with the subjunctive even when it introduces a simple fact. All three conjunctions, even in the sense of 'as long as,' are construed with the subjunctive, if any purpose or intention is implied — as *die insequenti milites quievere, dum praefectus urbis vires inspiceret*, on the following day the soldiers remained quiet, as long as (while, in order that) the prefect might inspect the forces of the city.

§ 357. *Antequam* and *priusquam* are joined with the indicative when it is simply to be stated that one action precedes another in time ; the subjunctive, on the other hand, is used when the event does not or did not actually happen before the other — as *priusquam de adventu meo audire potuissent, in Macedoniam perrexi*, I reached Macedonia before they could hear of my arrival ; *nunquam eris dives, antequam tibi ex tuis possessionibus tantum reficiatur, ut eo legionem tueri possis*, you will not be rich until (before) you gain so much from your possessions that you can keep a legion with it.

Note 1. Antequam and *priusquam*, especially in a narrative, are sometimes joined with the subjunctive, though they denote simple priority, and also when they express that which usually happens before a certain event occurs — as *tempestas minatur antequam surgat*, a storm (usually) threatens before it arises. Respecting the present indicative with these conjunctions, see § 334, note 5.

2. When the expressions *ante, citius, potius, prius quam* are used to

express that something is impossible, or is to be avoided by all means, they take the verb in the subjunctive, the event being conceived as not happening — as *Zeno Magnetas dixit in corpora sua citius saevituros, quam ut Romanam amicitiam violarent,* Zeno said that the Magnesians would sooner rave against their own bodies, than violate their friendship with Rome; *omnia perpessus est potius quam conscios delendae tyrannidis indicaret,* he suffered anything rather than betray those who knew of the design to overthrow tyranny. Respecting *quam qui* with the subjunctive, see § 314, note 1.

§ 358. The concessive conjunctions *quamvis* (however much, although a compound of *quam,* how much, and *vis,* thou wilt) and *licet* (although, properly speaking, a verb, after which *ut* is omitted) are construed with the subjunctive, like *quantumvis* and *quamlibet,* while *quamquam* (although) is joined with the indicative; e.g., *quamvis neges, tamen tibi credere nullo modo possum,* however much you may deny, still I cannot believe you in any way; *licet mihi invisus sit, tamen eum non persequar,* although he is hateful to me, still I will not persecute him.

Note 1. Instead of *quamvis,* we also find *quam* with other persons of *volo,* which, on account of its meaning, is likewise construed with the subjunctive — as *quam volent in conviviis faceti sint,* however witty they may be at their repasts.

2. Poets and late prose writers sometimes reverse the above rule, using *quamvis* with the indicative, and *quamquam* with the subjunctive — as *Pollio amat nostram, quamvis est rustica, Musam,* Pollio loves our Muse, although she is rustic; *dīs quamquam geniti essent,* although they were the sons of gods. *Quamvis* is also used as an adverb, and, as such, of course has no influence upon the mood of the verb — as *quamvis multos proferre possum,* I can mention as many as you like.

§ 359. The conjunctions *quasi, velut si, tamquam si* (sometimes *tamquam, sicut,* or poetically *ceu* alone), *perinde ac si, aeque ac si, non secus ac si,* are joined with the subjunctive, as they introduce a clause which is only a conception of the mind; e.g., *sic cogitandum est, tamquam aliquis in pectus intimum inspicere possit,* our thoughts must be such, as if any one could look into our innermost heart; *quid ego his testibus utor, quasi res dubia aut obscura sit?* why do I make use of these witnesses, as if the matter were doubtful or obscure? The tense in such clauses always depends upon that of the leading clause. See § 364.

§ 360. Relative clauses which simply add an explanation of some word or circumstance contained in the leading clause, have the verb in the indicative. But when a relative clause, besides containing a simple explanation, implies at the same time the idea of intention, purpose, result, or consequence, cause, &c. the subjunctive is employed. In all these cases the relative involves the idea of *ut* (in order that, so that) or

quum (as, since), which accounts for its requiring the subjunctive. The following special cases will more clearly develop
this rule :—

1. The subjunctive is used in a relative clause when it expresses the intention or purpose of the action contained in the
leading clause. In this case the relative is equivalent to *ut
is*, 'in order that he ;' e.g., *legatos Romam misit, qui (ut ii)
auxilium a senatu peterent*, he sent deputies to Rome, who
should ask the Roman senate for succour ; *nobis natura rationem dedit, qua (ut eā) regerentur animi appetitus*, nature
has given us reason by which the passions of our soul might
be controlled ; *Galli Druides habent, qui (ut ii) rebus divinis
praesint*, the Gauls have Druids to superintend their religious
affairs ; *non habet unde (ut inde) solvat*, he has no means wherewith to pay.

Note. What has been said here of the relative pronoun holds good
also of relative adverbs implying intention, purpose, or object, such as
cur, quare, quamobrem, unde, when they are preceded by such expressions as *causa est, ratio est, argumentum est;* e.g., *multae sunt causae,
quamobrem hunc hominem cupiam abducere*, there are many reasons why
I wish to lead away this man ; *quid causae fuit, cur hostes non sequereris ?*
what reason was there why you did not follow the enemy ? *non est*
(causa), *cur mihi invideas*, there is no reason why you should envy me.

2. After the adjectives *dignus, indignus, aptus*, and sometimes
also *idoneus*, the relative is used with the subjunctive, if
that of which a person is worthy or unworthy, or for which
anything is fit, is expressed by a verb—as *dignus* or *indignus est qui laudetur*, he is worthy or unworthy of being
praised ; *digna res est, quam diu multumque consideremus*,
the thing is worth being long and seriously considered ; *non
satis idoneus videtur, cui tantum negotium committatur*, he
does not seem quite fit to be intrusted with so important a
business. In these cases also the relative involves the idea
of *ut*.

Note. Poets and late prose writers sometimes join these adjectives
with an infinitive, either active or passive, according to the meaning —
as in Horace, *fons rivo dare nomen idoneus.* Sometimes *ut* takes the
place of the relative — as *quum indigni visi simus, ut (qui) a vobis re-
dimeremur.*

3. The subjunctive is used in relative clauses which serve to
complete the idea of a certain quality, and to express its
effect ; in such cases the relative is equivalent to *talis ut*,
'such that,' and the demonstratives *talis, tantus, hic, ille,
is, ejusmodi, hujusmodi*, or *tam*, sometimes actually precede
the relative, but sometimes they are understood ; e.g., *inno-
centia est affectio talis animi, quae (ut) noceat nemini*, harm-

lessness is that (or such a) state of mind which hurts no one ; *qui potest temperantiam laudare is, qui (talis ut) summum bonum in voluptate ponat ?* how can he praise temperance who (who is of such a kind that he) places the highest good in pleasure ? *non sumus ii, quibus nihil verum esse videatur,* we are not persons of that kind that nothing appears to be true to us ; *dicis aliquid (ejusmodi) quod ad rem pertineat,* you are saying something which (is of such a nature that it) bears on the point at issue.

Note 1. The subjunctive is used in similar relative clauses after a comparative, which are introduced by *quam qui,* equivalent to *quam ut.* In English, such sentences are expressed in quite a different manner — as *famae meae damna majora sunt quam quae (ut ea) estimari possint,* the injury done to my reputation is too great to be estimated ; *major sum quam cui (quam ut mihi) possit fortuna nocere,* I am too great to be able to be injured by fortune.

2. On the same principle the subjunctive is used in relative clauses, in which a general statement is limited in a certain way, especially those beginning with *qui quidem* — as *oratores Attici, quorum quidem scripta constent,* the Attic orators, at least as far as their writings are certain. So also *quod sciam,* as far as I know ; *quod meminerim,* as far as I remember ; *pergratum mihi feceris, si eum, quod sine molestia tua fiat, juveris,* where *quod sine molestia tua fiat* signifies, ' as far as you can do it without trouble,' or ' if you can do it without trouble,' the relative implying a condition or proviso.

4. After such general and indefinite expressions as *sunt* (there are persons), *inveniuntur, reperiuntur* (there are found men), *non desunt* (there are not wanting persons), *exstitit, exstiterunt, exortus est, habeo, est (ubi), nemo est, nihil est,* and the like, the relative may be joined with the indicative as well as with the subjunctive. The latter is used when the relative implies a quality — as *sunt, qui discessum animi a corpore putent esse mortem,* there are persons (of such a kind, so stupid or so wise) who believe that death is the separation of the soul from the body ; *fuere qui crederent,* there were persons of such a nature as to believe ; *sunt qui dicant,* there are persons of such a character as to assert. In all these and similar cases the relative implies the idea of *ut.* When the relative is joined with the indicative, a simple fact is stated without any intimation of quality, so that *sunt quos juvat* is equivalent to *juvat quosdam,* some persons take a delight ; *est ubi peccat,* equivalent to *interdum peccat,* he sometimes blunders.

Note. In many cases it depends entirely upon the writer's intention as to whether he is to use the indicative or subjunctive, according as he wishes simply to state a fact, or at the same time to express his opinion in such a covered and cautious manner as to leave the reader to guess it from the context.

5. The relative is followed by the verb in the subjunctive when it implies a supposition or condition, so that it involves the idea of *si* — as *nihil bonum est, quod hominem non meliorem faciat*, nothing is good unless it makes man better. In such a case, however, the writer, if he chooses, may use the indicative, employing the relative in its pure sense, without suggesting any condition — as *nihil bonum est, quod hominem non meliorem facit*, nothing is good which does not make man better. Compare above, No. 3, note 2.

6. Relative clauses have the verb in the subjunctive when they introduce a reason for what is contained in the leading clause; in such cases the relative is almost equivalent to *quum* (as, since) — as *O, fortunate adolescens, qui tuae virtutis Homerum praeconem inveneris!* O, fortunate youth, who (since thou) hast found in Homer a herald of thy valour! *miseret tui me, qui hunc tantum hominem facias inimicum tibi*, I pity you who (since you) make this great man your enemy.

Note 1. In many cases it is left to the writer's discretion as to whether by the relative clause he wishes to introduce a cause or reason, or merely a simple explanation. In the latter case the verb must be in the indicative, so that he may say either *magnam tibi gratiam habeo, qui ad me veneris* (because thou hast come), or *qui ad me venisti*, who hast come to me.

2. A relative denoting a reason or cause is often strengthened by the addition of other particles—as *quippe qui, utpote qui, ut qui, praesertim qui ;* and all these expressions are generally joined with the subjunctive, though some writers also use the indicative with them.

3. As *quum* sometimes has the meaning of although, so also *qui* implying *quum*, is sometimes equivalent to *quamvis*, and is then joined with the subjunctive — as *ego, qui sero Graecas litteras attigissem, tamen complures dies Athenis commoratus sum*, although I had commenced the study of Greek late, yet I stayed several days at Athens. Compare § 355, note 2.

7. Relative clauses have the verb in the subjunctive when the sentiment which they introduce is to be characterised as belonging to another person, and not as the sentiment of the speaker himself — as *Socrates exsecrari eum solebat, qui primus utilitatem a jure sejunxisset*, Socrates used to curse the man (whoever he was) who had first severed that which is useful from that which is just. Socrates here takes the opinion of some one else who asserted that some person had actually done so, but does not express it as his own opinion. —*Paetus omnes libros, quos frater suus reliquisset, mihi donavit*, Paetus has given me all the books which his brother might have left. Here Paetus, in thinking of the number of books left, does not state his own opinion, but says, ' whatever may

be the books left by my brother, as I am informed that there are books.' *Quos frater suus reliquerat*, would be 'all the books which his brother had left behind.' It is often a matter of little consequence whether in such a clause the indicative or subjunctive be used.

8. In historical narrative the subjunctive is sometimes used in a relative clause when actions of repeated occurrence are spoken of — as *quemcunque lictor jussu consulis prehendisset*, whomsoever the lictor had seized by the command of the consul; *semper habiti sunt fortissimi, qui summam imperii potirentur*, those who assumed the highest power have always been believed to be very valiant; *nemo Pyrrhum, qua tulisset impetum, sustinere valuit*, no one could resist Pyrrhus, wherever he made the attack. In all such cases the indicative may also be used, and is found almost as frequently as the subjunctive.

§ 361. The subjunctive is used in all clauses introduced into a dependent clause either by a relative pronoun or a conjunction, provided they form an integral part of it. By a dependent clause is meant one expressed by the accusative with the infinitive, or having its verb in the subjunctive. A clause forming an integral part of such a sentence is absolutely necessary, and without it, the whole does not and cannot convey a distinct meaning; e.g., *quod me admones, ut me integrum, quoad possim, servem, gratum est;* here the words *quoad possim* form part of the advice, and cannot be separated from it without destroying the meaning: *in Hortensio memoria tanta fuit, ut, quae secum commentatus esset, ea sine scripto verbis eisdem redderet;* here *quae secum commentatus esset* form an inseparable part of the clause introduced by *ut: Aristoteles ait, bestiolas quasdam nasci, quae unum diem vivant;* here *quae vivant* forms an inseparable part of the statement made by Aristotle. It sometimes, however, occurs that a writer or speaker, within a dependent sentence, introduces a remark or explanation of his own, and in this case the indicative is used, provided the conjunction introducing the remark admits of it — as *quis potest esse tam aversus a vero qui neget, haec omnia, quae videmus, deorum immortalium potestate administrari?* Here the words *quae videmus* contain a remark introduced by the speaker, and which is in no way connected with the dependent clause *haec omnia* . . . . , *administrari.*

Note. In some cases the difference is but small, whether such an inserted clause be treated as part and parcel of the one in which it is introduced, or whether it be treated as an independent remark added by the speaker — as *eloquendi vis efficit, ut ea, quae ignoramus* (or *ignoremus*), *discere, et ea, quae scimus* (or *sciamus*), *alios docere possimus ;* but in others the distinction is of serious import, and there are few cases in which the rule is not scrupulously observed, though even in Cicero we find the indicative where we should expect the subjunctive — as *Tertia est sententia, ut, quanti se ipse quisque facit* (for *faciat*), *tanti fiat ab amicis*, because the clause beginning with *quanti* is an integral part of the one beginning with *ut*. It more commonly occurs in historical composition that an inserted clause, though it forms a part of an *oratio obliqua*, is yet expressed by the indicative. The conjunction *dum* is in the same manner often used with the present indicative, though introducing a clause inseparably connected with a dependent clause — as *Dic, hospes, nos te hic vidisse jacentes, dum sanctis patriae legibus obsequimur;* but it is more correct in such cases to use it with the subjunctive.

CHAPTER LII.

THE TENSES OF THE SUBJUNCTIVE.

§ 362. The tenses of the subjunctive, generally speaking, have the same meaning as the corresponding tenses of the indicative, so that here we have to set forth only the peculiarities in the use of the tenses of the subjunctive.

§ 363. First of all, it must be observed that the Latin language is more strict than the English in the use of its tenses in subordinate clauses. This is manifest : —

1. In the use of the future perfect (the place of which, in the subjunctive, is supplied by the perfect subjunctive), for which we use either the present or the future — as *adnitar, ne frustra vos hanc spem de me conceperitis,* I shall exert myself that you may not in vain conceive this hope of me. Here the future perfect *conceperitis* signifies that at a future time you may not find that you have formed a wrong hope of me. *Si potestas facta erit, discedetur,* as soon as it is possible, there will be a parting. Here the parting (a future act) cannot take place till after the power has been given, so that logically the future perfect must be used. Compare above, § 338.

When past actions are spoken of—that is, when the verb of the leading clause is in the perfect (or the historical present) — the action of the subordinate clause, which must be completed before another can begin, is expressed by the pluperfect subjunctive — as *Divico cum Caesare agit, Helvetios in eam partem ituros atque ibi futuros, ubi eos Caesar constituisset atque esse voluisset,* the actions implied in *constituisset* and *voluisset* must be completed before those implied in *ituros* and *futuros* can take place. So also *dicebam, simulac timere desiisses, similem te futurum tui.*

In hypothetical sentences expressing mere possibility, the subjunctive of the future perfect is often used, where we employ the present or future, when it is to be expressed that the action of the protasis must be completed before that of the apodosis is to begin — as *si hoc feceris, mihi pergratum erit,* if you will do this, it will be very agreeable to me. So also *aliquis dixerit* (for *dicat*), 'some one may say,' representing the act of saying as possibly already past.

2. In English, two actions are often represented as simultaneous, though in reality the one expressed by the verb in the subordinate clause must be completed before the one expressed by the verb of the leading clause can begin. In such cases the Latin language more correctly uses the pluperfect in the subordinate clause — as, 'when he entered the house, he perceived,' *quum domum intrasset, animadvertit;* 'when he arrived in the Forum, he said,' *quum in Forum venisset, dixit.*

Note. Notwithstanding this general accuracy of the Latin language, the verbs of asking are often used in the imperfect, where we should expect the pluperfect, it being necessary that the act of asking should be completed before the answer is given—as *Socrates, quum rogaretur* (for *rogatus esset*), *respondit,* when Socrates was asked, he answered.

§ 364. In independent or leading clauses which have the verb in the indicative, the choice of the particular tense depends upon the nature of the statement; but in subordinate clauses, the choice of the tense is regulated by the tense in the leading clause. The general rule is — When the verb of the leading clause is in the present or future, the verb of the dependent or subordinate clause must be in the present or perfect subjunctive; and when the verb of the leading clause is in the imperfect, perfect, or pluperfect, that of the subordinate clause must be in the imperfect or pluperfect subjunctive — as *video, quid facias,* I see what you are doing; *video, quid feceris,* I see what you have done; *videbo, quid feceris,* I shall see what you have done; *nemo erit, qui nesciat,* there will be no one who does not know; *videbam, vidi* or *videram, quantum jam effecisset,* I saw, or had seen how much he had already effected; *nemo erat, qui nesciret,* there was no one who did not know. If the subordinate clause is connected with a clause expressed by the accusative with the infinitive, the tense of the verb of the subordinate clause depends upon that

18

which governs the accusative with the infinitive — as *indignum te esse judico, qui haec patiaris,* I think you unworthy to suffer these things; *indignum te judicavi (judicabam* or *judicaveram) qui haec patereris,* I thought you unworthy to suffer these things.

Note 1. A subordinate clause introduced by the conjunctions *ut* (in the sense of ' so that'), *quin,* and *qui non,* sometimes has the verb in the perfect subjunctive, though the verb of the leading clause is in a past tense. This, however, is the case only when the statement contained in the subordinate clause is conceived as a distinct historical fact by itself, and not merely as connected with that of the leading clause — as *Aemilius Paulus tantum in aerarium pecuniae invexit, ut unius imperatoris praeda finem attulerit tributorum;* here *attulerit* expresses the independent fact, that the booty of Paulus did put an end to the tributum, and that the· cessation of its payment continued in the speaker's time; *afferret* would mean that the booty of Paulus at the time in which he lived did away with the tributum, and the action contained in *afferret* would be viewed only as the result of another, and not as an independent event by itself; *inventus est scriba quidam, Cn. Flavius, qui cornicum oculos confixerit et fastos populo proposuerit.* Here, again, *confixerit* and *proposuerit* represent these actions as independent historical facts, while the imperfect subjunctive would introduce them only in connection with the leading clause. Corn. Nepos uses the perfect subjunctive even where we should expect the imperfect.

2. When the leading clause has the verb in the historical present (for the perfect), it may be treated as a real present or as a perfect, and the verb of the subordinate clause may accordingly be in the present or the imperfect subjunctive—as *tum demum Liscus proponit, esse nonnullos, quorum auctoritas apud plebem plurimum valeat* (or *valeret); Caesar, ne graviori bello occurreret* (or *occurrat), maturius quam consuerat, ad exercitum proficiscitur.* Sometimes the two modes of speaking are combined in the same sentence, as in Caesar, *Bell. Gall.* i. 7. The imperfect subjunctive after a real present is only a peculiarity which must be explained by the meaning of the sentence rather than by its form—as *video igitur multas esse causas, quae istum impellerent,* for *impellant,* because *esse* also implies the idea of *fuisse; verisimile non est, ut homo tam locuples religioni suae pecuniam anteponeret,* per· haps because *verisimile non est* is equivalent to *fieri vix potuit.*

3. In indirect questions the perfect subjunctive must be used if the question, in its direct form, would require the perfect or imperfect indicative—as *quis nescit, quanto in honore musica apud Graecos fuerit?* the direct question being, *quanto in honore musica apud Graecos fuit?*

§ 365. Subordinate clauses expressed by the subjunctive only because they form an integral part of a dependent sentence, have the verb in the perfect subjunctive; if in direct speech, it would be in the perfect indicative — as *quis putare potest, plus egisse Dionysium tum, quum eripuerit civibus suis libertatem, quam Archimedem, quum sphaeram effecerit?* it being in direct speech *nihilo plus egit tum, quum eripuit . . . . quum sphaeram effecit ·* nego me, postquam in urbem venerim, domi tuae fuisse,* because we say *postquam in urbem veni.* If, however, the verb governing the accusative with the infinitive is in a past tense, the verb of the inserted clause must be in the pluperfect — as *negavi me, postquam in urbem venissem, domi tuae fuisse.*

§ 366. When the verb of the leading clause is in a past tense, the verb of the subordinate clause is put in the present subjunctive, if the action implied in it is expressly conceived to take place, or to continue at the present time — as *Siciliam Verres ita vexavit ac perdidit, ut ea restitui in antiquum statum nullo modo possit,* that it (now) cannot be restored ; *posset* would mean that then (at that time) it could not be restored. In many cases, however, where the action or condition must be conceived as existing in past as well as in present time, the imperfect subjunctive is used, though it would be more in accordance with our idiom to use the present — as *tum subito Catilina scelere demens, quanta conscientiae vis esset, ostendit ;* the inserted clause here expresses not only 'what the power of conscience then was,' but also what it is now, and what it is at all times. So also *ad eamne rem vos delecti estis, ut eos condemnaretis, quos sicarii jugulare non potuissent ?*

Note 1. A subordinate clause denoting intention has the verb in the present subjunctive, when the one to which it is subordinate has a perfect denoting a repeated action, and expressing mere priority in time — as *quum misimus* (whenever we sent), *qui afferat agnum, quem immolemus.*

2. It sometimes occurs that the verb of the subordinate clause does not accommodate itself to that of the leading clause, but to that of some inserted or explanatory one — as *curavit Servius Tullius, quod semper in republica tenendum est, ne plurimum valeant plurimi ;* here *valeant* accommodates itself to *tenendum est* instead of *curavit.* Such cases are not numerous, and rather inaccurate, but may be explained by the reference to present time expressed in the present subjunctive.

CHAPTER LIII.

THE IMPERATIVE MOOD.

§ 367. The imperative represents an action or condition in the form of a command, request, or admonition. It has only two tenses — the present and the future: the former expresses a request or command in reference to present time, or without any reference to a particular time; and the latter a command or request that something is to be done in future, or when an occasion shall occur ; hence it is the appropriate form of expressing a command in laws, wills, contracts, or in writings composed in imitation of the style employed in such documents — as *vive felix!* live happily! — *subvenite misero mihi, ite obviam injuriae!* help me, wretched man, and resist the act of injustice! — *regio imperio duo sunto, iique consules appellantor*, there shall be two men with regal power, and they shall be called consuls; *servus meus liber esto*, my slave shall be free; *poëmata dulcia sunto, et quocunque volent, animum auditoris agunto*, poems must be sweet, and must carry the mind of the hearer whithersoever they please.

Note. Instead of the present imperative, we sometimes find the future indicative, expressing the firm conviction that the request will be complied with. This is the case especially in familiar conversation — as *sed valebis, meaque negotia videbis, meque ante brumam expectabis; siquid acciderit novi, facies, ut sciam.*

§ 368. Instead of the imperative present, it is very common to use the subjunctive, especially in the second person singular when an indefinite person is addressed — as *aut bibat, aut abeat*, let him drink, or go away; *meminerimus nos esse mortales*, let us remember that we are mortal; *status, incessus, vultus, oculi teneant decorum*, let your attitude, gait, countenance, and eyes, be decorous; *injurias fugiendo relinquas*, escape from injuries by flight. When a definite person is addressed in the second person singular, it is more common, at least in prose, to use the imperative than the subjunctive. Compare § 347, note 1.

§ 369. A negative command in legal phraseology is expressed by the future imperative with *ne*, and ' nor' is expressed by *neve* — as *nocturna sacrificia ne sunto*, there shall be no sacrifices at night; *hominem in urbe ne sepelito neve urito*, thou shalt not bury nor burn a man in the city.

Instead of the imperative present in a negative command, it is customary to use, in the third person, the subjunctive of the present or the future perfect; and in the second person in the active, the future perfect; and in the passive the perfect, or more rarely the present; the negative in these cases is likewise *ne* — as *puer telum ne habeat*, the boy shall not have a weapon; *hoc ne feceris*, do not do this; *nihil gratiae causa feceris*, do not do anything with partiality; *illum jocum ne sis aspernatus*, do not despise that joke.

Note 1. Poets often use the imperative present with *ne*—as *ne saevi*, do not rave. Sometimes also they use *non* and *neque* for *ne* and *neve;* in case of a subjunctive for an imperative, *non* and *neque* are found even more frequently. In later times, moreover, it was customary to use *ne* with the second person of the present subjunctive, which in the earlier times had been done generally only when an indefinite person was addressed.

2. A negative command is very often expressed by a paraphrase with *noli* or *nolito*—as *noli credere*, do not believe ; *nolite existimare*, do not think. The same is sometimes done by *fac ne, cave ne,* or *cave* alone — as *cavete ne omittatis*, take care not to omit ; *cave dixeris*, take care not to say. An affirmative command, on the other hand, is sometimes paraphrased by *cura ut, fac ut,* or *fac* alone—as *cura, ut quam primum venias*, take care to come as soon as possible.

§ 370. A sentence which in direct speech is expressed by the imperative, becomes the subjunctive when the speech becomes *oratio obliqua* — as *hoc mihi dicant* stands for *hoc mihi dicite* in direct speech. See § 388, note 2.

CHAPTER LIV.

THE INFINITIVE MOOD.

§ 371. The infinitive expresses the action or condition implied in a verb in the form of an abstract generality. The infinitive, from its meaning, may also be regarded as a verbal substantive, which, however, generally speaking, exists only in two cases, the nominative and the accusative, and differs from other substantives by its governing the case of a verb. The infinitive, both in the active and passive, has only three tenses ; the one, commonly called the infinitive of the present, simply represents an action in progress, and is therefore the infinitive not only of the present, but also of the past and the future — as *amare* and *amari*. The infinitive of the perfect represents the action as completed, and serves as the infinitive both of the perfect and pluperfect — as *amavisse* and *amatum (am, um) esse.* The infinitive of the future simply represents an action as yet to come, whatever may be the point of time from which the action is viewed, *amaturum esse* and *amatum iri.*

Note 1. In subordinate clauses expressed by the accusative with the infinitive, it has indeed a definite subject; but the infinitive can neither accommodate itself to the person nor to the number of the subject, unless the infinitive is compounded of a participle with *esse*, in which case the participle must agree with its subject in case, number, and gender.

2. Poets sometimes use the perfect infinitive active, like the Greek aorist, instead of the present infinitive, especially after verbs denoting a desire or ability—as *fratres tendentes opaco Pelion imposuisse Olympo; magnum si pectore possit excussisse deum; collegisse juvat.*

3. The verb *memini* (I remember) is followed by the present infinitive, though a past action is expressed, provided the speaker intimates
that he was present as an eye-witness of what he relates — as *memini
Catonem anno antequam est mortuus, mecum et cum Scipione disserere*,
I remember that Cato, the year before his death, discussed with me
and Scipio; *memini patrem optimis esse viribus*, I remember the time
when my father possessed the greatest bodily strength. But when an
event is mentioned, of which the speaker himself was not a witness,
the perfect infinitive is used. The same is sometimes done even in
cases of the former kind for the purpose of avoiding ambiguity.

4. Instead of the future infinitive, both in the active and passive, we
often find a circumlocution by *fore, ut* or *futurum esse, ut* — as *clama-
bant homines, fore, ut ipsi sese dii immortales ulciscerentur*, men ex-
claimed that the immortal gods themselves would take vengeance.
This circumlocution must be resorted to in those cases in which a verb
has no supine nor future participle, and is very common after the verb
spero—as *spero fore ut venias*, I hope you will come. *Fore* joined to a
past participle has the meaning of an infinitive of the future perfect —
as *Carthaginienses debellatum mox fore rebantur*, the Carthaginians
believed that the war would soon be finished.

§ 372. The subject of an infinitive is, with a few exceptions,
in the accusative. Respecting the nominative with the infinitive after the verbs *dicor, videor*, and others, see above, § 246;
and respecting the nominative with what is called the historical
infinitive, see below, § 390.

§ 373. As the infinitive has only two cases, the nominative
and accusative, it may be used either as the subject of another
verb (also as a predicate), or as its object. It is the subject
when an action is the thing of which something is predicated—
as *patriam amare cujusvis est civis*, to love one's country is the
duty of every citizen; *bene sentire recteque facere satis est ad bene
'eateque vivendum*, to entertain proper thoughts and act rightly is
enough to live well and happily; *apud Persas summa laus est
fortiter venari*, among the Persians it is the highest praise to be
a gallant hunter; *consulem fieri magnificum est*, to become consul
is glorious; *patriam a cive prodi turpissimum est*, it is a most
base thing that the fatherland should be betrayed by a citizen;
here the infinitive *prodi* is the subject, and *patriam* is the subject
of the infinitive.

Note. As the infinitive has no genitive, it cannot be joined with substantives as in English, and 'the desire to see' accordingly cannot be
translated by *desiderium videre*, but must be expressed by the genitive
of the gerund, *desiderium videndi*. See below, § 395. When, however,
an adjective is joined to a substantive, it may be followed by an infinitive, which then stands to it in the relation of an apposition—as *acerba
necessitudo te persequi*, 'the bitter necessity of persecuting you,' where
persequi stands in apposition to *acerba necessitas*. There are, however,
some examples of this kind, even when a substantive is not joined by
an adjective—as *consilium capio proficisci*, I form the plan of setting out;

consilium iniit reges tollere, he formed the design to abolish the kings; *copia mihi est in otio vivere,* I have the power to live in ease. In these and similar expressions, *consilium capio* or *ineo* is equivalent to *constituo,* and *copia mihi est* is equivalent to *possum.*

§ 374. The infinitive stands as an object (accusative) after many verbs which express an incomplete idea, and require another verb to complete it. Verbs of this kind are those denoting will, power, custom, inclination, beginning, continuing, ceasing, neglecting, and others — as *volo, nolo, malo, cupio, studeo, conor, nitor, contendo, tento* (in poetry also *quaero* and *amo), possum, queo, nequeo* (in poetry *valeo), audeo (sustineo), vereor (metuo, timeo), scio, nescio, disco, debeo, soleo, adsuesco, consuesco, statuo, constituo, decerno, cogito, paro, meditor, instituo, coepi, incipio, pergo, persevero, desino, maturo* (I hasten), *recordor, memini, obliviscor, negligo, omitto, supersedeo, non curo* (in poetry *parco, fugio).* The impersonal verbs *libet, licet, oportet, decet, placet, visum est, fugit* (me), *pudet, poenitet, piget, taedet,* as well as the expressions *necesse est* and *opus est,* are likewise followed by an infinitive, though with them the infinitive is the subject rather than the object. Lastly, there are certain expressions which have the same meaning as some of the above verbs, and are accordingly followed by an infinitive, such as *animum induco, habeo in animo, in animo est, certum est,* and the like. Examples are so numerous that it is superfluous to quote any.

Note 1. Verbs denoting resolution or determination are sometimes followed by *ut* instead of an infinitive—as *Athenienses constituerunt, ut urbe relicta naves conscenderent,* the Athenians resolved, after leaving their city, to embark on board their ships. So also we find *animum induco facere,* and *ut faciam; opto fieri aliquid,* and *ut fiat aliquid.*

2. Poets sometimes join the infinitive with such verbs as express a complete idea, and are therefore usually followed by *ut* or a preposition, and such as express an inclination in a figurative way — as *ardet abire fugā,* he longs to escape by flight; *incumbunt sarcire ruinas,* they are busy in repairing the loss; *certat tollere honoribus* for *certat ut tollat; laborat trepidare.* Sometimes such expressions occur even in prose — as *conjuravere patriam incendere,* they conspired to set fire to their native city.

3. An objective infinitive is sometimes found with adjectives which usually govern a genitive, dative, or ablative, or are followed by a preposition, and in such cases the infinitive may be said to be in the genitive, dative, &c. — as *cupidus discere* for *discendi; cedere nescius, avidus committere pugnam; fruges consumere* (for *ad fruges consumendas) nati; dignus laudari* (ablative); *indocilis pati, audax perpeti, callidus condere, eluere efficax;* but cases of this kind are almost entirely confined to poetry.

4. The verbs *volo, nolo, malo, cupio, opto,* and *studeo,* instead of being followed by an infinitive alone, sometimes have a whole clause for their object, in which the subject is put in the accusative and the verb

in the infinitive. This is always the case when the verb dependent on *volo, nolo,* &c. has a different subject from that of *volo, malo,* &c.; e.g., *volo praestare* signifies 'I wish to excel,' the real object of *volo* being *praestare;* but *volo me praestare,* 'I wish that I should excel,' the whole clause beginning with 'that' being conceived as the object of *volo.* So also *sapientem civem me et esse et numerari volo,* where all that precedes *volo* is conceived as its object. *Licet,* also, though rarely, is followed by the accusative with the infinitive — as *licet me isto tanto bono uti,* I am allowed to use that great advantage.

§ 375. The verbs *doceo, jubeo, veto, sino, arguo,* and *insimulo,* are followed by an objective infinitive, to express that which one teaches, orders, forbids, &c. In like manner the verbs *cogo, moneo, hortor, dehortor, impedio,* and *prohibeo,* are sometimes followed by an infinitive, though they are more commonly construed with the conjunctions *ut, quin,* or *quominus;* e.g., *doceo te loqui,* I teach you to speak; *jussit me ad se venire,* he ordered me to come to him; *consules jubentur exercitum scribere,* the consuls are ordered to levy an army; *Caesar legatos discedere vetuerat,* Caesar had forbidden the legates to go away; *Nolani muros portasque adire vetiti sunt,* the Nolans were forbidden to go to the walls and gates; *ratio ipsa monet amicitias comparare (ut comparemus),* reason itself admonishes us to form friendships; *quid me impedit haec dicere (quominus dicam)?* what prevents me saying these things?

Note 1. From these examples it will be seen that in the passive also these verbs retain the infinitive, which is in fact the second accusative, just as in *doceo te literas,* and *doceris literas a me.* Compare § 254.

2. *Jubeo,* in the sense of 'I order,' or 'I command,' is rarely construed with *ut* and the subjunctive, or with the subjunctive alone; but in the sense of 'I decree,' or 'I sanction,' it is commonly followed by *ut*—as *senatus decrevit populusque jussit, ut quaestores statuas demoliendas locarent. Veto* also is but rarely construed with *ne* or *quominus.* Late writers use *jubeo* also with the dative instead of the accusative. When the person who is ordered or forbidden anything is not expressed, *jubeo* and *veto* may be followed by the infinitive active — as *Hesiodus eādem mensurā reddere jubet,* where we may supply *te* or *hominem* as the object of *jubet.* But when the infinitive itself has an object (accusative), it is more common to change the construction into the passive — as *jubet virtutem coli,* he orders virtue to be cultivated. *Sino* is sometimes followed by the subjunctive with *ut,* and sometimes without it.

3. Poets and later writers use the infinitive also after many other verbs, instead of *ut* with the subjunctive, which is the practice of the best prose writers. Verbs of this kind are *impello, suadeo, concedo, permitto, impero,* though even Caesar has *de republica loqui non conceditur.* In like manner the poets use the verbs *do* and *reddo* in the sense of 'I grant,' 'I give the power,' with the infinitive — as *Graiis dedit ore rotundo Musa loqui; quantum mihi cernere datur.* For the infinitive after certain adjectives instead of the gerund or supine, see above, § 374, note 3, and below, § 396, note 3.

4. It very rarely occurs that an infinitive is governed by a preposition, but it is found especially with the expression *interest inter* — as *inter optime valere et gravissime aegrotare nihil prorsus interest.* So also *nihil praeter plorare.*

§ 376. When a substantive or adjective is added as a predicate to an infinitive referring to some preceding word either expressed or understood, the substantive or adjective agrees with the subject.

1. When, accordingly, the infinitive refers to a subject in the nominative, as is the case with the verbs enumerated in § 374, the substantive or adjective is in the nominative — as *cupio esse clemens,* where *clemens* agrees with *ego* implied in *cupio; Bibulus studet fieri consul; habeo in animo solus proficisci.*

2. When the infinitive has an accusative for its subject, as after the verbs mentioned in § 375, the substantive or adjective referring to that subject must be in the accusative—as *coegerunt eum nudum saltare ; pudet me victum discedere ; jubet me diligentem esse.*

3. When the infinitive belongs to a dative, the accompanying substantive or adjective is in the same case — as *mihi negligenti esse non licet,* I am not allowed to be idle ; *nec fortibus illic profuit armentis nec equis velocibus esse,* it was of no use to the herds there to be courageous, nor to the horses to be swift.

Note. The verb *licet* is sometimes followed by an accusative with the infinitive instead of the dative — as *civi Romano licet esse Gaditanum;* and the accusative is necessary if *licet* itself is not accompanied by its dative—as *non licet esse negligentem,* especially when a general principle is stated, and *licet* does not refer to any definite person — as *pro patria morientem non licet desperare.*

§ 377. As an infinitive alone may be the subject or object of another verb, so also an infinitive, accompanied by its own subject, may be either the subject or object of another verb. This is the construction of the accusative with the infinitive. A clause expressed by the accusative with the infinitive is commonly introduced in English by the conjunction 'that,' or 'the fact that.' If the infinitive, besides its subject, has also an object in the accusative, it is advisable to change the construction into the passive, in order to avoid ambiguity — as *aio te hostes vincere posse* may mean, 'I say that you can subdue your enemies,' and also 'I say that your enemies can subdue you,' whence it is preferable to say either *aio te ab hostibus vinci posse,* or *aio hostes a te vinci posse.*

§ 378. A clause expressed by the accusative with the infinitive, is the subject of another verb when the whole of it is con-

ceived as a single idea or noun of which something is predicated
— as *victorem parcere victis aequum est.* Here the clause *victis
victorem parcere* is the subject, and *aequum est* is the predicate.
So also *apparet nos ad agendum esse natos ; accusatores multos in
civitate esse utile est.*

Note. Instead of the accusative with the infinitive representing the
subject of a sentence, a clause is sometimes introduced by *quod*, ' the
fact that.' See below, § 381.

§ 379. A clause expressed by the accusative with the infinitive is the object, when a verb, instead of a single noun, has a
whole clause for its object. As I may say *video patrem*, so I
may also say *video patrem diu aegrotasse*, where *patrem diu
aegrotasse* is as much the object of *video* as in the preceding
sentence the noun *patrem.* In this case the English language
sometimes admits of the same construction, as, ' I wish him to
be here,' ' I know him to be a trustworthy person.' An accusative with the infinitive of this kind, therefore, may occur
after all verbs which can have a whole clause as their object.
This is the case especially after verbs of perceiving, declaring,
thinking, believing, &c. — such as *video, audio, sentio, animadverto, scio, nescio, intelligo, perspicio, comperio, suspicor, disco,
doceo, persuadeo, memini, credo, arbitror, puto, judico, censeo,
duco, spero, despero, colligo, concludo, dico, affirmo, nego, fateor,
narro, trado, scribo, nuntio, ostendo, demonstro, significo, polliceor, promitto, minor, simulo, dissimulo,* and many others ;
also after such expressions as *fama est, spes est, auctor est,
communis opinio est,* and all others containing the meaning of
any of the above verbs ; e.g., *Platonem Cicero scribit Tarentum ad Archytam venisse,* Cicero writes that Plato went to
Archytas at Tarentum ; *sentit animus se sua vi moveri,* the
mind perceives that it is moved (to act) by its own power ;
*e multis rebus intelligere possumus mundum providentia divina
administrari,* we can perceive from many things that the
world is governed by divine Providence ; *fama est Gallos ad-
ventare,* there is a report that the Gauls are approaching ; *oraculum editum erat patriam liberam fore rege occiso,* an oracle
had been given that the country would be free if the king were
killed.

Note 1. In the same manner an accusative with the infinitive is frequently pointed to by a pronoun or adverb (*sic, ita*) in the preceding
clause, and then stands to it in the relation of an apposition or explanation—as *hoc ipsum dicere solebat, nihil esse bonum, nisi quod honestum
esset; ita existimare debemus, nihil esse honestum, nisi,* &c.

2. Many verbs, having a different meaning from any of those mentioned above, are now and then used in such a way as to suggest to
the mind of the reader another verb requiring the accusative with the

infinitive — as *ad collegam misit, exercitu opus esse*, he sent word (or some one to say) that there was need of the army. Respecting *concedo* and *dubito*, see above, § 252, note 4, and § 275, note 3.

3. The verbs of hoping, promising, and threatening, are commonly followed in English by the present infinitive, when the leading verb as well as the infinitive have the same subject; but as the idea implied in such an infinitive refers to future time, the Latin language requires the future infinitive with its subject in the accusative — as *promisit se venturum*, he promised to come; *spero me eos visurum esse*, I hope to see them; *minabatur se abiturum esse*, he threatened to go away. Sometimes, however, *spero* and *polliceor* are construed, as in English, with the present infinitive — as *sperans deterrere*, hoping to deter.

4. The verb *audio* may be construed with the accusative with the infinitive, or with a participle instead of the infinitive — as *audio te dicere*, I hear (that is, I am told) that you say; but *audio te dicentem*, I hear you speaking. But the latter meaning is sometimes also expressed by the infinitive, or by a clause introduced by *quum*—as *audivi quum diceres*.

5. In English it often happens that the word which should be the subject of the infinitive, is introduced into the leading clause by some preposition; *e.g.*, 'as for my brother, I know that he is at Rome.' This cannot, generally speaking, be imitated in Latin, where it is necessary to say, *fratrem Romae esse scio*. There are, however, cases in which the subject of the infinitive is similarly introduced into the leading clause by *de* — as *de hoc Verri dicitur, habere eum perbona toreumata; de Antonio jam ante tibi scripsi non esse eum a me conventum.*

§ 380. An objective accusative with the infinitive is governed by verbs expressing a wish, permission, or command, that something should be done — as *volo, malo, nolo, cupio, opto, studeo, postulo, placet, sino, patior*, also *jubeo, impero, prohibeo,* and *veto* (compare §§ 374, 375); *e.g., majores corpora juvenum firmari labore voluerunt*, our ancestors wished that the bodies of the young should be strengthened by labour; *senatui placet Crassum Syriam obtinere*, the senate decrees that Crassus shall obtain Syria; *Caesar castra muniri vetuit*, Caesar forbade the camp to be fortified; *nullos honores mihi decerni sino*, I allow no honours to be decreed to me.

Note 1. Many of these verbs are sometimes followed by *ut* instead of the infinitive; *prohibeo* sometimes takes *ne* or *quominus*, and *jubeo ne*. Compare § 375, note 2. Respecting the difference between *cupio clemens esse*, and *cupio me clementem esse*, see § 374, note 4. The best authors use the verbs *permitto, praecipio, mando, interdico, oro, precor*, and many similar ones with *ut*, while later writers more commonly use the infinitive after them. *Censeo* is followed by *ut* in the sense of 'I advise.'

2. The verbs *volo, malo, nolo*, and *cupio*, are often joined with the perfect infinitive passive, to express the thing wished for as already completed—as *sociis maxime consultum esse vult*, he wishes that especial care be taken for the allies; *monitos (esse) vos volo*, I wish to remind you.

§ 381. An objective accusative with the infinitive is used

after verbs denoting content, discontent, or wonder — as *gaudeo,
laetor, glorior, doleo, angor, sollicitor, indignor, queror, miror,
admiror, fero aegre,* and *moleste fero.* All these verbs, however,
may also be followed by the conjunction *quod,* either with the
indicative or the subjunctive — as *gaudeo id te mihi suadere,* or
*gaudeo quod id mihi suades; nihil me magis sollicitabat, quam
non me ridere tecum,* or *quam quod non riderem tecum; Laetor,
quod Petilius incolumis vivit in urbe,* or *Petilium incolumem
vivere in urbe.*

Note. Subjective clauses of the accusative with the infinitive are
likewise sometimes expressed by *quod* instead of the infinitive, and in
this case *quod* may always be rendered by 'the fact that,' *non pigritiā
facio, quod non meā manu scribo,* the fact that I do not write with my
own hand, does not arise from idleness ; *hoc uno praestamus feris, quod
experimere dicendo sensa possumus,* by this fact alone we excel animals,
that we can express our thoughts in words. In most cases there is a
different meaning — as *utile est patrem adesse,* 'the presence of the
father is useful,' but it does not necessarily mean that the father is actually present; whereas *utile est, quod pater adest,* signifies the father
is present, and his presence is useful. The former therefore contains
a simple opinion, but the latter contains besides also a fact. Sometimes
quod signifies, 'as regards the fact that,'—as *quod scribis, te ad me venturum, ego te istic esse volo,* as regards your writing, that you will
come to see me, I wish you to remain where you are.

§ 382. In sentences expressing wonder, astonishment, of a
complaint at something happening, the accusative with the infinitive is used without there being any verb on which it is
dependent. When such an expression is put in the form of a
question, the first word generally takes the interrogative suffix
ne — as *te in tantas aerumnas incidisse!* that you should have
fallen into such great distress! *adeone hominem esse infelicem
quemquam ut ego sum!* that any man should be to that degree
unhappy as I am! *mene incepto desistere victam?* should I, conquered, give up what I have begun?

Note. It is not improbable that in all cases of this kind the accusative with the infinitive may be objective, and dependent upon some
expression understood, which is suppressed by the excited state of
mind of the speaker. We might in the above examples supply, for
instance, such an expression as 'is it possible,' *fieri ne potest,* or 'it is
hardly credible,' *vix credi potest.*

§ 383. When the passive of a verb of saying, thinking,
ordering, forbidding, or the verb *videtur* (it seems), should be
used impersonally, and followed by a clause in the accusative
with the infinitive (as in *dicitur patrem venisse*), the noun which
is the subject of the infinitive is drawn into the leading clause,
and is made the subject of its passive verb — as *pater dicitur
venisse,* and any adjective or noun added to the infinitive, and
referring to the subject in the nominative, must likewise be

in the nominative — as *dicitur pater esse mortuus; Hortensius magnus orator fuisse dicitur; luna solis lumine collustrari putatur; malum mihi videtur esse mors.* The same construction exists in English, as in ' he is said to be a good man' for ' it is said that he is a good man;' ' he is believed to be a very honest person' for ' it is believed that he is a very honest person.' Compare § 247.

Note. The simple tenses of the verbs *dicitur, traditur, existimatur, putatur, creditur,* &c. are but seldom used impersonally with the accusative with the infinitive — as *eam gentem traditur Alpes transisse;* but it is more often the case with *nuntiatur* and *dicitur,* when these verbs are accompanied by a dative — as *nuntiatur mihi hostes flumen transisse.* The verbs of saying and believing are more commonly used impersonally (with the accusative with the infinitive) when they are in a compound tense—as *traditum est, Homerum caecum fuisse;* but also *Julius Sabinus voluntaria morte interisse creditus est.* In the case of a gerundive with *esse,* the accusative with the infinitive is used almost invariably—as *nuntiandum est, omnes hostes devictos esse.*

§ 384. This method of using the passive verbs of saying, believing, &c. personally is also applied to other passive verbs expressing more specific kinds of saying or knowing, as *scribor, demonstror, audior, intelligor, judicor* — as *audiebatur Caesar victor esse in Gallia,* it was heard that Caesar was victorious in Gaul; *scutorum multitudo deprehendi posse indicabatur,* it was announced that a number of shields might be discovered. It is more common to use such verbs impersonally with the accusative with the infinitive.

Note. Poets and later prose writers extend the use of such personal passives much further than the earlier writers; thus we find *colligor placuisse* for *colligitur me placuisse; compertus sum fecisse* for *compertum est me fecisse.*

§ 385. When the subject of a clause expressed by the accusative with the infinitive is a personal or reflective pronoun referring to the subject of the leading clause (as in *dico me esse, dicit se esse*), the pronoun is often omitted with verbs of saying and believing — as *confitere, eā spe huc venisse,* confess that you have come hither in this hope; *quum id nescire Mago diceret,* when Mago said that he did not know this.

Note 1. This omission is particularly frequent in the case of *me, se,* and *te,* but occurs more rarely in the case of *nos* and *vos.* It is found almost invariably when one accusative with the infinitive is dependent upon another, and both have the same pronoun for their subject — as *licet me existimes desperare ista posse* (me) *perdiscere.* The omission is particularly frequent with the infinitive future active, in which case *esse* also is very often omitted — as *Alcon, precibus* (se) *aliquid moturum* (esse) *ratus, transiit ad Hannibalem.*

2. The poets sometimes, imitating the practice of the Greek lan-

guage, use the nominative with the infinitive, when the leading verb and the infinitive have the same subject — as *sensit medios delapsus in hostes* for *se medios delapsum esse in hostes.*

§ 386. Explanatory clauses inserted by means of a relative pronoun in a sentence expressed by the accusative with the infinitive, have, according to circumstances, the verb either in the indicative or subjunctive. See § 361. But when the relative pronoun supplies the place of a demonstrative, so that the clause introduced by it is only a continuation of the statement expressed by the infinitive, the relative clause also has the verb in the infinitive; e.g., *Postea autem Gallus dicebat ab Eudoxo Cnidio sphaeram astris coelo inhaerentibus esse descriptam, cujus omnem ornatum et descriptionem Aratum extulisse versibus.* Here *cujus* is equivalent to *et ejus,* and the clause introduced by it stands to *dicebat* in the same relation as *sphaeram esse descriptam.*

Note. The same is sometimes, though very rarely, the case with clauses introduced by relative conjunctions—as *quum, quia, quanquam,* when they supply the place of *et* and a demonstrative; e.g., *Jacere tamdiu irritas sanctiones, quae de suis commodis ferrentur, quum interim* (that is, *et interim*) *de sanguine et supplicio suo latam legem confestim exerceri.*

§ 387. When the subject of a clause in the accusative with the infinitive is put in connection with another subject by means of *quam, idem qui, tantus-quantus,* and similar expressions, the latter subject, by a kind of attraction, is likewise put in the accusative, although, properly speaking, a finite verb is understood — as *suspicor, te eisdem rebus, quibus me ipsum, commoveri,* where we should have expected *quibus ipse (commoveor) ; Platonem ferunt primum de animorum aeternitate sensisse idem, quod Pythagoram,* for *quod Pythagoras senserat ; Terentium censeo elegantiorem fuisse poetam, quam Plautum,* for *quam Plautus fuit.* If, however, the verb is repeated with the second subject, the nominative must be used. When two clauses are in this way connected by *quam,* and each has its own verb, the second should have its verb in the finite form ; but it nevertheless sometimes occurs that, by a species of attraction, it is likewise transformed into the accusative with the infinitive — as *Nonne tibi affirmavi, quidvis me potius perpessurum, quam ex Italia ad bellum civile me exiturum,* instead of *quam exirem* or *quam ut exirem.*

§ 388. An accusative with the infinitive very often occurs without there appearing to be any of the verbs or expressions mentioned in the preceding rules. This is the case when a person is introduced stating the substance of what he said or thought, without his identical words being adduced.

In these cases, however, it is easy to supply some such word as ' he said' or ' thought;' e.g., *Romulus legatos circa vicinas gentes misit, qui societatem connubiumque novo populo peterent; urbes quoque, ut cetera, ex infimo nasci* (dicens); *deinde, quas sua virtus ac dii juvent, magnas opes sibi magnumque nomen facere.* This use of the infinitive to state a person's thoughts or sentiments indirectly is termed the *oratio obliqua,* while in the *oratio recta* not only the substance of a man's opinion, but his very words are stated.

Note 1. In all cases of this kind the verb governing the infinitive must be discovered from the context, or it is implied in some verb actually occurring. Examples of the *oratio obliqua* are of frequent occurrence in the Latin historians.

2. Sentences which in the *oratio recta* would be expressed by the imperative mood are given in the *oratio obliqua* by the subjunctive—as (dixit) *sin bello persequi perseveraret, reminisceretur pristinae virtutis Helvetiorum,* which in the *oratio recta* would be *si bello perseveras, reminiscitor pristinae virtutis Helvetiorum; Vercingetorix perfacile esse factu dicit frumentationibus Romanos prohibere; aequo modo animo sua ipsi frumenta corrumpant aedificiaque incendant,* where in direct speech we should have *aequo modo animo vestra ipsi frumenta corrumpite aedificiaque incendite.* Compare § 370.

§ 389. Questions which in direct speech would be expressed by the indicative in the first or second person, are in the *oratio obliqua* expressed by the accusative with the infinitive; but if in the direct form, they belong to the second person; they are expressed by the subjunctive (imperfect or pluperfect); e.g., *Quid se vivere, quid in parte civium censeri, si, quod duorum hominum virtute partum sit, id obtinere universi non possint?* In direct speech it would be — *quid vivimus, quid in parte civium censemur? Si veteris contumeliae oblivisci vellet, num etiam recentium injuriarum memoriam deponere posse?* (*num etiam recentium . . . . deponere possum?*) *An quidquam superbius esse quam ludificari sic omne nomen Latinum?* (*an quidquam superbius est?*) *Quid de praeda faciendum censerent?* (*quid de praeda faciendum censetis?*)

Note 1. Questions thus expressed by the accusative with the infinitive are generally equivalent in meaning to a negative assertion—as *se non vivere, se in parte civium non censeri; recentium injuriarum memoriam se deponere non posse; nihil superbius esse;* and this seems to be the reason why they are expressed by the accusative with the infinitive; for where the subjunctive is used, the question does not admit of such an explanation.

2. Questions which in direct speech are expressed by the subjunctive, retain the same mood in the *oratio obliqua,* but the tense is usually the imperfect or pluperfect — as *quis sibi hoc persuaderet?* which in direct speech would be *quis sibi hoc persuadeat?*

§ 390. It is a peculiarity of the Latin language, that in

animated historical narratives and descriptions, the present infinitive is used instead of the imperfect. This is commonly called the historical, and more correctly the descriptive infinitive, for by means of it a writer is enabled, as it were, by a few broad strokes, to bring before the mind of his reader a rapid sketch of a series of scenes or pictures. Hence we very rarely find one descriptive infinitive alone, but usually two, three, or more. This construction is the only one in which we may truly say that the subject of the infinitive is in the nominative, and not, as usual, in the accusative; e.g., *Hoc ubi Verres audivit, usque eo commotus est, ut sine ulla dubitatione insanire omnibus videretur. Quia non potuerat eripere argentum, ipse a Diodoro erepta sibi vasa optime facta dicebat; minitari absenti Diodoro, vociferari palam, lacrimas interdum vix tenere.* Examples are very numerous in all the Latin historians.

Note. This infinitive is sometimes used even after the conjunction *quum* to express the sudden beginning of an action—as in Livy, *senatus expectabat, quum Appius, quam asperrime poterat, jus de creditis pecuniis dicere,* when Appius suddenly began to pronounce sentence.

CHAPTER LV.

THE GERUND AND GERUNDIVE.

§ 391. The gerund supplies the place of a verbal substantive in all cases except the nominative and vocative (the place of the nominative is supplied by the infinitive); but it differs from ordinary substantives by the fact that it governs its case as a verb, and is not followed by the genitive of another substantive — as *studium obtemperandi legibus,* the zeal to obey the laws; *ad fruendum frugibus terrae,* for the purpose of enjoying the fruits of the earth; *consilium scribendi epistolam,* the plan of writing a letter; *amicitia dicta est ab amando.*

Note. There are a few instances in which the genitive of a gerund, like an ordinary substantive, is followed by the genitive of a noun, as in Cicero (*De Invent.* ii. 2, *Univ.* § 9, *in Verr.* iv. 47, *Philip,* v. 3, *De Fin.* v. 7), and more frequently in the early poets and Gellius. This, however, is a mere anomaly, which it is not easy to explain; but it does not warrant the conclusion of some of the earlier grammarians, that in such cases as *consilium mei interficiendi* the word *interficiendi* is to be regarded as a substantive governing the genitive *mei; interficiendi* being no gerund at all, but the gerundive agreeing with *mei,* the genitive of *meum* used substantively.

§ 392. When the gerund is a transitive verb, having its object in the accusative, as in *consilium condendi urbem*, the common practice is to change the accusative into the case of the gerund, and the gerund into the gerundive, making it agree with its noun — as *consilium condendae urbis*, the plan of founding a city. So also *persequendis hostibus* for *persequendo hostes*, by pursuing the enemy. When the gerund is governed by a preposition, this change of the gerund into the gerundive is almost invariably adopted — as *ad placandos deos* for *ad placandum deos; in victore laudando* for *in laudando victorem.* The dative of the gerund with an accusative for its object is likewise very unusual whence it is better to say *oneri ferendo* than *onus ferendo.*

Note. In all other cases it is left to the discretion and taste of the writer as to whether he is to use the gerund or gerundive; but it is advisable to retain the gerund when its object is a neuter adjective or pronoun — as *studium aliquid agendi*, the desire to do something; *cupiditas plura habendi*, the wish to have more things; but we also find *studium veri inveniendi*, 'the desire to discover the truth' where *verum* has the meaning of an abstract noun.

§ 393. As the gerund, as far as its meaning is concerned, is nothing but the oblique cases of the infinitive, and as the infinitive cannot in all cases be used as an ordinary substantive, the gerund also is subject to a similar limitation.

The accusative of the gerund is used only after prepositions, especially *ad* and *inter*, in the sense of 'during' or 'amid' — as *inter ludendum*, during the play; *ad scribendum*, for the purpose of writing; *ad tolerandum labores*, for the purpose of enduring the labour.

Note. The instances in which the prepositions *ante, in, circa*, and *ob*, occur with the gerund, are very rare.

§ 394. The dative of the gerund is used after certain verbs and expressions to denote the object or purpose. Such verbs are — *studere, praeesse, impertire, operam dare, diem dicere, locum capere;* e.g., *praesum agro colendo,* I superintend the cultivation of the field; *consul placandis diis dat operam*, the consul is engaged in appeasing the gods. The dative is also used after adjectives denoting fitness and usefulness — as *utilis, inutilis, noxius, par, aptus, idoneus, firmus, natus, accommodatus*, and others; e.g., *area firma templis porticibusque sustinendis*, an area firm enough to build temples and porticoes on it; *aqua utilis est bibendo*, water is useful for drinking; *intentus venando*, bent upon hunting. It is, however, more customary after such adjectives to use the preposition *ad* with the accusative of the

19   N

288   LATIN GRAMMAR.

gerund. The object or purpose is also expressed in the titles of certain Roman officers by the gerundive supplying the place of the gerund—as *decemviri legibus scribendis ; triumviri agris dividendis ; curator muris reficiendis ;* and after *comitia* — as *comitia consulibus creandis,* an assembly held for the purpose of electing consuls.

Note. The verb *esse,* joined with the dative of a gerund, signifies ' to be able'—as *esse solvendo,* to be able to pay ; *oneri ferendo erant,* they were able to bear the burden ; *esse tolerandae obsidioni,* to be able or fit to hold out against a siege. The verb *sufficere* is used in the same way. Late writers often use the dative of the gerund for the gerundive as its substitute) to express a purpose or intention after verbs of motion — as *misit exercitum distrahendo hosti* for *ad distrahendum hostem.*

§ 395. The ablative of the gerund is used either as an ablative of the instrument, or with the prepositions *in, ab, de,* and *ex.* In the first case, the gerund, when it has an object, is commonly changed into the gerundive, and in the second almost always ; e.g., *hominis mens discendo alitur,* the mind of man is fed by learning; *Caesar dando, sublevando, ignoscendo gloriam adeptus est,* Caesar acquired glory by giving, helping, and forgiving ; *loquendi elegantia augetur legendis oratoribus et poetis,* elegance in speaking is increased by reading the orators and poets ; *summa voluptas ex discendo capitur; in voluptate spernenda virtus vel maxime cernitur ; homines ad deos nulla re propius accedunt quam salutem hominibus dando.*

Note 1. The ablative of the gerund is sometimes an ablative of manner or time, intimating that two actions are going on simultaneously— as *Quis est, qui nullis officii praeceptis tradendis philosophum se audeat dicere ?* Such expressions as *contentus possidendis agris* for *possessione agrorum;* or *pro ope ferenda* (instead of bringing succour) for *omisso opis ferendae consilio,* are anomalies which occur very rarely.

2. The English ' without,' joined with a verb, cannot be translated by *sine* with a gerund. If simultaneous actions are mentioned, the word ' without' may be omitted, and the present participle be used — as *haec dico nullius reprehensionem verens,* I say this without fearing any one's censure ; but it is more general to use the ablative absolute, or the conjunctions *quin, ut non,* or *nisi;* e.g., *consul non expectato auxilio collegae* (without waiting for the help of his colleague) *pugnam committit; haec dijudicari non possunt, nisi causam cognoverimus* (without our having examined the case) ; *adspicere eum non possum, quin sentiam,* I cannot look at him without feeling.

§ 396. The genitive of the gerund is used after substantives and those adjectives which govern a genitive (see § 277). After substantives, it is either an objective genitive, or defines more particularly the general idea implied in the substantive ; e.g., *ars docendi,* the art of teaching ; *cupidus discendi,* eager to learn ; *pugnandi cupiditas,* the desire to fight ; *parsimonia est scientia vitandi sumptus supervacuos, aut ars re familiari moderate utendi ; Germanis neque consilii habendi, neque arma capiendi spatium datum est ; in suspicionem incidit regni appetendi ; Cicero auctor non fuit Caesaris interficiendi ; principes civitatis non tam sui conservandi quam tuorum consiliorum reprimendorum causa Romā profugerunt.*

Note 1. Instead of *se conservandi*, we must, with the gerundive, say *sui conservandi*, the word *sui* being the genitive of the neuter *suum*, and being used both as a singular and as a plural. Compare § 391, note.

2. The genitive of the gerund is never governed by a verb, and those verbs which govern a genitive take a verb in the infinitive—as *recordor facere, pudet me dicere.*

3. Certain substantives which should be followed by the genitive of the gerund, may, when accompanied by the verb *esse*, assume the force of an impersonal verb, and are then followed by the infinitive — as *tempus est abire*, it is time to go ; but *tempus proelii committendi non neglexit*, he did not neglect the (proper) time of fighting a battle. So also *consilium est, consilium capio. Consilium inire*, as well as the passive form *consilium initur*, is almost invariably followed by the genitive of the gerund, or by the gerundive supplying its place. Poets are very free in the use of the infinitive after substantives and adjectives instead of the genitive of the gerund, or the prepositions *ad* and *in*. After the substantives *facultas, locus*, and *signum*, we sometimes find the preposition *ad* instead of the genitive of the gerund — as *oppidum magnam ad ducendum bellum dabat facultatem*, the town afforded a great opportunity for protracting the war.

4. The genitive of a substantive accompanied by the gerundive is sometimes joined to the verb *esse*, to express the purpose or object which anything serves — as *regium imperium initio conservandae libertatis atque augendae reipublicae fuerat*, the kingly government had at first served to preserve liberty, and strengthen the republic. Sometimes, especially in later writers, such genitives are found, which must be explained by the ellipsis of *causa* or *gratia*—as *Marsi miserunt Romam oratores pacis petendae; Germanicus in Aegyptum proficiscitur cognoscendae antiquitatis.*

5. The gerund being the representative of the infinitive active, has itself an active meaning ; but there are some cases in which it might seem to have a passive or at least reflective meaning—as *censendi causa haec frequentia convenit*, this multitude assembles for the purpose of undergoing the census; but in such cases the gerund may be said to be used for an abstract noun—as *Antonius, hostis judicatus, Italia cesserat; spes restituendi nulla*, where *restituendi* has the same meaning as *restitutionis.*

§ 397. The gerundive of transitive verbs is in form an adjective, and signifies that something must be done — that is, it expresses necessity — as *vir haud contemnendus*, a man not to be despised ; *patria defendenda est*, our country must be defended : *homines docendi sunt*, men must be instructed ; *agri colendi sunt*, the fields must be cultivated ; *hoc necessario faciendum est*, this must necessarily be done. If the agent who must do anything, or by whom anything must be done, is added, it is always expressed by the dative — as *hoc mihi faciendum est*, I must do this, or this must be done by me; *tria videnda sunt oratori*, an orator has to bear in mind three points; *video jam hoc mihi esse omittendum*, I see that I now must omit this; *Carthaginem delendam esse censeo*, I am of opinion that Carthage must be destroyed.

Note. When joined with a negative particle or *vix*, the gerundive sometimes expresses possibility and not necessity — as *dolor vix ferendus*, a pain scarcely to be borne; *vix credendum erat*, it could hardly be believed, for *vix credi poterat.*

§ 398. The gerundive of intransitive verbs is used only in the neuter gender with the tenses of *esse*, and forms a kind of impersonal expression denoting the necessity of performing the action expressed by the verb. The agent here, as with transitive verbs, is expressed by the dative—as *mihi eundum est*, I must go; *nunc est bibendum*, now drinking must take place; *proficiscendum mihi erat in castra*, I had to go into the camp; *obtemperandum est legibus*, one must obey the laws; *pane utendum est*, bread must be used.

Note 1. When a verb governs a dative, and the agent also is expressed by the dative, there may often arise an ambiguity — as *his hominibus nobis est consulendum*, these men must take care of you, or you must take care of these men. In order to avoid such ambiguity, the agent may be expressed by the ablative with the preposition *ab* — as *his hominibus a nobis consulendum est.*

2. The verbs *utor*, *fruor*, *fungor*, and *potior*, though they govern the ablative, have yet their complete gerundive like genuine transitive verbs — *sapientia non paranda nobis solum, sed etiam fruenda est; ad perfruendas voluptates; spes potiundorum castrorum; rei utendae causa.* Early writers, on the other hand, sometimes use the neuter of the gerundive in the same impersonal way as that of intransitive verbs — as *mihi hac nocte agendum est vigilias*, I must this night keep watch; *aeternas poenas in morte timendum est*, eternal punishments are to be dreaded in death.

§ 399. Certain verbs denoting to give, surrender, leave, take, or receive — as *do, mando, trado, impono, relinquo, propono, accipio, suscipio, loco, curo*, and others — often have an object accompanied by a gerundive, denoting the purpose or object for which the action is performed — as *hostibus mortuos sepeliendos tradidit*, he surrendered to the enemy the dead to be buried, or for the purpose of burying them; *hunc librum mihi legendum dedit*, he has given me this book to read; *laudem gloriamque P. Africani tuendam conservandamque suscepi*, I have undertaken to protect and preserve the honour and glory of P. Africanus; *loco templum aedificandum*, I give the building of the temple in contract; *muros reficiendos curavit*, he caused the walls to be rebuilt; *Caesar pontem in Arari faciendum curavit,* Caesar caused a bridge to be made on the Arar.

In the passive, such object, with its accompanying gerundive, is of course changed into the nominative — as *murus reficiendus locatus est,* the restoration of the wall was given in contract.

Note 1. Poets sometimes use a present infinitive active in the place of such a gerundive — as *tristitiam et metus tradam protervis in mare Creticum portare.* In prose also we find *do* or *ministro alicui bibere,* 'I give to a person to drink;' and *jussi ei bibere dari,* I ordered drink to be given to him.

2. The verb *habeo* is sometimes construed in Latin with another verb in the gerundive — as *habeo aedem tuendam,* I have a temple to protect; *habeo dicendum,* I have to say; *habeo statuendum,* I have to determine. In the sense of 'I can,' it is sometimes construed with the infinitive of *dico, scribo, polliccor,* and similar verbs — as *haec fere dicere habui de natura deorum,* this is about what I had to say respecting the nature of the gods; *nihil habui ad te scribere,* I have nothing to write to you.

CHAPTER LVI.

THE SUPINES.

§ 400. A supine is likewise a verbal substantive. It belongs to the fourth declension, and has only two cases — the accusative (in *um*) and the ablative (in *u*). It also differs from an ordinary substantive, inasmuch as it governs the same case as the verb to which it belongs — as *legati venerunt res repetitum,* ambassadors came to reclaim their property.

§ 401. The supine in *um* has an active meaning, and is used after verbs of motion, to express the object of the motion — as *legati in castra venerunt questum injurias,* deputies came into the camp to complain of the acts of injustice; *Fabius Pictor Delphos ad oraculum missus est sciscitatum, quibus precibus deos possent placare,* Fabius Pictor was sent to Delphi, to the oracle, to inquire by what prayers they could propitiate the gods; *Philippus, cum spectatum ludos iret, occisus est,* as Philip was going to see the games, he was killed.

Note 1. In like manner we find the expression *aliquam alicui nuptum dare,* to give a woman to some one in marriage. *Eo perditum* and *eo ultum* answer to the English 'I am going to ruin myself,' 'I am going to take revenge.'

2. The supine is not used as often as might be expected in Latin, and most writers generally prefer using *ut, ad,* or *gratia* — as *legati*

venerunt ut quererentur, ad querendum, querendi gratia, or *questuri.*
Poets sometimes use the mere infinitive instead of the supine — as
Proteus pecus egit altos visere montes.

§ 402. The supine in *u* has a passive meaning, and is used
with certain adjectives to denote that a quality is attributed to a
subject with reference to the action expressed by the supine;
e.g., *pleraque dictu quam re sunt faciliora,* most things are more
easy to say than to do; *honestum factu, turpe factu,* honourable
to do, disgraceful to do; *uva peracerba gustatu,* a grape very sour
to taste; *jucundum cognitu atque auditu,* pleasant to know and
to hear.

The words most commonly used with this supine are — *fas,*
nefas, opus, honestus, turpis, jucundus, facilis, difficilis, incredi-
bilis, memorabilis, utilis, dignus, indignus.

Note. This supine is likewise of comparatively rare occurrence.
The neuter adjectives *facile, difficile,* and *proclive,* are joined with the
supine in *u* even where we should expect an infinitive as the subject to
them — as *difficile dictu est* (for *dicere*), *quanto opere conciliet homines*
comitas affabilitasque sermonis; ad calamitatum societates non facile est
inventu (for *invenire*), *qui descendant. Fas* and *nefas* are used in the
same manner. The supine in *u* with *dignus* and *indignus* is very rare,
and instead of *nihil dictu dignum* we much more frequently find *nihil*
dignum quod dicatur. (§ 360, 2.) *Facilis, difficilis,* and *jucundus,* are
often used with the preposition *ad* and the gerund, instead of the
supine—as *res facilis ad intelligendum,* a thing easy to be understood;
verba ad audiendum jucunda, words pleasing to hear. Poets even use
the infinitive after these adjectives—as *facilis legi,* easy to be read.

CHAPTER LVII.

THE PARTICIPLES.

§ 403. A particle is in form an adjective, but differs from
other adjectives by the fact of its expressing also time, and
governing the case of the verb from which it is formed.

In the active there are two participles: the one commonly
called the present participle represents an action or condition
as in course of progress, and accordingly, if present actions
are spoken of, it may be regarded as a present participle — as
accusat me dicens me ad hostes transfugisse, he accuses me,
saying (present) that I deserted to the enemy; if past actions
are spoken of, it may be termed the participle of the imperfect — as *accusavit me dicens* (imperfect) *me ad hostes trans-*

fugisse, he accused me, saying (for he said) that I had deserted to the enemy. The future participle represents an action or condition as intended or as to take place in future time — as *milites adversus urbem profecturi per totam noctem in castris se tenebant,* the soldiers intending to march against the city kept themselves all night within the camp. The active voice has no participle for a completed action.

The passive, if we except the gerundive, has only one participle which expresses a completed action — as *injuria illata,* an injury has been done ; *domus ornata,* a house which has been adorned ; *bene de republica meritus,* one who has well deserved of the republic.

Deponent verbs have all the participles both of the active and of the passive — as *hortans, hortatus, hortaturus,* and *hortandus.*

Note. The present and past participles, from the nature of their meaning, are very often used as pure adjectives, and, like them, have their degrees of comparison — as *amans, amantior, amantissimus; doctus, doctior, doctissimus.* The future participle, on the other hand, is never used as a pure adjective, except in such cases as *res futurae, anni venturi.* The present participle of transitive verbs, when used as a pure adjective, governs the genitive—as *amans patriae.* See § 277, 1.

§ 404. The Latin language employs participles much more frequently than the English, and many explanatory or subordinate clauses expressing manner, reason, concession, condition, or any accompanying circumstance, may be expressed in Latin by a participle, and thus impart to the language a conciseness of which our own tongue is incapable — as *omne malum nascens facile opprimitur,* every evil is easily suppressed in its origin ; *inveteratum fit plerumque robustius,* when it has grown old it generally becomes stronger ; *M'. Curio ad focum sedenti Samnites magnum auri pondus attulerunt,* when M'. Curius was sitting by his hearth, the Samnites brought to him a great quantity of gold ; *Valerium hostes accerrime pugnantem occidunt,* the enemy slew Valerius while he was fighting most courageously ; *Dionysius tyrannus cultros metuens tonsorios candenti carbone sibi adurebat capillum,* as Dionysius the tyrant dreaded razors, he used to singe away his hair with a burning coal ; *risum saepe cupientes tenere nequimus,* often we cannot suppress laughter, though we wish it ; *Romani non rogati Graecis auxilium offerunt,* the Romans, without being asked, offer their assistance to the Greeks ; *Verres absolutus tamen ex manibus populi Romani eripi nullo modo potest,* Verres, even if acquitted, yet cannot escape in any way from the hands of the Roman people ; *Caesar hostes aggressus extemplo fudit,* Caesar having attacked the enemy, routed them immediately, or Caesar attacked the enemy, and routed them immediately.

Note 1. A participle is often used instead of a subordinate clause beginning with *nisi*, if the leading clause contains a negative—as *non mihi nisi admonito* (for *nisi admonitus essem*) *venisset in mentem*, it would not have occurred to my mind, had I not been reminded.   In like manner, *quamquam, quamvis, quasi, tamquam, non ante quam*, or *non prius quam*, are often joined with a participle instead of a complete clause — as *Caesarem milites, quamvis recusantem, in Africam secuti sunt*, the soldiers followed Caesar into Africa, although he did not wish it.

2. As the present and past participles are often used as pure adjectives, they are also, like adjectives, sometimes used substantively; but this is done very cautiously, and only where no ambiguity can arise — as *jacet corpus dormientis ut mortui*, the body of a sleeping person lies like that of a dead man; *eodem temporis puncto nati dissimiles et naturas et vitas habent*, persons born at the same moment have different natures and careers of life.

3. A past participle is often joined to a substantive in such a manner as not to describe the person or thing in a certain condition, so much as the action itself in its state of completion—as *rex interfectus*, the (completed) murder of the king; *sibi quisque caesi regis expetebat decus*, each claimed for himself the honour of the king's murder—that is, of having murdered the king; *ante Christum natum*, before the birth of Christ; *post urbem conditam*, after the building of the city.   In these cases the participle supplies the place of a verbal substantive, and must therefore be employed, especially where no such verbal substantive is in current use.   Livy uses the neuter of this participle even of intransitive verbs as a kind of impersonal expression—as *Tarquinius Superbus bellica arte aequasset superiores reges, nisi degeneratum in aliis huic quoque laudi offecisset*, where *degeneratum in aliis* signifies, ' his degeneracy in other respects.'

4. The verb *habeo* is sometimes used with the past participle of verbs denoting knowledge or resolution, the participle either agreeing with some substantive, or being used substantively in the neuter gender—as *hanc rem perspectam habeo*, or *perspectum habeo*, I have this matter (as an understood one) clearly before my mind; *hanc rem perspexi* would only mean, ' I have clearly understood this matter.'   So also *persuasum habeo, cognitum habeo, bellum indictum habuit, fidem meam suspectam habet, jam statutum habeo.*

5. The past participle, especially of deponent verbs, is frequently used in the sense of a present participle denoting an action or condition in progress—as *melior est certa pax quam sperata victoria*, a certain peace is better than a victory (only) hoped for — that is, one which we are looking forward to; *Caesar iisdem ducibus usus, qui nuntii venerant, Numidas subsidio oppidanis mittit*, Caesar availing himself of the same guides who had come as messengers, sent the Numidians to the assistance of the people in the town.   This is done, especially in the historical style, when the verb of the leading clause is a historical perfect or present, and when the participle of the present is not used, as in the case of the verbs *reor* and *soleo*.

6. The neuter of some past participles, as *dictum, factum, responsum, actum, mandatum*, and others, is sometimes used completely in the sense of a substantive—as *praeclarum factum*, a glorious deed; *fortia*

facta, gallant deeds. But sometimes they preserve their nature of a participle, and are accordingly accompanied by an adverb instead of an adjective — as *recte facta*, good deeds; *facete dicta*, witty words. This is the case especially when such substantives have another adjective or pronoun accompanying them — as *multa prudenter acta et acute responsa*, many prudent actions and acute answers.

§ 405. It was remarked in Chapter XLV. that the ablative is used to denote the time when? place where? cause, manner, or any accompanying circumstance of an action. Now, if any of these things is expressed by a subordinate clause having a different subject from that of the leading one, that clause is put in the ablative — that is, the subject is put in the ablative, and the verb, being changed into a participle, is made to agree with the subject. A clause thus expressed is said to be in the ablative absolute, it not being governed by any other word; e.g., *rege expulso consules creati sunt*, after the king was expelled consuls were elected; *hae res Tarquinio regnante gestae sunt*, these things were done in the reign of Tarquinius; *sole stante terra vertitur*, the earth turns round while the sun is standing still; *Caesar homines inimico animo, data facultate per provinciam itineris faciendi, non temperaturos ab injuria existimabat*, Caesar thought that men of a hostile disposition would not abstain from acts of injustice, if permission were given to them to march through the province; *reluctante natura irritus labor est*, exertion is useless, if nature be against it; *Mucius Porsennam interficere, proposita sibi morte, conatus est*, Mucius attempted to kill Porsenna, although death stared him (Mucius) in the face.

Note 1. The English language also uses an absolute case (the nominative absolute) in such clauses as, 'the town being taken, the soldiers began to plunder;' 'he listened to me with attention, it being evident that he wished to know my opinion.' But it cannot be employed as frequently as in Latin.

2. Instead of a participle in a clause expressed by the ablative absolute, we sometimes find a verbal substantive, such as *dux, comes, auctor, adjutor, testis, judex, interpres*, and also the titles of office, *rex, consul, imperator, praetor, censor*, and the like — as *Carthaginienses, duce Hannibale, Romanos vicerunt*, the Carthaginians, under the command of Hannibal, defeated the Romans; *haec gesta sunt Cicerone consule*, these things were done in the consulship of Cicero; *mo puero*, in my boyhood. As, moreover, *esse* has no present participle, an adjective alone must sometimes be used — as *coelo sereno*, the sky being bright; *me ignaro*, without my knowledge; *deo propitio*, if God is propitious.

3. A clause in the ablative absolute is sometimes, like a participle (see § 403, note 1), introduced by the conjunctions *nisi, quamquam, quamvis, quasi, tamquam, velut, non ante quam*, or *non prius quam* — as *nihil praecepta atque artes valent, nisi adjuvante natura* for *nisi na tura adjuvat; Albani, velut diis quoque simul cum patria relictis* (for *velut dii relicti essent*), *sacra oblivioni dederant*.

4. As there is no past participle in the active voice, it is often neces sary, for the purpose of using the ablative absolute, to change a clause into the passive, so that in many cases the subject of the leading clause must at the same time be conceived as the agent in the clause ex- pressed by the ablative absolute—as *cognito Caesaris adventu, Ariovis- tus legatos ad eum mittit,* Ariovistus having heard of Caesar's arrival, sent ambassadors to him; *C. Sempronius causa ipse pro se dicta damna- tur,* C. Sempronius having conducted his own defence, was condemned.

5. Sometimes a participle in the neuter gender is used by itself to supply a whole clause in the ablative absolute. The participles most frequently occurring in this way are *audito, cognito, comperto, intellecto, nuntiato, edicto, permisso, auspicato, consulto* — as *Alexander, audito, Darium movisse ab Ecbatanis,* Alexander, after hearing that Darius had broken up from Ecbatana; *consul edicto, ut, quicunque ad vallum ten- deret, pro hoste haberetur, fugientibus obstitit; Hannibal cognito in- sidias sibi parari, fugā salutem quaesivit.* In all these cases the ablative of the participle represents a clause expressed impersonally, no definite subject being understood; but there are others in which the subject must be supplied from the context — as *additur dolus, missis, qui magnam vim lignorum ardentem in flumen conjicerent,* where *missis* is the same as *missis hominibus,* men having been sent who, &c.

6. The ablative absolute cannot be used when the subject of the subordinate clause is the same as that of the leading clause, and it is commonly avoided when the subject of the subordinate clause is at all mentioned in the leading one. We must accordingly not say *Manlius, caeso Gallo, torque eum spoliavit,* but either *Manlius caesum Gallum torque spoliavit,* or *Manlius, quum Gallum cecidisset, torque eum spoli- avit.* There are, however, instances of the ablative absolute in such cases, which seems to have been employed for the purpose of setting forth more emphatically the statement contained in them — as *Vercin- getorix, convocatis suis clientibus, facile incendit* (eos), for *Vecingeto- rix convocatos suos clientes facile incendit.*

7. The ablative absolute with a participle future active occurs very rarely, and still more rarely with the gerundive—as *quum contio plau- sum, meo nomine recitando, dedisset,* where *recitando* assumes the meaning of a present participle passive. An ablative absolute may always be resolved in English by some conjunction, and the Latins themselves sometimes use a subordinate clause with a conjunction instead of the ablative absolute, especially to prevent the occurrence of several ablatives absolute in the same sentence.

APPENDIX I.

ELEMENTS OF LATIN VERSIFICATION.

§ 405. A verse (*versus*, from *verto*) is properly nothing out a line, but, in its usual acceptation, a line regulated by certain laws. In most modern languages these laws refer to the manner in which accented syllables (which are always long) alternate with unaccented ones; but in Latin and Greek they refer to the manner in which long syllables must alternate with short ones. What syllables of a word are long and short has been stated in that part of this grammar which explains the various forms of words, and more particularly in Chapter II. Every verse, consists of a certain number of parts which are termed feet (*pedes*), and which determine the measure or metre (*metrum*) of the verse.

Note 1. It must not be forgotten that in the ancient languages prosody and accentuation are perfectly distinct — that is, that the long syllable need not be at the same time the one having the emphatic accent; and that, on the other hand, a syllable may be short, and yet have the emphatic accent. This circumstance produces with us a difficulty in reading the ancient languages correctly, because we are accustomed always to give the emphatic accent to the long syllable of a word, whereas the ancients in their pronunciation appear to have drawn a very marked distinction between a long unaccented and long accented, as well as between a short unaccented and a short accented syllable.

2. The regular movement arising either from a repetition of the same feet, or from the regular succession of different feet, is called the rhythm (*rhythmus*) of a verse.

§ 406. A foot consists of a combination of two or more syllables. The time required for pronouncing a short syllable is regarded as a unit, and called a *mora ;* a long syllable, requiring twice as much time, has two *morae.* Hence one long syllable is equal in value to two short ones, and very often one long syllable supplies in poetry the place of two short ones.

DISSYLLABIC FEET.

1. Pyrrhichius,	⏑ ⏑,	as in *gĕnŭs.*
2. Spondeus,	– –,	as in *bēllō.*
3. Trochaeus or choreus,	–́ ⏑,	as in *laétŭs.*
4. Iambus,	⏑ –́,	as in *dĕós.*

1. Tribrachys,   ᴜ ᴜ ᴜ, as in *mĕmŏrĭs*.
2. Molossus,   – – –, as in *Ālbānī*.
3. Dactylus,   ⸺́ ᴜ ᴜ, as in *nŭmĭnĕ*.
4. Anapaestus,   ᴜ ᴜ ′, as in *mĕmŏrā*.
5. Amphibrachys,   ᴜ ′ ᴜ, as in *ămārĕ*.
6. Amphimacer or Creticus,   ⸺́ ᴜ ⸺́, as in *lēgĕrănt*.
7. Bacchius,   ⸺́ ⸺́ ᴜ, as in *āccēnsă*.
8. Antibacchius   ᴜ ⸺́ ⸺́, as in *dŏlōrēs*.

Feet consisting of four or more syllables cannot, properly speaking, be regarded as single feet, but are combinations which may be resolved into dissyllabic feet. The number of such compound feet is sixteen : —

1. Proceleusmaticus,   ᴜ ᴜ ᴜ ᴜ, properly a double pyrrhich.
2. Dispondeus,   – – – –, a double spondee.
3. Choriambus,   – ᴜ ᴜ –, a choreus and an iambus.
4. Antispastus,   ᴜ – – ᴜ, an iambus and trochaeus.
5. Diïambus,   ᴜ – ᴜ –, two iambus.
6. Ditrochaeus,   – ᴜ – ᴜ, two trochees.
7. Ionicus a majore,   – – ᴜ ᴜ, a spondee and a pyrrhich.
8. Ionicus a minore,   ᴜ ᴜ – –, a pyrrhich and a spondee.
9. Epitritus primus,   ᴜ – – –, an iambus and a spondee.
10. Epitritus secundus,   – ᴜ – –, a trochee and a spondee.
11. Epitritus tertius,   – – ᴜ –, a spondee and an iambus.
12. Epitritus quartus,   – – – ᴜ, a spondee and a trochee.
13. Paeon primus,   – ᴜ ᴜ ᴜ, a trochee and a pyrrhich, ⎫
14. Paeon secundus,   ᴜ – ᴜ ᴜ, an iambus and a pyrrhich, ⎬ or equivalent to a creticus.
15. Paeon tertius,   ᴜ ᴜ – ᴜ, a pyrrhich and a trochee, ⎪
16. Paeon quartus,   ᴜ ᴜ ᴜ –, a pyrrhich and an iambus, ⎭

Feet consisting of syllables of the same kind, as ᴜ ᴜ, – –, ᴜ ᴜ ᴜ, and – – –, are not genuine feet, for no verse can possibly consist of such feet exclusively ; but they are often employed to supply the place of other feet, especially of such as are of equal value, as ᴜ ᴜ for ᴜ –, – – for – ᴜ ᴜ, ᴜ ᴜ – and ᴜ –, ᴜ ᴜ ᴜ for ᴜ – or – ᴜ, and the like.

§ 407. The long syllable in every genuine foot is the most important, and is for this reason said to be in the *arsis* — that is, the rising ; the short syllable or syllables are said to be in the *thesis* — that is, a sinking. In the above lists of simple feet, the arsis has been marked by an accent (′), as ⸺́ ᴜ, ᴜ ⸺́, ᴜ ᴜ ⸺́, ⸺́ ᴜ ᴜ. In feet which are not genuine, the place of the arsis depends upon the nature of the foot represented by the non-genuine foot — as, for example, if $\cup \; \cup \; \cup$ stands for an iambus, $\cup \; \_\!\_$, the two last short syllables conjointly are in the arsis, $\cup \; \cup'\!\cup$; but when $\cup \; \cup \; \cup$ stands for a trochee $\_\!\_ \cup$, the first two short syllables conjointly are in the arsis. $\cup'\!\cup \; \cup$. In like manner a spondee has the arsis on the first syllable, when it represents a dactyl, and on the second, when it represents an iambus.

Note 1. When the arsis in a foot precedes the thesis, the movement or rhythm is, as it were, descending; and when the thesis precedes the arsis, the movement is an ascending one.

2. We are accustomed to pronounce the syllable which has the arsis, as if it had the emphatic accent — that is, as if it were the accented syllable of a word, though in prose and in ordinary conversation it never occurs to us to pronounce such a syllable as accented. Thus we read *Arma virúmque canó, Trojaé qui primus ab oris*, although in prose we pronounce *cáno* and *Trójae*. We cannot suppose that the ancients in reciting verse thus violated the laws of accent, and must therefore conclude that they pronounced a syllable in the arsis in a different manner from what we are accustomed to do, and that in reciting a verse they only marked the difference of long and short syllables, and gave the accent only to those syllables which really had it, irrespective of their length or shortness. The terms *arsis* and *thesis*, accordingly, have no reference to the rising and sinking of the voice, but are taken from the raising and sinking of the baton with which time is beaten in music.

3. It very often happens that a short syllable of a word, especially a final syllable ending in a consonant, is made long by the mere fact of its being in the arsis of a foot. But short monosyllabic words are never lengthened by the arsis.

§ 408. In verses consisting of iambuses, trochees, or anapaests, two feet (a *dipodia*) are taken together and form one metre (*metrum*), so that a verse consisting of six iambuses is called an iambic trimeter (an iambic verse containing three metra), and one consisting of six trochees, a trochaic trimeter, and one consisting of six anapaests, an anapaestic trimeter. A dactyl constitutes a metre by itself, whence verses consisting of five or six dactyls are called pentameters and hexameters.

§ 409. A verse consists either of a repetition of the same foot, or of a combination or mixture of different feet. The former is called a simple verse, the latter compound or mixed. It must, however, be understood that in a simple iambic verse, for example, all feet need not be iambuses, but the iambuses may alternate with their equivalents, spondees, anapaests, and tribrachs, all of them retaining the iambic movement, $\_\!\_ \; \_\!\_, \; \cup \; \cup \; \_\!\_, \; \cup \; \cup'\!\cup$.

§ 410. The last syllable of a verse is generally indifferent

(*anceps*) — that is, it may be either long or short; and if it be
long, its place can never be supplied by two shorts. A verse
often ends in such a way as to leave the last foot incomplete, in
which case the verse is termed *versus catalecticus.*

Note. When the last foot, which is incomplete, consists of only one
syllable, the verse is called *catalecticus in syllabam;* when the last foot,
instead of consisting of three syllables, contains only two, it is called
catalecticus in dissyllabum; but these two syllables may be regarded
as a complete dissyllabic foot by itself.

§ 411. *Caesura,* a cutting or incision, is the division of certain verses into two or more parts, arising from the fact of a
word ending in the middle of a foot. At the point where the
caesura takes place, the voice pauses a little, though without
interrupting the movement of the verse, the incompleteness of
the foot insufficiently indicating that something more must be
coming. There are certain verses in which an incision occurs
at the end of a foot, but then the remaining part of the verse is
usually of a catalectic nature. A caesura is necessary in certain places of certain verses, and greatly contributes to their
euphonic flow; whereas an unpleasant sensation is produced
when the words coincide with the feet, which in fact destroys
the harmony of the verse, as —

> *Sparsis* | *hastis* | *longis* | *campus* | *splendet et* | *horret.*

Note. A caesura is sometimes defined as the incision produced when
the end of a foot falls in the middle of a word, so that one part of the
word belongs to one foot, while the other belongs to the following
foot. If only one long syllable passes over into the next foot, the caesura
is termed a *strong* one; if one long and a short one, it is termed a
weak caesura, as in the following hexameters: —

> *Blāndă quī|ēs vīct|īs fūr|tĭm sūb|rēpĭt ŏ|cēllīs.*
>
> *Ūtĭlĕ* | *sit faū|stūmquĕ prĕ|cōr quŏd ĭ|māgĭnĕ* | *sōmnī.*

§ 412. The correctness of a verse consists in every syllable
being used in its proper quantity, and the necessary caesura
occurring in its proper place. It must, however, be observed
that certain licenses were regarded by the ancients as admissible; for example, *illĭus, unĭus,* for *illīus, unīus; rĕligio,*
rĕliquiae, for rēligio, rēliquiae; stetērunt for *stetĕrunt* (see
§ 141, 3), especially in the case of such words or proper
names which without such license could not be used in certain kinds of verse — as *altĕrius, Prĭămĭdes,* instead of which
we find *alterīus* and *Prīamides.* To this we must add the fact,
that a short syllable ending in a consonant, and sometimes
also the suffix *quĕ,* are made long by being in the arsis of a
verse (hexameter), and that *ie, iu,* and *ua,* are used as one syllable, as —

Hic hasta Aeneae stabāt; huc impetus illam —
Et Messapus equum domitōr, et fortis Asilas —
Antheusquē Mnestheusque ruunt, omnisque relictis —
Pectora, nec misero clipei mora profuit aerēi —
Moenia quique imos pulsabant ariēte muros —
Genuā labant, gelidus concrevit frigore sanguis.

Note. In like manner we sometimes find a long syllable used as short, which is termed *systŏle,* while the use of a short syllable as long is called *diastŏle.* The old comic poets (Plautus and Terence) avail themselves of far greater licenses than the poets of the best age of Roman literature ; for they often make syllables short which are long by position, and contract or elide syllables in a way which can be accounted for only on the supposition that they imitated the pronunciation such as it was heard in every-day life.

§ 413. The hiatus must be avoided in poetry as much as possible. A hiatus arises when one word ends in a vowel (or *m*) and the next begins with a vowel, without its being possible to elide the former without destroying the verse — as in

Causa mali tanti, oculos dejecta decoros;

where the *i* in *tanti* ought to be elided, but cannot without destroying the verse.

Note 1. When one verse ends in a vowel, and the next begins with one, no hiatus arises, there being a pause at the end of a verse ; sometimes, however, the vowel of a preceding verse is nevertheless elided, if the next begins with a vowel, as in Virg. *Aen.* xi. 609 and 610.

2. There are, however, cases in which a hiatus is not very offensive, and where, accordingly, the poets do not much care to avoid it. Such cases are — 1*st,* When a word ends in a long vowel or diphthong which is in the arsis, and forms the caesural syllable, as —

Orchades et radi|ī et amara pausia bacca.

2*d,* When a word ends in a long vowel, or a diphthong being in the thesis, and thereby becoming short, as —

Credimus! | ān, quĭ ă|mant, ipsi sibi somnia fingunt ?
Insŭlăe | Ionio in magno.

3*d,* When a word ends in a short vowel in the thesis, and at the same time forms the end of a sentence, or when the same word is repeated, as —

Et vera incessu patuit dĕă. Ille ubi matrem.

The *m* in words ending in *m* is very rarely found unelided.

3. Interjections consisting of a single vowel can never be elided, though a long one may be used as short. The diphthong *ae* at the end of a word is rarely elided before a short vowel, so that other means must be resorted to in such cases to avoid the hiatus.

§ 414. The most important of all simple dactylic verses is the hexameter, also called the heroic verse, because it is the usual metre employed by the ancients in the heroic epic. It consists of six dactyls, the last of which is defective or catalectic, consisting either of a trochee or a spondee, so that the whole verse is catalecticus in dissyllabum. The place of each of the first four dactyls may be supplied by a spondee; but the fifth foot is rarely a spondee, because it obscures the nature of the dactylic movement; but when the fifth is a spondee, the fourth is always a dactyl. The hexameter regularly has a caesura in the third foot, either after the arsis (the first long syllable), which is called the strong caesura, or after the first short syllable of the dactyl, which is called the weak caesura, as —

Arma vi|rumque can|o ‖ Tro|jae qui | primus ab | oris
Id metu|ens vete | risque ‖ me | mor Saturnia belli.

Note 1. Besides epic poetry, the hexameter is used in didactic poetry, satires, poetic epistles, and sometimes also in lyric compositions.

2. The caesura after the arsis of the third foot is called *penthemimeres* (from the Greek πενθημιμέρης), because it occurs after the fifth half foot; and the caesura, after the first short syllable of the third foot, is said to be the arsis after the third trochee. Sometimes there is no caesura in the third foot, but after the arsis of the fourth, which is called *hephthemimeres*, because it occurs after the seventh half foot, as —

Illi | se prae|dae accin|gunt ‖ dapi|busque fu|turis.

At other times there is a caesura both in the third and fourth foot; and when the former is weak, the latter must be regarded as the proper caesura.

3. The particle *que* at the end of a hexameter is sometimes elided when the verse following begins with a vowel. See § 413, note 1. In a well-constructed hexameter, a new sentence very rarely begins with, or in the last foot.

§ 415. The following dactylic verses are often used, especially by Horace in his lyric stanzas, in conjunction with other verses : —

1. The versus Adonius, – ◡ ◡ | – ◡, as —

Ōcĭŏr | aūrā.

2. The Archilochius minor, – ◡ ◡·| – ◡ ◡ | ◡, as —

Pūlvĭs ĕt | ūmbră sŭm|ŭs.

3. Dactylus tetrameter catalecticus, – ◡ ◡ | – ◡ ◡ | – ◡ ◡ |–◡, as —

Ō fōr|tēs pē|jŏrăquĕ | pāssī.

§ 416. The pentameter is a verse consisting of two parts, each composed of two dactyls and one syllable of a broken foot, and in the first part this syllable is always long, forming a strong caesura. The place of the two dactyls in the first part may be supplied by spondees. No poem consists of pentameters only ; they are always used alternately with hexameters ; and two verses, one of which is a hexameter and the other a pentameter, are called a distich, as —

Pŏstĕră | lūx Hŷă|dās Taū|rīnaē | cōrnŭă | Iŏvĭs,
Ēvŏcăt | ĕt mūl|tā ‖ tērră mă|dēscĭt ă|quā.

Note. Hexameters alternating with pentameters are used especially in elegies, whence such a combination is also called elegiac verse ; but it is also employed in epigrams, and by Ovid in didactic poetry.

§ 417. The most common anapaestic verse is the anapaestic dimeter — that is, a verse consisting of four anapaests, two forming a metre. A pause or incision occurs between the second and third foot, the second foot always ending with a word. The place of the anapaests may be supplied by spondees or even dactyls, though a dactyl rarely occurs in the last foot. Such verses occur only in the choruses of Seneca's tragedies.

Note. Anapaestic dimeters always occur in succession, so as to form a stanza, and are continued until the sentiment to be expressed is completed. It must be observed that the last syllable in these verses is not anceps, but always long ; that when the last word of a verse ends in a consonant, the vowel contained in it is long by position, if the first word of the next line begins with a consonant ; and lastly, that a hiatus between one line and another is not admissible. See Seneca, *Hippol.* 1124, foll.

§ 418. Trochaic verses are likewise divided into dipodiae — that is, two feet are counted as one meter. The most common trochaic verse, which occurs in animated scenes of tragedy, is the catalectic tetrameter (*versus tetrameter trochaicus catalecticus* or *trochaicus septenarius*), consisting of seven trochees and one syllaba anceps at the end ; and a pause or incision usually occurs at the end of the fourth foot, which ends with a word. Instead of trochees, tribrachs may be used in all feet, and in the second, fourth, and sixth feet, the place of the trochee may be supplied by a spondee.

Note 1. Comic writers are not always very scrupulous about the pause at the end of the fourth foot, and often employ spondees in all feet except the seventh ; they even introduce a dactyl or anapaest instead of the spondee, so that the verse presents a great variety of forms.

2. Horace also uses the trochaic dimeter catalecticus, consisting of three trochees and a syllaba anceps at the end, as —

Trūdĭ|tūr dĭ|ēs dĭ|ē.

§ 419. Iambic verses, like anapaestic and trochaic verses, are measured by dipodiae — that is, two iambuses are counted one metre, and the first foot in every dipodia (if the verse be not very short) may be a spondee instead of an iambus, without disturbing the iambic movement.

(*a*). The most common iambic verse is the iambic trimeter (*iambicus trimeter*), also called *senarius*, from its containing six feet. The place of an iambus may be supplied in the uneven feet (the 1st, 3d and 5th) by a spondee, and a tribrach may be employed instead of an iambus in every foot except the last. It sometimes occurs, though very rarely, that the first and third foot consist of a dactyl, or the first of an anapaest. The iambic trimeter usually has a caesura after the thesis of the third foot, or if this is not the case, after the thesis of the fourth. Its various forms are represented in the following table : —

ᴗ –	ᴗ –	ᴗ –	ᴗ –	ᴗ –	ᴗ ᴗ
– –	ᴗ –	– –	ᴗ –	– –	ᴗ ᴗ
– ᴗ ᴗ	ᴗ –	– ᴗ ᴗ	ᴗ –	ᴗ –	ᴗ ᴗ
ᴗ ᴗ –					
ᴗ ᴗ ᴗ	ᴗ ᴗ ᴗ	ᴗ ᴗ ᴗ	ᴗ ᴗ ᴗ	ᴗ ᴗ ᴗ	ᴗ ᴗ

Note 1. The iambic trimeter is the ordinary metre employed in the dialogue of dramatic poetry, and is found also in small lyric poems, either exclusively or mixed with other verses.

2. The comic poets sometimes take great liberties with the iambic trimeter, for they employ the spondee also in the even places (in the 2d and 4th foot), but never in the sixth, and the dactyl and anapaest are used by them in any of the first five feet. The comic poets, moreover, sometimes employ iambic tetrameters, which are either complete, consisting of eight feet (*octonarii*), or are catalectic (*septenarii*), consisting of seven feet and one syllable. These tetrameters usually have an incision after the fourth foot, and show great variety in the alternation of the feet.

(*b*). Horace makes use of iambic dimeters and catalectic trimeters. The former consist of four iambuses ; instead of the first and third iambus he sometimes employs a spondee, and in the first a dactyl, while the second is found resolved into a tribrach, so that the verse may consist of —

$$ \frac{\breve{\smile}\,–}{–\,\smile\,\smile} \ \Big|\ \smile\,\smile\,\smile \ \Big|\ \frac{\breve{\smile}\,–}{\breve{\smile}\,–} \ \Big|\ \smile\,\frac{\breve{\smile}}{\smile}, \text{ as} — $$

Īmbrēs | *nĭvēs*|*quĕ cōm*|*părăt.*

The catalectic trimeter consists of five iambuses and one syllable. The first and third foot may be spondees, and the second a tribrach : —

$$ \breve{\smile}\,– \ \Big|\ \smile\,– \ \Big|\ \frac{\breve{\smile}}{–}\,– \,|\, \smile\,– \,|\, \smile\,– \,|\, \breve{\smile} \ \text{ as} — $$

Trăhŭnt|*quĕ sĭc*|*căs mā*|*chĭnāē* | *cărĭ*|*nās.*

Another iambic metre likewise found in Horace is the Alcaic verse of nine syllables (*Alcaicus enneasyllabus*), ⌣ _ | ⌣ _ | _ _ | ⌣ _ | ⌣, as—

Ēt scīn|dăt hāēr|ēntēm | cŏrōn|ăm.

Note 1. There is a species of iambic trimeter verse called the *choliambus* or *scazon* — that is, the limping iambic verse, from the circumstance that the last iambus is changed into a trochee or spondee.

2. Choriambic verses are of an iambic nature, and contain one or more choriambuses in the middle; but there is one instance in which Horace (*Carm.* iii. 12) begins such a verse with an anapaest, and then continues the choriambuses to the end of the verse.

§ 420. The verses hitherto spoken of are simple, consisting of a repetition of the same feet or their representatives. Compound verses are those which consist of different feet, which produce a more artificial or complicated movement; but it is nevertheless generally easy, either from one verse alone or from a comparison with those with which it is connected, to discover the movement which predominates. When the dactylic movement passes over into the trochaic, the verse is called a logaoedic verse. A dactylic or logaoedic line is something preceded by an introductory foot of two syllables, called the basis of the verse, and sometimes the middle of a verse is choriambic, while the end is logaoedic. All compound verses are of an animated kind, and are peculiarly suited to lyric poetry. The principal compound verses, especially those used by Horace, are —

1. The Aristophanicus, _ ⌣ ⌣ | _ ⌣ | _ ⌣, as—

Lȳdĭă | dīc pĕr | ōmnēs.

2. The Alcaic decasyllabus, _ ⌣ ⌣ | _ ⌣ ⌣ | _ ⌣ | _ ⌣, as·

Nēc vĭrĭ|dēs mĕtŭ|ūnt cŏ|lūbrās.

3. The Pherecrateus, _ _ | _ ⌣ ⌣ | _ ⌣, as—

Vīs fŏr|mōsă vĭ|dērī.

4. The Archilochius major, _ ⌣⌣ | _ ⌣⌣ | _ ⌣⌣ | _ ⌣ ⌣ | _ ⌣ | _ ⌣ | _ ⌣, as—

Sōlvĭtŭr | ācrĭs hĭ|ēms grāt|ā vĭcĕ | vērĭs | ēt Făv|ōnī.

5. The Glyconicus, _ _ | _ ⌣ ⌣ | _ ⌣ | ⌣, as—

Nīl mŏrt|ālĭbŭs | ārdŭ|ūm ēst.

6. The Alcaicus hendecasyllabus, ⌣ _ | ⌣ _ | _ ‖ _ | ⌣ ⌣ _ | ⌣ ⌣, as—

Dūlcē ēt dĕcōr|ŭm ēst ‖ prō|pătrĭă | mŏrī

7. The Sapphicus, _ ⌣ | _ _ | _ ‖ ⌣ ⌣ | _ ⌣ | _ ⌣, as—

Īntĕg|ĕr vī|tāē ‖ scĕlĕr|ĭs quĕ | pūrŭs.

8. The Sapphicus major, $- \cup \mid -- \mid - \cup \cup - \mid - \cup \cup \mid - \cup \mid - \underset{\smile}{-}$,
as—

Cūr tĭ|mēt flā|vūm Tĭbĕrīm | tāngĕrĕ? | cūr ŏ|lĭvŭm?

9. The Asclepiadeus minor, $-- \mid - \cup \cup - \parallel - \cup \cup \mid - \cup \mid \underset{\smile}{-}$, as—

Māecē|nās ătăvīs | ēdĭtĕ | rēgĭ|būs.

10. The Asclepiadeus major, $-- \mid - \cup \cup - \parallel - \cup \cup - \parallel - \cup \cup \mid$
$- \cup \mid \underset{\smile}{-}$, as—

Quīs pōst | vīnă grăvēm | mīlĭtĭām aut | pāupĕrĭem | crĕp|ăt?

Note 1. In the Sapphicus the caesura sometimes occurs after the first short syllable of the dactyl.

2. The verses commonly called asynarteti, which consist of two parts loosely connected, so that at the point where they are divided a hiatus is admissible, and the last syllable of the first part is anceps, are perhaps more properly treated as two verses. Such verses are the elegiambus, $- \cup \cup - \cup \cup \underset{\smile}{-} \parallel \underset{\smile}{-} - \cup - \underset{\smile}{-} - \cup \underset{\smile}{-}$, and the iambelegus, $\underset{\smile}{-} - \cup - \underset{\smile}{-} - \cup \underset{\smile}{-} \parallel - \cup \cup - \cup \cup \underset{\smile}{-}$.

§ 421. Lyric poems do not generally consist of a repetition of the same verse, but either two different verses alternate, and form distichs, or several verses form a strophe, stanza, or couplet, so that the poem consists of a number of such strophes. These distichs and couplets are called metres.

The distichs used by Horace are —

1. The second Asclepiadean metre, consisting of a Glyconicus and the asclepiadeus minor.

2. The greater Sapphic metre, consisting of an Aristophanicus and the greater Sapphic verse.

3. The first Archilochian metre, consisting of a dactylic hexameter and the Archilochius minor (see § 415, 2).

4. The second Archilochian metre, consisting of a dactylic hexameter and an iambelegus (§ 420, note 2). If the iambelegus is treated as two verses, this metre ceases to be a distich, but consists of three lines.

5. The third Archilochian metre, consisting of an iambic trimeter and an elegiambus; this metre may likewise be regarded as consisting of three lines.

6. The fourth Archilochian metre, consisting of the greater Archilochius and a catalectic iambic trimeter.

7. The Alcmanian metre, consisting of a dactylic hexameter and a catalectic dactylic tetrameter.

8. The second iambic metre, consisting of an iambic trimeter and an iambic dimeter.

9. The first Pythiambic metre, consisting of a dactylic hexameter and an iambic dimeter.

10. The second Pythiambic metre, consisting of a dactylic hexameter and an iambic trimeter.

11. The trochaic metre, consisting of a catalectic trochaic dimeter and a catalectic iambic trimeter.

Note. The uninterrupted use of the lesser Asclepiadean verse is generally called the first Asclepiadean metre, and the continued use of the iambic trimeter is termed the first iambic metre.

The strophes or stanzas used by Horace are —

1. The Sapphic strophe, consisting of three Sapphic verses followed by an Adonius.

2. The first Asclepiadean strophe, consisting of three lesser Asclepiadean verses followed by a Glyconicus.

3. The second Asclepiadean strophe, consisting of two lesser Asclepiadean verses, one Pherecrateus and one Glyconicus.

4. The Alcaean strophe, consisting of two versus Alcaici hendecasyllabi, one Alcaicus enneasyllabus, and one Alcaicus decasyllabus.

Note. In the Sapphic strophe it sometimes occurs that a vowel at the end of a line is elided, when the next begins with a vowel, and also that a word is divided between the second and third Sapphic verse.

APPENDIX II.

ABBREVIATIONS OF LATIN NAMES AND WORDS.

1. PRAENOMINA.

A. = Aulus.
Ap. or App. = Appius.
C. or G. = Caius or Gaius.
Cn. or Gn. = Cneius or Gneius.
D. = Decimus.
K. = Kaeso.
L. = Lucius.
M. = Marcus.
M'. = Manius.
Mam. = Mamercus.
N. or Num. = Numerius.
P. = Publius.
Q. or Qu. = Quintus.
S. or Sex. = Sextus.
Ser. = Servius.
Sp. = Spurius.
T. = Titus.
Ti. or Tib. = Tiberius.

2. OTHER WORDS AND EXPRESSIONS.

Aed. = Aedilis.
Cal. or Kal. = Calendae.
Cos. = Consul.
Coss. = Consules.
D. = Divus.
Des. = Designatus.
F. = Filius.
Id. = Idus.
Imp. = Imperator.
Leg. = Legatus or Legio.
N. = Nepos.
Non. = Nonae.
O. M. = Optimus Maximus.
P. C. = Patres Conscripti.
Pl. = Plebs.
P. R. = Populus Romanus.
Pont. Max. = Pontifex Maximus.
Q. F. F. Q. S. = Quod felix faustumque sit.
Q. B. F. F. Q. S. = Quod bonum felix faustumque sit.
Resp. = Respublica.
S. P. Q. R. = Senatus populusque Romanus.
S. C. = Senatus consultum.
S. = Salutem (in letters).
S. D. P. = Salutem dicit plurimam.
S. V. B. E. E. V. = Si vales bene est, ego valeo (in letters).
Tr. Pl. = Tribunus plebes.

These are the chief abbreviations which occur in the classical writers and in ancient inscriptions. There are a great many more, especially in inscriptions, but their explanation belongs to that part of antiquarian studies called Palaeography.

(308)

INDEX.

(309)